TAUTAI

Tautai

Sāmoa, World History, and the Life of Ta'isi O. F. Nelson

Patricia O'Brien

University of Hawai'i Press
Honolulu

Paperback edition 2022

Printed in the United States of America

Library of Congress Cataloging-in-Publication Data

Names: O'Brien, Patricia, author.
Title: Tautai : Sāmoa, world history, and the life of Ta'isi O.F. Nelson / Patricia O'Brien.
Description: Honolulu : University of Hawaiʻi Press, [2017] | Includes bibliographical references and index.
Identifiers: LCCN 2016047765 | ISBN 9780824866532 (cloth ; alk. paper)
Subjects: LCSH: Nelson, O. F., 1883–1944. | Nationalists—Samoa—Biography. | Samoa—Politics and government.
Classification: LCC DU818.N45 O27 2017 | DDC 996.14092 [B]—dc23
LC record available at https://lccn.loc.gov/2016047765

ISBN 9780824893910 (paperback)

University of Hawaiʻi Press books are printed on acid-free paper and meet the guidelines for permanence and durability of the Council on Library Resources.

To the three brightest stars in my universe,
Bruce, Aelfred, and Lachlan,
this book is dedicated to you.
Ma lou alofa atoa.

Contents

Acknowledgments

A few months ago, my youngest son said something that gave me pause. Perplexed at the seemingly endless process of writing this book, he asked me when I was going to finish it because "you've been writing it for more than half my life." He was absolutely right. I started when he was three, and he's now eight. Though I had been thinking I had made good progress with the book, his observation brought home how much this book has impacted him and his brother (and their parents). For us, this book has been a tale of four cities. We have lived in Wellington, Washington, DC, and Canberra, and I have spent a lot of time in Apia—every day in my imagination and long stretches in person.

We arrived in New Zealand from Washington, DC at the start of 2012 as I was the J. D. Stout Fellow in New Zealand Studies at Victoria University Wellington (VUW) for that year. My research project, thanks to the assistance of Jocelyn Charmers, a librarian at the National Library of New Zealand, rapidly became focused on Ta'isi when she directed me to the Pacific Manuscripts Bureau microfilm of Ta'isi's letters (PMB 712). Before I could read them, I had to get authorization from Ta'isi's grandson, the Sāmoan head of state. With the aid of colleagues at Va'aomānu Pasifika at VUW, Teresia Teaiwa and then Tamasailau Suaalii-Sauni, I was soon in contact with Tui Atua Tupua Tamasese Ta'isi Efi and then sitting at Ta'isi's desk in Tuaefu reading his papers. As I read his papers it became even more apparent how powerful and important this story was, and that it needed to be told. I could only achieve this by working closely with the extensive Ta'isi family.

Family is at the heart of this book. As the heirs to Ta'isi's story, the Ta'isi *aiga*'s cooperation with this project has been critical. They have been invaluable in helping me piece together this history, and they have enhanced this story immeasurably by giving insights and information unavailable in paper sources. Throughout the process of research and writing, the family has generously given me access to documents and photographs, participated in robust discussions, answered my questions, and provided insights upon request, but then stepped back to allow me to make my own evaluations and conclusions. I have regularly updated them on findings and forwarded documents I found in the course of my research. There have been many meetings in Sāmoa, New Zealand, and Australia, and we have exchanged copious e-mails, texts, and phone calls. They have attended lectures I have given, sometimes involving considerable travel, and in Wellington in July 2015, stairs. They have challenged me to look deeper and consider factors overlooked. This book is the product of that exchange. I do not forget that during the writing of this book the family has endured a great deal, which makes their attention to this project all the more generous. I thank them for all their assistance and for granting me the liberty to do my historical work without constraint.

In Apia, my heartfelt thanks go to the Head of State, Tui Atua Tupua Tamasese Ta'isi Efi, and Masiofo Filifilia for their generous support of this enterprise throughout. I cannot thank them both enough for everything they have done to aid my research. It has been a great privilege to have access to Ta'isi's personal papers and to reconstruct such an important and untold history. I will not forget the day when Tui Atua first showed me Ta'isi's office, and we were looking out the window at the view of Mauga Folau and a brilliantly colored *segasegamau'u* bird landed just outside the window; an avian visit I took as an auspicious sign. Tui Atua's own scholarly work, his unrivaled knowledge of Sāmoan genealogies, history, custom, and particularly his emphasis on the importance of the indigenous reference, has been a guiding star for this book from the outset. I thank the many acts of kindness and support from the other Ta'isi grandchildren resident in Sāmoa: Irene Piliopo Maiai, who generously shared letters exchanged between her grandparents with me and a lot of her time, as has her cousin Viopapa Annandale Atherton. Joe Annandale and Sose Annandale, who live on Upolu's southern shore, have kindly attended lectures I delivered in Apia. Their Australian-based sister, Calmar, has attended lectures and shared her knowledge from Canberra. In the extended family in Apia, Joan Tamasese, Judge Clarence Vui Nelson, and Nynette Nelson have also shared reminiscences and given me many kinds of support, as has Emma Kruse Va'ai. Tiffany Nelson-Sauni was a devoted researcher for me in 2012; her work has been invaluable. I thank the Tuaefu household—Tupu Tovio, Peleseuma Toufi, and Tenisia Tovio—for the many ways they have shown me hospitality. Tenisia also assisted me in reconstructing the Tuaefu Library over a number of very long, hot days in 2012. MaryLou Ofoia, from the head of state office, has assisted me in many vital ways and taught me many things since 2012 for which I am very grateful. In 2015 Zita Anderson showed me many kindnesses. On Savai'i, I thank Tugaga Tevesi David, Seti Sā, and Sarah and Kuki Retzlaff for helping me understand a Safune perspective to this history. There have been many others who have assisted my research when I've been in Sāmoa. One who stands out is Tiufea G. Mata'ia. Throughout my visits to Apia, Tiufea was a great presence, and when the Ta'isi and the Pōmare families were reunited for the 2013 Pōmare Day at Owae Marae in Taranaki, Tiufea was unforgettable as the family orator. He did not live to see this book realized, but he is very much a part of its story.

In Wellington I have been extremely fortunate to have the invaluable assistance of Fialaui'afualeafi Tamasese. Fialaui'afualeafi has a masterful recall of history that she has generously shared with me since 2012. Her son, Mea'ole Keil, has also been a wonderful support and facilitator. Her granddaughter Faai'ulelei and her husband, Uale Mai Vala, I fear must have grown to dread my repeated appearances in Wellington as their Wainuiomata home was invariably the venue for *toana'i* (the immense Sāmoan feast after church on Sundays). On these occasions much historical work was conducted. Siuga Paula Masoe has also been a great supporter and resource for this book since 2012. I thank Siuga for everything she has done to aid its progress.

In Auckland there are many Ta'isi *aiga* deserving of recognition. Tugaga Misa Telefoni Retzlaff has been an incredible support from the start. As well as being a frequent correspondent, he has traveled to represent the family at numerous lectures I've given and has been an indispensable sounding board for many of my questions and ideas. His wife, Sarah, I thank for her kindness and forbearance. I first met Ta'isi's Auckland-based granddaughters Sina Schmaulken and Paulele Ulberg in June 2012 when they drove overnight from Auckland to hear a lecture I gave at VUW. Since this meeting, there have been others with their extended families, and Sina has been a fount of stories and information. In 2013 I met many generations of the Auckland-based Ta'isi family thanks to the organizing efforts of Edwina Ulberg. Some of them had demanding exams the next day but still came out on a winter night to meet me. On this occasion I also met granddaughter

Lelani Keil and grandson Kurt Meyers, who then shared vitally important family letters with me. I also met cousin Loloma Johnston that night. Loloma then traveled with me, my mother, and my son to Taranaki for Pōmare Day, sharing many perspectives on Ta'isi and his extended family along the way. Many new conversations began from visits to Auckland. One was with Tony Brunt, thanks to Tugaga Misa Telefoni. Since then Tony has been extraordinarily helpful on all matters relating to the visual history incorporated in this book. His knowledge of the photographic history of German Sāmoa and beyond is unsurpassed, and Tony has provided many other vital insights, connections, and observations. In 2015 I met the only remaining grandchild I had not yet, Leone Forsgren of Pago Pago, who attended my lecture in the Fale Pasifika at Auckland University with her family.

The Ta'isi *aiga* have shaped this book in countless ways. This book has also been shaped and made possible by three fellowships. Before I was awarded the J. D. Stout Fellowship at VUW, I was the recipient of the Jay I. Kislak Fellowship in American Studies at the John W. Kluge Center at the Library of Congress, Washington, DC, in 2011 and then again in the summer of 2013 after I returned from New Zealand. Though this project explored different times and places, the work done during this fellowship was instrumental in giving me a richer view of colonial history that informed this book throughout (and it also gave me much-needed research time after years of an unbroken teaching schedule at Georgetown University). I thank the Kluge Center's then director, Carolyn T. Brown, and the special assistant to the director, Marylou Reker, for all their support during this fellowship.

When I was awarded the J. D. Stout Fellowship at VUW in 2012, this book was born. I thank the Stout Trust for their support throughout my tenure. My heartfelt thanks also go to my colleagues at VUW. Stout Center director Lydia Wevers is the *mauga* (the mountain) at this book's center. I cannot thank her enough for all her support before, during, and after my year at the Stout Center. Also at the Stout Center in 2012 were James Belich, who offered sage advice, Richard Hill, and Rachel Buchanan. With Rachel, the rich connections between Ta'isi and Sir Māui Pōmare, Parihaka, and the Sāmoan Mau were made. Rachel continued to be a vital interlocutor for this book up to the very end when she read the manuscript and provided, once again, invaluable feedback. In the wider VUW community, Charlotte McDonald, Roger Blakeley, Malcolm McKinnon, April

Henderson, Luamanuvao Winnie Laban, and especially David Capie and Sally Hill were supportive and helpful in many ways. I am especially indebted to Tamasailau Suaalii-Sauni, who has been a *tautai* since the book's inception and answered many questions. I am also very grateful for the friendship of Wellingtonians Barbara and Ian Hill, Charlotte Beaglehole, and Gareth Smith.

After my year at VUW, I returned to Washington to my position at Georgetown University. A summer research grant from the Edmund A. Walsh School of Foreign Service allowed me to accept the invitation of Miria Pōmare and the Pōmare whanau to speak about the friendship of Ta'isi and Sir Māui Pōmare at the 2013 Pōmare Day in Taranaki, a great honor that I thank them for. Over my many years at Georgetown, I was always greatly appreciative of the support of John McNeill, Carol Benedict, Carole Sargent, Micah Muscolino (now at Oxford), many other colleagues and friends, and the many wonderful students I had the privilege to teach there.

In late 2013 I was awarded an Australian Research Council Future Fellowship, which set us on a course for Canberra and the Australian National University. Here I have been privileged to be a part of another supportive scholarly environment. In the School of History I thank Angela Woollacott, Douglas Craig, and Nicholas Brown for all their assistance; and our reading group, Carolyn Strange, Ben Mercer, Alex Cook, Jeanine Leane, Gemma Betros, Tanya Colwell, and Frank Bongiorno, for being an important part of this book's development. My PhD student, Nicholas Hoare, has also engaged in highly valued discussions on the subject matter of this book, alerted me to the location of the Richardson papers and compiled the bibliography (with due compensation). Stella Armstrong was a troubleshooter extraordinaire, and Karen Smith, Louise Knox, and Mark Fletcher have all given critical help along the way.

My colleagues in the National Centre of Biography and the Australian Centre for Indigenous History in the ANU School of History have also provided much food for thought as I wrote this book. In the College of Asia and Pacific, I am particularly indebted to Kylie Moloney of the Pacific Manuscripts Bureau, Robert Cribb, and Vicki Luker, as well as my other Pacific history colleagues. Beth Battrick was invaluable in getting the manuscript into good shape in 2015. In Canberra, Chris Wallace, Joanna Sassoon, and Teresa Giuca and beyond Canberra, Joy Damousi, Noah Riseman, Ana Carden-Coyne, Sharon Cavanagh-Luskin, Kim McKay, Vicky Haskins, Sherif Gamal, Jonathon

Neill-Dore, and Russell Cheek, all of whom I thank for their interest, questions, support, and, most important, good humor. Our time in Canberra has been greatly enhanced by being a part of the village that is Turner ACT. I thank all our friends who welcomed us into this community, especially Helen and Percy Bell and Velissa Aplin, and gave me much-needed support so I could work on the book.

Research was conducted at many institutions, and I thank all those who have provided me with such generous assistance along the way. In particular, at the National Library of New Zealand, Jocelyn Chalmers and Roger Swanson have been exceptionally helpful, as have the many others I have worked with through to the final stages. At Archives New Zealand (ANZ), Donal Raethel and the team of archivists helped me during the many hours spent there. Brian Johnson, who was researching at ANZ, was particularly generous sharing his knowledge of the intricacies of government files on Sāmoa. At Auckland Public Library, Keith Giles has been very helpful, as were the librarians at the University of Auckland Special Collections, especially Stephen Innes. At VUW Law Library, Aisling O'Hagan provided excellent assistance. In Geneva, Jacques Oberson helped me navigate the League of Nations Archives. I am greatly indebted to Ambassador Pär Ahlberger and Katarina Prime Linmarker of the Embassy of Sweden, Canberra, and Julia Lindkvist of the National Archives of Sweden, for their invaluable assistance with helping me navigate Swedish-language sources and the Swedish dimension to this story. There have been many in Australia, New Zealand, and Sāmoa who assisted in the painstaking process of organizing images. In particular I thank Estelle Strickland, who got the book's final image to me; Steven Percival in Apia and Sophie Napier at ANU have also provided vital assistance on this front. Special thanks for exceptional hospitality are more than due to Angela Wanhalla and Lachy Patterson in Dunedin; Jon Kay Kamakawiwoʻole Osorio, Cha and Jack Tihati Thompson, and Sa'iliemanu Lilomaiava-Doktor in Honolulu; and Alison Bashford in Cambridge. All the many public lectures I have given throughout the writing of the book have provided an invaluable forum to test ideas and receive feedback. I thank all those who participated in these events and urged me to dig deeper in telling this history. For organizing lectures and visits special thanks are due to Ryan Jones, Leasiolagi Malama Meleisea, Tony Ballantyne, John Stenhouse, Alumita Durutalo, Craig Howes, David Hanlon, Peter Hoffenberg, Sujit Sivasundaram, Christina Twomey, and Toeolesulusulu Damon Salesa.

I also owe a great debt of thanks to the team at University of Hawai'i Press, especially Masako Ikeda, and the editing team at Westchester Publishing Services, for bringing this book to fruition.

And last but by no means least, my family deserves my thanks. My parents, Sandra and John, have given many kinds of support for which I am very grateful. To my husband, Bruce Vaughn, and sons, Freddy (Feleti) and Lachlan, I cannot thank you enough for taking this book's global journey with me since 2012. For that I will be ever grateful, and for much, much more besides.

PO'B
Canberra 2016

Key Historical Figures

Ta'isi Olaf Fredrick (O. F.) Nelson

The subject of this book is referred to by his *matai* title, Ta'isi, a title bestowed on Olaf Fredrick "O. F." Nelson, by the village of Asau in 1923. In using his *matai* title, this book follows the Sāmoan convention of using this name as a mark of respect in all formal and many informal settings. Ta'isi continued to be called Fred Nelson or Feleti Nelsoni, his *igoa itaulealea* ("everyday calling name" or Christian name) by close family and friends, as well as by his detractors, who steadfastly challenged his right to assert his status within Sāmoan society denoted by his *matai* title. According to the latter, his European parentage canceled out his Indigenous heritage, a view Ta'isi confronted continuously. Because this work aims to "decolonize" this history, it centralizes Ta'isi's Sāmoan identity and follows Sāmoan naming conventions. Therefore, this work refers to him as Ta'isi unless directly quoting from a source where he is referred to by his *igoa itaulealea.*

Ta'isi's Aiga (Family) in Birth Order

August Nelson (1838–1909)—father
Sinagogo Masoe (m. Nelson) (1859–1918)—mother
Lucy Nelson (m. Kruse) (1874–1924)—sister
Gustava Nelson (m. Wetzell) (1879–1946)—sister
Josephine Nelson (m. David) (1881–1918)—sister
August Nelson Junior (1889–1918)—brother and father of Frank Nelson (mother—Jane Meredith) and August "Gussie" Nelson (mother—Fusipala Tuiletufuga Ale)
Rosabel Edith Nelson (née Moors 1889–1959)—wife
Priscilla Muench (née Moors)—sister-in-law

Viopapa Lucy Nelson—Ta'isi's eldest daughter (1904–1937) (her mother was Leata of Safune, m. E. J. Grey of Suva)

Ta'isi and Rosabel's Children in Birth Order

Irene Gustava Noue Nelson (m. Tupua Tamasese Mea'ole)—mother of Fialaui'afualeafi, Olaf Fredrick ("Efi") now known as Tui Atua Tupua Tamasese Ta'isi Efi, Peter Tusi, Irene Piliopo (m. Maiai)

Olive Virginia Malienafau (m. Fredrick Betham)—mother of Barry and Leone (m. Forsgren)

Joyce Rosabel Piliopo "Billie" (m. Richard Carruthers; Hermann Retzlaff)—mother of Lelani (m. Keil), Tuitautai, Hermann Theodore (known as Misa Telefoni), and Erich (died in infancy)

Ta'isi Nelson—son (1915–1919)

Sina Hope (m. Edward Annandale)—mother of Viopapa (m. Atherton), Calmar, Joseph, Teuila, and Sose

Calmar Josephine Taufau (m. August Meyers)—mother of Sina (m. Schmalkuchen), Paulele (m. Ulberg), Kurt

Extended Aiga

Pitofau Masoe—(m. Masoe Ti'amamana) cousin who lived at Tuaefu with three generations of family

Fa'agutu Tugaga (m. Atoa Polito, who worked for O. F. Nelson and Co. and was active in the Mau)—cousin who lived adjacent to Tuaefu

Masoe Tulele—son of Pitofau and Masoe Ti'amamana who was active in the Mau and cared for Tuaefu in Ta'isi's absences

Leading Sāmoan Political Figures

Afamasaga—prominent chief who was stripped of his title by Administrator Richardson and referred to from then on by the administration as Lago Lago

Faumuina Fiame—president of the Mau from 1930

Lauaki—leader of the *Mau a Pule,* exiled by German governor Solf to Saipan in 1909, died en route back to Sāmoa in 1914

Malietoa Tanumafili I—*tama aiga,* leading Sāmoan supporter of the administration

Mata'afa Iosefo—*tama aiga* whose popular support sparked the 1899 civil war
Ala Tamasese—widow of Tupua Tamasese Lea'lofi III and leader of Women's Mau
Toelupe—leader of the fono of faipule
Tupua Tamasese Lea'lofi III—*tama aiga,* president of the Mau killed in Black Saturday Massacre 1929
Tupua Tamasese Mea'ole—*tama aiga,* succeeds older brother to Tupua title from 1930, Mau leader and Ta'isi's son-in-law from 1935
Tuimalealiifano—*tama aiga,* senior Mau leader, injured in Black Saturday massacre

O. F. Nelson and Co. Figures and Business Associates

C. V. Allom—general manager of Head Office Apia
Rudolph Kruse—(nephew)
Harry W. Moors—(brother-in-law)
L. D. Stewart—manager of Sydney office of O. F. Nelson and Co.
Rex Pleasants—secretary of Auckland office (traveled to Europe with Ta'isi in 1928)
G. E. L. (George) Westbrook—Sāmoa-based trader and merchant

New Zealand Prime Ministers

William Massey—Prime Minister 1925 (Reform Party) and Minister for External Affairs 1923
Gordon (J. G.) Coates—Prime Minister 1925–1928 and Minister for External affairs August–December 1928 (Reform Party)
Joseph Ward—Prime Minister and Minister for External Affairs 1928–1930 (United Party)
George Forbes—Prime Minister and Minister for External Affairs 1930–1935 (United Party)
Michael Savage—Prime Minister and Minister for External affairs 1935–1940 (Labour Party)
Peter Fraser—Prime Minister 1940–1949 (Labour Party)
Helen Clark—Prime Minister 1999–2008 (Labour Party)

Government Ministers

Francis H. D. Bell—Minister for External Affairs 1923–1926, Prime Minister May 1925, leader of Legislative Council, conservative power broker
Frank Langstone—Minister for External Affairs 1940–1942
E. P. Lee—Minister for External Affairs 1920–1923
William Nosworthy—Minister for External Affairs 1926–1928
Māui Wiremu Piti Naera Pōmare—Minister for the Cook Islands 1916–1928, Ta'isi's friend and confidant

Government Officials

Carl Berendsen—Secretary of the Department of External Affairs (from 1928)
J. D. (James Dunbar) Gray—Secretary of the Department of External Affairs (1919–1928)

Sāmoa Administrators

Robert Logan (1914–1919)
Robert W. Tate (1919–1923)
George Spafford Richardson (1923–1928)
Stephen S. Allen (1928–1931)
Herbert E. Hart (1931–1935)
A. C. (Alfred Clarke) Turnbull (1935–1946)

Other Key Political Figures, Public Figures, and Associates in New Zealand, Sāmoa, Australia, and the League of Nations

Percy Andrews—editor of *Samoa Guardian*
Arthur L. Braisby—Sāmoa inspector of police
Joseph Hector McNeil Carruthers—Premier of New South Wales (1904–1907), member of New South Wales Legislative Council (1887–1932)
H. V. Evatt—leading Australian barrister, High Court judge, and future Australian Labor Party leader who gave Ta'isi legal advice
Charles Fergusson—Governor-General of New Zealand 1925–1930
P. B. (Patrick) Fitzherbert—editor of *NZ Samoa Guardian*

E. W. Gurr—exiled from Sāmoa in 1928 for five years
Harry E. Holland—leader of the New Zealand Labour Party 1919–1933
F. G. Lewis—Australian Methodist minister appointed Sāmoa secretary of native affairs in 1928
J. H. (John Hector) Luxford—Chief Justice Sāmoa
Alfred McCarthy—Crown Solicitor Sāmoa Administration
James Parr—New Zealand High Commissioner, London and representative at League of Nations
E. A. Ransom—Acting Prime Minister 1930
A. G. (Alfred George) Smyth—trader exiled from Sāmoa in 1928 for two years

Lawyers Associated with Ta'isi

F. D. Baxter—Sāmoa-based lawyer
Stafford Cripps—UK Kings' Counsel
John Findlay—NZ Kings' Counsel
Gustav Klinkmueller—Sāmoa-based German lawyer
D. R. Hoggard—lawyer in John Findlay's chambers
John Roberts—London-based solicitor
Alfred Hall Skelton—Auckland-based lawyer
Thomas Slipper—Sāmoa-based lawyer

Glossary of Sāmoan Terms

Note on the spelling of Sāmoa: When quoting sources I have spelled Sāmoa as it was spelled in those sources, almost always "Samoa." Spelling conventions now use a macron over the first *a* to indicate the long vowel sound in *Sāmoa.*

aiga—family
fa'asamoa—the Sāmoan way, Sāmoan custom
faipule—village representatives selected by administrators until 1936
fale—traditional Sāmoan house
fono—meeting
fautasi—traditional longboat
'ie toga—highly valued fine mat woven from pandanus by women artisans given on special occasions like ifoga, marriages, funerals, ta'alolo
ifoga—forgiveness ceremony
malaga—tour of villages
matai—head of family
pākehā—a New Zealander of European descent
pālagi—foreigner to Sāmoa, tends to denote a white person (singular)
papālagi—plural for pālagi
ta'alolo—an elaborate, formal presentation of gifts in support of an occasion and/or presentation of a VIP
tama aiga—one of the four paramount chiefs (Tamasese, Malietoa, Mata'afa, Tuimalealiifano)
tāupou—preeminent unmarried woman of a village
tautai—navigator

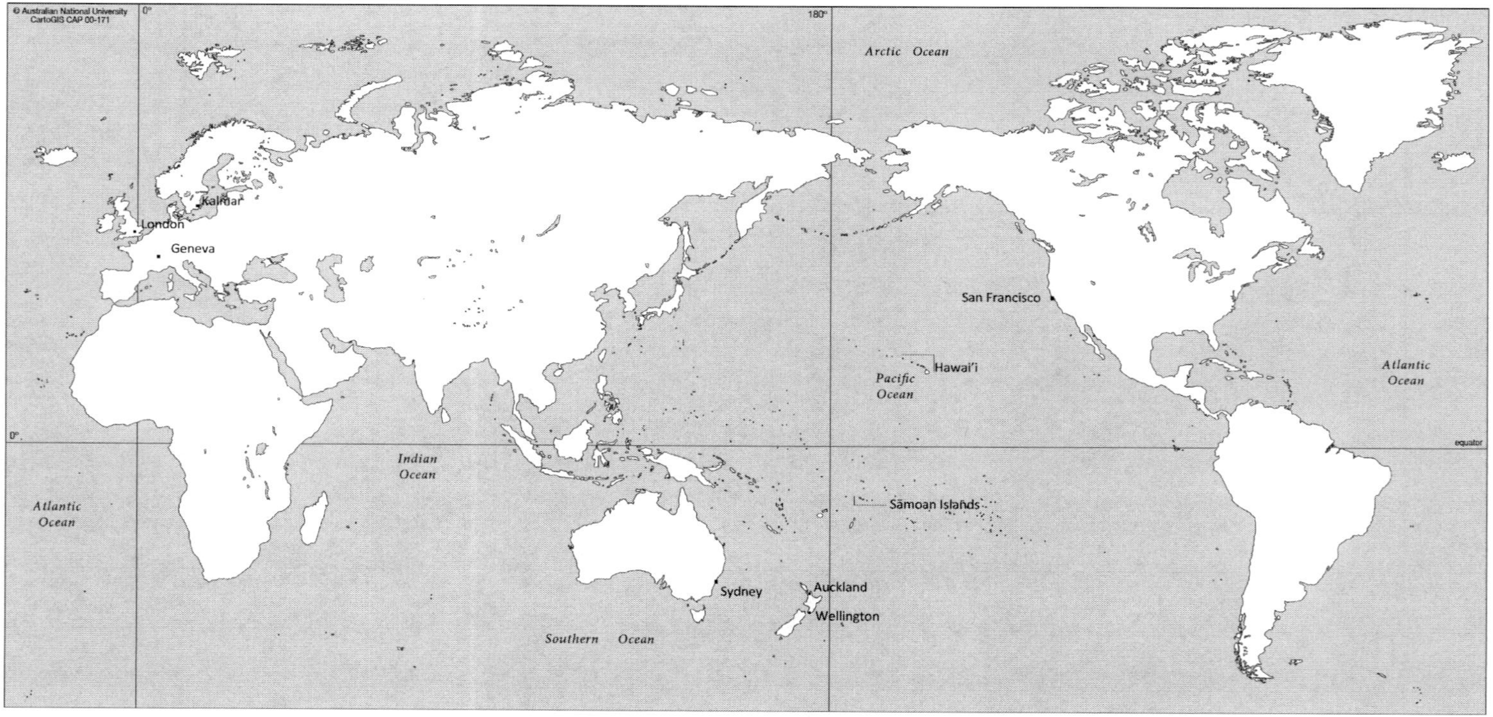

© Australian National University
CartoGIS CAP 00-171
0°
180°
Arctic Ocean
Kalmar
London
Geneva
San Francisco
Hawai'i
Pacific
Ocean
Atlantic
Ocean
0°
equator
Indian
Ocean
Atlantic
Ocean
Sāmoan Islands
Sydney
Auckland
Wellington
Southern Ocean

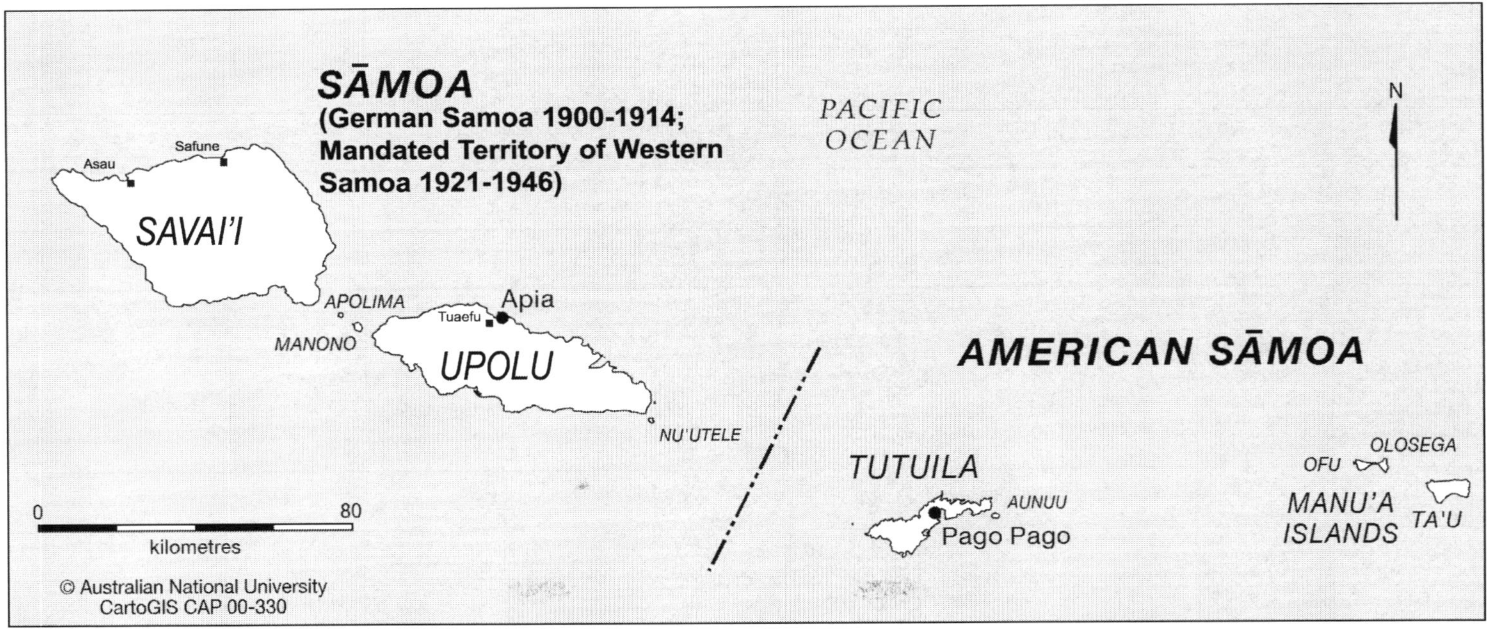
SĀMOA
(German Samoa 1900-1914;
Mandated Territory of Western
Samoa 1921-1946)
PACIFIC
OCEAN
N
Asau
Safune
SAVAI'I
APOLIMA
MANONO
Apia
Tuaefu
UPOLU
NU'UTELE
AMERICAN SĀMOA
TUTUILA
AUNUU
Pago Pago
OFU
OLOSEGA
MANU'A
ISLANDS
TA'U
0
80
kilometres
© Australian National University
CartoGIS CAP 00-330

Prologue

This book tells the astonishing story of a man born in a little village on a small Pacific island who was formally educated until age thirteen, became one of the richest men in the Pacific, and then fought the greatest empire the world has known. Driven by a quest for justice and universal democracy, he refused to accept the colonial mantra that his people were incapable of governing themselves. Though his life was deeply impacted by conflict—by wars in his island home and wars that engulfed the world—he was devoted to peace. He strenuously fought the militaristic aftershocks of the Great War in the Pacific with a war of words, by aiding a campaign of nonviolent civil disobedience, and through a slew of imperial challenges from Apia to Wellington, London, and Geneva. He defied notions of white racial superiority that were the bedrock of an imperial system at its zenith. He upset many powerful people and governments. For his efforts he was ostracized, humiliated, financially ruined, exiled (twice), tried, and imprisoned.

This is the story of Ta'isi O. F. Nelson and his world.[1] His life was a saga wrought by the great driving forces of his time—empire, war, the 1918 influenza epidemic, the Great Depression, nationalism, internationalism, and all-powerful colonial ideas. This book chronicles Ta'isi's great causes, love of his country, Sāmoa, as well as his intimate world, his life as the paterfamilias to his greatest love, his family.

Being such a central figure in the story of twentieth-century Sāmoan history, Ta'isi has made appearances in previous histories; this book is duly indebted to historians who have authored the foundational story of his times.[2] Yet this body of work has given us an incomplete picture of Ta'isi. Some historians have been swayed by biased sources.[3] Others have made assertions about him without clearly revealing where their evidence comes from, or they have missed the global scope of his life, networks, and achievements.[4] Some claims about him are incorrect yet are continuously recirculated as if they were facts.[5] The received historical view of Ta'isi has been confused, incomplete, and questions about him have remained unanswered. Was he an exploiter of his people? Was he a power-mad capitalist driven by a lust for commercial dominance? Was he a naive idealist striving for an impossible goal? Why *was* he an agitator?

This book aims to answer these questions by going deeper into the story of this man. It uses new sources and adopts new perspectives, and so tells an untold story about this man, his family, and the global communities he inhabited. Ta'isi continuously transcended categorizations and borders; so does this book.[6] It takes insights from an eclectic range of sources and approaches. It interrogates notions of race, empire, gender, power, and towering national myths shaped by these ideologies. Also it pays close attention to the Sāmoan foundations to this story. Many of Ta'isi's grandchildren, great-grandchildren, and extended family have provided insights and information, answered questions, and shared family stories that have fleshed out the "paper sources"—previously untapped personal letters and documents and other archival data—that form the book's backbone.[7] This book is richer, indeed it has been made possible, because of their invaluable support.[8]

As Ta'isi's life was connected to many people across many nations, this book is the culmination of an international exchange of ideas and information spanning seven countries—Sāmoa, New Zealand, Australia, the United Kingdom, the United States, Sweden, and Switzerland. It binds deep histories of the Pacific to contemporary questions about the past, and epic stories of humanity to the life of one man: Ta'isi O. F. Nelson.

Tautai

Chapter One

Converging Worlds

Sāmoa and Europe Clash (1883–1909)

Safune is one of a cluster of villages nestled on the northern shore of the Sāmoan island of Savai'i. These villages sit between volcanoes and ocean, the two great forces that have dominated and sustained life here for centuries. These two forces have brought bounty and delivered regular displays of their astounding power through spectacular eruptions and destructive storms. Safune is set on the picturesque Siliafai Lagoon at a break in the reef that encases much of Savai'i's coast. This channel has been a point of ingress and egress for people for as long as this land has been inhabited.[1] In the nineteenth century, new people began arriving, and disparate worlds met.

It was here that Ta'isi Olaf Fredrick Nelson was born on February 24, 1883. Fred Nelson, or Feleti Nelesoni as Sāmoans knew him, was the fourth child and first son for his parents, Sinagogo Masoe and August Nelson. Like his older sisters and his future younger brother, Ta'isi was the embodiment of converged worlds that blended ancient Sāmoan hierarchies with distant European communities. The Nelson children's paternal lineage stretched from Safune to the town of Ödängla, Mönsterås, in Kalmar Province on Sweden's southeast coast.[2] These converged worlds produced new generations filled with potential, promise, and unprecedented parentage, and also precipitated great trauma.

By the year of Ta'isi's birth, Sāmoa was enmeshed in global currents of people, commodities, ideas, and power shifts. These currents and shifts triggered fundamental changes. They happened at such a pace that in the decades before his birth Sāmoa was gripped by clashes made all the more deadly by the introduction of new weapons—guns, gunboats, and foreign actors—into traditional and cyclical conflicts between rival Sāmoan groups. The civil wars that had racked the islands before Ta'isi's birth were suppressed into a short-lived "sullen peace" in 1883.[3] The first years of Ta'isi's life saw events in Sāmoa similar to those echoed across the Pacific, as well as those that were nothing less than extraordinary. The ramifications of these bloody times shaped Sāmoa and left a deep and indelible imprint on Ta'isi. To make sense of the world Ta'isi was born into, we need to step back from Safune and look at the forces that shaped Sāmoa in the decades before Ta'isi's birth and that would continue to shape his life and his life's work.

By the nineteenth century, colonialism had only lightly impacted Sāmoa.[4] But changes were coming. One hundred years before Ta'isi's birth, the establishment of British colonies in Australia from 1788 had a profound impact on Sāmoa and its region. The Australian colonies were penal settlements initially driven by both a pastoral and an oceanic frontier. The pastoral frontier grew through a systematic process of seizing lands occupied for many millennia by the continent's Indigenous peoples. Sheep ran on lands that had never seen a hoof, and wool was exported back to the industrial mills in northern England. Ships returned from the British Isles laden with thousands of immigrants, a proportion by force and many more by choice, to Australian shores, where they forged settler societies akin to the United States, Canada, and South Africa. Like these other settler societies, Australia was premised on exploitation of Indigenous peoples and the acquisition of their lands. Australia's settler society was also premised on exploitation of convicts, predominantly working-class men and women from the British Isles, exiled to the Pacific to labor and provide the bottom rung in a new society on the other side of the world.

Although wool would become to Australia what tobacco was to the United States, the first exports from the colonies were the pelts of seals and kangaroos sold in the extraordinarily lucrative China markets. Other resource rushes followed, focused on finding more commodities to sell to China. Sandalwood, bêche-de-mer, and tortoiseshell were sought all over the Pacific. Sāmoa was not rich in these commodities, and the rushes sparked by them had greater impact on contiguous island groups. Yet the traffic of men who manned the ships involved in these trades found its way to the harbors of Sāmoa. Whaling was the greatest of all Pacific resource rushes. Unlike others, its harvest was not directed toward China markets but predominantly toward the eastern United States. Whaling drew thousands of men on hundreds of ships to the Pacific from the 1790s until the steep decline in whale populations drove the whalers into more distant and dangerous grounds off the coast of East Asia by the late 1840s.

Men of the lower orders of society manned the Pacific's resource rushes. Many of them were believed to be men of ill repute, escaped convicts from the Australian colonies, escaped or ex-slaves from the United States, or just the plain poor and uneducated.[5] Christian moralists fretted about the impact such men were having on Indigenous people throughout the region. In the Australian colonies, missionaries blamed these lower-class men for the extreme violence meted out to Aboriginal People contesting the takeover of their lands and the endemic culture of sexual violence against Indigenous women.[6] In the islands, these men were charged with exporting the most degraded form of European culture with them, one lubricated by drink, licentiousness, and brutality.

A network of port towns from Sydney[7] in Australia, Honolulu and Lāhainā in Hawai'i, Levuka in Fiji, Kororāreka in northern New Zealand, Papeete in Tahiti, and Apia in Sāmoa vied for the dubious honor of being the "Hell of the Pacific." Missionaries narrated alarming tales of degradation. Sailors were supposedly ungoverned by European laws or personal moral codes, riding roughshod over Indigenous communities wherever they made contact. There was truth to their tales; however, the more dire the picture, the better it served the missionary purpose of soliciting financial (and spiritual) support for taking Christianity to the region's Indigenous peoples. Missionaries insisted Christianity alone was the panacea for vice.[8]

The reality was considerably more complex. Many Indigenous communities initially exercised considerable control over these foreign men. They participated in, and benefited from, the proceeds of port economics. Indigenous rulers initially set the terms of trade. European goods—especially guns—became highly sought-after items in exchange for food, water, and sex. The infusion of guns into traditional rivalries in island groups had devastating effects throughout the Pacific, not least in Sāmoa.

Though British missionary societies had been active in the Pacific since the 1790s, it took some thirty years before Christianity arrived in the Sāmoan islands. The landing of London Missionary Society (LMS) figure John Williams, at Sapapali'i on Savai'i in 1830, is a much-celebrated event to this day. Williams left Tahiti to do God's work in the Sāmoan islands. It also happened to be the work of the British Empire; missionaries fostered ongoing links between Britain and the islands. Nine years after John Williams' arrival, the United States staked an interest in the Sāmoan islands when the US Exploring Expedition, captained by Charles Wilkes, arrived in 1839. Wilkes established relations with Sāmoan chiefs, especially on the island of Tutuila, that would later grow into a critical alignment. Wilkes appointed John Williams' son (John C. Williams) to be the first US consul in Sāmoa in 1839. Britain matched this US consular posting in Sāmoa with one of its own in the same year. National loyalties were brittle in those days; John C. Williams would switch to serving Britain as its consul in Sāmoa from 1858.[9]

The British government's 1837 assessment of the impact on Indigenous peoples throughout the range of British settler activity (very interestingly, avoiding comment on India or China, where British merchants were engaging with the insidious opium trade) reinforced the view that contact between the "dregs of humanity" and Indigenous peoples was nothing less than a national disgrace. Too often, the 1837 *Report on the Condition of Aborigines in British Settlements* stated, "their territory [has been] usurped, their property seized, their numbers diminished, their characters debased." It continued, "European vices and diseases have been introduced and they have been familiarized with the use of our most potent instruments for the subtle or violent destruction of human life . . . brandy and gunpowder."[10] The impact in Sāmoa of these "gigantic evils" was illustrated by the testimony of Reverend Thomas, a Wesleyan missionary stationed in Tonga, who claimed a whaler had killed two score people in Sāmoa in late 1832. "Our hearts almost bleed for the poor Sāmoa people," he wrote. "They are a very mild, inoffensive race . . . and as they are near to us, we have a great hope of their embracing the truth . . . that the whole group will do so." This hope was bolstered by the fact "a part of them have already turned to God." The conduct of "our English savages" by contrast, "has a tone of barbarity and cruelty in it which was never heard of or practiced by" Sāmoans.[11]

Piety dissolved considerably when the realpolitik of survival in the islands became all too apparent for the successors to the first missionary wave. The second wave had to contend with quite different conditions. Imperial agents were sent into the islands to satiate the territorial ambitions of, first, Britain and France, whose presence had quickly followed unruly whaling crews. One of the first sites for Anglo-French rivalry in the South Pacific was New Zealand. In the late 1830s, British consuls and missionaries stationed in the far north, close to the infamous whaling port of Kororāreka, worked to stymie French imperial activities on the Akaroa peninsula on the east coast of the south island. New Zealand was the great prize after the British outfoxed French imperial designs in southern Australia.[12] New Zealand's temperate climate was perfectly suited for another settler colony supported by a pastoral economy, and both Britain and France wanted a share of it. The Māori ultimately decided the victor, opting to sign the *Treaty of Waitangi,* making Queen Victoria the protector of New Zealand in 1840. Britain interpreted this treaty differently. To them the Māori had signed away their sovereignty, opening the way for British occupation and the systematic dispossession of Māori from their lands as the settlers built a pastoral economy that, like Australia, was dominated by wool. Battles raged across New Zealand from 1845 until 1916, when the last shots were fired in the New Zealand Wars.[13] Settler-Māori conflict would shape New Zealand in an infinite number of ways. It would also impact Sāmoan history when New Zealand settlers began to see the Sāmoan islands as a natural extension of their territory from the 1870s.[14] New Zealand's history of conflict between settlers and Indigenous peoples would cast a long shadow, and it would be echoed in the Sāmoan uprising against New Zealand rule in the 1920s in which Ta'isi played such a central role.

After the *Treaty of Waitangi,* French imperial ambition turned away from New Zealand and toward the islands. In 1842 French admiral Du Petit Thouars used the pretext of the mistreatment of French Catholic priests by the queen of Tahiti, Pōmare IV, to annex the islands of Tahiti. He also claimed the islands of the Marquesas in the same year. British missionary George Pritchard (of the LMS) was the close adviser to Queen Pōmare. In widely publicized British accounts of this instance of French gunboat diplomacy, Pritchard was portrayed as the defender of the Protestant faith and British imperial claims, as well as the protector of the young, vulnerable queen, who was likened to a Pacific Queen Victoria.[15] Despite holding out for some time, Queen Pōmare ultimately acquiesced to French rule when the promised intervention by Britain on her behalf never eventuated. George Pritchard was ejected from Tahiti and returned to England. Shortly after, he returned to the Pacific as the British missionary-consul to Apia in 1845. In the same year, French Marist priests arrived in Apia, too, and there were palpable fears that France would replicate the tactics it used to annex the eastern Polynesian islands. Visits by French warships alarmed Pritchard, seeming to confirm his suspicions.[16] France's imperial ambition eventually manifested itself elsewhere: it annexed New Caledonia in 1853. When France turned this island outpost into a penal colony from the 1860s, panicked British settlers in Australia and New Zealand called for the expansion into the island Pacific.

George Pritchard cut a different figure as a missionary and consul in Apia than he did in Tahiti. Pritchard straddled the first and second waves of missionary activity in the islands, and he shows how the missionary enterprise shifted to a more mercenary venture. In Tahiti he was the paragon of British Christian manhood (according to British accounts). In Sāmoa, his standing among Sāmoans was checkered; his standing with the LMS became even worse.[17] By the time Pritchard assumed his Sāmoan role, the lines between traders, missionaries, and consuls had already become blurred; he would blur the lines further still. In action that would have been unthinkable to missionaries railing against the unmitigated harm alcohol caused to colonized peoples and European seaman in the Pacific only thirteen years before, Pritchard began importing liquor into Apia in 1850. When he imported another shipment in 1852, he was expelled from the LMS. Disgrace had to be weighed against profit; Pritchard chose the latter. The British consul in Apia had turned his consulate into a tavern, a place "unfit for a respectable Englishman to live in or for the English flag to fly in front of," according to one observer.[18] John C. Williams, son of the founding Christian missionary and then US consul, was accused of trading in arms.[19] Both Pritchard and Williams temper the virtuous image of the British Empire touted eighty years later during the Mau, when New Zealand officials presided over prohibition and scorned those—Ta'isi in particular—who criticized restrictions on alcohol.

By the 1850s, the port trade in Apia had grown greatly and the potential profits, though sinful and tainted, were too tempting for men like Pritchard. Midway through the nineteenth century, Pacific society was shaken by seismic shifts, spurring immense changes to the pace and scale of Pacific migrations altering the human landscape, and the environmental one, too, throughout the region.[20] Gold discoveries in California in 1849, then southeast Australia in 1851 and New Zealand in 1861, were an immense draw to humanity, launching new population centers on the Pacific Rim with breathtaking rapidity.[21] The "golden Pacific" years saw change staggering in its pace and scale. Railways linked the United States from one "shining sea" to the other in 1869. People and goods flowed from Europe across the United States to thriving cities in California; many did not stop there. Ships fanned out on maritime highways to Asia and ports in Australia and New Zealand. The maritime highway between these settler societies was traversed by ever-increasing numbers of men (and far fewer women). The Sāmoan islands were caught up in this expanding web of networks and commercial linkages.

While Pago Pago also grew from the 1870s when it became a US coaling station, Apia continued to be the Sāmoan hub for foreign influence. The population of foreigners living there grew, expanding what was dubbed "the beach": a heterodox community of incoming men (overwhelmingly) who lived outside the traditional Sāmoan village system. Apia's broad harbor was one reason for it being favored by "the beach" as their place of residence, the shore land was also largely unoccupied by Sāmoans due to previous conflicts and so the transfer of land here was more straightforward than it would prove in other areas. Apia provided provisions for shipping and the onshore recreations that alarmed moralists: drink and sex.[22] In addition to this economy structured on services and provisioning, another element to the Sāmoan economy had been developing from the 1840s. In 1842, John C. Williams had pioneered the first export of Sāmoa: coconut oil.[23] Whale oil was declining in availability in the 1840s, and an alternative source was needed for its multifaceted uses in industry and cosmetics.[24] The answer to this deficit in oil grew on trees. The first coconut oil was exported from Sāmoa in 1842. From this beginning the copra industry would grow to be the country's most important commodity. As it was described in 1929 (possibly by Ta'isi) "what wool is to the New Zealand farmer, so is the product of the cocoanut to the Samoan."[25] Initially the export of coconut products was constrained by a number of factors. It was not until the 1860s and a coalescence of intersecting local, regional, and global factors that allowed the coconut trade to flourish.

The years of the "golden Pacific" coincided with the shift away from resource harvesting—most notably whaling—to the beginnings of the "plantation Pacific" that would span the ocean's tropical region. By the 1850s plantation economies brought to the Pacific similar insidious effects to those that had shaped the Atlantic world for centuries. The first region to transform into a component of the plantation

Pacific was Hawai‘i, after the Great Māhele of 1848.[26] This event monetized land, facilitating its rapid transfer from Indigenous possession to that of planters, the majority of whom hailed from the United States. Within four decades, two-thirds of all land had passed into *haole* (white) hands, driving the creation of an elite planter class. Many in this new Hawaiian planter class were descendants of New England Protestant missionaries who began their work in the islands from 1820.[27] Hawai‘i rapidly became a factory of sugar production powered by its rich volcanic soils and the labor of peoples from Japan, China, Portugal, and then, at the end of the nineteenth century, Korea and the Caribbean island of Puerto Rico. The rapid economic ascent of Hawaiian planters came at the expense of Indigenous Hawaiians. Every aspect of their culture and lives was adversely impacted by this profound shift from possession to dispossession in a few decades. This process culminated in the end of Indigenous governance when planters seized power from Queen Lili‘uokalani in 1893, leading to the US annexation of the group in 1898. Intermarriage between different ethnic communities was extensive in Hawai‘i (giving rise to the misconception that Hawai‘i was a "racial paradise"). Yet the planter class that quickly emerged after 1850 and would, in less than half a century, wrest power from Indigenous Hawaiians, had the least instance of intermarriage with Hawaiians. Though there were notable exceptions to this practice—like some prominent marriages between planters and noble Hawaiian women—essentially the Hawaiian planter class was small and racially homogeneous, with its members jealously guarding their "whiteness."[28]

The course of Hawaiian history in the second half of the nineteenth century was an object lesson for other Pacific polities about the perils (or opportunities, depending on where you stood) of unchecked planter power. Planter politics immensely impacted Sāmoa and Ta'isi's life. Sāmoa's harbors and rich hinterlands attracted growing numbers of newcomers, who brought fresh waves of culture, power dynamics, and economic conditions with them. One of these newcomers was Nils Peter Gustafsson, who would later anglicize his name to August Nelson: Ta'isi's father. Nelson was born on the croft Sandvik Ödängla, Mönsterås, in Kalmar Province, Sweden, in 1838. Born to an affluent widow, Stina Kajsa Olsdotter, and a married farmhand, Gustav Persson, Nelson suffered unbearable ostracism for being illegitimate and so escaped to sea as a thirteen-year-old in 1850.[29] Like thousands of others, he was drawn by gold fever to the mining frontiers of Australia and then Otago, New Zealand.[30] Having made some money at the diggings Nelson was drawn to another frontier, that of the island Pacific, arriving in Sāmoa in 1867. His movements mirrored the immense human migrations occurring around the Pacific at the time.

By the time August Nelson arrived in Sāmoa, the pace of change in the islands was accelerating. The coconut oil export trade shifted into higher gear in the late 1850s when a third player of the imperial game joined Britain and the United States: Germany. Germany made its presence felt quickly through pioneering plantation economics around the Pacific. The Hamburg-based company, J. C. Godeffroy and Son, shaped the history of swathes of the Pacific, not least of which Sāmoa. The company's commercial activities were closely followed by forms of German governance and then, in 1900, formal annexation of the western Sāmoan islands. J. C. Godeffroy and Son arrived in the islands in 1857 and from 1864 introduced a new method of processing coconuts to minimize freight costs and maximize profits. Rather than exporting coconut oil, as had been practice since 1842, the head agent for J. C. Godeffroy and Son from 1864, Theodor Weber, devised a new process: dry the coconut at island-based plants; then ship the copra (dried coconut flesh) to Europe and extract the oil there, using the residual fiber for livestock fodder.[31] Profits soared when copra, rather than oil, was exported. Weber also ushered in another far-reaching shift in the industry. To circumvent the insecure supply of coconuts from Sāmoans, who valued the coconut highly for diet and a myriad of other vital uses, he introduced the concept of coconut plantations. As with sugar plantations in Hawai'i and, by the 1860s sugar plantations in Fiji and Australia's Queensland coast, the advent of coconut plantations in Sāmoa sparked a rush for land and raised the question of who was going to labor on the plantations. As seen in plantation economies in the Atlantic world, this question and its answers were extremely fraught; they impacted Sāmoa's history from this point in multiple ways.

Apia became the headquarters of Godeffroy and Sons. In 1878, Godeffroy and Sons became the stock company known as Deutsche Handels-und Plantagen-Gesellschaft der Sudsee Inseln (German Trade and Plantation Company of the South Sea Islands) commonly referred to as DHPG or colloquially as "the company." DHPG became a complex of plantations and labor traders that bound Sāmoa with New Guinea and Micronesia after 1884. The DHPG operated plantations across these island groups and was headquartered in Apia. The economic and strategic importance of Apia, coupled with the growing (though still small) population that made up the Apia beach, drove efforts to institute law, order, and respectability into the port town. The reform of Apia dates from this time. The presence of British, US, and German interests meant that parallel and competing jurisdictions developed in Apia. In turn they overlay and competed with Indigenous law and custom.[32]

Though Apia was arguably no longer the "Hell of the Pacific" by the time Nelson arrived in 1867, he did not opt to join Apia's "beach." In 1868, August Nelson founded the firm Nelson and Company with one trading outpost at Fasitootai on Savai'i. This outpost would lead to many others that would come to dominate Sāmoan commerce in coming decades. After five years he built a forty-ton schooner "to facilitate and extend his business" and opened another station at the village of Gagaemalae on the south coast of Savai'i. As he prospered, he opened another station in Safune in 1878 on the north coast that became the "controlling station" for his firm. Nelson had become what one Englishman at the time described as a "Savai'i squire."[33]

August Nelson made a life for himself on Savai'i. He learned the language, reputedly speaking it with the precision of a native speaker.[34] Business success was one path to respectability, and it greatly facilitated another: marriage. The ravages of war depleted the population of young Sāmoan men, further enhancing the eligibility of *pālagi* men as husbands; however, the young women intended to be their wives did not always see matters this way.

One young woman who was the village belle and *tāupou* of Asau caught Nelson's attention. She was Sinagogo Masoe, a young woman descended from esteemed familial lines. Her mother was Viopapa, daughter of Tugaga of the village of Safune. She was also connected to the village of Samauga through Mala'itai Pa'ovale. Her father, Masoe, was the *matai* (head of family) of Asau. Sinagogo's family could see the great benefits Nelson offered to their family with his prospering commercial enterprise and insisted Sinagogo put the wishes and prospects of her family first. Sinagogo did not agree and ran away to the hills. Her brothers pursued her and again presented her with her family's wishes that she marry this *pālagi* man. If she carried out her duty, great prestige would be bestowed on her and her descendants, particularly her eldest son. Sinagogo acceded to her family's wishes and married Nelson, whom she came to love deeply. After they wed, they adopted four-year-old Lucy (born 1874), whom they acknowledged as their eldest child. They established their home in the village of Safune, where they had four children together: Gustava in 1879; Josephine in 1881; and then her sons, Olaf Fredrick (Ta'isi) in 1883 and their youngest, August Junior, in 1889.[35]

Nelson's trading stores became a family business. The men in the Masoe family were employed rowing longboats to transport goods around Savai'i.[36] Nelson was also involved in land speculation, and his inclusion into the extended Masoe family aided this side of his business greatly. Nelson was the northern Savai'i agent for Frank Cornwall, the former LMS printer who was involved in landing and then slave driving Kanak laborers in the 1870s, as well as unscrupulous land speculation on an enormous scale; he ventured to buy some "three hundred thousand acres in Savai'i and A'ana" building "the first massive block of British claims in Samoa" amounting to about 40 percent of all Sāmoan land.[37] Nelson's familial connections were intrinsic to Cornwall's success; the latter freely admitted this to the Sāmoan Land Commission of the early 1890s, who investigated the manner in which he, and others, had acquired huge tracts of land.[38]

Though August Nelson was integrated into a highborn family and his business grew, his prosperity took place against a backdrop of increasing friction in the islands. Although the European presence was small by population size, it was highly disruptive, bringing new elements to the traditional and cyclical conflicts between rival Sāmoan groups. Unlike Hawai'i or Tahiti, ruled by the Kamehameha and Pōmare, respectively, no dominant leader had emerged in the Sāmoan island group in the nineteenth century to vanquish traditional opponents and unite the island groups under a single ruler. Rather, two rival groups emerged by the 1820s: Sā Malietoa and Sā Tupua. Sā Malietoa was allied with orator groups of Pule, while Sā Tupua was allied with the orator groups of Tumua.[39] Much of the conflict in Sāmoa that followed was triggered by disputes over titles and lands that were intricately intertwined, as each side vied for dominance over the other.[40] As Europeans entered the picture, guns, cannons, and warships added new complexities and lethality to fighting. Conflict was a consistent part of the Sāmoan landscape in the nineteenth century, interspersed with periods of brokered peace. Wars further advantaged Europeans who bought up lands—such as those around the Apia waterfront—deserted as a result of fighting.[41]

The ever-increasing presence of the three imperial rivals—the United States, the United Kingdom, and Germany—in Sāmoa jostling for power from the 1870s made the islands crowded and volatile. Imperial attempts to secure the prized lands needed for plantation agriculture exacerbated existing Sāmoan divisions around family, power, and resources; government representatives and individuals played Sāmoan rivals on all levels against one another. The DHPG agent who became German consul, Theodor Weber, sought to profit from the situation. Weber, like Cornwall, bought immense tracts of land for his company, some twenty-five thousand acres of land in just three years between 1869 and 1872. Warships were brought in to support the competing land claims, drawing all three powers deeper into what one historian dubbed the "Samoan Tangle."[42]

All parties sought greater stability and security in the islands, making centralized government, an alien concept in Sāmoa, appear a panacea to the persistent problem. The idea was attractive, but its implementation impossible to satisfactorily effect for all competing parties. Though Sāmoans had lost immense tracts of land and suffered from the frequent conflict, they did not want to also lose political power in their own country. So in 1873 a provisional government was formed, vesting power in seven high-ranking chiefs, known as the Ta'imua, that was to "conduct relations with foreign powers, to maintain law and order in Apia and to appoint certain district officials." The Ta'imua worked with a "lower house" of *faipule,* or district and village authorities, who retained their traditional powers and aimed to bring village opinion to "bear upon government policy."[43] Another iteration of Indigenous governance was enacted in 1874 to circumvent the difficulties of having seven chiefs in the Ta'imua (which had doubled to fourteen). Two joint kings, with one representing Sā Malietoa and the other Sā Tupua, were appointed. The provisional government had the greatest difficulty dealing with "multinational claims to Samoan land." Claims competed; their legality was contested, and this "caused great power rivalry which ensued over Samoa."[44]

Several Europeans had a disproportionate influence on reshaping the Sāmoan political landscape. Weber from the DHPG was one. Another was Colonel A. B. Steinberger, who "masqueraded as a fully-powered American envoy" and worked to further American interests, becoming premier of the government in 1875. He was then deported by the settler community in 1876.[45] Steinberger's deportation sparked more conflict and an opportunity for Germany to undertake some classic gunboat diplomacy of trying to force the ratification of German land claims. Further warship visits reinforced European interests as the Sāmoan government tried to retain sovereignty in the face of great pressures, and the three powers maneuvered around one another. They did not want to spark a clash over the islands, nor did they want to give ground. Rivalries for the position of king, or deputy king—a position enacted in 1879—and then the formation of a rebel government caused war to break out again in 1881, but another "sullen peace" was brokered.[46]

This was the world Ta'isi was born into in 1883. Contenders for the kingship—Malietoa Laupepa, Mata'afa Iosefo, and Tupua Tamasese Titimaea—disputed one another's claims and would eventually raise armies to fight after 1887 (Malietoa and Mata'afa were both exiled in the Marshall Islands at different times). On the imperial level, the year after Ta'isi's birth saw the 1884–1885 Berlin Conference formalize imperial acquisitions and assert Germany's desire to rapidly acquire previously unclaimed imperial territories. This sparked the "scramble" for Africa and the Pacific. In Sāmoa, this reignited conflict; the country descended again into acrimony and war from 1887. This is the period that Robert Louis Stevenson wrote about in his *A Footnote to History*. Stevenson was the famed Scottish writer whose masterworks *Treasure Island* (1883), *The Strange Case of Dr. Jekyll and Mr. Hyde* (1886), and *Kidnapped* (1886)[47] made him an enduring literary celebrity. In 1889 he arrived in Apia to take up residence in the hope the climate would improve his chronic ill health. He landed in the aftermath of the most extraordinary event of all in this period of Sāmoa's history. The hurricane of March 1889 ripped through Apia Harbor, destroying six of the seven American and German warships anchored there in a show of strength. The British warship had just escaped the harbor before the tempest roared in. More than two hundred US and German seaman were drowned when the warships were destroyed. The destroyed ships, especially Germany's *SS Adler*, became monuments to the hubris and overinvestment of the three powers in Sāmoa, as they rusted in Apia Harbor for decades to come.[48] In the wake of the disaster, the three powers retreated to the negotiating table in Berlin to cut a deal. The Treaty of Berlin of 1889 ended Sāmoan autonomy and ushered in the era of shared rule of the islands between Britain, Germany, and the United States, the condominium. The treaty attempted, again, to find a solution to the unrest and to guarantee the rights of the three powers. An uneasy peace again ensued.

By the time of the great calamity in Apia Harbor in March 1889, Ta'isi was a schoolboy at the Marist Brothers' Commercial School, a school set back from the shore. If he did not witness the hurricane itself, he would have watched the great wrecks rust in the seawater as he proceeded through his schooling with the French Marist brothers.[49] Under their tutelage Ta'isi shone as published school rankings show. In 1894 when he was in fourth class, he came second in spelling, geography, and English composition and first in arithmetic and grammar.[50] In his final year, 1896, he also got several mentions in the *Samoa Weekly Herald*. Not only did he perform a number of songs and recitations at the prize-giving ceremony; he was awarded prizes for Christian doctrine and geography (second places) and first place for arithmetic, grammar, orthography (the art of writing), algebra, and stenography.[51] And here Ta'isi's formal education ended at age thirteen.

Ta'isi was immediately employed as an office boy with the biggest operation in town, DHPG, where his aptitude was noticed. Ta'isi banked invaluable knowledge, learning firsthand how the firm ran its multifaceted business that operated ships, plantations, and laborers, importing and exporting goods. He would have also observed the political dimensions to DHPG's operations; commerce, politics, and empire were inextricably intertwined for this firm. Great power politics intruded into Ta'isi's employ at DHPG. Even though he was ordered to learn German, he was not proficient and "refused to speak German," leading the company managers to suspect him of being "pro-British."[52] August Nelson was approached with the proposal of enlisting Ta'isi in the German navy and making him a German subject. Nelson "would not influence me in any way, and I declined," Ta'isi later recalled.[53]

In 1898 the latent tensions that had been kept under check since 1889 erupted again when Malietoa Laupepa died. Again Ta'isi witnessed the destructive forces of war—between global superpowers and rival Sāmoans—at close range. The highly popular Mata'afa Iosefo returned from exile, raised an army, and fought forces supporting the heir apparent for the kingship—Malietoa Tanumafili I.[54] The uneasy peace negotiated in Berlin collapsed; civil war erupted again in January 1899. Apia was divided with trenches and fortifications demarcating the rival strongholds—Malietoa's forces at Mulinu'u and Mata'afa's in Vailele. And once again, the three powers were drawn back into the fray. Sāmoa continued to be a pawn in an imperial game of chess that was increasingly playing out in the domestic politics and

Figure 1.1. Ta'isi when he was an office boy for DHPG in 1898. He is on the left lying down. *NZ Samoa Guardian,* May 12, 1932.

foreign relations of the three powers, the Australasian British dominions, as well as France and Russia. This game now involved Egypt, the Congo, the Philippines, Puerto Rico, Hawai'i, Tonga, the Gilbert Islands, and increasingly southern Africa ahead of the outbreak of the Boer War.[55]

In Sāmoa German forces supported Mata'afa with Britain and the United States now supporting Malietoa. After Mata'afa was declared ineligible to be king by a European court on the final day of 1898, fierce fighting erupted in Apia as 1899 dawned. Warships again converged on Apia Harbor with the USS *Philadelphia* firing the first shell in naval bombardments of Apia. After this pounding, the threat of increased hostilities and Malietoa's coronation in late April (Tupua Tamasese Lea'lofi I was made vice-king), Mata'afa agreed to a ceasefire, with the conflict ending on May 13.

The great power's resolution to the Sāmoan conflict was affected in Washington, DC, in December 1899 with the signing of the Tripartite Convention. The United States took control of the eastern islands of Tutuila and the Manu'a group. Germany annexed Upolu, Savai'i, Manono, and Apolima. Britain withdrew its interests (but only for fourteen years, as events transpired). The kingship was abolished, but

Figure 1.2. The US Navy bombards Apia in April 1899. Sir George Grey Collections, Auckland Libraries, AWNS-189904073-1.

this did not eradicate traditional rivalries. Sāmoa was now partitioned, and Ta'isi's world became a German possession.

Ta'isi felt the sting of this new order personally "about a week after the German flag was raised" when he was dismissed from DHPG at age seventeen. The manager's suspicions about Ta'isi's lack of loyalty to the Kaiser were compounded by an "affray" between Ta'isi and a "few of my friends" at the "Lindenau . . . a dancing-place and restaurant" in Apia. "I had some trouble with some Germans there, including German men-of-war's men," and they were all served with notices to pay fines. Ta'isi and his friends refused to pay, instead opting to make an appeal to the court—a foretaste of Ta'isi's future activism. The DHPG manager warned Ta'isi if the German judge went against him, he would be dismissed. The judge told Ta'isi and his friends to "get rid of . . . anti-German sentiments" and decided against them. Ta'isi's subsequent dismissal from his job did not help endear the new German regime to him.[56]

After Ta'isi was sacked from DHPG, he left Apia for a number of years, returning to Safune, his birthplace. He joined his father's company: it was subsequently renamed A. Nelson and Son in 1905, when Ta'isi was made a junior partner.[57] He lived in Safune until 1908,

Figure 1.3. Ta'isi's immediate family circa 1900. Front row: Lucy/Luse (Kruse), Sinagogo, August, and August Junior. Back row: Gustava (Wetzell), Ta'isi, Josephine (David). With permission of Tui Atua Tupua Tamasese Ta'isi Efi.

where he was further schooled in *fa'asamoa* as well as in operating the trading business, which benefited greatly from his industry. Ta'isi watched the spectacular eruptions of Matavanu from August 1905 to 1910 that entombed huge tracts of land to the east of Safune. These volcanic eruptions were a portent for growing political discontent centered in Savai'i against German rule that reached a climax in 1908. Ta'isi watched this protest from a distance, but it left a lasting impression on him.

While he lived again in Safune, Ta'isi fell in love with a woman named Leata, whom he married according to Sāmoan rites.[58] In 1904 Ta'isi became a father when his daughter Viopapa was born.[59] When Ta'isi left Safune for Apia in 1908, his relationship with Leata ended. He joined his parents, who also moved to Apia when they opened a store in Matafele that same year.[60] Viopapa came to Apia, too, and was cared for by her grandmother. While living in Safune deepened Ta'isi's Sāmoan roots, he was also trying to connect with his father's homeland. Ta'isi wanted to be registered as a Swedish subject (he

Figure 1.4. Ta'isi, seated in front of his parents, with his extended *aiga* circa 1906. With permission of Siuga Paula Masoe.

achieved this and was "Swedish" until 1924). In his contact with the Swedish government via their consulate in Sydney, Ta'isi expressed his frustration at the ambiguous status of Sāmoans at this time: "it is very awkward to think that one cannot claim the protection of any country at all," he wrote to the Swedish consul general, Count Mörner, in 1908.[61]

Now living back in Apia, Ta'isi's affections turned to a young woman newly returned from her schooling in San Francisco. Rosabel Edith Moors was born in September 1889, the second daughter of the formidable Harry J. Moors, an American-born businessman. Rosabel was as formidable as her father, and she was reputedly the favorite of his six children.[62] Like Ta'isi, Rosabel's parentage reflected Sāmoa's converging worlds. Harry J. Moors was born in Detroit in 1859 and was the "black sheep" of the family. He came to Sāmoa in 1875 and, like so many others, hoped to do better for himself. In this endeavor he succeeded. Moors was a trader and a copra planter. He was also heavily involved in early labor recruiting into Sāmoa and then as an employer of Gilbert Islanders and then Chinese.[63] In his recruiting past, Moors may have been associated with his notorious fellow American

William "Bully" Hayes, who was known for defrauding, swindling, and terrorizing Indigenous communities he raided for plantation labor.[64] Unlike Hayes, Moors became a person of influence and consequence as his economic prospects improved greatly. He befriended Robert Louis Stevenson when he came to Sāmoa, and Moors would write about his famous friend. Moors continued throughout his life to be a diligent man of letters.[65]

A key aspect of Moors' business success in Sāmoa, like Nelson's, was a prudent marriage. Moors married Fa'animonimo (known as Nimo), who was born to Sāmoan parents but adopted by a missionary couple, the Johnsons, who educated Nimo in Scotland. Nimo spoke her whole life with a Scottish brogue, and, though she was Sāmoan, she was "very much *pālagi*."[66] Moors' store, located prominently on the Apia waterfront, did a thriving trade along with Moors' other businesses. He became wealthy enough to send some of his offspring to revered American schools after they completed Catholic schooling in Apia. Rosabel attended Saint Mary's in Apia and then was "finished" at Mills College in San Francisco. As well as a top-notch education, her father spoiled Rosabel in other ways. Her life mirrored that of other wealthy, indulged young women. She had an abundance of material possessions, including a Thoroughbred horse that was one of her most prized possessions. She was said to have an imperious demeanor to match. Ta'isi fell in love with her, and the passionate pair married in July 1909.

Chapter Two

Kaiser or King?

German Empire, War, and Its Brutal Aftermath (1910–1920)

At age twenty-six, Ta'isi embarked on married life with Rosabel. They started out living above A. Nelson and Son's now larger store in Matafele on Apia's commercial strip. Matafele was a big step down for Rosabel from her family's palatial residence at Ululoloa, high in the lush hills above the township of Apia. Though the new couple was passionately in love, the reduced circumstances grated on Rosabel. Meeting Rosabel's social and financial expectations became a contentious element in their marriage, but one Ta'isi tried his best to appease. Rosabel sought the European luxuries she was accustomed to and schooled Ta'isi in these matters. After all his years of village living, Rosabel thought her new husband required considerable refinement.[1]

Rosabel was the latest formidable woman to enter Ta'isi's life. As the younger brother, Ta'isi had numerous obligations to his three older sisters and his mother, Sinagogo. Rosa, as her family knew her, challenged her mother-in-law's position; the two women evidently never got on. Sinagogo was reputedly a very Sāmoan mother who still took it upon herself to physically discipline her adult son, even in front of employees when she thought it necessary. Ta'isi would accept his mother's punishment as an expression of her maternal rights, but asked her to carry it out away from his employees' eyes, in private.[2] The altered circumstances of Ta'isi's life in 1909 were also marked by the death of his father in May. With August's passing, Ta'isi was now the head of the large, extended family, with all the attendant responsibilities.

The politics of Ta'isi's intimate world were complex. By this time, so too were the politics of intimacy throughout German-ruled Sāmoa. The German colonial regime had begun to police intimate relations across racial divides as part of its increasing interference in a range of other facets of Sāmoan life. The year after Ta'isi wed Rosabel, a marriage like that of his or her parents—between a Sāmoan woman and a European man—required the governor's approval. Germany was worried about the rise of an articulate group in Sāmoa whose loyalties might not lie with the Kaiser, and wanted to stymie the demographic increase of mixed-race (*afakasi*) people like Ta'isi and his siblings. This policy would also retain a racially "pure" Sāmoan population; another objective touted by Germany's long-serving governor of Sāmoa Wilhelm Solf, who ruled from 1900 to 1911, and his successor Erich Schultz, who ruled until September 1914.[3] For the existing offspring of European fathers and Sāmoan mothers, Solf fashioned a policy that permitted these people to gain "European" or "white" status that supposedly canceled out their Sāmoan heritage.[4] Yet people's lives, like Ta'isi's, were not so simple; their Sāmoan-ness endured.

The governor's interference at this level in the lives of those he ruled over was not unfamiliar in many colonial contexts, German or otherwise. The politics of race and power were impacting colonies across the globe in the twentieth century in new ways owing to the infusion of eugenics into an already immense corpus of racial ideologies and practices. Eugenics, the science of improved breeding that would have its gruesome heyday in Germany's Third Reich from the 1930s, was having a marked impact on colonial thinking during the period of German Sāmoa. Mixed-race people or *afakasi* were a particular focus of this science that was as elastic and contradictory as all of its ideological predecessors. Eugenics also confounded logic and any empirical evidence that undermined a human pyramid of racial superiority with Europeans at the apex. According to this thinking, mixed-race people were both an improvement on Indigenous peoples *and* a degeneration of the white race.[5]

In this politicized atmosphere of intimacy and race, Ta'isi and Rosabel started their family together. In 1910, the couple welcomed their first daughter, Noue.[6] In the next eight years they would have five more children: Malienafau in 1911, Piliopo on Christmas Day 1913, their only son Ta'isi in June 1915, Sina Hope in 1916, and Taufau on July 8, 1918.[7] Ta'isi and Rosabel were immensely proud of their

Figure 2.1. Rosabel, Noue, and Ta'isi circa 1911. Sir George Grey Special Collections, Auckland Libraries, 31-66440.

young family, who were the subject of studio portraits. These portraits show a conscious attempt to convey respectability and prosperity. In conveying their affluence and style, the Nelson family challenged stereotypes and colonial racial ordering, which dictated a lesser status for the people "between" European and "native."

Over the years these portraits were taken, the colonial landscape in Sāmoa shifted. Some of Ta'isi's children were born under German rule, while the younger ones were born under New Zealand rule. What did it mean to live under the two regimes? To make a comparison we need to look at what German colonial rule entailed. The picture that emerges shows that New Zealand did not learn from German mistakes; it replicated them. So what were the German mistakes? The promise of peace and prosperity were foremost expectations for German rule of Sāmoa in 1900, but as the history of colonialism has consistently shown, the benefits of colonial rule were always grossly uneven in their distribution.

Figure 2.2. Malienafau, Sina, Noue, Ta'isi, Piliopo circa 1917. Sir George Grey Special Collections, Auckland Libraries, 31-2590.

Many historians view the Germans as akin to modern Spanish conquistadors, hell-bent on profit and power at any cost to the people they subjugated.[8] Violence and cruelty were the tools of domination in this version of German colonialism, a version given added impetus by imperial competitors eager to deflect similar charges against their own colonial enterprises. The history of Southwest Africa is a case in point supporting the thesis that German colonialism was a reign of violence. Here Germany fought wars of dispossession against the local Herero and Nama peoples (in 1904–1907 and 1904, respectively). These wars resulted in staggering causalities: an 81 percent decline in the Herero population in three years and 50 percent decline for the Nama in one year.[9] But German colonialism (like its British counterpart) was not one blanket set of policies and practices applied uniformly; it was a strange beast.[10] Place, politics, differing imperial ambitions, divergent ideas of race, and colonial and Indigenous personalities deeply impacted the way German colonialism played out in Africa, Asia, and the Pacific. If Southwest Africa was the worst-case example of the

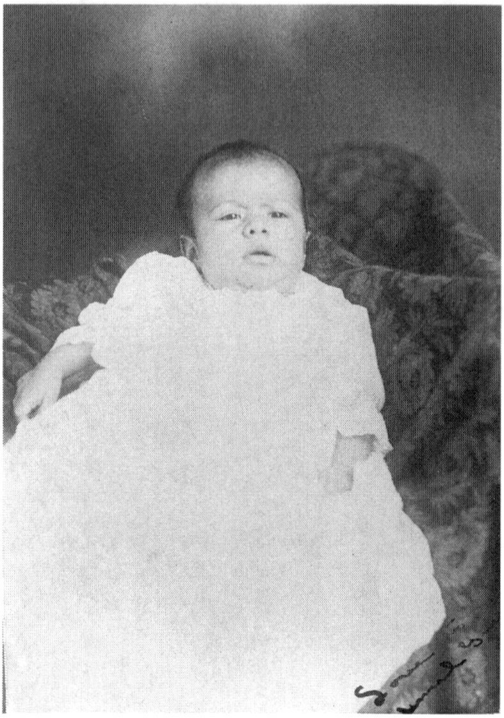

Figure 2.3. Taufau circa 1918. Sir George Grey Special Collections, Auckland Libraries, 31-71702.

conjunction of colonial avarice, the idea of racial superiority, and the unrestrained actions of individuals in the field resulting in extraordinary carnage, Sāmoa was arguably the best-case example. Sāmoa was an exception in the story of German colonialism; yet the occupation was still dogged by resistance during its fourteen-year duration.

Why was Sāmoa an outlier? Some historians explain that Sāmoans occupied a place on German racial scales that elevated them above all other Indigenous peoples in the German colonial network. Sāmoans were considered to be "soft savages," ennobled by their physical beauty and cultural sophistication. Their assertive and strong social organization and martial culture, demonstrated numerous times in the decades leading up to Germany's rule, also garnered respect. Explanations for the exceptionalism of German Sāmoa also include particular mention of the governor, Wilhelm Solf. Solf has been attributed with bringing the best colonial practices of well-intentioned benevolence and paternalism to Sāmoa. His rule was not supported by a military force, and, according to this version of German Sāmoa, Solf ruled through negotiation and consultation, as he was informed by the latest anthropological ideas aimed at protecting and preserving an admired Indigenous group.[11]

Solf envisaged a tropical commercial empire with small numbers of Germans forming a planter class that would rule over protected Sāmoans who produced a large percentage of copra for the German-controlled market. Indentured laborers imported from China, who worked the German government plantations, supported Sāmoa's production, ensuring that the deleterious effects of grueling tropical labor were not borne by the Sāmoan people. Solf's policies supported the preservation of Sāmoan culture and landownership, but with one considerable caveat. The Sāmoan culture Solf worked to preserve had to mesh with German ambition, assuring its colonial power and prestige. When it did not mesh, Solf introduced changes to law, cultural practice, and economics that generated consistent opposition to German rule from Sāmoans, as well as planters and traders, like Ta'isi, throughout his tenure.

German Sāmoa had been simmering with discontents since Germany raised its flag at Mulinu'u in 1900. In late 1904 Sāmoans led by the *afakasi* Sāmoan Pullack tried to staunch the flow of political power away from Sāmoans to Europeans, by establishing a Sāmoan-run copra enterprise to which every male Sāmoan was to make a financial contribution. The goals of the Sāmoan cooperative known as the *Cumpani* or *Oloa* were to return economic power back into Sāmoan hands and reduce the ability of Germans, especially the DHPG, to profit from Sāmoan-grown copra. The German administration saw a number of alarming developments in this scheme that undermined the very basis of colonialism. It empowered Indigenous people economically, promising to enrich them and put them in direct competition with European traders. It set up a quasi-taxation system that challenged the power of the colonial administration and united the often heavily divided Indigenous population through mutual self-interest. It also thoroughly undermined Solf's paternalistic colonial vision. If Sāmoans could be enterprising, economically independent, and politically empowered, where could European colonial power reside and what would become of the notion of European superiority? Governor Solf tried to stamp out the movement swiftly through preventing participation by leading chiefs attached to the administration, prohibiting the collection of funds, and exiling Pullack, the instigator. While it seemed initially that Solf had crushed this movement and its threat to the imperial order, in fact he spurred greater resolve and Sāmoan protest, which from 1908 generated the greatest crisis of his governorship.[12]

Growing political discontent centered in Savai'i, picking up where the *Oloa* left off. In 1908, the *Mau a Pule* emerged to protest the drastic erosion of Sāmoan self-governance, interference in sacred cultural rituals and the imposition of taxes; many of these measures were imposed by Solf after the *Oloa*. The *Mau a Pule,* headed by Lauaki, threatened to rupture the fragile peace that had existed since the German annexation. The rebel movement challenged German rule and its Sāmoan supporters, led by Mata'afa Iosefo, with armed revolt. German property was attacked and Lauaki increasingly challenged Solf's authority. By 1908 Solf called for military reinforcements. Ships, sailors, and marines came from German concessions in China.[13] A force of police-soldiers came from the Solomon Islands. Tensions mounted, and war seemed imminent. Given the asymmetry between German military might and that of Sāmoans, particularly in the wake of what had occurred in Southwest Africa in preceding years, the prospect of conflict must have seemed a certain bloodbath. Bloodshed was averted when Lauaki, eight other chiefs, and their families accepted exile to the German colony of Saipan in March 1909. The seventy-one exiles remained on Saipan until late 1915. New Zealand authorities, alive to the great sense of grievance Sāmoans felt about this exile, sent a ship to retrieve them after they took over control of Sāmoa; Lauaki died on the way home.[14]

Ta'isi was living in Safune when he met Lauaki, who was so highly esteemed he was a "kingmaker" in the ongoing leadership disputes of the late nineteenth century. Governor Solf also appointed him as a *faipule.* When Ta'isi's uncle Tugaga of Safune died in 1902, Lauaki led the party of *faipule* at the funeral service reciting the genealogy of the Seumanutafa family to show its powerful connections with the Tugaga family. Lauaki's deep knowledge of history and his oratorical skill left an impression on the young Ta'isi. Ta'isi encountered Lauaki again around 1906 when he was on a *malaga* (village tour) around Savai'i. Lauaki came to Safune to end a long-running dispute and took everyone in the village by surprise by performing an *ifoga* (forgiveness ceremony). The people of Safune accepted his offer of forgiveness required to end the long-running dispute and then "gave Lauaki the largest reception of the whole malaga." It was costly, "but the hatchet was buried ever after. Lauaki was able by eloquence to draw tears of joy as well as blood," Ta'isi remembered. Then the *Mau a Pule* erupted.

During the "excitement . . . before Lauaki was deported," Ta'isi met with Dr. Schultz, then deputy governor, in a private sitting room of the old International Hotel. Ta'isi, then twenty-five, "made bold to tell Dr. Schultz that [he] thought Lauaki a great man who was sincere in his intentions for the good of the Samoans." If the Germans viewed Lauaki's representations "sympathetically as they deserved," he "could have added to the lustre and glory of German administration in Sāmoa by his influence and co-operation," Ta'isi told Schultz. Lauaki would only do this, of course, once "he was satisfied that the proper status of the Sāmoan was adequately recognised and reasonable scope was made open for the aspirations of the Sāmoans for advancement towards self-determination and self-government within a reasonable time." Ta'isi recalled that Schultz was noncommittal. There would be no conciliation; Lauaki's punishment was severe. Ta'isi would identify with his plight two decades later as history seemed to repeat.[15]

Ta'isi's outspokenness when he saw injustice continued. Following the deportation of Lauaki and others involved in the *Mau a Pule*, a group of citizens in Apia lodged a stinging protest against Governor Solf's rule in the form of a petition to the Reichstag in 1910. "Ten years ago, when the German flag was raised in Samoa, most of the inhabitants believed that there would come a peaceful prosperous advancement," the protest letter began. Instead of this promise, "the most unsound conditions rule in these islands" that are "oppressive and unprofitable and have retarded the advancement and happiness of the colony."[16]

Discontent with Governor Solf's governance rippled through the Sāmoan commercial community, although in more muted ways than the open Sāmoan rebellion Solf crushed the previous year.[17] Beyond the DHPG complex, other businessmen became increasingly critical of the monopolistic and politically favored position the company enjoyed. Ta'isi bristled against the situation that supported DHPG dominance at the expense of businessmen like himself. The ideal of "peaceful prosperous advancement" under German rule, as the petition began, had not materialized.

The 1910 petitioners, defining themselves as "European" and "white," set their interests out as distinct from those of "natives." Ta'isi signed as "Fr Nelson" along with George Westbrook, T. Niebuhr, Alfred Preuss, and L. Schmidt. Ta'isi's voice is entangled with that of others in this 1910 petition. One admiring commentator believed Ta'isi led the group in penning this protest, showing he was always a patriot. New Zealand argued he lead the protest, too, a sign he was always a troublemaker. Ta'isi himself claimed to have had "nothing to do with the drafting of the petition at all." "I was respected by the whole of the people and I was asked to become a member of the committee," he would later explain.[18] In this petition were the seeds of his later political campaign, particularly the belief that Western democratic systems should be a central part of the Sāmoan political landscape, and that Sāmoans should be self-governing to a considerable degree.

Though they were only five in number, the petitioners claimed to speak for the "majority of white residents." They outlined a litany of complaints described as only "some of the many grievances and drawbacks which this colony has had to bear." The colony was overrun with expensive officials, it claimed. There were 435 white residents and 400 "half-castes registered as white" in Sāmoa by 1910, but some fifty-eight government officials—an increase of more than 200 percent since 1902.[19] The cost of these officials, the petition stated, commandeered more than half the annual income of the colony. Added to this, the officials worked only four- to five-hour days and took long furloughs. The petition directly attacked Governor Solf's habit of taking "almost annual vacations" that "derange the affairs of the colony" in his absence. The petition's portrayal of German administrators as lackadaisical whites in the tropics was not without irony. Colonial ideas stressed that Sāmoans were not capable of the industrious work required to fuel the entire copra plantation economy, and so indentured laborers were brought in to undertake that sweated labor.[20]

The petition argued that the fiscal burden of the colonial service was compounded by the imposition of taxes that were unduly burdensome to traders operating outside the DHPG. These traders—including the petition's signatories—had formed the Traders' Association, a bloc of businessman intent on combatting the commercial and political dominance of the DHPG. The DHPG was favored in the tax regime, it argued. Sāmoans, missionaries, planters, and government officials "pay but a trifle" in taxes, while traders were being hit by an 800 percent increase in their tax burden since the previous year.[21] Sāmoans were being taxed at 4 marks per capita, whereas these traders were paying 117 marks per capita. Unsurprisingly the petition called for the shifting of revenue collection away from this group of traders to the DHPG and "native Samoans." A proposed export tax on copra would solve this problem and "would be scarcely felt by them" (that is, the natives), and would make a small dent in DHPG's "heavy dividends."

In addition to this leading grievance, the letter also complained about the "undue influence" that the administration and its supporting group in the community had over the press. Differences of opinion with Solf's rule were stifled to the detriment of the colony. Also, the hospital was inefficient and expensively managed, more schools and teachers were required, and the very advantageous position of the DHPG as far as selling land was concerned was deeply unjust. The DHPG had a virtual monopoly on selling large tracts as Sāmoans were prohibited from selling their lands under the land ordinance Solf introduced.

The solution for these ingrained problems, the traders argued, was self-government. They proposed that the Government Council, which "chiefly represents the interests of a certain firm," be reformed. The council should be elected by "the ratepayers, from whom these nominations should emanate," also "the meetings of this council should be public." The work of this envisaged council should include financial matters and taxation, and "it should have an advisory voice in connection with Native affairs."[22] The petition was, in its sum, a stinging critique of Solf's administration, as well as of colonialism itself. "We are of the opinion," it continued, "that the German Government has acquired colonies for the purpose of finding employment for German capital, and homes for its surplus inhabitants where they can be warmly received and helped without discommoding the Native people." Yet "our present disordered state" did not resemble this ideal.

Any student of colonial history would detect the clarion call of anticolonialism: the economic self-interest of colonists expressed in the "no taxation without representation" mantra that had sparked a rolling series of anticolonial movements in the Americas from 1776. There were important lessons here for colonial powers some eighty years later. Repression and the withholding of economic, social, and political rights on the basis of race were tactics central to colonial power, but embedded within them were the attitudes that sparked opposition and often brought about imperial demise. One lesson was to keep racially divided colonial communities politically and socially separate. United against a colonial power, these communities were perilous. Germany, and then New Zealand, was aware of this danger in Sāmoa. Though Solf handed over the governorship to Schultz in 1911, the increasingly reactionary stance of the administration toward dissent continued, as did the increasing interference in the everyday lives of Sāmoans.

Though Germany had fretted over a revolt from either the Indigenous or settler communities that might overthrow them, the end of German rule in Sāmoa (and in its other colonies) played out quite differently. Britain's declaration of war against Germany on August 5, 1914, immediately drew Sāmoa into a global allied assault against German territory. Within a day of the declaration of war, New Zealand, which automatically followed Britain into the war with Germany, was called on to perform a "great and urgent imperial service."[23] It was tasked with capturing the German wireless station near Apia and occupying this German colony for the duration of the war. New Zealand scurried to ready two ships for the task. Not knowing where the German Pacific fleet was, the New Zealand contingent was supported by Australian and French ships before they steamed into Apia Harbor on August 29. New Zealand troops landed and met no resistance. As much as Germans wished to cling to their lucrative colony, Governor Schultz admitted that "our forces consisted of twenty soldiers and special constables, and our fortifications are one gun . . . our only other defensive weapon were fifty rifles" that dated from the 1871 Franco-Prussian war.[24] The Germans surrendered, and New Zealand raised the Union Jack on August 30, recommencing British colonial interest in the Sāmoan islands after being suspended for the preceding fourteen years, since Germany took exclusive control of the western islands. In a war in which millions of lives would be lost, the first blow against Germany was a bloodless event, even after German warships entered Apia Harbor in mid-September only to leave without firing a shot.

The loss of German Sāmoa was a minor event in the appalling cataclysm that was to become the Great War. However for Germans in Sāmoa, particularly for the DHPG, it was a small-scale tragedy. New Zealand set about immediately rounding up Germans, readying some for deportation to New Zealand to live out the war in internment camps in Auckland or Wellington. New Zealanders replaced Germans in the civil service. Though New Zealand initially maintained a "business as usual" approach to the Sāmoan economy, by 1916 it learned that German traders were continuing their connections with Germany, and so an abrupt end to German commerce in Sāmoa was enforced. Assets owned by Germans and German firms were expropriated. In

Sāmoa, as in other colonies, these assets would be sold off to fill Allied coffers. The vast complex of German plantation and trading concerns in the Pacific came up for sale.[25] Others in Sāmoa had to choose between loyalty to the German Kaiser or his cousin, the British king; a baffling choice that perhaps made sense in Sāmoa where entanglements of family, power, and shifting allegiances were well known.

Sāmoans at first welcomed the change from Germany's colonial administration to New Zealand's military occupation. Headed by Lieutenant Colonel Robert Logan, the military occupation eased the pressure created by Solf and Schultz, who had tried to force changes to traditional power systems at the village and national levels. Sāmoans found themselves better able to self-govern as New Zealand stepped back and "*laissez-faire* replaced paternalism" as a governing approach. Logan did not interfere, as Solf controversially had done, in highly important sacred fine mat exchanges, especially when "the Fautua, Tupua Tamasese Lealofi died on 13 October 1915."[26] But not all Sāmoan residents were pleased with New Zealand's military occupation. Harry J. Moors (Rosabel Nelson's father) was a strident critic of it and of Colonel Logan; he sent a blizzard of complaining letters to the New Zealand government. Logan suspected Moors was angling for the United States to extend its Sāmoan territory by absorbing the western islands into its eastern Sāmoan territory.[27] Moors did not endear himself to Logan's successor, either; he would describe Moors as "a naturalized American nuisance" whom New Zealand should deport.[28]

The desirability of US rule increased from January 1918 with the issuance of President Wilson's Fourteen Points. Point Five gave explicit support to the self-determination of colonized peoples. These words fueled uprisings throughout the colonized world. Though self-determination did not become a reality for most colonized people after the conclusion of World War I, it did become an aspiration. The United States was seen as the champion of this ideal, although many colonized peoples from the Philippines, Hawai'i, African Americans, and Native Americans would continue to experience inequality that belied the inspiring rhetoric.

For his part, Ta'isi initially disagreed with his father-in-law about New Zealand's rule. Logan noted in January 1918, that while the Americans were trying to steer postwar Sāmoa into US hands, "the Swedish [most likely a reference to Ta'isi] and other nationalities would be 'very greatly British.'"[29] Ta'isi's initial support of New Zealand was self-interested; New Zealand rule was very good for business. When Logan began dismantling German economic power, Ta'isi was perfectly positioned to seize the materializing opportunities. He bought up German assets (though not without restriction), and his net worth grew greatly. Without Germans linked to the DHPG dominating Apia politics, Ta'isi assumed a far more prominent role in that realm, too. When Ta'isi and his staff sat for a photograph in 1918 to mark the golden jubilee of the firm his father started in 1868, A. Nelson and Son was replacing the DHPG as the dominant commercial concern in Sāmoa. High wartime prices and other favorable conditions augmented his economic and political rise. The snapshot of Ta'isi's business contrasted greatly with that of the DHPG taken twenty-two years earlier, when only German men played a role in its operations with the exception of the two office boys, one of whom was Ta'isi (figure 1.1). Now in 1918, the leading firm in Sāmoa reflected the community's diversity (even women) in its personnel. Not only did this distinguish Nelson and Sons from the DHPG of the past; it also set them far apart from their competitors in employing people other than whites.

Figure 2.4. The Nelson Company fiftieth jubilee staff photograph, 1918. Ta'isi is seated in the middle of the second row. "One Hundred Years of Service to Samoa," special supplement of *Samoa Times,* November 29, 1968, 1. Alexander Turnbull Library, Wellington.

Ta'isi's economic and political good fortunes were marred in mid-1918 by tensions in his personal life. While Ta'isi was absent on business, Rosabel left the family home and all of their young children, except the toddler Sina, in May 1918. She returned to her mother's house at Ulufoloa. Rosabel was heavily pregnant with Taufau (who was born in July), and in her heightened emotional state all Rosabel's frustrations with her life with Ta'isi brimmed over. She told him she needed rest, but he was desperately worried about the impact her absence was having on their children and the "scandal" and "dishonor" her leaving their home was causing.[30] Rosabel's appeal for rest compounded into accusations that Ta'isi had been untrue to her; he was "brokenhearted" at the suggestion. He told her, "You have unjustly wronged a man who loves you and who has always been true to you." She was being unreasonably "jealous and suspicious" without cause; however, he continued to plead with her to return. He also noted that Rosabel was prone to compare her "mother's and sister's portions favourably with your deplorable lot." They had their own homes, but Rosabel resented that their residence above the store in Matafele was not her own. As well as recriminations there was also great tenderness in their exchanges at this time. Rosabel told Ta'isi, "If I live to be a hundred I could never love another man." Ta'isi was deeply wounded by things Rosabel said and did; Rosabel admitted her condition made her "a little nasty and unhappy."[31] Though Rosabel returned to their home, the incident was a prelude for the trouble that lay ahead for the couple.

Marital troubles paled into insignificance with what came to Sāmoa in November 1918. The ship *Talune* arrived in Apia on November 7, bringing the Spanish influenza with it. The pandemic, estimated to have killed between fifty and one hundred million people worldwide, killed more people per capita in Sāmoa than anywhere else in the world. The ship had left Auckland, sailed to Suva, and then was allowed to dock and disembark passengers in Apia even though four people on board were exhibiting severe symptoms of illness. The disease had been raging in the Northern Hemisphere, following the returning troops from battlefields to home fronts with devastating effect. New Zealand was feeling its ravages by the time the *Talune* departed Auckland. Apia's Port Health officer, Captain Frank Atkinson, met the ship on November 7, but he "had no experience in connection with the duties of the Port Health Officer, nor had he received any instructions from the Principal Medical Officer on the matter."

Atkinson also had not been informed "that influenza had become a 'notifiable' disease in New Zealand" on November 6. Alarming evidence of the presence of influenza on the ship was overlooked and the *Talune* was granted pratique; passengers moved off the ship, mingling with people on land without restriction.[32]

Ta'isi was one of the first to see someone with the disease. Reverend Paul Cane, Ta'isi's friend, came ashore from the *Talune* and went to the Bank of New Zealand before calling on Ta'isi at his offices. Ta'isi was shocked by the state his friend was in. "He was very sick. In fact he was foaming at the mouth," he recalled.[33] Ta'isi called a car, and Reverend Cane was taken to the hospital. He survived, but in the coming days other *Talune* passengers died. Sāmoans then began contracting the disease at a startling rate. Without adequate medical attention or information about what was afflicting them, they began perishing at a shocking pace. Colonel Logan refused assistance from American Sāmoa, ten hours' steam away, and cut off communications in "a moment of exasperation."[34] Ta'isi and his immediate family began to suffer, too. Ta'isi contracted the disease and was at "death's door" for months.[35] His mother, Sinagogo, was visiting him and became bedridden at Ta'isi's Apia residence. Ta'isi got word that his brother August, at Palauli on Savai'i, was extremely ill. So was his wife, Jane Sueina (née Meredith), and Ta'isi's sister Josephine (David). In one week, all four—Sinagogo, August, Jane, and Josephine—would die. The death of August and Jane orphaned their only son, Frank. From then on, Ta'isi shared the care of this boy with his maternal grandfather, S. H. Meredith. Ta'isi's brother had another son, also named August, who became known as Gussie or Kasipo'a. His mother was Fusipala Tuiletufuga Ale, and Ta'isi would share in the care of this boy, too.[36]

The pandemic continued to devastate the population. By the end of 1918, 7,542 people had died, though the 1919 commission formed to investigate it found it likely that 8,500 people had perished from the population of 38,302, or 22 percent. The 1919 *Samoan Epidemic Commission* leveled blame at Captain Atkinson and the *Talune*'s captain, Mawson. Of Colonel Logan, the commissioners accepted his rationale for refusing assistance. It also praised his "splendid work in visiting Native villages, seeing to the feeding of the Natives and personally burying the dead." The heroic efforts of the garrisoned soldiers onto whom also fell the grim duty of burying the dead and administering any relief to those suffering from influenza were also praised. A number of these soldiers also died in the catastrophe. History has been less sparing of Logan and other members of New Zealand's military occupation. Logan is portrayed as the inept head of an inexperienced and incompetent colonial regime that permitted the decimation of the population under their charge. The extraordinary comparison with American Sāmoa, where there was not a single casualty from the pandemic, only brought New Zealand's performance into sharper relief. Though Logan was not publicly blamed for the epidemic's devastation, his term as administrator was abruptly terminated at the end of 1918; Colonel Robert W. Tate replaced him.

Meanwhile the pandemic continued to take lives into 1919. Ta'isi was still so ill in February 1919 that Tate noted he was leaving Sāmoa for "convalescence and further medical treatment"; Ta'isi recovered.[37] His adored son, also Ta'isi, then only four, was not so lucky. He "was so impaired in health by the effects of influenza that he died some nine months later from a slight attack of colitis."[38] Little Ta'isi died in September 1919, another casualty of this calamity as were more than twenty-five hundred other Sāmoan children.[39] The death of this beloved son devastated his parents; it was a blow from which neither would ever fully recover.

As the fight against the pandemic continued in Sāmoa, the New Zealand military occupation administered a colony that was growing increasingly restive. Attempts at regaining self-government reemerged. One example of this was a revival of the 1904 *Oloa* concept in which Sāmoans hoped to form a trading company giving them greater independence through economic empowerment by putting more control for prices for copra and goods into Sāmoan hands. Colonel Logan gave the go-ahead for the formation of the limited liability company, the Toeaina Club, but his successor, Colonel Tate, effectively stopped the venture nine months later. He considered it "the greatest political danger."[40] The decision to economically disempower Sāmoans through stopping the Toeaina Club planted a new seed of bitterness. Trading rights then became an exclusive privilege of those with European status, like Ta'isi.

The epidemic coupled with ending the Toeaina venture meant Colonel Tate would preside over a period of intense discontent with New Zealand's rule that only deteriorated further; this protest movement was known as the Mau of *faipule*. From the outset of his term as administrator, which began in January 1919, Robert Tate could have been in no doubt about Sāmoan anger. When he set foot in the territory, he was presented with a petition requesting that the islands be transferred to the United States or, failing that, Britain. Despite this, the natural beauty of Sāmoa initially captivated him; he described it as "veritably a garden of Eden." Tate's rapturous enthusiasm evaporated when he realized the extent of Sāmoans' seething anger; within seven months he was describing with alarm "the volcano we are sitting on."[41]

The petition handed to Tate on his arrival coupled with the irrefutable mortality figures from the epidemic were indeed distressing for New Zealand, as it took its place among other nations from January 1919 in Paris for peace talks. Despite Sāmoans' grave misgivings about New Zealand's governing performance, the decision was made in Paris that New Zealand would continue its rule of Sāmoa under the auspices of the League of Nations, an arrangement mirrored in numerous parts of Africa and the Pacific. Occupying nations would continue to rule their new territories in the mandate system so that the map of former German colonies was divided up into class B mandates, Tanganyika (Britain), British Cameroons (Britain), Togoland (France), Cameroun (France), Ruanda-Urundi (Belgium), and class C mandates, Southwest Africa (South Africa), German Possessions in the Pacific Ocean lying north of the Equator (Japan), New Guinea (Australia), Nauru (Britain, Australia, and New Zealand), and Western Sāmoa (New Zealand). Sāmoa would be New Zealand's national proving ground.[42]

In this postwar era, Ta'isi begins to emerge as a distinct historical figure. The combination of his economic and social rise in Sāmoa, as well as the newly imposed conditions of colonial rule by New Zealand, pushed him into prominence. He became a writer of letters and a more vocal spokesman for Sāmoan interests. Tate made particular mention of him from the start; Ta'isi was clearly an outstanding person in Tate's views. On their second meeting Tate described him as "a big well-educated half caste merchant, a young man, bulky in person with a clear voice and precise diction like one of our half-castes." He possessed "superlative attributes" the new administrator initially considered very useful: "I learn from Mr Nelson," he wrote in February 1919.[43]

Closely following Tate's arrival in Sāmoa, numerous other figures came to the islands to assess the state of the colony after four years of New Zealand rule and gather intelligence to construct a governing path. In July 1919 New Zealand's governor-general Lord Liverpool called in on Sāmoa during a tour of New Zealand island dependencies, which at this point also included the Cook Islands, Niue, and Nauru. Dr. Māui Pōmare, who would become a central part of Ta'isi's life story, accompanied the governor-general on this visit.[44]

Dr. Pōmare had been the minister for Cook Islands in the William Massey government since 1916 and was a prominent national figure in Māori affairs. Since being elected the Member of Parliament for Western Māori in 1912, he was particularly known for his involvement in issues relating to Māori health.[45] As a prominent Māori politician fascinated with cultural connections across the Pacific between Polynesian peoples, Dr. Pōmare showed a keen interest in New Zealand's Sāmoan affairs. When he arrived in Apia in mid-1919, he was introduced to Ta'isi and they had a conversation about the "future administration of Samoa." Dr. Pōmare asked Ta'isi to write to him with his "views on the matter."[46] Ta'isi did so in August in two letters that mark the formal beginning of the deep friendship that would grow between the two over the next eleven years.

In the first letter Ta'isi addressed the topics of native affairs, the municipality of Apia and European affairs, the formation of the governor's council, and the possibility of Sāmoan representation in the New Zealand parliament. Common themes were woven through his proposals on these four matters; one was that representative positions for Sāmoan and European governance should be elected, and another was that the New Zealand administrator should oversee the running of Sāmoa by Sāmoans, rather than interfering in this process too intrusively. Ta'isi argued that native affairs should be kept "sacredly aloof from other affairs" and a parliament of elected *faipule* should form one level of government, with the administrator having "a veto on all decisions of this house."[47] The administrator should also appoint two chiefs from the Malietoa and Tupua families to act as his advisers. These positions should be well paid and come with housing in Apia befitting "the dignity of their rank." Though he strongly advocated that Sāmoans "learn the principals of voting [to] pave the way for further extensions in this line in the future," Ta'isi was adamant that these two advisory positions had to be appointed by the administrator so not to "revive factional disputes" of the past. He also argued that Sāmoan customs should be strongly encouraged and the "prestige of chiefs" upheld by the government. For the affairs of Europeans in Apia, Ta'isi argued for the formation of a municipal council with members "elected by all who are classed as Europeans in

Samoa and will deal with all matters appertaining to the town and with European affairs generally." Like the *faipule,* the administrator should have power of veto over "any decisions . . . for the first five years at least." In addition, the administrator should have an advisory council made of three administrator-appointed members and three representing "planting, trading and native interests." He was also in favor of Sāmoan representation in the New Zealand parliament so long as it did not interfere with the "powers of local bodies."[48]

In his second letter, Ta'isi got to more complex and vexed matters of racial status and rights, native lands, and the governance of Savai'i. On this last point, he firmly opposed the current arrangement where the "Deputy Administrator of Savaii is the executive, legislative and judicative power for that island." This arrangement "should be abolished." Of Colonel Tate, Ta'isi wholeheartedly endorsed him, saying, "He has the confidence of all classes here and would be appreciated as first civil administrator if your Government deems fit to appoint him." Regarding native title to land, he strongly supported the current system that did not allow the sale or conversion of native-owned lands into freehold land, thus preventing the dispossession of Sāmoans that had caused the ruin of Indigenous people throughout the colonized world.[49]

On the other points, given his own position as an afakasi who would be bestowed *matai* titles in coming years, the views Ta'isi expressed in this letter undercut his own position. He argued in favor of the simplistic divisions of the Sāmoan population along racial lines, largely based on education. "Half-castes who have been brought up as natives with no prospect of receiving European education should be classed as natives," he argued. "All descendants of mixed marriages between natives and Europeans should be classed as Europeans hitherto." His rationale for this being that it "eliminates the chance of having semi-educated half castes meddling in native affairs which have always been regarded a source of danger," and it allows "the old pioneers who made their homes here and married native women to bring up their children in a manner befitting their own status." He also noted that he encouraged the ability of Sāmoans who were not of mixed parentage but who had received a European education to have the option of attaining European status, which would mean "they would lose the rights and privileges of natives." Few Sāmoans had done this, except "native women who by marrying Europeans became by law Europeans forfeiting all their native rights of succession to lands and titles of their families." Though he was speaking precisely of his own circumstances and those of his recently departed mother, he thought this system "a very good one for Samoa and [it] should be allowed to stand."[50]

In only a few years, Ta'isi would refine and then repudiate many of these views. How can we explain such a major shift in this very critical, and personal, stance? The answer lies in the way New Zealand opted to rule Sāmoa. In the months after his first meeting with Dr. Pōmare, Ta'isi and other Sāmoans realized New Zealand was not going to opt for a progressive form of rule in any sense. This realization dramatically impacted Ta'isi's self-perception and thoughts on categories of race, indeed on all matters relating to New Zealand rule.[51]

After Dr. Pōmare's visit and this first exchange between these future friends, Sāmoa's fate continued to be decided and formulated in Geneva, Paris, London, and Wellington. On June 28, 1919, with the signing of the Paris Peace Treaty, Germany relinquished all claims to its former colonies and with that the governance for Western Sāmoa passed to "His Majesty in his Government of the Dominion of New Zealand." On March 11, 1920, the British government was "pleased accordingly to authorise and empower the Parliament of New Zealand to make laws for the peace, order and good governance" of Sāmoa.[52] From this point on, New Zealand began generating legislation to affect its rule. The legislation New Zealand produced harkened back to old imperial methods that vested enormous powers in the administrator, his officials, and the colonial government at the expense of the inhabitants' political rights. Forms of democratic representation and other aspects of progressive rule that Ta'isi promoted in his 1919 letters to Dr. Pōmare were ignored in Wellington.

When Ta'isi and others in Sāmoa became aware of the lack of concessions to democratic processes or other wishes for their country, there was a sharp change in tone in their discussions with New Zealand government and its representatives. The first iteration of New Zealand's legislative framework, the *Samoa Constitution Order,* was made public in early 1920, though it would not come into force until May, creating the impression that its contents were negotiable.[53] Its release was followed by a New Zealand parliamentary delegation in March 1920. Led by Sir James Allen, who had been charged by the Massey government with overseeing the transition of Sāmoa to a League of Nations mandate, the delegation also included Harry Holland. Holland was the recently elected member for the seat of Buller, prominent advocate of the labor cause, future leader of the Labour Party, and the unlikely ally of Ta'isi in the fight against New Zealand rule. Holland had already signaled his interest in Sāmoa via his two publications, *Samoa: A Story That Teems with Tragedy* (1918) and *Indentured Labour: Is It Slavery?* (1919), which criticized New Zealand governance of Sāmoa to date. His professed stance was that "the fullest rights of internal self-government must be guaranteed to the Samoan people" once war conditions end.[54] The Holland-led Labour Party increasingly clashed with the Massey government as the government gradually revealed their plans for running Sāmoa in 1920 and 1921.

Sāmoans took the parliamentary delegation's visit in good faith as a consultative exercise to gather responses to New Zealand's governing intentions. Sāmoans and Europeans duly formulated documents responding to the *Samoa Constitution Order.* The delegation's first order of business was to meet with *faipule* at Mulinu'u on March 5. Although the Sāmoan leaders made polite statements of welcome, their message to the delegation contained quite potent requests and warnings in a twenty-seven-point address to the parliamentarians (though it barely made any reference to the epidemic except to request that the graves of the victims be improved). The first point bluntly stated that if "dissatisfaction of the Samoan becomes greater with the Administration it will then be possible for the Samoans to appeal that Samoa be ruled from England by the Colonial Office." The *faipule* wanted more schools, educational opportunities for Sāmoan boys in New Zealand, and a better steamer to "ply between the islands of Samoa." Provocatively they requested "that the salaries of the Samoans employed together with white officials in the Government . . . shall be comparatively equal" and that these Sāmoan officials should also "receive trip allowances and furlough passage fees as allowed to white officials." The *faipule* wanted to make laws that would affect whites and Sāmoans alike.[55]

Sir James Allen responded reassuringly: "I give you the promise of New Zealand that no oppressive rules will be imposed upon you" and "it is our desire that you continue your government—your own local government—in very much the same way as it has been carried on in the past." He then launched into paternalistic imagery of New Zealand as the "father" of his "son" Sāmoa and set about denying most requests. On the possibility of the colonial office ruling Sāmoa, if New Zealand failed to satisfy Sāmoans, Allen told the *faipule* that "if you are ruled from England . . . we cannot come and meet you and hear what you have to say." He also informed the *faipule* that their proposed legal powers over whites along with wage equality and generous travel allowances could not be allowed as they were not "fair" to whites. One of the few points of agreement between New Zealand and Sāmoans was on the issue of prohibition on the importation of alcohol. Allen noted that this was in line with league rulings on the matter and he thought in this one instance (unlike wages, benefits, or legislative powers of Sāmoans over Europeans) "what is good for the Samoan is good for the white man also."[56]

The delegation then visited cocoa, coconut, and rubber plantations, where they investigated the most pressing issue to face the colony from the point of view of those involved in the plantation economy: the supply of indentured labor. The delegation posed a line of questioning to the plantation managers they interviewed that consistently followed the issues of who was the better and most valued worker—Chinese or Solomon Islander (referred to as "black boys")—as well as the sexual orientation and activity of Chinese laborers who were identified by numbers.[57] The issue of Chinese sexual relations with Sāmoan women, particularly those relationships that produced children, was of equal importance for the delegation as their plantation work and would be addressed in forthcoming legislation.

After the plantation visit, the delegation confronted a hostile Citizens' Committee in Apia on March 10 with Ta'isi acting as the committee's chairman. The "citizens of British Western Samoa" had appointed this committee during a public meeting in late January 1920. Like the *faipule*, the Citizens' Committee had compiled a document to present to the delegation; a series of reports on the most pressing issues arising from what was known about the *Samoa Constitution Order*. The committee painted a picture of Sāmoa being, like Shakespeare's state of Denmark, a rank and unweeded garden: quite literally overgrown. Plantations productive in 1914 now lapsed into a distressingly wasted state after nearly six years of New Zealand rule. The influenza epidemic had stopped work almost entirely for a period of weeks, allowing a surge in pests, especially the "dreaded rhinoceros-beetle and cocoa canker" that were "ravaging our trees and threatening our very existence," according to one planter.[58] The depleted Sāmoan population coupled with a depleted foreign workforce meant plantations across Sāmoa had not been able to regain the upper hand in their daily fight against pests and weeds.

The first and foremost order of business of the committee was "to bring most forcibly before you . . . how vitally necessary to the future prosperity of the colony the supply of indentured labour is." Their report then set out, in considerable detail, an analysis of Sāmoan lands and their ownership and use, shipping returns, commodity prices, and revenues received from Sāmoa's various markets, and a catalog of the main plantations and the numbers of indentured laborers they employed in 1914 versus the number in 1919 (many plantations lost more than half their workers). High wartime prices for commodities were matched by high prices for rice and other foods needed to feed workers. The high commodity prices were heading for a catastrophic fall as labor numbers had plummeted owing to forced wartime repatriations, influenza deaths, and the inability to replenish numbers with new recruits. After the epidemic it was virtually impossible to find Sāmoan labor. As far as foreign workers were concerned, planters uniformly agreed that they greatly preferred Solomon Islanders for their workforce. This was due to the Solomon Islanders' harder work, lack of vices, and supposed lack of interest in Sāmoan women. As one plantation manager put it, "The black man is a better man than the Chinaman." Also in their favor was the fact that a Solomon Islands laborer was usually paid only about one-quarter what a Chinese laborer was paid (although this was not openly admitted).[59]

When met with the dire circumstances of the plantation economy, and with the Citizens' Committee attributing all blame to New Zealand for their situation, Allen attempted to divert their anger. He explained that New Zealand's requests to Britain and Australia for the continuing flow of Solomon Islanders into Sāmoa had been flatly denied. On the question of Javanese labor, Allen's "memory is not quite clear . . . but if it is correct we also communicated with them [the imperial government] about Javanese labour and we were told we could not get Javanese labour." He tried to reassure the anxious committee to be "fair" to New Zealand and accept "that every effort was made to get you the labour." Cook Islanders were not available, although "some Niue-Islanders" (he emphasized their number would be small) would be spared to come to Sāmoa to work twelve-month stints. The only remedy was to continue Chinese indenture, despite the anxiety about vice and cross-racial sexual relations. The Chinese government had consented and Prime Minister Massey, uneasy about the matter, had charged the delegation members to go to Sāmoa and assess the situation for themselves. Allen's view was that it was New Zealand's duty to Sāmoans and whites that sufficient labor be provided "somehow or another . . . for the further development of your country."[60]

Though labor issues consumed the greatest portion of the meeting between New Zealand parliamentarians and the Citizens' Committee, other issues were raised, such as the formation of a municipality of Apia (as Ta'isi had proposed to Dr. Pōmare) governed by an elected council. The committee report noted that Sāmoans had village governance, and so "it is the opinion of the residents that the time has arrived when they should have some form of local government, and a municipality of Apia would meet the case." The report also raised the possibility of a legislative council, and made clear the committee's opposition to the administrator appointing members: "we do not know of a single instance where a nominated Council has proved satisfactory to the public." The committee also sought other planks of a Western democracy: a free press (the editor of the *Samoa Times* described the egregious government censors he had to deal with) and better education. They were particularly insistent that a secondary school in Apia be established "for the children of Europeans and half-castes." They wanted more financial transparency from the administration and the "'hush' and 'shrouded in mystery' policy of the past five years . . . totally eradicated." They also questioned the expensive overpolicing of Sāmoa by the newly arrived Sāmoa Constabulary.[61]

The committee also vehemently opposed the prohibition on alcohol. They argued that alcohol was actually necessary for good health in the tropics; "any one who has lived in the tropics for more than two or three years will admit that a certain amount of alcohol is necessary for the system." The committee felt certain that "almost any member of the medical fraternity" would support this claim. Not only was alcohol good for health; it also saved "thousands of lives" during the epidemic. Those not afflicted by influenza who undertook the gruesome work of "relieving the sick and burying the dead . . . only managed to keep going through the stimulating effects of alcohol." Whiskey lived up to its Celtic description, *uisce beatha,* or "the water of life," during the epidemic; without it, it "would have been physically impossible for any white man to have handled the putrid corpses some of which had been lying" in their houses for days. So the relief work could not have been carried out, and "as a consequence the death-rate would have been fully 50 per cent higher than it actually was." The committee refuted the government's position that the terms of the mandate meant a general prohibition had to be imposed in

Sāmoa. The fact that American Sāmoa was dry was not argument in support of replicating the same in Western Sāmoa, the committee continued, as American Sāmoa was a naval station and "automatically dry according to American legislation."[62]

Allen seized on the committee's views on prohibition to question Reverend Clarke of the LMS, a Citizens' Committee member, on whether he agreed with this aspect of their report. Ta'isi had assured Allen that all committee members had agreed with the report's contents and knew what they were signing. Reverend Clarke replied, "I cannot, on behalf of the London Missionary Society, associate myself with the views expressed on the subject of prohibition"—an ironic position, given that it was an LMS missionary (George Pritchard) who began the Sāmoan liquor trade back in 1850, as previously discussed. No one (unfortunately) could recount this significant fact when the question was raised about how long liquor had been available in Sāmoa before its prohibition.[63]

The alcohol issue, which would become a central component of New Zealand's campaign to malign Ta'isi's character, was here used by Allen to discredit the work of the committee by insinuating that it was not representative of the views of the wider community. Ta'isi assured him it was. Allen was adamant that the prohibition of importing alcohol would stand, though he noted that they had not taken the next step and stopped its consumption. If it was required for medicinal, sacramental, industrial, or scientific purposes, it could still be attained. He then said, "I am going to ask you this, as white men like myself" and implored the men present to think of the sacrifices made by those men who went to war, and whether they, too, could now make a "sacrifice—give up some little luxury and pleasure to help the free and dignified race of Samoans?" The report did not include any responses to his request.

Ta'isi was most vocal in these exchanges with the parliamentarians on the issue of creating a municipality of Apia run by an elected council and the legislative council—the two innovations that would deliver a measure of self-government to Europeans in Sāmoa. Allen ducked and wove about why one of the foremost democratic nations in the world (men, women, and Māori could vote by 1900) should not extend these fundamental rights in Sāmoa. He was "in favour of the municipality when the time comes," but "the time is not ripe in my opinion." On the legislative council being composed of elected officials, Allen noted, "I agree entirely with the principle that there be no taxation without representation." But he added, "We cannot always carry out our principles." It was too soon after the war to make decisions about voting rights, Allen argued. "We have not settled down after the war, and until we have settled down and know exactly who the whites are and what they are, and who the half-castes are and what they are, it is not safe, in my opinion, to provide for the election of members of the Legislative Council."[64]

In the 1920 parliamentary delegation reports, responses, and exchanges, virtually all the demands from Sāmoans and the Sāmoan European community were refused by the delegation. Allen's patronizing and paternalistic tone would increasingly become the standard of the New Zealand government and its various officials as it moved into its role as a mandatory. The government went through the theater and pretense of listening to Sāmoan communities, but, as would become clear when the *Samoa Constitution Order* was enacted in May 1920, their views were not taken into account at all. From this point, the future battle lines were being drawn. Allen's promise that "no oppressive rules will be imposed upon you" by New Zealand rang very hollow for all Sāmoans, not least Ta'isi.

Chapter Three

The "Troublesome Garden of Eden" (1920–1923)

Shortly after the New Zealand parliamentary delegation departed in March 1920, Ta'isi and Rosabel left Sāmoa for a trip to Europe. Still grieving from the loss of their son six months earlier, not to mention the loss of other family members to influenza, the couple took a trip that included Sweden and Britain. They first made their way by ship to the United States, traveled by train across the continent, and then took another ship to Europe. Homeward bound they took the same journey in reverse, arriving in Sāmoa by late 1920.

During Ta'isi's absence, Sāmoan communities had time to digest the *Samoa Constitution Order* and better understand how it was altering relations between the administration and the people. Sir James Allen had promised "no oppressive rules will be imposed upon you" by New Zealand when he led the parliamentary delegation in March 1920.[1] The May enactment of the *Constitution Order*, with all the egregious elements Sāmoans complained about still in place, incensed the community. Sāmoans now saw this delegation's cynical "listening tour" as a patronizing exercise. It was perceived as a breach of faith between the New Zealand parliamentary delegation and a cross section of Sāmoan society.

By the time Ta'isi returned to Sāmoa in late 1920 the mood was grim. The protest movement, the Mau of *faipule*, had gained momentum. Despite this salutatory protest, Sāmoan concerns continued to go unheeded, so the protest movement grew. Tate, who had waxed lyrical about the beauties of Sāmoa upon his arrival, soon realized it was a "troublesome Garden of Eden."[2]

New Zealand's military occupation ended and the League of Nations mandate era commenced on January 1, 1921. Despite its promise of renewal, the mandate's birth was mired in the ill feeling carried over from the past two years. The situation had deteriorated to such an extent that Ta'isi felt compelled to go to the top of the New Zealand government and begin an exchange with Prime Minister Massey when the civil administration was only eight days old. Ta'isi was in Auckland, and he hoped his communications might lead to meetings with government officials, rapid action, and a resolution to the tensions.

Though New Zealand had "full power" over Sāmoa by this time, Ta'isi was not intimidated. His passionate 1921 letters show he considered himself an equal to New Zealand officials and politicians, no matter how high they had climbed the ladders of power. In the eyes of colonial administrators, Ta'isi did not know his place in this colonial world. He spoke on behalf of both the Sāmoan and European communities, as he saw them as an integrated and mutually interdependent community. He told Massey his motivation in writing to him was entirely based on his sense of patriotism, "being a Samoan by birth, blood and sentiment, my interests in the welfare of Samoa and its inhabitants are as deep-rooted as anybody's can be for his country." So he took "the opportunity of placing before you and the New Zealand government my views on the situation," which Ta'isi hoped "will be accepted in the spirit in which they are given."[3]

Ta'isi let Prime Minister Massey know "the lack of confidence between the Samoan Administration and the inhabitants of the group (natives and Europeans) which was evident during the Military Administration has become more acute that ever on the advent of the Civil Administration." He continued, "I cannot believe that the conduct of the Administration of Samoa till now is in accordance with New Zealand's laid down policy for the Government of these Islands." Although he believed "New Zealand's intentions towards Samoa are of the very best," the "growing discontent . . . has been taken as prejudice . . . and has prompted [New Zealand] to govern Samoa regardless of the feelings of the inhabitants."[4]

Ta'isi ordered Sāmoan grievances into nine categories: policy, representation, native affairs, lands, Europeans, trading rights, labor, national status, and medical services. For every interlocking grievance, he attacked the current administrative stance with vigor. He repeated many of his earlier formulations for good governance made to Dr. Pōmare in July 1919 or to the parliamentary delegation in March 1920. He emphasized the need for a board of citizens to be established "to supervise the expenditure of Government revenues" and the need for democratic representation of the people of Sāmoa "now that most Germans have been repatriated." He also made key changes to his earlier expressed views: the long-proposed legislative council should now represent "natives, traders and planters"; previously, Ta'isi advocated for separate political arrangements for "native" Sāmoans and Europeans. This was a significant refinement of his outlook, elevating native Sāmoan political reach to the higher level of national governance rather than just overseeing the Indigenous Sāmoan community. He did not see the legislative council replacing the house of *faipule*. It would continue to govern native Sāmoan affairs but, he reminded Massey, the house of *faipule* had no legal provision, nor had its powers been defined as it had not even rated a mention in the *Constitution Order.* Ta'isi again stressed that the house of *faipule* should also be comprised of elected members, not ones appointed by the administrator. It was seen as another instrument of the administrator and a source of increasing objection.

On the all-important issue of land, Ta'isi conveyed the widespread sense of "gross injustice" about the powers vested in the administrator to take "any European or Native land in Samoa . . . by Ordinance . . . for any public purpose specified in the Ordinance."[5] "The Natives fear that the Government may dispose of some of their land under the rights of this clause, without reference to the owners," a circumstance Ta'isi could not believe was the actual case. He advised the language be altered to ensure there was no misinterpretation of the government's intent. If the administrator ever acted on this right, he warned, "this feeling now evident everywhere will undoubtedly materialise in a dangerous manner."[6] Native Sāmoans were also very discontented that trading rights had been withheld from them, thereby perpetuating a racially stratified economic structure whereby Sāmoans could only be producers of raw materials and not participate in the market where they might influence prices.

Regarding the question of the municipality of Apia, which Sir James Allen had shot down during the parliamentary delegation, Ta'isi again stressed the value of reinstituting an arrangement that "would only be a revival of the privileges extended to Europeans by the three powers as far back as 1889."[7] The other "great bone of contention" was prohibition. Ta'isi opined, "I feel that until this measure has been adopted in New Zealand itself this grievance should be removed by allowing consumption of liquor by Europeans," though with "strict government control" to limit abuse.[8] As far as business was concerned, New Zealand's legislative blueprint greatly reduced the opportunities of business people to levels below what they were under German rule. "This only brings before the citizens more than ever the many disabilities which the new Constitution will impose as compared to the German regime," he wrote—words sure to rile Massey and his government.[9]

Ta'isi argued that all these issues had fed Sāmoan discontent. He underscored that labor and the medical department were both "very important" and if not dealt with correctly would continue to rapidly corrode sentiment toward New Zealand. The lack of resolution of the indentured labor issue continued to impair the investment of capital in Sāmoa and the economic straits that Ta'isi and others in the Citizens' Committee outlined in March 1920 would continue to prevail. He described the medical department (that should be a centerpiece of the beneficial colonialism) as "deplorably mismanaged." Its poor services and inefficiencies was "one of the main causes of the present unrest amongst the natives and thus requires immediate attention." Again Ta'isi compared the current state of New Zealand–run services poorly against what Germany provided. He also pointed to the other great vulnerability in New Zealand's recent medical performance in Sāmoa during the epidemic. In a very prescient statement, he told Massey that "the ravages of the influenza epidemic will ever be laid at the door of [the] New Zealand administration and will not be erased from the native mind for many years to come."[10]

On top of all these sources of discontent, Ta'isi, by virtue of his unusual position as a Sāmoan world traveler, had uncovered the difficulties arising from the absence of Sāmoa's national status. His recent travels highlighted the ridiculous level of unworkable definitions about Sāmoan nationality and New Zealand government inabilities to confer British subject status. Ta'isi had been seeking British subject status since 1916 without success.[11] When he was in Europe, he told Massey, he took up this issue in London, having not got satisfaction by working through New Zealand government channels.[12] What Ta'isi's experience revealed was that even though Sāmoa was administered by New Zealand on behalf of His Majesty, "a native of Samoa was not entitled to British protection overseas," and, counterintuitively, "Samoa was not part of the British Dominions." Sāmoa had no national status itself under colonial arrangements and had no empowerment to confer documents. Ta'isi urged Massey to look into rendering "natives of Samoa the diplomatic and consular protection afforded to British subjects as well as European settlers of longstanding" who sought British subject status. Ta'isi felt sure that this step would "tend to increase British sentiments amongst all classes of the community."[13] Not only would a British passport ease travel complications; Ta'isi had to return to the birth country of his father, Sweden, for national recognition and to secure a travel document. His ships also had to fly the Swedish flag "because my father was born in Sweden some 83 years ago."[14] When the *Samoa Times* advertised leases of expropriated German plantations in September 1921, the notice stated that "applications to lease are limited to Samoans and British subjects." By this definition, Sāmoan-born people of mixed parentage were ineligible: they were neither Sāmoan nor British subjects, according to the constitution.[15]

When Ta'isi concluded this first letter to Massey he hoped the prime minister would be as "anxious" as he was to "remedy grievances existing and remove the causes which brought them about." "To this end I beg that you select a board of inquiry" composed of two New Zealanders, two Sāmoan residents, and two outsiders to report their findings "at an early date."[16] He offered to discuss these matters personally while he was in New Zealand, but this required Massey to respond with relative haste. He signed off and awaited Massey's reply at his Auckland office.

He waited a week. No response came. By January 15 Ta'isi, impatient for some response from the prime minister, stewed about the multiple problems in Sāmoa not receiving adequate attention in Wellington. He took the lack of response to mean the crisis in Sāmoa was of little consequence to Massey. Massey may also be snubbing him for his forthright tone, Ta'isi thought. Regardless of his misgivings about the tenor of his previous letter, Ta'isi began his next tersely. "I take it for granted that you have no intention to reply to my letter," he wrote, adding, "if the tone of my letter was objectionable to you, I can assure you that there was no intention to offend you in any way." He felt so strongly about the state of things in Sāmoa "that I think it my duty to exploit every avenue which may lead to a satisfactory settlement, and prompts me to take a further liberty to intrude in what may seem to you to be outside my province." He reiterated the seriousness and scale of discontent in Sāmoa among both "natives and Europeans," warning that "I cannot foretell the consequences if nothing is done to check the growing feeling of discontent." He also sought to diminish any perception that he was the source of the trouble New Zealand had experienced in the past and at present in ruling Sāmoa. He acknowledged he had translated the petition handed to Administrator Tate upon his arrival in 1919 bidding that Sāmoa be transferred to the United States or Britain. The petition had been "referred to me when I was ill in bed with influenza . . . and I translated [it] from Samoan into English at the request of the natives." Ta'isi had urged that the clause asking for Sāmoa to "be handed to America" be withdrawn and "the whole petition ultimately annulled," he told Massey. But, he cautioned, if things continued to deteriorate, "another general petition will be made for a complete change of government, and whereas feelings hitherto have been in favour of a change from New Zealand to direct British rule I should not be surprised if a request is made for a transfer to America or some other Power."[17]

Ta'isi felt quite certain that if the weight of public opinion in Sāmoa continued to shift away from New Zealand, articulated in another petition, New Zealand's "position in Samoa [will not be] tenable in the face of such a petition" regardless of whether the colony was held through the League of Nations or the Allied Powers. He genuinely believed the international order favored self-determination and forms of popular rule, and he clearly thought in 1921 that Sāmoans could shape their own future through political protest of sufficient magnitude. But Ta'isi was at pains to point out to Massey that he did not "wish in any way to figure in the transformation which is necessary to ensure success." In spite of his palpable anger at Massey and the New Zealand administration, he reassured the prime minister, "I still hold out hopes that New Zealand will rise to the occasion and bring about a solution of the great problems which now confront Samoa." He ended this missive with the thought that the solution could only be "effected by meting out to Samoa that measure of fair treatment in a careful study of the requirements of the inhabitants, which has made British Rule famous the world over."[18]

Ta'isi did not know when he fired off this hotly worded letter on January 15 that William Massey had responded to his first letter two days earlier. Massey "carefully noted" Ta'isi's views and assured him that the New Zealand government "has no desire to do other than in every way possible promote the interests and well-being of Western Samoa and of its inhabitants and particularly of the indigenous population." Sāmoa had been "imposed" on them, but all the government's efforts would be directed to fulfilling this obligation. Massey dismissed Ta'isi's careful and detailed delineation of problems in Sāmoa. He was "quite unable to agree" with Ta'isi on any point and considered his conclusions as misinformed owing to his "absence from the group." The suggestion of a board of inquiry would not be considered. Massey refuted there had been six years of New Zealand rule. It had only been since May 1, 1920, "when the *Samoa Constitution Order* came into operation that New Zealand has been in a position to formulate any definite policy." Even still, he continued, New Zealand was awaiting "the decision of the Supreme Council of the Allied and Associated Powers with respect to German indemnities and reparations" that was further hampering New Zealand's ability to effect its own policies. He hoped he could visit Sāmoa in the near future, and he would then consider any "representations that may be submitted having for their object the progress and development of the mandated territory." He concluded by noting that he had referred the matter to the Minister for External Affairs, E. P. Lee, rejecting (in less than one page) Ta'isi's impassioned pleas for more prime ministerial attention or to engage in an ongoing dialog.[19]

When Minister Lee addressed Ta'isi's letter two days after Massey had done so, he, too, let Ta'isi know that "it appears to me you have been misinformed" about a "lack of confidence existing between the Samoan Administration and the inhabitants of the Group (Natives and Europeans)." Administrator Tate had just completed tours of Upolu and was met with a "cordial" reception everywhere. Lee paid lip service to the government line that there was no problem in Sāmoa. Then he contradicted himself by admitting there *was* significant "native dissatisfaction." So much so that he had authorized the setting up of a commission of enquiry. "A native boycott of European foods and goods has been in progress for some considerable time and has now reached such a stage" that this inquiry was charged with investigating "the whole question of prices and cost of living."[20] Ta'isi was correct in his assessment of the situation in Sāmoa, but Lee dared not admit it. He wanted to maintain the appearance that New Zealand was as omniscient as any colonial power should be, a position of hubris and denial that was the root of future problems.

Despite his contradictory position, Lee addressed most of Ta'isi's other concerns. However, he added little new to Sir James Allen's responses when he faced similar questions in 1920 about prohibition, the municipality of Apia, or the democratization of the legislative council. On this last issue, Lee said a census would be taken in 1922, and "after its results are known it will be possible to further consider the matter." On the expropriation of land, Lee wrote, the government "has no intention whatever of expropriating any Samoan land," but then he added, "it may be necessary from time to time for the government to take land . . . for public purposes." The medical department had suffered in Sāmoa because of overstretched wartime resources, but he was hopeful that things would now improve. The matter of preventing "native" Sāmoans from trading "is one which has caused the Administration a good deal of concern." He referred back to the 1918 Toeaina Club that he saw as "an attempt . . . to induce Samoans to take shares in a European company." "In fact," Lee challenged Ta'isi, "it was your firm [that] drew attention to this matter and protested strongly against this movement as being altogether contrary to public policy," the view put forth by Tate that did not square with Ta'isi's commentary on the matter. Lee did agree with Ta'isi on one point: "the question of labour is a very important one." The administration's remedy (continuing Chinese indenture) would also be "safeguarding to the full the interests and well-being of the Native population," whose welfare was "particularly" important to New Zealand.[21] This "safeguarding" of the Native population from a continued Chinese presence in Sāmoa (code for sexual relations between Sāmoan women and Chinese men) would be the one significant change from the *Constitution Order* to the *Samoa Act*. The *Samoa Act* would criminalize marriage (and so sexual relations more broadly) between Chinese men and Sāmoan women.[22]

Ta'isi responded to Massey's and Lee's correspondence by hoping that a proposed prime ministerial visit to Sāmoa, including Minister Lee, would be an opportunity to expand on the conversation he had started. To emphasize the ongoing urgency, he passed on the contents of a recent telegram relaying the state of the native boycott. In Upolu the situation was "slightly improved" though on Savai'i "it has become worse." "This requires no comment from me," Ta'isi goaded, "but I trust the administration has been able to cope with this matter."[23]

Ta'isi's second letter did not impress Massey. The prime minister penned a response letting Ta'isi know that "while the New Zealand government has no objection to reasonable comments . . . it will not permit any person in Samoa to question the sovereignty and authority which it holds under His Majesty from the Allied and Associated

Powers."[24] This letter was not sent. Even though Ta'isi did not receive this particular letter, its message spoke loud and clear about the government's stance toward its Sāmoan critics. "Reasonable comments" were acceptable, though the interpretation of what was "reasonable" continually narrowed from this point as New Zealand battened down against the growing clamor of Sāmoan complaints. Soon no criticism would be "reasonable." Ta'isi's letters were likened to the copious and unsolicited advice by his father-in-law, Harry J. Moors. Moors had been sending such correspondence to the New Zealand government since 1914. "This is very much the same as we communicate to Mr Moors," one official noted, suggesting Ta'isi's warnings about contesting or transferring New Zealand sovereignty were the same incendiary refrain generated by Moors, who had always strongly pushed for US rule over all Sāmoan islands.[25] Unlike Moors, Ta'isi had no loyalties to the alternate power.

Ta'isi continued to write to New Zealand ministers and officials in 1921 before the *Samoa Act* came into force at the year's end. He was undeterred by the hostile reception he received as he wanted to take the opportunity to shape legislative frameworks while they were still being formed, in the hope of avoiding the conflict and unrest that had so plagued Sāmoa's recent past. Ta'isi knew New Zealand's distinguished heritage of democracy well and found it hard to reconcile this with how far a democratic government would stray from fundamental tenets for its own society when governing another. He would become painfully aware of the shortcomings of the great democracies—Britain, France, and the United States—who advanced democracy on their own home soil (albeit for those with the right class, gender, and racial criteria) but imposed often harsh colonial regimes in foreign lands. Many nationalist leaders around the world took at face value the exalted rhetoric of Western civilization and its democratic ideals, believing that political rights and freedoms would be—had to be—universally applied.

Ta'isi was one of these people. To accept the different circumstances, one had to accept colonized people were less deserving of political rights. He never entertained the thought that Sāmoans were lesser people; such a notion was abhorrent to him. He kept warning of the problems with the *Samoa Constitution Order* in 1921, noting in November that the only solution was "to scrap the whole constitution and frame a new one more in keeping with the rights, privileges and aspirations of the Natives and residents."[26] New Zealand did not heed the warning. When the *Samoa Act* came into force on December 7, 1921, it was almost a complete copy of the *Constitution Order*.[27] It was perfectly clear how little the New Zealand government listened to entreaties articulated by Ta'isi or the *faipule* and other Sāmoans about the flaws in the *Samoa Constitution Order* and New Zealand's administration. Ta'isi was staggered prompting him to reshape his political agenda. That New Zealand made "no provision" in this act for "the people of Samoa to have a voice in the government of the country" set a course for future clashes.[28]

Why did Ta'isi put himself forward as a spokesman and interlocutor between Sāmoans and the New Zealand government? According to him, he was sought out by both Sāmoans and Europeans because he was a unique entity. Sāmoans had sought him out to translate documents (like the 1919 petition to Administrator Tate) and interpret New Zealand government edicts that were enforced before they were published in Sāmoan.[29] In his letters to Massey and others in 1921, Ta'isi cites reports from chiefs and others in Sāmoa from which Ta'isi pieced together the view he presented to the New Zealand government. He considered himself, as he told Massey, to be "Samoan by birth, blood and sentiment." By 1921 Ta'isi had the Toleafoa *matai* title bestowed on him by the village of Lefagaoali'i in Samauga Savai'i. This title, belonging to the Mala'itai family, was passed down from Mala'itai Pa'ovale to Ta'isi in recognition of his maternal connections through his mother, Sinagogo Masoe. Mala'itai Pa'ovale, who had made Sinagogo his *taupou,* conferred the Toleafoa title on her son.[30] For European Sāmoans, the Citizens' Committee that met with the parliamentary delegation in March 1920 selected Ta'isi as their chairman. In February 1922 when the Citizens' Committee was again reconstituted in anticipation of the forthcoming visit of the prime minister and minister for external affairs, Ta'isi was again elected chairman (the prime ministerial visit did not occur).[31] He was popular and had stature in a cross section of Sāmoan communities; Ta'isi was also a noted forward thinker in realms beyond politics and commerce. For instance, in 1921 he was appointed Sāmoa's commissioner on the World's Board of Aeronautical Commissioners, which looked to a future of air travel but was presently concerned with organizing an around-the-world "aerial derby."[32]

Sāmoa's "native" and "European" communities were not mutually exclusive and detached from each other. They were intertwined at the community, familial, and individual levels, and Ta'isi exemplified that. Starting with Colonel Logan in 1914, New Zealand officials had sought Ta'isi out for advice and assistance. When Dr. Pōmare came to Apia in 1919, it was Ta'isi he asked about how New Zealand should precede with its Sāmoan rule. When Colonel Tate assumed his administrator responsibilities, he sought out Ta'isi for knowledge and advice. Ta'isi's situation as a person of high standing with native Sāmoans, European Sāmoans, and New Zealand was unparalleled. His linguistic skills—he could speak and write eloquently in English and Sāmoan—also naturally qualified him for this position.

From 1921 the New Zealand government became increasingly concerned with Ta'isi.[33] His bicultural life and identity had been an asset, but his rising power in Sāmoa made him a difficult person for New Zealand to control: his roots in Sāmoa were deep and intricate, and he came from esteemed stock. He was proving obdurate by clinging to principles of democratic political representation. He was, to Tate's disgust, "native loving Nelson."[34] Tate found "his real attitude . . . almost impossible to discover," but Tate could not accept Ta'isi's advocacy on behalf of "native interests" that Tate feared were "only platitudes and his desires and his practice are only to use the Samoans for his own personal profit."[35] Yet Tate had invited Ta'isi to become a founding member of the legislative council in 1920 along with other appointed men in the administration. Tate was amazed and frustrated when Ta'isi refused this invitation because "he has knowledge which would make him very useful to us if he threw in his lot with us." If Ta'isi was driven by "personal profit," why did he not throw "in his lot" with the administration that would accelerate this goal? Tate could not understand this decision; he would later write "why did he [Ta'isi] not take the opportunity to elevate himself on our shoulders through the Leg. Council?" The only answer Tate could find showed how his thinking was so atrophied by racial ideas: "the answer is because he is a halfcaste and does not possess the qualities of a white man but is really half Samoan in mentality."[36] Ta'isi rejected his offer of joining the legislative council because he fundamentally objected to being a government appointed representative; he insisted that this forum should be elected. To have accepted Tate's overtures would have meant increased influence and patronage from the administration, but he would have had to sell out the Sāmoan community; he refused to do this.[37] This was a powerful statement demonstrating Ta'isi's "real attitude."

Ta'isi's social position and political stance were sure to grate on those people deeply and profoundly wedded to imperialism, such as Massey and almost every member of conservative New Zealand who dominated government, society, and the Sāmoan administration. Ulster-born William Massey was an ardent imperialist. His favorite author was none other than Rudyard Kipling, the great spinner of imperial tales set in British India and author of the iconic 1899 poem "The White Man's Burden," which implored the United States to take up its racial and imperial duties in the Philippines. (Tate was also steeped in Kipling, whom he regularly cited. He referred to his "w. m. burden" in Sāmoa.[38]) For Massey and his cohort of ministers and officials, New Zealand had a burden to uplift and improve Sāmoans; an assignment conferred by Britain and the League of Nations. By the time Ta'isi wrote to him in 1921, Massey had been prime minister of New Zealand for nearly ten years. He had led New Zealand through the Great War and through the final act of the New Zealand Wars that had wrenched the country since 1845. In 1916, police attacked the Ngāi Tūhoe community living on Maungapōhatu, the sacred mountain, to arrest the community's rebel leader, Rua Kēnana, and assert Pākehā sovereignty over this holdout Indigenous community.[39]

Ta'isi was a peculiar figure in Sāmoa and the Pacific as he was in the spectrum of colonial worlds. He upended racial constructions with his business acumen, success, and his obvious brilliance. British imperialism had always encountered indigenous elites, particularly in old-world empires in Asia and Africa, who were moneyed and had considerable political and military power. In New World colonialism, which was predominantly settler or plantation colonies, circumstances differed markedly. Indigenous peoples experienced colonialism via slavery, indenture, or their dispossession in favor of incoming European populations. In Sāmoa and other tropical colonies, people classified as Indigenous were prevented from engaging in wealth-making enterprises. Racial ideas ensured that upward social mobility for non-Europeans was as rare as their economic progress. Indigenous Australia did not have an elite class. In the early years of the Australian British colonies, Aboriginal people were bestowed the status of "king" or "queen," often as a mark of gratitude for assistance to colonists.[40] Colonialism benefited very few, if any, Indigenous people in Australia. Polynesia, on the other hand, did have Indigenous hierarchies: Hawai'i's Kamehameha line is perhaps the most prominent.

This family acquired riches through the proceeds of resource harvesting, trade, and then the Great Māhele, when they liquidated extensive landholdings. Extravagant living dissipated much of it by the time of the US annexation of the islands. In New Zealand, British officials played elites against one another, and the course of colonialism typically did not result in net gains in wealth, as land was sold on unfavorable terms or confiscated by the Crown. The Kīngitanga, the Māori King Movement, established a Māori political elite in the central North Island in 1858 that opposed British rule. The Kīngitanga's strenuous opposition to settler and government encroachment on their lands was punished by considerable land confiscations in the rich Waikato region. By the 1920s few Māori individuals or communities had gained from British colonialism, and so New Zealand experience with Indigenous elites was limited.[41] Ta'isi's soon-to-be great friend Sir Māui Pōmare and a small cohort of others, such as Sir James Carroll, Sir Āpirana Ngata, and Te Rangi Hīroa (Sir Peter Buck), were exceptions.

Administrator Tate was increasingly anxious about Ta'isi's economic power in Sāmoa by September 1921. Ta'isi had indicated his interest in the expropriated DHPG plantations by questioning the wording of the advertisement that precluded non-British subjects or people not classified as Sāmoan from making a bid for these assets. Tate thought it wise to change the language to include "persons born in Samoa" as well as Sāmoans, so that Ta'isi and others could bid, he told Minister Lee. However, he wanted to ensure that these properties were not disposed to "undesirable people." Tate noted that "lately Mr Nelson has acquired the business interests of Mr Moors [his father-in-law], and now controls a very large number of trading stations in both islands." If Ta'isi "were to acquire any appreciable number of D. H. and P. G. Trading Stations, he could easily become a menace by establishing a monopoly." So he advised that New Zealand use its "fullest power" to reject any tenders that may be suitably high but were not in the longer term interests of economic and political balance from New Zealand's point of view.[42]

Ta'isi's communication of Sāmoan grievances had little impact on the *Samoa Act* as it was passed in December 1921. Yet Ta'isi's words echoed through New Zealand's first report to the League of Nations finalized in late 1921. This report, like every report to the League, was an exercise in self-justification. It acknowledged problems and challenges but then explained how New Zealand's presence mitigated or improved circumstances. For instance, in explaining events of 1918 the report admitted, "The influenza epidemic was disastrous, causing the death of many thousands of people, and but for the presence of the garrison, and the excellent services the garrison rendered, the results would have been more disastrous." The report also granted that the epidemic was "a ground for great grievance . . . they blamed their loss to New Zealanders occupying the place" but would have blamed any other power who was occupying their country at that time. The impacts of the epidemic were "that their temperamental cheerfulness received a severe blow" and as "a great number of the older chiefs died, younger and less experienced men succeeded to the positions as chiefs." The result was that "nothing could have occurred to have so prepared the minds of the Native people for the insidious action of agitators," who stoked a community whose organization was "shattered, its manner of life disturbed, and was blind to any profit or advantage it had gained, and saw only its losses and inconvenience." The native people did not appreciate "the fact that [the epidemic] visited many other parts of the world in the same unexpected manner" and as they had "suffered nothing of the actual horrors of war," all their anger was unreasonably directed at New Zealand.[43] Significantly the report failed to note damaging findings against key New Zealand officials made by the 1919 *Samoan Epidemic Commission*. The report showed the New Zealand government was in agreement with Ta'isi on one point: the epidemic had profoundly reshaped Sāmoan conceptions of New Zealand giving rise to significant political agitation.

Moving on from this fertile ground for discontent, the report addressed many of the grievances Ta'isi's had repeatedly laid out through 1921, which the secretary of the Department of External Affairs, J. D. Gray, deemed "trivial."[44] "An impression exists," the report stated, "that the Legislative Council has no power; but on the contrary, it is vested with real power." "No local legislation" is "possible without its concurrence," the report argued, and it is "an advance on the German system." On native self-government, the report admitted that "there seems to be a desire among a certain section of the Samoans . . . for complete self-government." However, not only was this sentiment "probably . . . not widespread"; it was "impracticable in the present state of Samoan development and education." On this topic it added, "There is an agitation afoot to invest the *faipule* with not only the powers which the Legislative Council now has, but also with such administrative powers as would give them complete powers of government in all respects . . . affecting the white community and the Native community." Again, the report deflected this demand by claiming "the measure of self-government which the Samoans now enjoy is considerable." With "improved" education there could be a "gradual extension of the present system" that was already generous and favorable to Sāmoan political rights. The report noted the demise of Sāmoan business enterprises through mismanagement. It gave an extensive review of the Department of Health, quoting the chief medical officer's claim that medical services had "clearly gained the confidence of the Samoan people." On education, the report recited the wonderful results of schooling, though it acknowledged the enormous debt owed to mission schools, and admitted that the main government efforts were directed to a few schools in Apia and "comparatively little has been done for the children of districts outside Apia" where the greater part of the population lived.[45]

Many efforts to educate and uplift Sāmoans were stymied. The report suggested, "The Samoan does not realize the absolute necessity for punctuality and regularity in attendance of systematic work." These same racial traits impaired Sāmoan progress because of the shortage of a willing and capable Sāmoan workforce for plantation labor. The report rationalized the need for Chinese indentured laborers for capital works and labor on government plantations. The report also recorded the downside of this scheme: Chinese overrepresentation in criminal activity in the use, possession, and smuggling of opium and gambling. What the report omitted to mention was that under the *Samoa Act* marriage between a Chinese man and a Sāmoan woman would be a criminal offence punishable by a twenty-pound fine or six months imprisonment.[46] The overall effect of New Zealand's line of argument in this first mandate report was to indicate discontent existed but to characterize the problem as contained and limited. Where there were shortcomings with New Zealand's administration, the fault lay elsewhere, often with Sāmoans themselves. Emboldened by this attitude and the legislation to support it, the New Zealand government forged an adversarial path. Ta'isi lay in this path.

Though Tate had been making representations on Ta'isi's behalf to resolve the British nationality question (because he thought it a pragmatic policy to keep Ta'isi on side), in April 1922 Tate delivered an incendiary speech to the fono of *faipule* in an effort to win them over to the administration. He said, "Traders who claim to be friends are in reality your enemies. Your only friend is the government . . . they [the traders] make money out of you and mislead you . . . a proof of these large profits is that one of them [implicating Ta'isi] has just returned from a tour around the world."[47] Tate knew there was antipathy between Toelupe, a leading figure in the *faipule,* and Ta'isi; he would exploit this to the administration's advantage.[48]

When Ta'isi learned of this speech, he was incredulous. "I could not believe this at first," he wrote to Tate. "The integrity of my firm is so well established by very many years of fair and honourable dealing in Samoa and elsewhere . . . that remarks of the above nature from anyone will fail to shake it." Yet Ta'isi feared that his "personal honour" was involved and his "professions of goodwill to the natives questioned." "In all my protests against your administration I have carefully abstained from personal references, and I have contested every effort on the part of others to bring personalities into it," he insisted.[49] Tate had lowered the bar considerably with this personal attack, though Ta'isi politely sought Tate's confirmation of the words he used. Tate denied the "alleged statements . . . were made by me" but confirmed he did say "there are white and half-caste residents and traders who pretend to be your friends who make their money out of you." Tate explained he then said that "as I look around I see nothing (except Mr Nelson's promise of £1000 for education) which the residents and traders have done for Samoans . . . what I see is that these people can build fine houses and take trips to Europe and Australia." Tate attempted to argue that these words did not "discountenance" any personalities and he "made no personal attack upon you." In fact, "when I used your name it was in an appreciatory manner." Tate also accused Ta'isi of having never having approached him "in suggesting improvements of administration or errors of policy." Instead Ta'isi had gone over his head to Wellington.[50]

Unsurprisingly Ta'isi was not placated by Tate's response: "your address to the *faipule* was—to say the least of it—impolitically and unnecessarily prejudicial to the commercial fraternity in Samoa, and particularly to myself." Ta'isi appealed to Tate's sense of British propriety to "vindicate my personal honour." If this were done, Ta'isi would then "set out before you my views of Samoa's requirements . . . as well as attempt to prove why your administration, now constituted, will ever fail to achieve success, and promote contentment and happiness in Samoa."[51] An unrepentant Tate wrote back to Wellington, "I am by no means satisfied that he is not guilty of the practices of misrepresentation about which I warned the *faipule*," but Tate did not have any evidence to support this suspicion. "Whether Mr Nelson is guilty or not is known better by the *faipule* than by anybody else," he reasoned, but would proceed with the assumption of Ta'isi's guilt regardless.

Tate's next move was like dousing a fire with gasoline. In September 1922 he signed the *Samoan Offenders Ordinance* into law. Many Sāmoans saw this ordinance as "vicious."[52] The *Samoan Offenders Ordinance* referenced Governor Solf's 1901 proclamation that prohibited Sāmoan chiefs from exercising their traditional rights of banishment and instead vested that power in the governor. This proclamation was the trigger for the protest movements that plagued Solf's term. New Zealand did not take its historical lessons, and replicated the egregious edicts, reaping similar results.[53] The administrator's "full power" was now even greater through the imposition of a more invasive colonial order. The administrator could impose "a sequence of banishments and degradations without trial of sacred and high Chiefs" and banish any Sāmoan from their village, which "short of being killed [was] the traditional ultimate punishment."[54] It could also deprive chiefs of their *matai* titles, stripping them of their authority and humiliating the individual and his family.[55]

Tate's growing hostility did not deter Ta'isi from incorporating his firm in Sāmoa in November 1922.[56] The company his father started in 1868 became O. F. Nelson and Co. in the business of General Managers and Island Traders, Merchants and Commission Agents, Importers and Exporters with offices throughout Sāmoa, Auckland, Sydney, and London, known colloquially as Nelisoni's. Ta'isi's star was still ascending as 1922 came to a close despite Tate's blatant efforts to stall its rise. A man of Ta'isi's economic and social stature needed an appropriate home. His grand German colonial-style mansion, Tuaefu, designed by local architect Fred E. Syddall, was undergoing its finishing touches in 1922.[57]

Tate was a guest at the new home in early 1923 just before his posting was coming to an end. Though he attended with "great disinclination" in the end, he said, "I was glad I went." Nelson was "as nice as nice could be," though "as far as the government is concerned he is as oppositionist as ever." The men talked "land tenure and native custom" before lunch and after they listened to singing and watched a "basket ball match by the little female piebalds," who had learned the game at their Auckland schools. Tate and his companion were the only ones there who were not "half castes," obviously a rare and uncomfortable situation for the administrator. Tate was also struck by Tuaefu; Ta'isi "has his place very much nicer than I would have expected," Tate wrote. "The terraces, tennis courts, basket ball court and the grounds generally are well laid out and well kept; the furniture etc are good." Rather than challenging his racial prejudices, Tate's impressions of Tuaefu made him realize that Vailima, Robert Louis Stevenson's former home where he was housed, had to be renovated to keep pace. "I realized that the practice of economy at Vailima was an error . . . it is in comparison ill kept and shabby." "His paint is clean and smart ours is awful because our roof is wrong and the rain water runs down the walls . . . Nelson has fans and good electric fittings—ours you have seen . . . money must be spent on Vailima," he complained. As Tate's successor would articulate after inspecting the house in 1923, "Vailima should reflect the prestige of the New Zealand government and the Samoa Administration." Implicit within this thinking was that Vailima had to reflect the prestige of the white race also.[58] To date historians have propounded the view that Tuaefu was built to rival Vailima. By Tate's own description, Vailima was in a sorry state and no object of envy. In fact, Vailima was upgraded in 1923 at considerable expense (expenditure that would prove controversial) to rival Tuaefu, a critical difference.

At Tuaefu Ta'isi hoped to make a home for his daughters and, especially to create a residence befitting Rosabel. Tuaefu sat across the Fuluasou River from the Moors' estate at Ululoloa; the situation of this mansion was no coincidence. It was also situated at the "base of Mount Papase'ea" (also known as Mauga Folau) and commanded "an exquisite view of the sea and the beautiful surroundings of tropical vegetation."[59]

Tuaefu reflected more about Ta'isi and his personality than his love of family and display. Though he was the most successful man in the country, he was far from complacent. He had many luxurious possessions, from the latest cars to fine English china. Of all these, his four-hundred-volume library, housed in his second-floor office, was perhaps his most valued.[60] It was also testament to his ongoing industrious, self-improving quest to be an educated and informed man with a well-stocked mind. To this end he had books entitled *Public Speaking and Influencing Men in Business, How to Win Friends and Influence*

Figure 3.1. Ta'isi at Tuaefu with men from the American Narwhal Expedition at Tuaefu, May 1923, photograph by Murry N. Fay. Copyright unknown. Please contact author if you are the copyright holder.

People, and *Things Worth Knowing.* As well as these self-improving texts, his collection had *Encyclopaedia Britannica, The Wonderland of Knowledge,* and other encyclopedic publications.[61]

Ta'isi also had more erudite reading. He had a considerable collection of works by British authors and poets and historical works, as well as a first edition of Herman Melville's *Omoo: A Narrative of Adventures in the South Seas* that detailed the French takeover of Tahiti in 1842.[62] There were multivolume collections on the Great War (*Nelson's History of the War*) and collections on other famed historical episodes and figures such as the multivolume *Beacon Lights of History: The World Heroes and Masterminds* and Theodore Roosevelt's *Outdoor Pastimes of an American Hunter.* Several other titles by this American political figure indicated Ta'isi's admiration of him. He also possessed H. G. Wells' four-volume *The Outline of History* and *An Englishman Looks at the World.* Though the titles were wide-ranging, there were also consistent themes: imperial history was one of them. He had Edmund Gibbon's *The History of the Decline and*

Fall of the Roman Empire, The Treaty of Waitangi or How New Zealand Became a British Colony, and, even closer to home, the 1917 publication *The New Pacific: British and German Aims* and the 1918 work *New Zealanders in Samoa*. The course of Irish history was also of particular interest among Ta'isi's readings on empire, evidenced by his possession of *Young Ireland in Exile* and *Michael Collins and the Making of the New Ireland*. He had many volumes on the Pacific, the other theme of his collection. He owned many books on Pacific exploration and contact as well as contemporary works like Bronislaw Malinowski's *Argonauts of the Pacific* and Frederick O'Brien's *Mystic Isles of the South Seas*. Ta'isi also possessed works on Pacific indigenous myths and legends and ethnologies of Māori and Polynesians like Elsdon Best's classic *The Maori—Memoirs of the Polynesian Society*.[63]

Ta'isi's books reveal a lot about his personality and his intimate world of thought and intellectual diversions. New Zealand's characterization of "the Samoan" to the Permanent Mandates Commission in 1922, cited earlier, as a person who "does not realize the absolute necessity for punctuality and regularity in attendance of systematic work," was faulty when it was applied to any Sāmoan, and certainly did not apply to Ta'isi.[64] He was a stickler for hard work, efficiency, and abiding by the clock. It was no coincidence that his contribution to the public memorial for those killed in World War I, and also to his son, was the workings of a large clock. "The Nelson Clock" tops the tower (paid for with funds raised by a cross section of the community by such things as singing contests) that continues to dominate Apia's cityscape.[65]

For all his strict work and personal habits, which he would drill into his daughters, Ta'isi was also a famed gregarious host, as even Tate had to admit. Tuaefu was designed so he could entertain multitudes in style. Elegant dinner parties, tennis, billiards, and singing were on offer to guests officially invited with formal note cards. Ta'isi hoped to enhance Sāmoan society by loaning out guidebooks from his library on dance or how to play whist.[66]

He was also deeply religious. He had a small Methodist chapel built on his estate for his family and other neighbors. Here he went through the rituals of faith that were so greatly embellished by the beautiful musicality of Sāmoan singing. His favorite hymn was "The Rock of Ages," in Sāmoan.[67] For all his religious devotion and civic-minded generosity, evidenced by his £1,000 donation for local (that is, "native Sāmoan") education that was given to Methodist Reverend George Skinkfield, tensions were rising between Ta'isi and the Australian Methodist Church leadership (the Sāmoan Methodist Church was a branch of the New South Wales Conference of the Methodist Church of Australasia, headquartered in Sydney, until 1964). Tate explained the cause of the "fierce controversy" between Ta'isi and his church's clergy that deteriorated along with the broader political situation in Sāmoa as the Methodists increasingly sided with the administration.[68] Tate wrote that in the course the men's correspondence over this handsome donation, Skinkfield "offended him [Ta'isi] sorely by telling him he could not 'ride the white horse and the brown horse together.' "[69] The reverend, like the administrator, could not understand Ta'isi's indestructible connection to "native" Sāmoans. The clergyman's suggestion that he make a choice between supporting Europeans or Sāmoans, and Ta'isi's visceral reaction to the suggestion, speaks volumes about Ta'isi's politics and identity.

Tuaefu reflected these. Alongside the European mansion was the Sāmoan *fale,* where members of his extended Masoe family, headed by his cousin Pitofau Masoe and her husband Masoe Ti'amamana, lived. On the adjacent estate, another cousin, Fa'agutu Tugaga, who was married to Atoa Polito, lived with their large family. The dual aspects of Sāmoa—the Sāmoan and the European—blended here on this estate, also representing Ta'isi's two indivisible sides. While it was a showcase of European taste, it was also a site for Sāmoan rituals with his large extended family. Tuaefu was a place that accommodated impressively large and frequent gatherings—especially on Sundays after church—that remain a hallmark of *fa'asamoa.* Feasting was a grand, weekly event, and here Ta'isi relied heavily on his Tuaefu *aiga* to grow, prepare, and share in the foods that were such a central part of *fa'asamoa.* There were many Tuaefu children who enjoyed the beautiful grounds as well as a swing set, a rarity in Sāmoa at the time, that delighted the youngest generations endlessly.[70]

Ta'isi was often accused of vanity as a way to disparage him as the political situation intensified. Though he was self-deprecating among family and close friends about his girth—he enjoyed his food—he also believed his body's traits revealed his highborn lineage. His long fingers and elegant hands, which he tended with care, he took as a definitive sign he was descended from aristocrats.[71] Anyone meeting him at Tuaefu in early 1923 could not have disputed Ta'isi's unique place in Sāmoa. But to Tate, and many other Europeans with extraordinary power over the country, "Nelson is only a halfcaste, poor chap, and that seems to mean only half discerning and half stable." Despite Ta'isi defying all the stereotypes through which Tate viewed the world, Sāmoans reciprocated with an even lower opinion of Tate: his nickname was "moga moga" or "the cockroach."[72]

These all-encompassing ideas about race underpinned every relation in the early days of the mandate. Though they were articulated privately, they were a latent force that would be unleashed as tensions escalated. The appearance that all was well in Ta'isi's world a glimpse of him at Tuaefu at this time might give was deceiving. Tuaefu would not be the happy home Ta'isi hoped it would be. In the world beyond Tuaefu's boundaries, problems shifted in some ways and persisted in others. What remained constant was that Ta'isi was inextricably connected to them.

Chapter Four

A New Era? (1923–1925)

Ta'isi—and many other Sāmoans—had been deeply frustrated with Colonel Tate's administration. Tate rebuffed copious complaints and did nothing to alleviate the burning anger that ran throughout his term when Sāmoa transitioned from being occupied by the New Zealand Expeditionary Force to being the Mandated Territory of Western Samoa governed by a civil administration. Tate's "constant anxiety" during his term was "Native unrest." "A considerable white and half-caste population" were angered "mostly on account of prohibition," he argued. "Their ideas and discontents became reflected in the natives who cannot see that we are here for their benefit while the whites are here for their own," Tate reasoned.[1]

Embedded in Tate's remarks were the real causes of the "unrest." He trivialized the unrest, narrowing its cause down to the politics of drink. More seriously, he saw the vast majority of Sāmoans—"the natives"—as so easily led by disgruntled "whites" that mere trivialities would rile them up and turn them against New Zealand rule. Sāmoans also could not see, Tate believed, New Zealand was there to serve and benefit them, protecting them from greedy Europeans only out for their own gain. Tate and numerous officials downplayed the wide-ranging Sāmoan complaints, while Prime Minister Massey refuted there were any complaints at all. The situation throughout Tate's tenure was muddled and brimming with denial about the root causes of so much discontent.

Tate showed how he would combat incessant criticism when he made the speech to the *fono* of *faipule* in April 1922. Ta'isi was outraged because of the speech's pointed attacks against him and his firm. Tate showed he was going to exploit fissures within Sāmoan society to dislodge Ta'isi from his leading position among many Sāmoans. Tate wanted to disunite native Sāmoan leadership—the *faipule*—with that of European Sāmoans; this he achieved. He also actively tried to turn Sāmoan anger away from New Zealand and toward other targets. Ta'isi was an easy target. His wealth was plain for all to see. Tate questioned how he got to be so rich. To explain Ta'isi's wealth he constructed a simple narrative with victims, a villain, and heroes. Ta'isi's wealth was gained, according to Tate, by exploiting the very Sāmoans whose interests he professed to represent. Tate offered no proof for his contention. Tate's narrative for Sāmoan distress would prove useful again when Sāmoan anger toward New Zealand reemerged.

For all the offense Ta'isi took to Tate's administration, particularly his incendiary speech to the *faipule,* Ta'isi maintained that he and Tate remained "firm friends" despite their "differences of opinion."[2] "It is true that we have not always agreed on political and other matters during your regime," Ta'isi wrote to Tate some years later. However, "to say that these [disagreements] . . . interfere[d] with our personal respect for one another is, in my opinion false."[3] The pleasant day Tate spent as a guest at Tuaefu before he left Sāmoa in 1923 was undoubtedly the source for Ta'isi's impression. As we know, Tate regularly conveyed his contempt for Ta'isi to New Zealand officials, a contempt rooted in his views on race.[4]

Regardless of how the relationship between these two men fared, the government realized relations needed to be reset. Tate's period of rule had been bedeviled by the "persistent" publication of critical media accounts in "English, American and Australian newspapers."[5] This kind of publicity was excruciating, and so New Zealand was keen to alter the story going out to an international audience about its imperial work. Wellington concluded that resolution to the problems in Sāmoa would not be reached with Tate at the helm. On top of this, Tate was lonely (his wife, Maude, was back in Wellington for health reasons), demoralized, and had wanted to be replaced since September 1921.[6] A suitable replacement was sought from late 1922. Unlike Logan's and Tate's terms, which were either partially or wholly under the terms of the military occupation, the new administrator would serve entirely under the League's mandate system. Yet the government still looked to a military man to fill the position of administrator.

By early February 1923 it was announced that it was "absolutely unanimous" Brigadier-General George Spafford Richardson CB, CMG, CBE, had been selected by the New Zealand government to be Tate's successor.[7] Born in Northampton, Richardson came to New Zealand in 1891 as an "instructor in gunnery and master gunner" to the dominion forces. In 1892 he married Caroline Warren, whose New Zealand lineage stretched back the earliest days of Pākehā settlement. It was in the New Zealand army that Richardson made a career, the Great War providing the means for him to reach rare levels of career distinction. He fought at Gallipoli, where he served at Cape Helles until the December evacuation from that mythic battle site. He served on the western front in France before being appointed as the general officer commanding the New Zealand Forces in the United Kingdom.[8] Since April 1915, when this corps landed on the Gallipoli peninsula in Turkey, the myth of ANZAC has been a powerful force shaping Australia and New Zealand national identity and ideas of masculinity. For Richardson, being an ANZAC gilded his stature as much as his worldview was refracted through the prism of the Great War.[9] These factors would be key driving forces in Sāmoan affairs during the mandate. The Great War and the colonial surge in the Pacific that followed it were inextricably linked by the men that led these efforts.

A dinner was held in Richardson's honor after his appointment in March 1923. In his dinner speech, New Zealand's solicitor general congratulated Richardson on becoming "the uncrowned king of Samoa." He said Richardson was "taking up part of the white man's burden in the Pacific," and it was hoped he would "prove to be one of the great pro-consuls of our scattered Empire." Richardson was moved by all the adulation at this dinner but assured the guests it would not "swell his head." Instead Richardson pledged to "act up to the highest traditions of the best British administrators, and to hold up before both the white people and the natives of the mandated territory the very highest ideals." He aimed to show the "natives of Samoa what the people of this Dominion had done for their blood-brothers, the Maoris of New Zealand, and to convince them that it was New Zealand's aim to do as much and more . . . for the people of Samoa."[10] He wanted to "induce the Samoans to love New Zealand and the Empire" because in early 1923 it was evident Sāmoans "loved" neither.[11]

As the outgoing administrator, Tate was also praised in media reports. The *Evening Post* noted that Colonel Tate had to cope with "exceptional difficulties in inaugurating civil government at a time when trade depression was being severely felt in the Islands." Despite his heroic efforts, Tate had been subjected to "much criticism and abuse," which he had stoically endured as he continued on his rightful governing course.[12] In his final report before his March 1923 departure, Tate described the extremely gratifying farewells he received. The American consul, Mr. Quincy Roberts, spoke highly of Tate and the New Zealand administration, a valued verdict Tate was eager to convey. Tate was equally keen to note Sāmoans bid him farewell with "fulsome" and grateful speeches. It was especially pleasing that Afamasaga, "whom you may remember as rather a troublesome person in native affairs," hosted the event along with Fautua Malietoa. Afamasaga "appears to have seen the error of his ways and to appreciate that he was used a tool." The *faipule* in their farewell speeches said, "The flame of loyalty to New Zealand, our guardian, burns brightly." Tate was "exceedingly surprised and gratified to receive an invitation from the Chamber of Commerce," chaired by H. J. Moors. Moors, who had criticized New Zealand rule from the outset, spoke handsomely, showing that the Chamber of Commerce "have a much higher appreciation of the Administration . . . than their correspondence and actions in the past have led us to believe." "Practically the whole of the commercial community was present at this luncheon," Tate wrote, but the "few absentees included the minority, whom we may expect to continue opposition and criticism."[13]

Tate did not make direct reference to Ta'isi, though he did obliquely refer to him as a critic and an absent Chamber of Commerce member. As Tate was making his last congratulatory rounds in Apia, Ta'isi was in Auckland. Here he attended a lunch hosted by the Auckland Chamber of Commerce and met Richardson. The relationship between these two men, which would be pivotal to the course of Sāmoan history over the next decade or more, began exceedingly well. Their initial meeting went so favorably that the two men continued their conversation as they walked down Queen Street together afterward. Richardson then invited Ta'isi to lunch at Auckland's Grand Hotel the following day. Again the men enjoyed each other's company so much Ta'isi paid Richardson the honor of seeing him off at the wharf as he steamed to Sāmoa with his wife, Caroline, and two of their six children, a few days later.[14]

As Richardson headed to Sāmoa, Ta'isi continued on to Sydney for business. When he was in Sydney he granted an interview to the *Sydney Morning Herald* as chairman and spokesman for the Sāmoa Citizens' Committee. He made clear in the interview that "what we want most is an elective Legislative Council, not a nominated one, to govern the group in accordance with the requirements of the people and its financial capacity." He criticized "foolish restrictions" on travel between the islands, where people had to apply for a permit to move between Upolu and Savai'i, and the restrictions on indentured labor. He and other Sāmoans hoped that Richardson was "invested with power to make changes that were urgently necessary for the welfare of Samoa." With "sensible administration," there was no reason Sāmoa's future "should not be bright," he argued.[15]

Ta'isi's remarks were quickly picked up in New Zealand. The *Evening Post* ran an article, "White and Brown," which challenged Ta'isi's call for an elective council as against the interests of "the native population." His proposals "would place the whole government in the hands of white planters and traders . . . unless Mr Nelson contemplates that members of the brown majority should have an equal voice with the white minority in the election." This seemed unimaginable in 1923 but was exactly what Ta'isi proposed. The *Evening Post* dismissed his other suggested reforms, in terms similar to that used by government officials in their correspondence, as the views of a "Samoan white man" that were unlikely to be "generally held."[16] Reports on Ta'isi's remarks competed in New Zealand with glowing accounts of Richardson's reception in Sāmoa after he arrived March 19. The new administrator was met with "enthusiastic" welcomes wherever he went. Sāmoans interpreted the change in leadership as a signal that their complaints had registered in New Zealand and the future would improve.[17]

Ta'isi's public criticism of New Zealand's rule hit the government where it was most sensitive—its international image. Despite his outspokenness, when Ta'isi arrived back in Apia "about a month later," the friendly encounters with Richardson that started in Auckland continued.[18] Richardson knew that if he was to have a smooth tenure as administrator, he needed Ta'isi's cooperation and assistance. This point was reiterated early on by J. D. Gray, the secretary of the Department of External Affairs, a key figure in New Zealand's rule of

Sāmoa. He wrote to Richardson in May 1923, noting that in addition to the Citizens' Committee, "they have formed now a Samoa Welfare League, and that Nelson had a good deal to say at its first meeting." Gray hoped Ta'isi would live up "to his high professions" and told Richardson if he managed to "hold his good will and co-operation throughout your term you will have achieved something that no other Administrator has so far succeeded in doing." Gray noted that he had the "greatest personal regard and liking for Nelson but in my experience he has been very unstable." Though Gray was in two minds about Ta'isi personally, for New Zealand's agenda, "I have always felt . . . that it was quite possible to get a lot of valuable help and work out of such men as Mr Nelson."[19]

Richardson was more than aware of the need to befriend Ta'isi. As his first order of business he requested that the New Zealand government (which in turn asked the Permanent Mandates Commission) look into Ta'isi's application for British subject status. (Ta'isi was still a Swedish subject at this time.[20]) This question affected Sāmoan citizenship generally and had generated a considerable paper trail from 1922, with Ta'isi being considered a worthy test case. Richardson gave Ta'isi's quest his fullest support, writing, "He is a man of the highest social standing . . . is respected by all sections of the community [and] has shown his loyalty [to Britain] by his personal assistance to the Administrator and handsome contribution to the Great War."[21] Fostering the loyalty of this individual, and others like him, was of "great political importance," Richardson emphasized. Richardson urged immediate action as "Mr Nelson feels his position keenly."[22] The government acted: it made representations to the Permanent Mandates Commission in April 1923 to resolve the quandary of the statelessness of citizens in former German colonies (now B and C mandates). New Zealand did not want Sāmoan citizens declared citizens of New Zealand, and they wanted an ambiguity about British status to remain, with Sāmoans described as "under British protection," as they were concerned about Germans in Sāmoa gaining coveted British national status.[23] The League determined Sāmoans would be British subjects but they would not be New Zealand citizens.[24] Ta'isi was duly granted British subject status in September 1924 as a precedent for other Sāmoans.[25] Perhaps as another sweetener to secure Ta'isi's good opinion, Richardson gave O. F. Nelson and Co. "the contract for shipping our copra [that is, from the Crown Estates] to London" in December 1924. This made the Burns Philp manager "very upset," but Nelson's "shipping arrangements were more favourable," Richardson informed Wellington—a decision that only augmented Ta'isi's position.[26]

Richardson was accurate in his assessment of Ta'isi's unique status in Sāmoa when he first became acquainted with the man and his country in 1923. As the head of the most prosperous firm in the country, and with all the trappings of Western material success, best exemplified by his new mansion, Ta'isi was Sāmoa's undisputed "leading citizen." In 1922 the Grand Lodge of New Zealand successfully requested that its jurisdiction be extended over the Sāmoan mandate, and it is probable Ta'isi joined the Freemasons, that great and mysterious bastion of British imperial male power that was also accessible to a select group of colonial elites, around this time.[27]

Richardson would have quickly recognized the status inherent in Ta'isi's wealth and position in the business community, the Citizen's Committee, Welfare League, and in the Freemasons. More perplexing to him would have been Ta'isi's status among the Sāmoan community. Ta'isi was already the holder of the Toleafoa title from Samauga.[28] In 1923 the village of Asau on Savai'i bestowed upon him the *ali'i* title, or high chiefly title, of *Ta'isi,* because of the esteemed rank his mother, Sinagogo Masoe, had held. More than his Toleafoa title, the Ta'isi title affirmed his eminent standing within his Sāmoan family and the Sāmoan community.[29] Comprehending the complexities of Sāmoan status embodied in matai titles was never a subject Richardson, or most other New Zealand officials, mastered. They consistently failed to see the fundamental importance of titles to *fa'asamoa;* any outside interference with how titles were bestowed was an outrage. This is a lesson New Zealand would learn slowly, incurring dramatic consequences along the way. Ta'isi's deep interest in Sāmoan culture—his culture—was also evident by his foray into scholarly circles at this time. In November 1923 he gave an address to the Samoa Research Society entitled "Legends of Samoa" that was published by the *Journal of the Polynesian Society* in 1925, coauthored with the journal's coeditor Johannes Andersen. Ta'isi revealed his fascination and study of Sāmoan legends went back to when he was seventeen and living in his birthplace, Safune on Savai'i. In his address he recounted legends as well as his quest to find more or different versions of legends—like "Sina and her Eel," which explained how the coconut came to Sāmoa—from different villages. He also explained the sacredness of these legends and how they were preserved in oral tradition and often contrasted with the versions written down by *pālagi*.[30]

Initially Richardson entertained Ta'isi regularly at his residence at Vailima. Ta'isi reciprocated by having the administrator and his family often to Tuaefu. Richardson would also call at Ta'isi's office at least once a week to "discuss various matters."[31] These "various matters" ranged across the spectrum of issues confronting the new administrator keen to quell the tensions ignited by his predecessor. For instance, the position of chief judge opened up in July 1923, when Judge Orr Walker resigned suddenly due to his wife's ill health. The chief judge was the deputy administrator, who acted in the position in the administrator's absence. He also was an appointee to the legislative council and wielded considerable power in the courtroom where no juries were constituted to dilute the judge's power. In seeking a replacement for this important position, Richardson sought Ta'isi's advice. He let Richardson know the "general view" about this position that "deeply concern[ed] the citizens and natives." Ta'isi advised that Orr Walker's replacement should be "a man of experience and legal knowledge . . . who could uphold the dignity of the Court and the prestige of the Administration." Ta'isi believed that "no one in the present staff in Samoa [could] satisfactorily fill the position." He thought this view was widely held, but he could not confirm this view with the Citizens' Committee or Welfare League before writing, but would do so, showing his consultative approach to the question.[32]

Richardson also sought Ta'isi's opinion about "matters of Native policy and other matters in connection to the administration." For instance, Ta'isi gave Richardson advice on education and how New Zealand should go about rectifying the lack of adequate schooling beyond Apia. When they first discussed this issue, Richardson favored English instruction in new schools throughout Sāmoa. Ta'isi did not, and he told Richardson as much. He prompted Richardson to think about what the implications would be to educate Sāmoans in English. Would they then seek office jobs? Or would they be content to stay with their coconut plantations as the majority of them would need to with the economy structured as it was? Richardson adopted Ta'isi's view about using Sāmoan as the language of instruction in his expanded education system.[33]

Ta'isi's campaign for political representation bore some fruit from 1923. A 1923 amendment to the *Samoa Act* permitted elections for three seats in the legislative council along with six appointees. The appointees would be the men who held the positions of secretary to the Sāmoan Administration, the chief judge, the secretary of native affairs, the collector of customs, the crown solicitor, and the treasurer. Administrator Tate, in anticipation of this concession to democracy being granted in Sāmoa, had earlier raised the issue about who should be permitted to vote. He was concerned that a distinction needed to be made among the numerically significant half-caste population that "range through every grade of society" from those "as reputable as any of the European population" to those "little removed from the Samoan . . . who are in no way qualified to exercise a franchise wisely." To affect the distinction between the different grades of "half-castes," Tate favored a property qualification that would "exclude persons of such a low grade as could not reasonably be enfranchised, unless the vote is also given to the whole of the Samoans." Though Ta'isi had argued for voting rights for all Sāmoans, Tate wrote, "To give the vote to the whole of the Samoans at the present time would, I think, be an absurdity."[34]

When the governor-general, Viscount Jellicoe, signed the Samoan Legislative Council (Elective Membership) Order in September 1923, a qualified elector was defined as a male person over the age of twenty-one who was the legitimate son of parents of European descent or was the legitimate son of a European father, who was registered as a European. Also, an elector had to hold freehold or leasehold taxable property in Sāmoa with a capital value of not less than two hundred pounds, and earn a taxable annual salary in Sāmoa of not less than two hundred pounds. New Zealand, the country that boasted of enfranchising women before any other nation, and where Māori (men *and* women) had voting rights, was not engaging in such radical maneuvers in Sāmoa. European and Sāmoan women and Sāmoan men, like people of "unsound mind" and convicted criminals, were not eligible to vote. To be eligible for election to one of the three seats, a person had to meet the voting eligibility criteria of gender, age, and wealth, and had to be a natural-born British subject or born in Sāmoa.[35]

Elections were held on January 24, 1924. The three clear winners were O. F. Nelson (Ta'isi), George Westbrook, and Arthur Williams. Richardson noted when he informed New Zealand of these early results, it was "remarkable that no informal votes so far" had been counted; presumably it was remarkable for people unused to exercising political rights.[36] Five hundred and nine votes were cast; six were disallowed. Ta'isi received ninety-seven votes and so became the first member of the legislative council. Ta'isi received messages of congratulations upon his election, and he told Sir Francis Bell in reply to one of these messages, that "I shall ever endeavour to promote the progress and advancement of Samoa and its peoples, and hope by so doing to be of service to the Administration of Samoa and the Government of New Zealand." The New Zealand government had taken "a step in the right direction" with a new legislative council with elected members, and "the confidence thus displayed will prove to be well warranted by the better understanding which it will create."[37] To add luster to these newly elected positions, and put the Sāmoan body in line with other legislative councils in the empire, the secretary of state for the colonies granted permission for members of the council to use the designation "Honourable" while they held office. This was an honorific Ta'isi would often use, even when he was technically not an active member.

On March 5, 1924, the legislative council sat for the first time with its elected members. Ta'isi was not present. He was en route to New Zealand on business. Richardson sent word ahead that Ta'isi was coming and asked officials, including the new governor-general, Sir Charles Fergusson, to see him.[38] Though he was not at the first meeting of the legislative council after his campaign for its democratization, Ta'isi would make his presence felt in future meetings. His role as the first member placed him second to the administrator in orchestrating the meetings, and he was rarely short of comment on proceedings as Richardson's administration unfolded.

Ta'isi's campaign for democracy was still only partially successful in 1924. He advocated for elected members to the legislative council, though only Europeans could be members and only European male electors were permitted to participate in this modicum of democracy. The existence of the legislative council, though minimal, was held out as an example of noblesse oblige on the part of the New Zealand government. Sāmoan participation was completely dismissed in spite of Ta'isi's advocacy for it since 1921. Despite the shortfall in his desired reforms, Ta'isi's election to the council must have come with some satisfaction. It promised a better future for Sāmoans and New Zealand after the years of the military occupation and then Tate's jarring rule without any visible benefits or improvements.

By 1924, given his economic dominance and his direct and indirect political influence with New Zealand's government and administration, as well as with Sāmoa's European community and within Sāmoa's traditional systems of authority, Ta'isi's star seemed ascendant. He was forty, and his good fortunes, acumen, and hard work aligned to make him the most prominent citizen in his country. But Ta'isi's efforts to create a magnificent domestic setting for his daughters and Rosabel at Tuaefu, with his extended Sāmoan family living traditionally on the estate, were unraveling. Rosabel's temperament was causing friction within the house and on the estate. She was an indulged person who could not abide by the communal tenets of *fa'asamoa*. Unlike Ta'isi, who had lived a village life in Safune as a young man, Rosabel's experiences rendered the Sāmoan way alien to her. Ta'isi had his daughter Viopapa from his relationship with Leata from when he lived in Safune. Twenty years later, Rosabel objected to Viopapa coming to live with her and her five daughters at Tuaefu, which was supposed to be Rosabel's undisputed domain. Viopapa supplanted Noue's position as the eldest daughter in the family, a position that came with responsibilities and deference, and so diminished Rosabel's position in turn. To make matters more difficult, Viopapa herself was reportedly a trying person. She had been raised by her grandmother Sinagogo, and may well have been indulged herself, being raised as an only child by her grandmother and with a wealthy father. Most troubling for Viopapa and her family was that she had health problems, suffering, at times severely, from what could be diagnosed today as an acute depressive disorder that became increasingly apparent in the coming years particularly following injuries sustained in a car accident in the UK as we will see. She was reputedly erratic in her moods and challenged her sisters, who were forced to accept and defer to her. They never overcame their resentment despite loving her. Ta'isi's love for his eldest daughter was strong, as it was for all his daughters. He was an affectionate and involved father, so much so that he placed his daughter's best interests above those of his indulged wife: a rare stance. Ta'isi's devotion to his family extended beyond his own offspring. He oversaw the upbringing of his nephews, the sons of his brother August Junior: Frank Nelson (whose maternal grandfather, S. H. Meredith, often clashed with Ta'isi) and August (Gussie) Nelson. As these boys had lost their father to the epidemic, Ta'isi had a special duty of care to them. He also took care of other family members as required by his *matai* position.

Figure 4.1. Ta'isi and Rosabel's daughters circa 1920. From the left: Taufau, Malienafau, Piliopo, Noue, and Sina. With permission of Tui Atua Tupua Tamasese Ta'isi Efi.

Ta'isi's view of family was inclusive, expansive, and rock solid. Rosabel's view differed diametrically. Rosabel's imperious behavior to her stepdaughter was replicated toward other members of the extended family who were not familiar with any concept of ownership other than the communal, Sāmoan one. Rosabel had beautiful things, and she did not want to share them with nieces and cousins fascinated by cosmetics, her fine clothes and shoes. The final straw for Rosabel was when one of the young girls on the estate took her prized horse for a ride without permission. Rosabel flew into a rage and physically disciplined the girl. Ta'isi could not abide her behavior. When Rosabel threatened to leave, as she had done in 1918, he did not stop her. Rosabel left Tuaefu, the mansion built for her, in 1924. She also left her five daughters. Her youngest, Taufau, was barely five years old. Rosabel spent long periods abroad during her daughters' youngest years, indulging her love of travel.[39]

Behind the apparent success of the Nelson family, Rosabel's departure would become another enduring source of pain. The death of

Figure 4.2. The grave of Ta'isi and Rosabel's son, Ta'isi, on the Tuaefu grounds. Photograph by author 2014.

her beloved son in 1919 still gnawed at Rosabel, as it did Ta'isi. Once Tuaefu was finished, a life-size monument to the little boy was erected in the lush gardens, a lasting shrine to his parents' love and grief. Though they separated, Ta'isi and Rosabel never divorced, and each continued to refer to the other as their spouse. Rosabel would not return to Tuaefu and her marriage for twenty years.

During these testing times in Ta'isi's personal life, Richardson revealed how he planned to address his task of meeting New Zealand's mandatory obligations in Sāmoa and induce "Samoans to love New Zealand." He was determined that Sāmoans would see material benefits of empire through improvements to education, better health services, and capital works. He wanted to make his bit of British Empire a showcase. These progressive inclinations did not extend to the reformed legislative council. Though he had overseen the modest increase in democracy, Richardson was not impressed with having to deal with elected members questioning his decisions or policy: a practice anathema to his experience as a military commander. In March 1925 he confidentially declared himself "fed-up with politics," and the legislative council was no more than a "make believe Parliament" and "a great sham." The next administrator should be a "trained politician," Richardson argued, because such a man could better deal with the "unpleasant" business of negotiating with elected members "more effectively than I or any soldier can hope to do." Elected members were only working for "self interests and popularity with their electors" rather than to "further the interests of Samoa."[40] "I get no help or advice from elected members," Richardson complained, "only criticism and an attitude of unnecessary alarm on the smallest pretext."[41] He also recorded his anger at the suggestion the Crown Estates should be managed differently than they currently were. The estates and their proceeds "belong to N.Z. a country which lost 17,000 men killed and over 40,000 wounded and spent £100,000,000 in the Great War" and still had to bear an immense pension liability "running into millions of pounds." Also merchants (like Ta'isi) who "say they like me . . . will be glad to see my back" because Richardson had "killed" the influence these white men had over Sāmoans in Tate's time, he claimed in early 1925.[42] Despite his growing disdain for the three elected members and for the pretense of power sharing he had to sustain, Richardson held his tongue for the sake of good relations.

Although there were tensions he endeavored to hide, Richardson decided by the end of 1925 to extend his tenure as administrator for an additional term (a knighthood perhaps gave Richardson the necessary inducement to stay on). He discussed his extended tenure in the last legislative council meeting for 1925 before he took extended leave in New Zealand. In making his decision to stay longer in his post, Richardson weighed up his "private interests" against his "duty to meet the wishes of the Government." He was "deeply concerned in one or two matters" that he had recently started and was "anxious to see their success." Some of these matters were "native matters," and, he told the legislative council, "you know what the difficulties are in a country like this in getting anything new done with the natives, or getting any big schemes put through for their own good." "The natives do not always see that the Administration is working entirely on their behalf," he continued, and this was particularly evident with his efforts to implement the land policy, which he cited as the most "outstanding question" unresolved. He felt if he "stayed a little longer I might be able to get that put through successfully," so he set aside his own interests for those of Sāmoa, and agreed to see things concluded.[43]

Arthur Williams, the third elected member of the council (who advertised his services in the *Samoa Times* as "plumber, tinsmith and general sheet metal worker"), greeted Richardson's magnanimous decision with lavish praise.[44] "I feel that at all times His Excellency has carried out his duties . . . in a manner compatible with what he has considered to be in the best interests of the community as a whole." "We all know the difficulties of government in a country like Samoa where we have to contend with two distinct races because the psychology of those two races is so much different," Williams said. "His Excellency took over the position" at a difficult time, when there "was a certain amount of suspicion in the minds of the people and we all know that there were certain flaws in the Constitution which I am very pleased to be able to say have been amended," Williams told the assembly. "Except one," Richardson interrupted. "More than one," Ta'isi chimed in. Williams then conceded; there "was this vexed question of prohibition which [was] introduced in an unconstitutional manner . . . and these suspicions die very hard, but every credit is due to His Excellency for his untiring energy." Any person who had sought an interview with Richardson got one, and he always gave "a prompt and courteous answer." The administrator's energy and approach led Williams to declare, "I think His Excellency's next term of office will be more successful than the first one." He even quoted lines from Berton Braley's poem "Now Do It," which urged admirers of men of action and achievement to not save their praise for a eulogy but to proclaim it while the men still lived. Richardson accepted Williams' ingratiating speech with a modest "thank you very much."[45]

It was then Ta'isi's turn to speak, and he opened by saying he "endorse[d] the remarks of the Honorable Third Member." He then gave an assessment of Richardson's first term that was supportive but tempered with forthright qualifications and little effusion. "When His Excellency Sir George Richardson arrived here some two and a half years ago," he began, "Samoa had just taken its first loan and most of that money had been spent on what the public called 'smoke,' insomuch that they could not see where the money went." As "no great improvement could be shewn [*sic*] to account for the expenditure of this money, the whole Territory was seething with discontent over accumulated grievances." Richardson's arrival brought a swift change, and the "people of Samoa could not help but note great changes for the better" and "it was recognised that a master mind guided the situation." Water lines were laid in villages; hospitals and schools were opened in districts. Richardson encouraged the building of model villages and emphasized the need to keep them and their surrounding lands clean along "sanitary lines." In Apia, the visible improvements to the seawall and roads were commendable, electricity and water flowed, the Crown Estates were "now paying handsomely," and Vailima "has been remodeled and beautified at a great pace." Richardson's policy of village orderliness (which has been roundly criticized by some historians) seemed to align with Ta'isi's philosophy about personal and civic improvement and striving that he thought best for the country. Ta'isi warmed to this idea but would later balk at the manner in which it was executed.[46]

Richardson was an "able administrator," but, Ta'isi stressed, his position was "virtually that of a dictator or an absolute monarch." Richardson was his own "Prime Minister and holds all the portfolios of the Cabinet subject only to the External Affairs Department of New Zealand." Given so much power, Ta'isi noted, "no man is perfect, not even an absolute administrator." To soften this criticism he added, "Neither are his critics." Ta'isi then laid out four sources of frustration that he and others had with Richardson's policies, style of rule, and the obvious flaws in the system he presided over. First, Ta'isi noted that the functioning of the legislative council, where the three elected members were consistently opposed and outvoted by the six appointees, "is not consistent with the good government of the Territory, nor is it in keeping with the Administrator's earlier promises that the views of the people will always be taken." This flawed process was indicative of the administrator's lack of sympathy with the people he ruled, but "successful government" could not operate without this "first essential."[47] "The people" that the administrator ought to sympathize with should also include "natives," Ta'isi argued, again. Richardson's "assumption of the representation of the natives in this Council instead of native representatives being elected or appointed is unwarranted."[48]

Ta'isi's criticisms also centered on the financial arrangements for the mandate and native policy. While he welcomed Richardson's reduction of civil servants' inflated salaries, which were unduly burdening Sāmoa, he also took "this opportunity of criticizing" Richardson's native policy. In particular, he targeted "the removal of titles and banishment of chiefs which, if at all allowed, should only be in cases of confirmed sedition and high treason." Ta'isi warned that this inflammatory method of enforcing compliance with government edicts was "at least over-indulged in and I feel will result in a reaction." "Certain officials . . . lord it over citizens and natives" reviving what he termed a "discredited autocracy." He was referring to the *Samoan Offenders Ordinance*, enacted by Tate but used to a far greater degree by Richardson. As noted earlier, this ordinance was itself a revival of one passed by Governor Solf in 1901 that sparked the most serious rebellion of Germany's fourteen-year rule, the *Mau a Pule*.[49]

Richardson stunned Sāmoans in April 1924 when he applied his powers under this ordinance to deprive Tupua Tamasese Lea'lofi III of his title and to enforce a banishment order on him. Though many other chiefs were targeted before and after this, Richardson knew that going after Tupua Tamasese was extremely provocative. He informed the minister of this action, describing it as "a bold move to take because he is a descendant of King Tamasese." Tupua Tamasese Lea'lofi's offence was that he "disobeyed an Order given by the Secretary for Native Affairs [Harry Griffin] and subsequently disobeyed two orders given by me, so I deprived him of his title and sent him to Savai'i where he commenced to cause trouble."[50] Griffin's defied order was that Tupua Tamasese Lea'lofi refused to remove a hedge he planted next to his house that reputedly obscured the view of a missionary living nearby.[51] Tupua Tamasese Lea'lofi would continue to resist Richardson into his second term, despite such harsh penalties, and galvanize "native" Sāmoan opposition.[52] Richardson had also punished other leading figures. In January 1925 he stopped Malietoa's eleven-pound-per-month salary from the administration and stripped the matai title and banished Atoa (Ta'isi's cousin by marriage who lived next to Tuaefu). The men had buried someone against Richardson's orders. Despite his stinging rebuke, Malietoa's relationship with Richardson repaired and he remained a constant supporter and correspondent with him long after his term as administrator ended.[53]

Despite Ta'isi's misgivings in late 1925 about Richardson's first term, he ended his address to the legislative council on an optimistic and gracious note. "If his second term will be as successful as his first, with a recognition of the people's rights, Sir George Richardson's name will go down to posterity as a very great Administrator, and to his credit will be attributed much of the future success and happiness of this country and its peoples." Ta'isi also paid tribute to Lady Richardson, an obscure figure in this history, for her "loving duty and loyal co-operation which is so essential to a man's success."[54]

In late 1925 Ta'isi and Richardson displayed a public face of collaboration and polite difference of opinion on matters that had been clearly and repetitively delineated on Ta'isi's part. This appearance was deceptive. Richardson was nursing considerable resentments that were undoubtedly directed at Ta'isi, but Richardson hid them. From Ta'isi's speech to the legislative council in late 1925, there could be no doubt that he was being transparent in his views about Richardson, the mistakes he made, and the unsatisfactory concentration of power into his hands. Ta'isi's candor speaks of his confidence that freedom of expression—the centerpiece of democracy—was not only permitted but encouraged. He was very wrong in this assumption. Richardson did not view the legislative council as a form of parliament where debate and oppositional positions were taken as a matter of course. He resented this, as his private communications showed. Ta'isi also underestimated Richardson's attachment to the notion of the white man's burden that was so thoroughly rooted in derogatory ideas about Indigenous peoples and inflated ideas about Europeans, their colonial duties, and value. Richardson's attitude was encapsulated in the 1925 publicity photograph of him with two small Sāmoan children—the great white man leading the infantilized race by the hand into a modern world under the British flag. Richardson was the exemplar of "white prestige," a concept that would be evoked repeatedly during his second term.[55] He was not only the administrator; he was a general, a Great War hero, and the personification of New Zealand and British Empire.

There had been glimpses of Richardson's views to date, but the mantra of native well-being and the evident beneficial improvements that had occurred under him had diverted attention from his shortcomings. Richardson really did believe in late 1925 that he had achieved his stated aim to "induce Samoans to love New Zealand and Empire." The overwhelming support he received on announcing he would continue as Sāmoa's administrator into a second term, seemed irrefutable evidence for this. 1926 would cast a different light on Richardson and his administration. After this legislative council meeting in late 1925, with its professions of affectionate collegiality, everything altered. Richardson left for New Zealand for several months, returning in 1926 with a changed attitude and to changed circumstances in Sāmoa.

Chapter Five

Before the Storm (1926)

The year 1926 slammed into Sāmoa. A fierce hurricane struck the islands on New Year's Day, conjuring up memories of the epic storm of 1889 that laid waste to German and American naval assets moored in Apia Harbor. The 1926 New Year's Day hurricane claimed few lives, but it dredged up huge waves and shredded coconut trees. So extensive was the damage, commentators predicted that the production of copra would be reduced by two thousand tons for the year.[1]

The storm affected more than the copra trade, the centerpiece of the mandate's economy; breadfruit and banana trees were extensively damaged. Hurricane damage to food-producing trees compounded the effects of a six-month drought in the second half of 1925 that dramatically reduced yields of the dietary staple of the islands: taro. Richardson reported to the legislative council that there were food shortages in "many" villages, especially in northern Upolu.[2]

It was an inauspicious start to the year that marked the beginning of General Richardson's second term as the mandate's administrator. When the storm struck, Richardson was still in New Zealand, returning in February to recommence his duties of governing Sāmoa with renewed vigor. He had a long list of items he wished to change or implement with great dispatch.[3] Richardson was buoyed by all the apparent gratitude for his first term publicly expressed in late 1925. Yet he knew his governing style did not please everyone. "It would be a mistake for me to imagine that I was pleasing everyone one here," he confided to his friend, the conservative political heavyweight Sir Francis Bell, in October 1925. "I have tried to do what is just and right regardless of the consequences in individual cases," he continued. Richardson reasoned that it was because of his even-handedness—"I have punished many Samoans and sacked a number of white officials"—that the majority of Sāmoans and Europeans appreciated and "respected" his judicious rule. Yet some were "afraid of me while some have no influence with the Natives while I am here & therefore would rather see me leave but dare not express their wish."[4] The "some" who had no "influence with the Natives" was probably a veiled reference to Ta'isi. Richardson suspected Ta'isi resented diminished influence, yet there was no evidence to support this suspicion. Ta'isi had maintained a frank discourse with Richardson about any misgivings he had, a practice he thought Richardson welcomed from the outset. Even though a seed of suspicion about Ta'isi and his political ambition was planted in Richardson's mind—a suspicion he shared with New Zealand government officials—the two men maintained a cordial relationship.

In March 1926 Ta'isi left Sāmoa for a seven-month absence. He spent most of his time away in Sydney, where he received treatment for an unknown medical condition. While in Sydney, he stayed at the Hotel Australia on Castlereagh Street, one of the best hotels in the city.[5] Ta'isi continued to run O. F. Nelson and Co. from his first-floor office at 318 George Street, in the heart of Sydney's commercial precinct. He was amid the hubbub of the city, and it suited him well. His health repaired, though he missed his daughters, who were at school in Auckland.[6]

During his time in Sydney he kept in touch with Richardson. Their letters did not betray any ill feeling: quite the opposite. In April Ta'isi wrote that the treatment he was receiving "has so far given me much benefit . . . and if this continues I should consider myself quite recovered and removed of all my ailings in a few months from now."[7] Richardson always wrote with concern for Ta'isi. In one letter he wrote, "I sincerely hope you will improve in health." He went on, "You are a young man; your cheerful nature and your good heart make you an important asset to Samoa."[8] They also discussed private family matters. Richardson reported his wife, Caroline, "is not in good form." Although she was "happy and cheery as ever . . . she suffers with nerves at night which causes loss of sleep." Children were discussed, with Ta'isi recounting how he got to know Richardson's son Ken when he stayed with Ta'isi at Tuaefu for about ten days. Richardson also revealed he was "keeping fit and not working hard at present."[9]

As well as their private worlds, the two men discussed a range of matters, from the possibility of boosting tourism and commercial shipping lines in Sāmoa to reports of a botched reception of visiting US naval vessels. Ta'isi knew raising this last issue with Richardson was a direct criticism. He noted, "I make boldly to speak in these lines well knowing how you appreciate to be told the real feeling of the people in such matters."[10] He failed to realize how much Richardson detested receiving frank views: Richardson immediately made his displeasure known. He strenuously denied the report (put about by the honorable third member of the legislative council, Arthur Williams, who had so extravagantly praised Richardson in late 1925). Richardson let Ta'isi know that "Mr Moors and several other Americans citizens waited upon me and wrote also to thank the Administration for all they had done." Richardson then chastened Ta'isi. "Had you been here things would have been settled amicably, and you would not have used acrimonious correspondence with your Administrator," he wrote. "If you had, the same course would have been taken."[11] Richardson was letting Ta'isi know his place.

Their letters also discussed the year's biggest event in Sāmoa: the much-anticipated visit of the latest New Zealand governor-general, Sir Charles Fergusson, his wife, Lady Alice, and their entourage. Richardson had anxiously awaited the opportunity to present his showcase colony to the governor-general. The two men admired each other greatly, not least because both were ex-military, came from comparable social echelons, and now found themselves in the service of the British Empire. Fergusson, whose father and father-in-law had been New Zealand governors, had served in the British army in the second Sudan campaign—where he sustained a serious injury in 1898—and ranked as a general in Ulster and World War I.[12] He was also a leading figure in the Freemasons. During Fergusson's term as New Zealand's governor-general from late 1924 to early 1930, he was the Grandmaster of the Grand Lodge in New Zealand, which had expanded into Sāmoa in 1922.[13] Fergusson's personal history made him both a pillar of British Empire and an old hand in addressing fraught colonial situations. He would bring the colonial lessons learned in the Sudan to bear on Sāmoa when tensions escalated from the end of 1926.[14]

Fergusson was supposed to tour Sāmoa in May 1925. Advanced planning had been carried out, and a detailed itinerary was made for this tour. Yet Prime Minister Massey's declining health and then death on May 10, 1925, meant the king's representative in New Zealand had to abruptly postpone his island tour for one year. Richardson thought it best to brief the governor-general on conditions in Sāmoa, though he did this knowing that Fergusson was "wise and experienced" in colonial matters. Richardson was at pains to point out "there are two sections of the Community—Natives practically 95% and to whom the country belongs, and the remaining small number who are chiefly half-castes (largely German and Samoan)." This circumstance required special tact. "This strain of German blood must affect the mental attitude of these 'Europeans'—as I always am careful to designate them in speeches—or sometimes 'Europeans, including those of *Mixed Descent.*'" "I never use the term 'Half-caste' either in conversation with locally born people or in my speeches," he said, but he did not explain why. Presumably Richardson was aware the term was disparaging, and wanted to avoid the governor-general causing offense unwittingly by using this expression in public. This was a personal policy Richardson dispensed with later in 1926, when he needed to undermine detractors of his regime. Their mixed racial status became a trump card Richardson played at every opportunity, as his predecessor had done.[15]

As well as this sage piece of advice about racial terminology from Richardson, Fergusson received a reading list from J. D. Gray, Secretary for the Department of External Affairs. Gray's list offered titles for each of the island groups the governor-general would visit. On Sāmoa, Gray suggested John Stair's *Old Samoa,* subtitled *Flotsam and Jetsam from the Pacific Ocean* (1897), Llewella Churchill's *Samoa 'Uma: Where Life Is Different* (1902), Robert Watson's *History of Samoa* (1919), and George Turner's *Samoa: A Hundred Years Ago and Long Before* (1884). For Fergusson's general information about the Pacific, Gray listed Frederick O'Brien's highly popular *White Shadows in the South Seas* (1919) and *Mystic Isles of the South Seas* (1921) and—hot off the presses—Robert Keable's 1925 book *Tahiti Isle of Dreams.*[16] Together, these readings would have done little to challenge any preconceived ideas Fergusson would have had about the islands, the role of Britain in them, or powerful and pervasive colonial stereotypes about island peoples.[17] Along with arcane ideas, Fergusson also brought "small gifts" to distribute in the form of boiled sweets, plug tobacco, and "a couple of thousand cigarettes in tins of fifty."[18]

Fergusson and his party had already visited Mangaia and Rarotonga in the Cook Islands and Niue before arriving in Apia on Sunday,

May 16, 1926 where he inspected schoolchildren and met relevant dignitaries. The next day's events started with a gun salute at eight o'clock in the morning marking the day Fergusson would invest Richardson with the knighthood he received in 1925. Arrangements were put in place to ensure Richardson's investiture "might take place as publicly as possible."[19] This day of imperial ceremony and celebration ended with a public film screening. Richardson had been waiting to show Fergusson the latest "highly artistic" film by Robert Flaherty for a year. *Moana: A Romance of the Golden Age* was a film of "educational and historical interest," Richardson assured Fergusson, which portrayed "the simple life of the Samoan people." As well as depicting an island romance, the film also attempted to recapture a precolonial moment without Christianity, sexual inhibition and modest Western clothing.[20] The governor-general and Richardson viewed *Moana* with a gathering of locals who were also "keen to see" the film shot in Safune (Ta'isi's home village) though the "Nelson wharf," jutting conspicuously out from the waterfront where the O. F. Nelson store and copra depot stood, were left out of Flaherty's camera frame.[21] The film confected a picture of romanticized primitivism, of simple folk going about their lives as their ancestors had done for centuries, deliberately obscuring evidence of the Safune villagers' integration into the modern world. The film's presentation of "simple natives" aligned precisely with the views of the two knights of the British Empire who sat in the Apia Market Hall surrounded by locals. It must have been

Figure 5.1. Governor-General Sir Charles Fergusson (seated center on left) is welcomed by Sir George Richardson (seated center right with hand on his knee) and Sāmoan leaders at Mulinu'u, Apia, May 1926. Sir George Grey Special Collections, Auckland Libraries, AWNS—19260610-42-2.

Figure 5.2. The Apia commercial center of Matafele at the time of the viceregal visit May 1926. The Nelson Clock Tower is on the left, and the O. F. Nelson and Co. headquarters is in the center festooned in Union Jacks. Frank O. V. Acheson Papers incorporating the papers of Sir George Spafford Richardson, MSS & Archives 96/1 5.2.1.2, Special Collections, University of Auckland Libraries and Learning Services.

a surreal scene as these men devoted to authoritarian rule and the white man's burden took comfort in seeing their arcane ideal portrayed on screen while a great challenge to the imperial order was brewing all around them; the first act of it would take place in the exact location in five months' time.

Over the next week, the crammed schedule Richardson devised for Fergusson did not fail to satisfy the governor-general in every particular. Fergusson was so impressed with Richardson that he felt the need to explain his enthusiasm to Lord Amery, Secretary of State for Dominion Affairs, so his report on this segment of British Empire would not be dismissed as mere exaggeration. "No one who visits these islands can fail to be impressed not only by the splendid ideals which animate," Richardson, Fergusson explained, "but also by the extraordinary success which has attended his efforts and by the unbounded confidence and affection with which he and Lady Richardson are regarded." Richardson's "mastery" of the Sāmoan language gave him a direct line of communication with "the natives" and was "quite independent of interpreters," Fergusson reasoned, though he could not detect the inadequacies in Richardson's command of the Sāmoan language that were a constant source of mirth for his charges. This linguistic asset along with his "high ideals . . . wide vision and ability of a high order" made Richardson an exemplary colonial administrator. So much so that Fergusson touted a scheme whereby Richardson and his team of administration officials could provide training for "New Zealand boys . . . who aspire to be Empire builders" in New Zealand's Pacific Islands.[22]

Fergusson conceded not everyone was happy with a "strong and determined" leader like Richardson. He cited Richardson's enemies as members of the community who "have battened on the natives in the past and have looked on Samoa and its people from the point of view of exploitation and of their own enrichment." Exploitation and enrichment were supposedly the main objective of Richardson's detractors, but prohibition was "still their great grievance." Fergusson was almost certainly alluding to Ta'isi when he said that he was "afraid that the Administrator does not get the support which is his due from the elected members of the Legislative Council" (Ta'isi, George Westbrook, and Arthur Williams). Fergusson told Lord Amery that the points of disagreement were with two "all important" parts of Richardson's policy. First, "that the mandated territory must be administered in the interest of the people of the country," and, second, "that the natives should be given a full voice in the management of their affairs and trained to take part in that management."[23]

Fergusson seemed to think that the elected members of the legislative council *opposed* native involvement in government, which was not the case. The three elected members wanted Sāmoan-elected representatives to have seats in the council, replacing the government-appointed *faipule*. Fergusson stated that the *faipule,* whose "traditional power over their people is unquestionable" (it *was* questioned, continually), were working "heart and soul in concert with the government" and that this relationship was producing effective results and represented the "soundest form of government."[24] The achievements of this "co-operation between the people and Government through the medium and influence of the Faipule" could be measured in many ways, Fergusson argued. Most notable were "the re-building of villages on a model plan, the improvement in roads, water supplies and sanitation, the formation of women's committees in the villages with a view to reducing infant mortality, the immense improvement to plantations, the new system of land tenure and the abolition of Faa-Samoa marriage customs."[25]

Fergusson also wanted Lord Amery to know about *Fetu o Samoa,* which had taken the place of the Boy Scout movement. Every schoolchild belonged, and the object was to inculcate the idea that the future of Sāmoa depended "on their own exertions" and a "loyalty to God, to King and Country, to fellow creatures, to themselves in Christian virtues." Fergusson said it was "inspirational" to hear thousands of assembled children and older people chant in unison with uplifted hands, "To-day Samoa is a great country. I am going to make it better." The schooling of children was also praiseworthy; the "syllabus of education is to my mind a model in its application to native races." With its emphasis on technical instruction—carpentry, plumbing, and handicrafts—this education fitted "all the requirements of their lives" in their own country. Only those who showed rare greater potential would be "encouraged to go higher" in their learning.[26]

In his report, Fergusson also returned to the intractable problem Richardson faced of traders and their role in oppressing the native majority. These unscrupulous people were working against Richardson's efforts to improve "the native system of (copra) cultivation" by mixing good-quality copra with bad and therefore offering a consistently low price of "£9 or £10 a ton." If the government bought the copra and marketed it instead, Fergusson contended, the traders would lose their opportunity to exploit and Sāmoans would be better off. They would then work harder and better to produce improved copra. He thought the mandate could follow suit with American Sāmoa and "eliminate the trader" by having the government run a copra buying and marketing monopoly. "No one probably desires to drive out the traders, but they must be made to give fair dealing," Fergusson reasoned. It seemed to him that traders' interests were incompatible with those of "the natives," who the mandate was to protect and govern.[27] Richardson's role as the protector of the natives was as critical in this economic aspect of the mandate as it was in all the other facets of governance Fergusson's report outlined. Only Richardson could be "trusted to deal firmly and justly to all parties" and so "the fullest support should be given" to all his endeavors.[28]

While Fergusson's effusive praise of Richardson's Sāmoa was being disseminated around the Empire, disturbing news was reaching Ta'isi who was still in Sydney. The "Native Department recently issued orders," he was told, "that all Samoans living in the villages near

Apia, and to which they did not belong, must return to their own villages unless they have permanent employment." Ta'isi was told that two of his best workers, Leagai and Lia, had not turned up at work in late June and were found to have been jailed for supposedly violating this order, even though they did have employment with O. F. Nelson and Co. They remained in jail for a week.[29] Ta'isi was shocked that the freedom of movement of Sāmoans and draconian measures to enforce it had reached these levels. Richardson had also issued seventeen banishments by mid-1926. Sāmoans were "seething with indignation" and let Ta'isi know about it; he was alarmed.[30]

Perhaps he should not have been so surprised this was happening in Sāmoa. Restrictions on movement, and the application of arbitrary and extraordinarily invasive laws resulting in incarceration and other punishments like banishment, were all too well known in Sydney where Ta'isi was living at this time. Indigenous peoples who lived in Sydney, indeed throughout the state of New South Wales, had been subject to the *Aborigines Protection Act* since 1909. This act was replicated in all other Australian jurisdictions except Tasmania, where the existence of an Indigenous population was denied (despite incontrovertible evidence to the contrary).[31] The act contained elements that would have been familiar to Sāmoans—like the prohibition of the sale or supply of alcohol—but most other parts were unheard of in the mandate. The *Aborigines Protection Act* empowered the Aborigines Protection Board, its employees, and the police to "protect and care" for "any full-blooded aboriginal native of Australia" or "any person having an admixture of aboriginal blood . . . in receipt of rations or . . . residing on a reserve." This care and protection entailed distributing blankets and clothing, managing reserves, and disposing of funds allocated by parliament for "the relief of aborigines" and "to provide for the custody, maintenance and education of the children of aborigines." The board could also prevent anyone from entering a reserve, and it could "remove from a reserve any aborigine who is guilty of any misconduct" or who was deemed capable of earning a living off the reserve. Those considered capable of earning a living off a reserve included "the child of any aborigine, or the neglected child of any person apparently having an admixture of aboriginal blood in his veins to be apprenticed to any master," and any wages they earned were collected by the board.[32]

The *Aborigines Protection Act* was one of the worst advents of settler colonialism. It was an integral component of white Australia and its control of nonwhite peoples within its borders. Australia's multiple but consistently similar state-based protection acts were coupled with federal restricted immigration legislation that prevented "undesirable" races entering or being permitted to stay in Australia. These "undesirable" races were classified as "aboriginal natives of Asia, Africa, or the Islands of the Pacific, excepting New Zealand."[33] That is, Māori were excepted. Why? To leave a path open for New Zealand to join the Commonwealth of Australia if it chose. This required New Zealand and Australian law to mesh, and so rights enjoyed by Māori in New Zealand had to be commensurate with rights in a potential federation with Australian states. This Māori exception gave latitude to other Polynesians who benefited from both the loophole and the understanding that all Polynesians were derivations of one culture; a view promoted in literature of the time as well as by Polynesians themselves, like Ta'isi and Māui Pōmare.[34]

Ta'isi slipped through this racial loophole. His classification as a European and a Swede, then from September1924 a British subject, elided his heritage as a Pacific Islander on paper. While he railed against New Zealand's increasingly harsh colonial attitude in the mid-1920s, Australia, particularly Sydney, remained a welcoming society for him.[35] His wealth gave him purchasing power and acceptability in elite circles that in turn endowed him with important connections. His indigeneity was not documented or recognized and so did not impede him in Australia. Ta'isi would later articulate arguments for why Sāmoans should not be subject to draconian racial laws and practices that he characterized as New Zealand's "mailed fist" by stressing the racial superiority of Sāmoans and their attainment of a requisite level of "civilization."[36] Though he actively sought information about the colonial plight of many people near and far from Sāmoa, he did not remark on the egregious treatment of Indigenous peoples within Australia's borders; there is a high probability he read about it in the local press at the time.[37]

Ta'isi appears to not have seen commonality between the plight of Australian Aboriginal People and Sāmoans. However, what was happening in both cases stemmed from the misguided and often malevolent imperative to "protect" colonial subjects. "Protection" and the belief in the white man's burden licensed governments and officials throughout the colonized world to concoct policies and practices that went to the epicenter of Indigenous lives, communities, and cultures and tried to alter them in any way they saw fit.[38] Richardson felt empowered to undertake this task, framing it as his "obligation" or "duty" to Sāmoans. His position resembled the all-powerful positions of Chief Protector of Aborigines in Australian states created by the protection acts (chief protector powers included the ability to remove children from parental care, which Sāmoan administrators did not possess). Ta'isi looked to New Zealand's relations with Māori as the template for relations with Sāmoans, when in fact the Australian case was closer in policy, practice, and its underpinning racial philosophies.

Ta'isi may not have considered on what was happening in Australia, but he was interested in the past and present experiences of Māori in Pākehā-dominated New Zealand. He had been to New Zealand many times and was well read (if the titles in his library are taken as a guide) on New Zealand history. Around the time he received news about the jailing of his employees, he was planning a trip to New Zealand on his way back to Sāmoa. On this trip he wanted to tour between Wellington and Auckland by road, a route that would have likely exposed him to numerous rural Māori communities. This plan prompted a series of interesting exchanges that provide insight into how Ta'isi was regarded by high-ranking officials in mid-1926. They went out of their way to accommodate requests that could be interpreted as Ta'isi treating them either as his staff or a good friend. Ta'isi's wealth gave him unique conundrums. In this case he wanted to bring his 1924 model Studebaker Super Six, which he bought in Sydney, to New Zealand, have it driven by a hired driver, and then sell it before returning to Sāmoa. He wrote to J. D. Gray asking about what taxes and other costs would be incurred in this arrangement, and "what prospect is there of my engaging a chaffeur [*sic*] who will be able to drive me and family to Auckland as well as drive us around Wellington while here." He also asked if Gray could book rooms in Wellington for his party, which would include "three of my daughters and a maid travelling with me."[39]

Gray, most obligingly, responded with a detailed breakdown of the complicated costs for import duties on the car (25 percent of the value), tolls, license costs, and the costs of hiring someone from the pool of government drivers (£240 per annum). He also informed Ta'isi that he had booked rooms for the party at the Midland Hotel as requested. Gray let him know he would personally try to meet him when the steamer arrived in Wellington. Gray also told Ta'isi about his recent visit to Apia with Sir Māui Pōmare in May 1926. They were both disappointed Ta'isi was not there, so they "were denied the pleasure of a personal call on you," but "we took the liberty of having a run round the drive of your beautiful residence." Gray told him that Māui Pōmare was "looking forward with the greatest pleasure to seeing you on your arrival" and that "he sends his warmest regards."[40]

As it happened, Ta'isi's road trip through New Zealand had to be abbreviated because a business associate from San Francisco was coming to Sydney to discuss the possibility of a US steamer company, Matson, including Apia on its trans-Pacific run. Ta'isi's involvement in securing this connection, to boost commerce and tourism to Sāmoa, was given support from officials in Wellington, as well from Richardson in Apia.[41] Gray told Ta'isi in reply that the government was more than aware of the need to provide a steamer to Apia and had taken tenders for one to be funded by the government. If Cabinet approved the expense, "which is in the vicinity of £60,000," Gray signaled that "I do not suppose the Samoan Administration would look with favour on a competitor in the Pago/Apia trade." Still he remained open to hear what Ta'isi could arrange with his meetings with the Matson representative, and he promised to keep Ta'isi informed of developments with the government steamer notion. Gray also hoped that Ta'isi might still be able to "slip down to Wellington" when he came to Auckland briefly in August.[42] At the end of July Ta'isi responded that he had no intention of fostering competition with a government steamer in his talks with the US company, and he would try to get to Wellington in August.[43]

From Apia, Richardson was doing his best to orchestrate a meeting with Ta'isi and the top government brass in Wellington. He wrote letters of introduction to the prime minister, the minister for external affairs, and other friends, such as Sir A. F. Roberts, a leading businessman in Wellington; Sir H. Beauchamp, one of the heads of the Bank of New Zealand; and Sir C. Holdsworth, managing director of the Union Steamship Company. Richardson also encouraged Ta'isi to call on the governor-general, promising, "You can be rest assured of a hearty welcome."[44] In the same letter, Richardson warned Ta'isi, "The flu is rapidly spreading over Samoa and is in all the islands" and suggested that "it might be better for your children if you delayed their return to Samoa for one month," when, hopefully, "we shall be clear." Richardson sang the praises of the women's committee, who had "been a godsend to the Natives and been the means of their taking precautions . . . and so minimizing the severity of the sickness."[45]

With this specter of another influenza epidemic sweeping Sāmoa, Ta'isi made his way to Wellington.[46]

On September 1 Ta'isi met with Prime Minister Coates, External Affairs Minister Nosworthy, and Sir Māui Pōmare, a meeting that became a watershed. The discussion went well beyond shipping and boosting tourism in Apia as Ta'isi took the opportunity to inform the leaders about the troubling state of affairs in Sāmoa. By highlighting problems—as he had always done, as an advocate for democratic representation and then as a representative—Ta'isi criticized the direction Sāmoa was being taken by the administration, as reported to him during his absence. Coates, Nosworthy, and Pōmare were sufficiently convinced of the gravity of the situation to agree Nosworthy should visit Sāmoa at the earliest date.

Ta'isi arrived back in Apia in late September 1926 to a rousing welcome after his absence of nearly seven months. On the evening of September 28, a large gathering of Sāmoans and government officials came together in Apia's Market Hall to mark Ta'isi's return home. According to custom, many speeches were made at this public function, but none could have been more remarkable than that delivered by the administrator. Richardson began with the hope Ta'isi had been "restored" to health and so "would be spared many many years to take your part in the affairs of this country." Richardson likened Ta'isi to "a bright outstanding star"; his speech only got more ingratiating from there. All the hyperbole aside, Richardson endorsed Ta'isi as a representative of Sāmoan people without reservation.

The administrator told the gathering that Ta'isi was the first locally born Sāmoan he met. His first positive impression, of a man with a "cheerful disposition" and a "very kind heart," had endured and contributed "so largely to Mr Nelson's popularity." "I should be quite prepared to introduce him with confidence to any society in any part of the world to fitly represent yourselves," Richardson went on, as he represented "Samoa with ability and dignity." In his role as a prominent citizen, someone successful in business and political life, Ta'isi was "a public man," who, like "a soldier in the open . . . [is] there to be fired at—and like every public man is fired at not only from the front, but from the rear." He cannot "protect himself behind sandbags" but with the "bullet-proof armour of rectitude." He "has my wholehearted sympathy and friendship and I hope that I shall always be able to retain that friendship long after I have left Samoa." His conduct, "hard work and thrift" that led to his personal success and prominence, should inspire the "young men of Samoa" to see "what is possible to do in this country under the British flag and the freedom of existing conditions here," Richardson continued. The British Empire, and the particular brand forged in New Zealand, with a "progressive pioneering spirit which caused men to take off their coats and work and struggle against difficulties," had steered Sāmoa on this course. Richardson then evoked a demigod of British imperial history as he was Ta'isi's namesake, Lord Horatio Nelson. He recalled gazing up at London's Nelson Monument as a little boy at "that very distinguished, although small, one-armed and one-eyed man" and pondering over the quote "England expects that every man this day will do his duty." Ta'isi encapsulated this call to duty to God, country, and neighbors, and he had "earned the public appreciation and public approval which he is receiving this evening." And to complete the entwined metaphors of stars, empire, and the British navy, Richardson noted, "I am only captain of your ship for a short period." He saw it as his duty "to command that ship and keep it on the course that has been set for me"; the engines are in "good running-order" and the crew "loyal" and doing "their best to help their captain." "Mr Nelson will, however, be with you always, and I wish him long life, happiness and may his prosperity increase."[47]

Within three weeks of this gushing speech, 250 people came together in Apia's Market Hall to prepare for Minister Nosworthy's forthcoming visit. Unlike the preparations before the parliamentary delegation in 1920, this meeting brought the sections of the community politically separated in the mandate—Sāmoans and Europeans—into one forum. Ta'isi chaired the meeting that lasted almost five hours. It had been called by all three legislative council elected members and was intended to "test the feelings of the people as to the advisability of making certain representations to the Minister." Ta'isi explained that he had met with the prime minister, Minister Nosworthy, and the minister for the Cook Islands (Sir Māui) and "represented certain features of the New Zealand administration of Samoa which were considered by the people of Samoa as not being to the best interests of the Territory." These representations were received "with sympathetic interest." Nosworthy had agreed to come as soon as possible, but a recent telegram conveyed by Richardson reported that Nosworthy was now delaying his visit until March or April. Ta'isi thought if the minister could see the "keen interest by the citizens," he might reconsider this delay. In anticipation of this outcome the public meeting was arranged.[48]

The meeting was orderly. Ta'isi set out the agenda, which had five points to be discussed: the legislative council, expenditure, assistance to planters, native policy, and prohibition. If other points needed to be discussed in the forum, they could be raised so the "common goal" of the gathering—"to assist the Powers that be to arrive at a satisfactory system of government for the good of all"—could be achieved, Ta'isi said. He also explained why "Native Samoans" were there; because they requested inclusion. Ta'isi agreed as they did not have their own elected members in the legislative council. Also, Ta'isi stated that "Twenty-six years of colonial government must place the Samoan Native in a position where he should be recognized to have sufficient intelligence to make common lot with the European in working out the future of his own native country." This progression had not happened, despite repeated attempts in the legislative council, with Ta'isi insisting that enfranchising native Sāmoans in this representative body "can be done here, as in other countries, without losing sight of the peculiar requirements of the two races in some things."[49]

Ta'isi then went on to define the legislative council and the forum called that night as the "opposition" to the government along the lines of the British parliamentary system. He explained that "the success of any Government to do the best for the people largely depends on the opposition it has in the Legislature . . . a good strong, sane and sound Opposition acts as a check on human weakness or its tendency to autocracy." Without a "strong Opposition," governments often do "rash things." He highlighted how freedom to criticize governments in New Zealand, Australia, and Great Britain was commonplace. In these countries "you see and hear people at street-corners and in parks speaking to large gatherings, criticizing and even condemning the Government of the day and the system of government." He noted to applause that "in Samoa you have only to open your mouth in criticism of some Government act when some one runs to headquarters and reports." Ta'isi was careful not to "blame any one in particular for these conditions . . . we must blame the status of Samoa or the system of government which that status is said to be entitled to." It was the duty of Sāmoans to advocate for "the gradual advancement of the political status of this country and its people." Because the elected representatives could never form a majority in the legislative council and therefore could not "control Government policy" or "bring about such reforms as you may direct them too . . . we have no alternative but to appeal to higher authority . . . vested in the New Zealand Government, and exercised through the Minister for External Affairs." Though some in the community had undermined the attempt to form a united opposition by claiming such actions were "Bolshevist" and were angering the administrator, Ta'isi felt sure His Excellency was "too sensible" of the great British democratic principles "to listen to such evil-minded talk."[50] If the meeting agreed to take Sāmoan grievances to the minister, then this would be done and a committee appointed to oversee Sāmoan representations.

Ta'isi expanded on the meeting's proposed agenda, organized around the five outlined areas. For the legislative council, the perpetual minority status of the three elected representatives and the lack of Sāmoan-elected representation were to be discussed. On expenditure, the meeting heard from Ta'isi that details of expenditure were shared with elected legislative council members as a courtesy and not a right, and they had no influence at all over how monies were spent. On assistance to planters, which Ta'isi noted included native planters (the majority) and European ones (many who have brought in foreign capital), there needed to be discussion on the two-pound export duty on cocoa, the "overhead charges on Chinese coolies," and the need to improve road access from plantations to ports. Native policy was the most convoluted and controversial item on the agenda. Ta'isi set the tone for discussion by describing the administration of native affairs as "deplorable." Here the list of grievances was long, but many were not new. Banishments, withdrawal of titles as punishment, the imposition of the one-pound-per-adult medical tax, drastic reforms such as the Fetu movement, the model villages "being rushed through," and the preaching of a doctrine of "hatred" against "the non-official European, particularly the trader" to natives, were the aspects of native policy he cited as the most objectionable. He wanted the administrator's contested professions of looking after native interests and traders to be put "to the test." And, finally, there was the issue of prohibition. "There will be some people who would . . . say that prohibition, though brought in last, is really the first and only real object of this meeting," Ta'isi warned. "Those who say that only prove their absolute lack of interest in the vital points essential to the progress of this country."[51] After Ta'isi's discussion of the meeting's objectives, the floor was opened to discussion.

Chief Faumuina Fiame responded first. He thanked the organizers for giving Sāmoans the right to discuss "matters affecting the government of our own country," a right that should have been given "long ago" as "we feel entitled to it." Faumuina said, "We fully appreciate the many good things done by the Administration, and the many good features of the administration of this country which tend to advance us in civilized government but," he added, "there are also several matters with which we are not quite satisfied." He prayed "that God may guide this meeting" and that it "may be the nucleus of a better understanding between all factions in Samoa—the Europeans, the Samoans and the Government."[52]

The rest of the lengthy meeting was taken up with discussion of the issues at hand. The colonial governance of Fiji was often raised to compare how matters stood in Sāmoa. Every time Fiji was evoked, the Sāmoan situation came off badly. The Fijian legislative council had ten appointed members and ten elected. Europeans elected seven members, Fijians two, and Indians one, and all members had "the same privileges on the Council." On expenditure, Sāmoa compared poorly with Fiji, where expenses were leaner. Sāmoan debt was amounting at a pace that many at the meeting found alarming. Chief Afamasaga chimed in that "one of the bones of contention" is that "we do not know where the money goes." If any financial information was given by the administration, it was in English. The meeting resolved to include this issue in their representation to the minister. Likewise labor and agriculture would be included. Native policy attracted passionate responses in all the aspects outlined by Ta'isi in his introduction. It was carried that this too would be included in communications with the New Zealand government.

Finally they got to prohibition, which Ta'isi characterized as "unconstitutional." Ta'isi and others noted that the people of New Zealand had "an opportunity for three years to impose prohibition on themselves, and every time it has been turned down by a popular vote." This raised the obvious question: "Why should they impose it on us?" Mr. Cobcroft told the meeting that he had traveled through Rabaul recently in Australia's Mandated Territory of New Guinea. "There is no prohibition there" and "I saw no ill effects and most certainly the Natives had not become addicted to the use of it." (Cobcroft was not correct in his observations—prohibition did apply to New Guineans but not Europeans in Australia's Mandated Territory of New Guinea.) And so the meeting agreed that prohibition be added to the other four issues for the ministerial-level dialog. The last order of business was to elect representatives in addition to the three members of the legislative council who together would comprise the organizing committee. S. H. Meredith, A. G. Smyth, E. W. Gurr, F. D. Baxter, A. R. Cobcroft, and K. Meyer were elected to represent Europeans. Faumuina Fiame, Tofaeono, Tuisila, Alipia, Afamasaga, and Ainu'u were nominated to represent Sāmoans. The meeting ended, and the 250 who attended made their way home.[53]

On November 12 a follow-up meeting was held after advertisements were run in the *Samoa Times*. Six hundred and sixty-three people attended. As Ta'isi opened the meeting with the words "in the last public meeting we . . . ," he was interrupted. Alfred McCarthy had been charged by Richardson to present a letter to Ta'isi that he wanted read in English and Sāmoan prior to "discussion taking place." Ta'isi permitted McCarthy to read the letter and for Laupu'e to translate. It began, "To the people of Samoa."[54]

Chapter Six

The Storm (1926–1927)

The letter Alfred McCarthy read aloud to the November meeting of Sāmoan citizens was the first shot fired in the battle that would consume New Zealand–Sāmoan relations for the next decade. While Ta'isi enjoyed the festivities welcoming him home after his long absence and proceeded with plans for Minister Nosworthy's visit, Sir George Richardson was following his own agenda of intelligence gathering and copious letter writing. Eight days after Ta'isi met with Prime Minister Coates, William Nosworthy, Minister for External Affairs, and Sir Māui Pōmare in Wellington on September 1, J. D. Gray wrote secretly to Richardson. Gray wanted to let Sir George know the meeting both men helped arrange did not go exactly as they had planned. Gray knew this because Ta'isi had told him. On the night Ta'isi left Wellington, he met with Gray at the Midland Hotel (where Gray had booked rooms for him at his request). "I got a fair idea from him of the matters raised" in the high-level meeting, Gray told Richardson.[1]

Ta'isi articulated many concerns about Richardson's performance; "it is obvious he does not see eye to eye with you in your Native policy," Gray began. Ta'isi "very forcibly expressed the view that your disciplinary measures" of certain chiefs were "drastic, high-handed and altogether over the odds." Ta'isi reported that Tupua Tamasese Lealofi was jailed by Richardson's orders alone just for "visiting Apia to see the Administrator," without any involvement of the courts. Richardson had neglected to report to Wellington on this and on other occurrences Ta'isi relayed at the meeting. To add to the delicacy of the situation, Nosworthy was newly appointed to his post at the helm of external affairs and had not yet had the opportunity to meet Richardson. Gray gathered that Ta'isi planned to "openly repeat" to Richardson the points he raised in Wellington upon his return to Sāmoa. When the minister made his promised trip to Sāmoa in the near future, these points would also be up for discussion. In the meantime, Gray did not want to give Richardson "a moment's worry" as "there is nothing in" the accusations. Even though Gray dismissed Ta'isi's "accusations," he was still cautious about the propriety of his writing directly to Richardson about them. "You will appreciate," Gray cautioned, that this letter and its content were "absolutely confidential."[2]

There was obviously a problem, Gray conceded, but it was not, in his mind, with Richardson. The problem lay with Ta'isi. "It has always been my firm conviction that Mr Nelson has never been what he might have been . . . a real leader of the Samoan people." Gray held the view that Ta'isi regarded "his material gain and interests as of paramount importance." Ta'isi met with "Sir Maui Pomare, the Hon. Mr Ngata, Tau Henare and one or two other Maori leaders and he was plainly impressed by them and their attitude to their own people," Gray told Richardson. "This visit has been an eye-opener to Mr Nelson in regard to his own attitude towards the Samoan people as compared with men of similar descent and standing in the Dominion," Gray thought, but Ta'isi "is a little bit too old to change" (Ta'isi was younger than all three of these named leaders). In Gray's view, Ta'isi was just not "imbued with this zeal and determination" to be a real leader of his people like the "Maoris of the type I have just mentioned." Any problems Ta'isi raised originated in his own shortcomings, and Gray reassured Richardson that when the minister made his visit, he would leave "with the same convictions as to the wisdom, value and benefit of the work you are doing in the interests of the Native people . . . as your other recent distinguished viceregal visitor."[3]

Richardson tried to respond to this latest intelligence with an even temper, but he could barely restrain his ire. He wrote back to Gray that he was "glad Nelson had a good time—I gave him introductions to friends which I would not have done but for the fact that I wished him to see that I & all of us do our part, and we act and talk 'in the open' & not from concealed positions—we have nothing to hide." Feeling betrayed by Ta'isi, Richardson was now preparing for battle, and he wanted to make it perfectly clear how Gray and other government officials and politicians should conduct themselves. "With regard to Native Policy," Richardson wrote with palpable anger, "I would like you and every Minister to have firmly impressed on yr [*sic*] minds that *no* native matters—grievances or otherwise—can be discussed with Europeans from Samoa." Ta'isi was entirely incorrect in his assertions, Richardson reiterated. "The natives are happy with their Govt (except offenders of course)." If there were complaints "they can submit their troubles to the fono of Faipules and will get every consideration." Richardson spelled out that "Nelson has been appointed by the Europeans to the European Leg Council—to look after European affairs." Richardson made perfectly clear not only how very limited Ta'isi's representative position was but also how defective Ta'isi himself was, owing to his racial characteristics that made him deceitful, mercurial and venal:

> Mr Nelson is a half caste who has made his fortune out of the Natives and is not their representative—He would like to be—god help Samoa and the Samoan race when the Govt allow native affairs to go out of their hands and into the hands of the European members of the Legislative Council—this would be government of the Natives by merchants and traders for the benefit of the latter.[4]

This letter from Richardson was extraordinary. Five days *after* writing this letter, which seethed with contempt for Ta'isi, Richardson attended the reception to welcome Ta'isi and his family back to Sāmoa after their long absence. At Apia's Market Hall Richardson stated categorically, "I should be quite prepared to introduce him with confidence to any society in any part of the world to fitly represent yourselves."[5] He had already written the exact opposite back to Wellington days before in his secret missive to Gray. Under these circumstances, how could Richardson accuse Ta'isi of deceit and inconsistency?

Was Richardson a "lying hypocrite" for making that speech if it did not reflect his "true opinion of Mr Nelson"?[6] Richardson later explained to Gray that he was approached to make a speech at the reception, and Richardson, being an obliging fellow, "said all I could to promote good feeling" and as a consequence "the meeting went off well." Richardson was incensed that even after his "eulogistic" speech Ta'isi, along with the two other elected members of the legislative council, still went ahead with their campaign to expose administrative problems.[7] Richardson had hoped he could diffuse comprehensive and, in some of its elements, long-standing criticism of his administration with extravagant—but hollow—praise of Ta'isi. Richardson's effusive speech was nothing more than a feint.

Ta'isi was not taking the bait. On October 5, the *New Zealand Herald* published his lengthy article "Conditions in Samoa," in which he responded to a report a month earlier that presented a glowing picture of Sāmoa in a state of great progress. Ta'isi disabused the notion that the Sāmoan plantation system was prospering along with a reduction by a third of the troublesome Chinese laborers. He explained instead that this reduction had occurred because many of the private planters had gone out of business and government plantations "have just survived a long period of losing years." Diversification of plantations from copra to rubber, cotton, or bananas was slow and not yet occurring at a rate needed for a healthy economy. Where there was economic health in Sāmoa, Ta'isi stressed, this was not "the outcome of any wonderful administration" but rather "the resourcefulness of its people." He then went into the issues that needed immediate reform. Most of these topics were not new to New Zealand newspaper readers, the New Zealand government, or administration: native Sāmoan representation on the legislative council; a review of the imbalance between appointed and elected legislative council members so a democratic and representative system of government could be realized; financial assistance to planters; government "interference in trade should cease"; and orders in council should not operate unless they have the consent of the legislative council, or in cases of emergency. Finally, all arbitrary measures such a prohibition of alcoholic liquors to Europeans, the removal of citizens' rights, hereditary titles, and banishments of native chiefs "should cease," and the "top-heavy" administration should be reduced in proportion to Sāmoa's size. Only by implementing these measures without delay, Ta'isi emphasized, will the New Zealand government be able to "maintain in Samoa that high prestige which has made British rule world-famous."[8] Ta'isi's challenge to the *New Zealand Herald*'s glowing report on Richardson's administration was, of course, unwelcome. Gray thought it was "moderately written" but disguised the true source of the grievance, prohibition.[9] Richardson could not have agreed more.

Ta'isi also went ahead and called the meeting for October 15, 1926, to organize for the minister of external affair's forthcoming visit. The meeting was advertised in the *Samoa Times*. Its aims were modest—all were welcome to discuss matters ahead of the minister's visit—but Richardson saw nothing but sinister intent. He wrote to the minister three days before the meetings to let him know that "political deputations" were getting mileage from the visit.[10] The day before the first meeting, Nosworthy "unavoidably postponed" the much-anticipated visit.[11] It was a telling fact that a minister for external affairs had not visited Sāmoa since mid-1921. With Nosworthy's postponement in late 1926, nearly six years would pass between visits.[12]

The meeting went ahead regardless and Richardson assigned Inspector Arthur Braisby to amass information for the administration's cause. Braisby quickly became a man who featured heavily in the ensuing Sāmoan troubles. He was the chief gatherer of intelligence—covert and overt—against Sāmoans opposed to New Zealand administration. In this role he wielded considerable power in constructing a narrative about the Mau (as it reformed from late 1926 onward) and its participants. Braisby's work, though ostensibly "police investigation," regularly strayed beyond information required for criminal cases. Braisby's qualifications for this central role were questionable and he is a prominent example of the second-rate—or third-rate—personnel the Mau constantly complained staffed New Zealand's administration of Sāmoa.

Braisby was born in Leicestershire in 1882. He served in South Africa in the imperial Regiment of the Yeomanry before he left the service for civilian employment four years later. He then migrated to New Zealand and enlisted in the New Zealand Expeditionary Force (NZEF) permanent staff in 1915. On his enlistment papers he gave his "occupation or calling" as "artist" as well as being a tram operator for Auckland Tramways.[13] His 1919 performance evaluation noted that though he was "zealous," of good character, and "smart and soldierly," he was not recommended for a promotion and his ability to "impart instruction" was ranked as "poor." He then left the NZEF in 1919 and transitioned into New Zealand's Samoa Service.[14] In Sāmoa, Braisby found a colonial milieu that suited him and his wife, Priscilla, so much so that they outlasted many other colonial officials and stayed in Sāmoa into World War II. Professionally he rose through the ranks to become Inspector of Police, a position he held when Ta'isi led the meetings in Apia in late 1926. Off duty, he often shot the second-best round at the Apia Rifle Club on weekends.[15]

Braisby wrote a long report (six pages) on the October 15 meeting. He noted that "140 Europeans and half-castes" and about "150

Samoan Natives" were present. "It was obvious," he wrote, "that the meeting had been well advertised among Natives as the number present was unusual for a meeting of this kind." "Lago Lago appeared to be the leading spirit among the Samoans" (whom Ta'isi addressed by his title, Afamasaga, one of the seventeen titles Richardson had stripped to date). Lago Lago, Richardson reported to Wellington, had stolen church funds and had manufactured intoxicating liquor and "sold it to his own race." "He wears trousers and apes the merchant and big man in Apia (i.e. Ta'isi) and resents being dealt with by his own race."[16] Braisby drew attention to the native submissions that were presented as typewritten statements showing that "the subject had been carefully arranged and the procedure understood," implying that the author of these documents was probably not a native Sāmoan. Braisby noted the subjects raised, the course of discussion, and how the election of the committee proceeded. He concluded that the meeting was "orderly," "no opposition was made to any of the subjects," and the program "had obviously been arranged in detail."[17]

After the meeting the elected members of the legislative council telegrammed the minister: "respectfully and urgently request reconsideration inviting you to visit Samoa November."[18] Richardson wrote to the minister two days later. He let him know the meeting "was orderly and well conducted by Nelson and no personal attacks made." "Obviously underlying factors are desire on part of some persons to change liquor laws and a few individuals to gain power by fomenting discord between Natives and thereby breaking influence of Faipules," Richardson reported. "The latter are very angry at what is to them interference by Europeans in their own Native affairs" and so, Richardson suggested, "you say regret unable to come till April and that Government will be pleased to consider any request they make through me."[19] When no reply came to their first telegram for a week—which they suspected was a result of the administrator not passing on correspondence—Ta'isi wrote to the minister again. He reiterated that the conditions in Sāmoa "urgently require investigation by a responsible Minister of the Crown."[20] The minister eventually responded—nearly one month after the first urgent telegram was sent—that the postponement stood and he would come in the autumn of 1927.[21]

The second meeting on November 12 went ahead with this intelligence about the minister's stance on his Sāmoan visit, and so the agenda changed to forming a delegation to take Sāmoan issues to Wellington if the minister could, or would, not visit for some months.

Braisby duly reported on this meeting too with more detail than his first, noting all the European participants by name, including the four "ladies" present, and that 332 Sāmoan men and women were there. In total the number of people attending was 430, though Braisby added that 75 of these were "young Native boys and girls who had casually entered the hall," which challenged the view that the protest movement was growing. Braisby noted Ta'isi opened the meeting and was immediately interrupted by Mr. McCarthy who read the letter from Richardson. Then Laupu'e conveyed the contents of the letter in Sāmoan. Ta'isi and the two other conveners were taken aback by Richardson's disapproval of the meeting and his request that native Sāmoans "refrain further from co-operating with the Europeans in their agitation on certain matters which do not concern Samoans."[22]

The conveners nevertheless proceeded with the meeting and Braisby noted how the discussion of topics fared. He looked around the room and drew conclusions about its makeup and organization. "It was noticed," he wrote, that "what might be considered to be the O. F. Nelson factor of the audience were placed on both ends of the hall. On one flank [note the military terminology] was Lago Lago with his Samoan committee support." "On the other flank" was "Lealofi Tamasese [*sic*] and Messrs Burnett, Kruse, Kohlasse and Atoa." Braisby perceived a rehearsed signaling between Ta'isi and the others. "As O. F. Nelson tapped the table with his hand, the walking stick of Lago rapped the floor at one end and Atoa at the other, and so the applause was developed." Not only could Braisby see Ta'isi's fingerprints on the meticulous organization and orchestration of the crowd's reactions by placing men on opposite "flanks"; he also "noted that amongst the audience was the majority of O. F. Nelson and Co.'s employees." This included a "big proportion of boatmen, wharf workers, taxi-drivers, persons against whom banishment orders have been made." A conspicuous number of "convicted criminals" were also present, Braisby reported. Missing were people from "west of Leulomoega . . . none from Malie or Faleula, no parties from Falefa, none from Aliepata (with one exception) . . . none from the south side of the island [Upolu], none from Savai'i or Manono" in his assessment, along with that of four other police who were present. So, Braisby concluded, "the Samoan audience may be considered to have been not representative."[23]

Richardson, meanwhile, had been enacting a multipronged attack against critics of his administration. He organized candidates to contest the upcoming election on November 30 of the three legislative council seats held by Ta'isi, Westbrook, and Williams. He also began concocting a line of argument about the political agitation. Richardson's script was that all other issues that caused the surge in protests were in fact a "camouflage" for the main cause of discontent—the prohibition of alcohol.[24]

The prohibition casus belli line pushed by Richardson, Gray, and then others within the government entailed sustained character assassination of Ta'isi and others. The legislative council's consistent challenge to prohibition mirrored debates taking place elsewhere in the West at the time. Led by the United States and the moral campaign to reign in a masculine drinking culture that afflicted society from the family home outward to the public realm, the imposition of prohibition in the United States from January 1920 was having serious ramifications. Bootlegging and hardened criminal activity were escalating; so the outcome of "cleansing" society of its ills through banning alcohol was not being realized. Added to this, the popular image of the criminal element emerging during the life of the Eighteenth Amendment (1920–1933) was decidedly racialized. Italian gangsters fought "quintessentially American" (that is, white) law enforcers and legislators. Drinking, crime, immorality, and aberrant forms of race and masculinity were all bundled together in 1920s popular imaginings of the incredible and gripping spectacle of prohibition America.

The mean streets of prohibition-era Chicago or New York and the comparatively quiet streets of 1920s Apia might seem completely incongruous. Drawing comparisons between legislative council challenges to prohibition in Sāmoa and American bootleggers might be described as drawing a very long bow. Yet, as their complaints against Richardson's administration grew louder, official attempts to taint the administration's detractors, Ta'isi in particular, with the stain of immorality and criminal activity became more concerted. If enjoying a drink was criminal, then Ta'isi was entirely guilty. He had a taste for fine Scotch whiskies (he had an impressive collection) and perhaps other alcoholic beverages, as well. Apart from taste, he considered drinking to be a prerogative of his masculine, economic, and racial status as someone "European" and a British subject. He resented government interference to this level in people's lives, including his own.

The politics of drink were also complicated by Ta'isi's religious beliefs. Ta'isi, as noted, was a devout Methodist. Strict Methodism and drinking were like oil and water, but Ta'isi's personal brand of Methodism was such that he could indulge and still consider himself devout. This position did not sit well with everyone in the Samoan Methodist Church. Ta'isi was deeply offended by Reverend Skinkfield's racial views, as previously discussed. Added to this, Australian reverend R. J. Maddox did not approve of either Ta'isi's policy on drinking or that he allowed tennis to be played on Sundays on the Tuaefu court.[25] Ta'isi was also a mainstay of Sāmoa's horse-racing scene. He owned many horses and gambled heavily at the races. Reverend Maddox no doubt took a dim view of this trifecta of unholy pastimes. In Sāmoa, as in prohibition-era United States, there was the "medicinal loophole" where doctors could prescribe alcohol for "health reasons." It is unknown whether Ta'isi had a doctor's note or if he took advantage of the other loophole that allowed Europeans to make their own home brew so long as the content did not exceed 3 percent alcohol by volume.[26] It is highly likely he continued to enjoy his scotch—now a politically defiant act—from his existing reserves (he was not required to surrender these but the administration would take them from him in the future).

The New Zealand government consistently argued that its imposition of prohibition was part of its duty as a mandatory power. The League of Nation's embrace of prohibition for mandated territories was a component of its effort to protect colonized peoples from the worst excesses of Western influences. Alcohol had undoubtedly led to the immiseration of countless Indigenous communities over the centuries of European colonialism. As Ta'isi, and others in many different colonial settings, experienced it, government restrictions on alcohol consumption for colonized Indigenous peoples was punitive, an additional form of control and discrimination. It is one of the great ironies of prohibition in New Zealand–ruled Sāmoa that a country that embraced drinking as a national trait imposed these restrictions in its colony. Like Australia, though perhaps to a lesser degree in this era, New Zealand's dominant masculinity was centered on male bonding and heavy drinking. Australia, of course, also had a League of Nations mandate to rule over. Unlike New Zealand, Australia permitted drinking by white men in its Mandated Territory of New Guinea, as noted, although drinking for Indigenous peoples there and in its separate territory of Papua, and for Indigenous peoples throughout mainland Australia, was criminalized. New Zealand argued their interpretation of this aspect of their mandatory duties was applied more fairly and not on a racial basis.

After the last the public meeting, which he had been unable to stop, Richardson began publicizing his complete disapproval of

Sāmoans and Europeans associating politically. He also began marking Sāmoans he thought required punishment for their association with the protest movement. High Chief (*tama aiga*) Tuimalealiifano was "suspended" as a *fautua* (adviser).[27] Three others "in the pay of the Committee"—Faumuina, Ainu'u, and Pitu—were banished from Savai'i for three months on November 25 under the powers of the *Samoan Offenders Ordinance* for distributing pamphlets and "trying to collect money from Natives to pay for a delegation to N.Z."[28] The committee continued to organize for the delegation to visit New Zealand, though Richardson ensured that the Native delegates were not allowed visas. They were only interested in a "free trip" to New Zealand anyhow, according to Richardson, rather than a legitimate purpose.[29]

After curbing critical Sāmoans via decree, Richardson then hoped to stop the three elected members of the legislative council on election day: November 30, 1926. Richardson's plan was foiled when electors did not cooperate. Ta'isi, Westbrook, and Williams were all safely reelected.[30] The *Samoa Times* reported that "for good or ill, the electors have given approval to the innovation of bringing native grievances into publicity at Europeans' political meetings."[31] Despite this setback, Richardson made sure that the voting power of these three remained in a two-to-one minority with the six appointed officials, thereby ignoring one of the main complaints of the political agitation.[32] Richardson steeled himself and told Gray he was laughing at the agitators and having "fun" at their expense "which they know, and it hurts them."[33] "The enemy" were brimming with "seriousness" about their cause, Richardson reasoned, and were deluded into thinking "the world is watching them" and that "they are a party as big as the N.Z. Labour Party—they think they are a Govt." "They know they will be ridiculed by Samoans if they fail—they will therefore Bluff-Bluff-Bluff," Richardson wrote to Gray with thinly veiled contempt.[34]

Even though Richardson claimed to be unfazed by what was happening, even saying that his measures had crushed the movement in late 1926 (the first of many premature declarations of the death of the protest movement), he set to work writing numerous letters and accounts to Wellington refuting the claims made against his administration.[35] He did not accept there were any legitimate complaints but he had to craft explanations for why the agitation emerged.

Richardson's expansive explanations still centered on Ta'isi, his racial status, and his stance on prohibition.[36] In his secret account of the protest, penned in December 1926 for the benefit of the Nosworthy,

Sir Francis Bell, and the governor-general only, Richardson wrote, "I have liked Mr Nelson for his ability and his apparent kind hearted disposition, but I have never really confided in him or trusted him because of my knowledge of his past methods [of speaking out against previous administrators and governors]."[37] When Ta'isi returned to Sāmoa in September, "I spoke on his behalf . . . and extended the hand of friendship to him with very suitable remarks to which he responded very nicely." But "within a few days" he began his political intriguing. This was due to Mr. Nelson being a "half-caste," which was now the first, and most important, piece of information Richardson dispensed about Ta'isi. Mr. Nelson is "a man of great influence . . . particularly among the half-castes." "He is an able, benevolent, but inordinately vain and ambitious man who a few years ago influenced certain Natives of Savaii to give him the Title 'TAISI' which is one of the highest titles in Samoa," Richardson explained. This title "has in the past given him influence with certain sections of the Natives and he has used it for commercial purposes by painting on all his stores as follows 'TAISI NELISONI,'" he continued. War conditions favored Ta'isi's family company enormously, and the high price of copra and New Zealand's obliteration of his German commercial competition catapulted him to unparalleled riches and influence. Now his "wealth enables him to entertain freely and lavishly" and, scandalously, "rumour states that these entertainments develop into drunken orgies for he appears to have a plentiful supply of liquor in spite of our precautions to check smugglers in this Territory."[38] Richardson failed to note he and his family had also been frequent recipients of Ta'isi's hospitality. There is no evidence supporting Richardson's risible accusation that Tuaefu was a site of debauchery.

Before he arrived in Sāmoa, the administrator explained, Ta'isi had been able to exert considerable influence on the *faipule*. Ta'isi had worked "clandestinely" influencing "the Faipule in their agitation a few years ago" when Tate was administrator. Richardson had put a stop to Ta'isi's influence. This group of administration-appointed leaders no longer "trust him" because "they consider he obtained [his high native title] by unfair means." Richardson also argued the *faipule* were now aware "of the part he [Ta'isi] formerly played in influencing them against New Zealand," and "they consider he has made his wealth at their expense." Ta'isi's inability to impact the *faipule* gave rise to his "resentment" of Richardson, and he had set out to undermine the administration and the *faipule* ever since, Richardson argued.

Ta'isi worked with other half-castes who sought to "get rid of white officials and employ local half-castes in their place." Germans had kept half-castes down, Richardson noted, and now they are "ambitious for power" but being "without ballast—do things wrong every time and make themselves foolish in the eyes of the world." All the agitators were either "married to natives or H.C. [half-castes] and have half-caste families and degenerate themselves."[39] Since the October and November meetings, Ta'isi "had a circular printed" and "appointed agents who were members of their committee to go around the islands and distribute the circulars" (the one Faumuina, Ainu'u, and Pitu were banished for distributing). Richardson considered this circular "to be seditious." It set out what occurred at the meetings, who attended, which Europeans and Sāmoans were on the committee, as well as the resolutions made. The parts of the circular Richardson considered particularly "seditious" used the words "cruel," "despotic," and "oppressive" in relation to the taking away of titles, banishments, or the banning of "important native customs."[40] This constituted "sedition," Richardson argued, because it was "aimed at inciting the Natives to lose confidence in the Government." Richardson knew this argument would not hold up in a New Zealand context. So he added, "what is sedition in an advanced community must not be taken as an absolute definition for a country where a backward race is being governed."[41] The New Zealand solicitor general, Arthur Farr, wrote in March 1927 he did not consider there to be anything "strong enough to constitute a seditious libel," in the pamphlet.[42] This definitive legal opinion did not alter the way Richardson or others described this pamphlet.

In this secret memo, Richardson defended himself against all accusations of poor financial management and of overstepping his powers in cultural matters or those laid out in the *Samoan Offenders Ordinance*, but still returned to the same conclusion that "the real grievance" was the "liquor question."[43] Sāmoans were being dragged into the agitation not because they "understood the business"; rather, they attended the meetings because of "curiosity or for fun."[44] But this explanation was far too simplistic and Richardson had to elaborate on his explanation for the source of the "agitation."[45] The webs of intrigue that Richardson and others in the government spun from late 1926 were fueled by a grand global conspiracy.

Richardson began insinuating that Ta'isi and others linked to the protest were in alliance with a resurgent Germany. Germany had rejoined the international community, becoming a member of the League of Nations, in September 1926. Within a few days, Ta'isi began to organize the protest against New Zealand's administration. This timing Richardson thought highly suspicious; he could see the hand of Germany all over the protests. In this grand conspiracy theory, Ta'isi was Germany's agent who stood to benefit politically and economically if its prized Sāmoan colony was returned. Richardson cast himself as the savior of Sāmoa, the one who stood in the way of this plot being realized. In his mind he was fighting his old foe of the Great War in a different place and under a different guise.

Richardson could see the influence of German allegiances in the reelection of Ta'isi, Westbrook, and Williams in November. In accounting for their win, Richardson wrote, "I am of the opinion that the successful candidates were elected chiefly on the vote of the half-caste and German electors. Most of the British residents voted for the three unsuccessful candidates." The majority "half-caste community . . . will always support candidates of their own nationality."[46] More suspicious was that Ta'isi had German relatives by marriage, "one of whom fought for Germany in the Great War" and he had regularly entertained Germans.[47] Concerns about German influence in Sāmoa amplified in early 1927 when the German government sought permission for the last German governor (Dr. Schultz) to visit ex-German Pacific colonies in April. New Zealand and Australia were both concerned that banning this visit would violate the 1925 *Locarno Pact* of which Britain and Germany were signatories; a pact aimed at maintaining peaceful relations. Prime Minister Coates wrote that given there was "considerable German intriguing in progress" in Sāmoa, it was necessary to press the point and gain British permission to put a stop to the tour that would have come at a time of escalating tensions.[48]

New Zealand authorities felt quite certain the protest was a German plot to "discredit New Zealand in the opinion of the world." The joint aim was to build support for "the demand for the transfer of the Mandate for Western Samoa from His Majesty the King in his right of government of this Dominion back to Germany."[49] Richardson fanned these suspicions but eventually admitted "I am unable to give any proofs of German propaganda in this Territory," and so this conspiracy theory receded by the middle of 1927.[50]

As well as accusing Ta'isi of traitorous relations with Germany and bootlegging, Richardson also hammered the argument that Ta'isi exploited Sāmoans. The basis for this claim was the price of copra that was around ten pounds a ton in late 1926. Richardson claimed this was "the lowest price in the Pacific." The price in American Sāmoa was twice that. In Tonga it was still substantially higher at sixteen pounds per ton, Richardson claimed.[51] This accusation of exploitation was an extremely damaging one. Tate, and now Richardson, used it to harm Ta'isi's reputation among Sāmoans: Ta'isi had gotten wealthy at their expense, the administration insisted.[52] Ta'isi owned about one hundred copra sheds dotted around the Sāmoan islands. These sheds bought and processed coconuts from local growers. Did he drive down the price of copra to maximize his profits? Richardson claimed he did. But commodity prices in a global market were more complicated than that. Ta'isi's argument was that he did profit enormously from copra during the war when prices were high, but since then "there has been little profit in copra." The slump in prices ("deflation is the trouble") meant that copra buyers had to offer "the highest possible price to induce them [Sāmoans] to cut the copra at all."[53] Ta'isi did not directly attack Richardson's argument—he was short of ways to do this in 1926—about the comparative price of copra in neighboring countries and so left himself open to the continued accusation of exploitation via the muddy waters of international commodity prices. The year 1927 would provide greater opportunities for Ta'isi to communicate his case about the price of copra, along with many other dimensions of the unrest.

What was more transparent than the prices of copra was how Richardson took aim at Ta'isi's business. Richardson hatched a plan to have the government begin purchasing copra at higher prices in December 1926. The chief judge of the High Court of Sāmoa, W. H. Woodward, warned Ta'isi in January 1927 that unless he walked away from the political movement, this punitive action would commence.[54] Woodward added that the government had stayed out of the business of buying copra from growers "out of consideration for Mr Nelson." Woodward overstepped what should have been his distanced position as chief judge on this occasion; Ta'isi also accused him of electioneering. (Woodward later pleaded guilty to assaulting a member of the Mau in 1927.) Ta'isi did not walk away, so the administration commenced purchasing copra in March 1927.[55]

The year 1926 had begun in Sāmoa with a furious storm. As it came to an end, the political trouble that had "travelled like a bush fire" around Sāmoa gathered heat and speed.[56] When Judge Woodward approached Ta'isi on December 16 on behalf of the administrator, threatening to harm him commercially by purchasing copra, Ta'isi expressed the opinion that the administrator should call a "conference & affect a reconciliation, but I have done nothing," Richardson reported to the minister. "There was nothing to discuss," and, more to the point, "if I held a conference they would only try to justify their action in interfering in Native matters and I do not intend that they should ever be consulted in Native affairs."[57] Nosworthy wrote back, assuring Richardson that "I fully share the confidence of my predecessor in yourself personally and in the manner in which you have discharged your responsible and onerous duties as Administrator." If the Ta'isi-led delegation came to see him in New Zealand, he would meet with them and "deal with their representations effectively."[58]

Like Richardson, Ta'isi was also in contact with a minister of the Crown about unfolding events in Sāmoa. While Richardson penned numerous letters in late 1926 to Gray, the minister for external affairs, the governor-general, and Sir Francis Bell, Ta'isi turned to his friend Sir Māui Pōmare. He informed Sir Māui about the first meeting in Apia. Sir Māui was pleased to hear that the "conjoint meeting with your people with the Europeans" showed that "the people were not ignorant as to what they wanted" and that the "whole discussion was temperate and orderly." "It is through these well thought-out meetings and discussions that you will get what you want," Sir Māui told Ta'isi. "The eyes of the world are centred on your small country and I am sure the guiding spirits of your ancestors will direct you in attaining your aims and aspirations." Sir Māui was also pleased "at last" to learn his friend's *matai* title (he would use it as his standard mode of address from then on). Given Ta'isi's political activism, Sir Māui playfully wondered whether "Ta'isi" had the meaning "to smite, beat or break up." "I hope it hasn't," Sir Māui joked.[59]

Ta'isi responded to Sir Māui in December 17 after the battle lines were drawn, with Richardson upping the ante on those who dared to protest against his administration. It was also the day after Ta'isi had his encounter with Chief Judge Woodward and was threatened with commercial retribution for his political activities. Ta'isi was angry but tried to curb this as much as he could. As he related what was occurring his indignation surfaced. He began by assuring Sir Māui that his title "Ta'isi" had no prophetic meaning nor did it denote "to smite, beat or break up." Instead it meant "a parcel," implying "always something in the cupboard for a friend signifying the very height of Samoan hospitality." He quickly moved to political matters and told

Sir Māui that his support for the cause was like "an oasis in the desert." New Zealand newspaper coverage of events consistently misrepresented or underreported what had been taking place. "I wonder what the Maori people would do even at this state of their Europeanisation and civilisation if one-half of those things were perpetrated on them," as were carried out on Sāmoans, Ta'isi wrote. He took particular issue with the conduct of Toelupe, who Richardson had appointed as the spokesman of the *faipule* and therefore of the Sāmoan people. This was objectionable, Ta'isi informed Sir Māui, as was a speech Toelupe supposedly made recently where he handed "over the emblems of sovereignty to New Zealand." "My dear Pomare," Ta'isi continued, "that speech was written out and handed to the Administrator without it being read to the Faipule" as "that was the only way . . . it could have been allowed." The artificial elevation of Toelupe to this position was becoming known "and the people are incensed about it." Ta'isi questioned, "How much would the 'Treaty of Waitangi' have held with the Maoris if that famous document had only been signed by one man who passed as the 'Chief Orator of Maoriland' and that his word was law with all the Maoris?" "The Samoans are just as much a free people as the Maoris and every bit as proud of their race and their liberty," and so they bristled against the different circumstances they found themselves subjected to under New Zealand rule, wrote Ta'isi.

He also asked Sir Māui, "Does New Zealand believe in militarism and military discipline in her people?" There was "more of it in Samoa now than had ever been experienced even during the Samoan wars" of the nineteenth century. Rather than meet and conciliate with people, Richardson had "relied on his military genius to settle the matter, but the grievances are too deep-rooted and the result of his high-handed actions has been that he is utterly discredited." Ta'isi recounted the punitive measures Richardson had undertaken since the second meeting, particularly the Sāmoan committee members who were denied passports to travel to New Zealand on the delegation, who had also been banned from Savai'i, even though they were from that island, for soliciting financial aid for the delegation, and for distributing sheets explaining the resolution of the meetings and the reason for a New Zealand trip. Again Ta'isi questioned the historical precedent, "Have Maoris born in the North island but staying in the South Island ever been prevented by law from visiting their native homes because their politics happen to hold with the opposition?"

"My Dear Pomare," he continued, "I am confident your people would not tolerate these oppressions for one day . . . British justice is a thing we have heard so much about but have seen so little," he said. Ta'isi prayed for Sir Māui's indulgence of his long letter as "a fellow Polynesian." He then launched into a series of vexed questions that hit at the heart of the Sāmoan dilemma:

> When will [Sāmoan] aspirations as a people be recognized? Why talk of teaching them self-government when they are keeping them in the dark and all efforts to enlighten them are resented by the government? Why should there not be a good understanding between the Samoans and the Europeans who are mostly either half-Samoans or married into the country? Why should the Europeans in Samoa and the Samoan Natives not be allowed to participate in the provision given in the famous "Bill of Rights" for the "liberty of the subject"?

"You will probably not agree with some of my contentions," Ta'isi acknowledged, "but you will however concede to me the honesty of purpose with which I am striving for the emancipation of the people of this country from the arbitrary laws which now govern them." "I have sufficient faith in 'human justice,'" he added, "to know that the case which the people of Samoa are now putting up is a just and fair one and that it will win out in the end." He estimated that "ninety-nine percent of the Samoan people are heart and soul with the whole of the present movement" and the "remaining one per-cent are those who are afraid of losing their government positions."[60]

Ta'isi's long, defining December 1926 letter to Sir Māui ended with warmth and humor. He enclosed photos of his family he neglected to send before. One was of Sina, and the other of Sina with her youngest and oldest sisters (Taufau and Noue). "The fat one of the three is my 'Baby' and a chip off the old block," he wrote with self-deprecating humor.[61] Ta'isi signed off wishing "aroha nui" to Sir Māui, Lady Pōmare, and their children, a "Happy Christmas and a Prosperous New Year."[62]

Richardson and Ta'isi sat down to their Christmas feasts in their respective mansions in the Apia mountains assured that their cause was the righteous one. Both men cast themselves as the protector of Sāmoa but with different aspirations for the political, cultural, and social rights that Sāmoans should enjoy. Both men saw fault lying with the other for the current political tensions. Richardson accused Ta'isi of treachery and inciting sedition, in order to enrich and empower himself, restore German empire, and secure the right to drink liquor with abandon. Ta'isi had repeatedly sought talks to discuss grievances, but Richardson offered only punishments for those who dared to participate in any political activity critical of his administration. There would be no discussion.

In the murk of flying accusations, rumor, and intrigue that swirled around Sāmoa that Christmas, one thing was perfectly clear. The friendship between these two men, whether it was ever genuine or merely expedient, was finished. The sudden breakdown of this relationship steered Sāmoa on a new and unknown course that neither man would have fathomed at the end of 1926. It had been an eventful year—1927 would be, too.

Chapter Seven

"He Is Not a Samoan" (1927)

Sir George and Lady Richardson hosted a lavish New Year's Eve party at Vailima to see in 1927. The *Samoa Times* reported that two hundred people attended the party, which was "brilliantly illuminated with electric light globes of diversified colour." Dancing and feasting was so remarkable that "by unanimous opinion, the function was set down as being one of the most enjoyable ever held at Vailima" in its storied history, the paper reported.[1] Not to be outdone, Ta'isi held a competing New Year's Eve ball at Tuaefu. His ball rivaled the administrator's function for extravagance and had a more inclusive guest list of people from beyond Sāmoa's European and colonial communities. Business associates, staff, friends, and family spent a festive evening at Tuaefu dancing and playing games. At the stroke of midnight, fireworks shot up from Tuaefu's grounds and lit up Apia's night sky.[2] Perhaps Ta'isi ordered pyrotechnics that would shoot so high the party at Vailima could not miss them. No doubt Richardson's guests could hear the cracks and booms like cannon fire coming from the other side of Mauga Folau. The year 1927 had begun.

The increasing tensions in Sāmoa were reflected in many other ways. The increasingly partisan *Samoa Times,* in which Ta'isi owned a minority 40 percent share, was a local forum where Ta'isi had written letters putting forth his position for some time. In contrast, the editor, G. P. Brown, and correspondents (often using pseudonyms) strenuously defended the administration.[3] In its first issue for 1927, the *Samoa Times* published another lengthy letter by Ta'isi in which he criticized the way the *fono* of *faipule* were conducted. Why were their meetings held "in camera" (in private)? Why were standard British practices not followed, allowing these meetings to be open? And, he asked, what really happened during Toelupe's recent speech, where he supposedly handed emblems of Sāmoan sovereignty over to the administrator? Why was the *Samoa Times* not reporting on these critical happenings?

Ta'isi also raised the comparative case of A. J. Cook, the general secretary of the British Miner's Federation, who was granted a passport to travel to Moscow for meetings with the Soviet government with which he had declared his political sympathy. An objective of the Soviet government was the overthrow of parliamentary governments, Ta'isi pointed out. Yet six Sāmoans were denied passports to travel with the proposed delegation to New Zealand to meet with the minister for external affairs even after they submitted the representations they wished to make to the administrator and the *faipule,* as directed. "What a difference between British Justice in England and British Justice in Samoa!" Ta'isi declared. "Does the famous Bill of Rights apply to Samoa, or is the 'liberty of the subject' too sacred to grant the Samoans? They have enjoyed it before. Probably there is not enough liberty now in Samoa to go around." And with that, Ta'isi ended his latest provocative letter in language he had aired with Sir Māui Pōmare a few weeks before.

The *Samoa Times* responded that in the "interests of freedom of speech" it had submitted Ta'isi's questions for official comment, almost certainly to Richardson. The official commentator who responded wished it to be noted that "no reply is considered to be necessary to any European resident who disregards the lessons of history by interfering in Native Affairs." The proceedings of the *faipule* meetings were always published in the *Savali,* the Sāmoan-language paper produced by the administration and distributed to "each Samoan family." No restrictions of speech or movement have ever been placed on the *faipule,* and to make such a suggestion "shows an entire lack of knowledge of psychology and erroneously assumes that the Administration has been unduly concerned over this small agitation on the part of a few European residents, whose methods and objectives are well known." Toelupe's speech was indeed given to all the *faipule* who appointed him to do so, and these *faipule* represented the "39,000 Natives of this Territory to make that speech on their behalf." Unsurprisingly, this response argued there was no basis for Ta'isi's attack on the *faipule* or the administration.

Regarding the refusal to issue passports to the six Sāmoan delegates and the case of Cook, the confused spokesman for the administration opened his riposte by arguing Cook was not British but a "Russian Pole," which was odd given Arthur James Cook was born in Somerset.[4] Furthermore, Cook had a "properly constituted authority to speak on behalf of the very large section of the community he represents" regardless of his aspiration for communist revolution. The six Sāmoans in question had no such authority. The "administration authority" then went into a tedious account of procedural errors Ta'isi made in applying for the passports from the minister that invalidated the application. In addition to these two reasons, this matter was concluded because the minister had now altered his view this delegation was required or welcome as he saw "no reason for any investigation into Native Affairs in Samoa at this present time." Consequentially "no passports will be issued to the Samoans referred to in Mr Nelson's letter." All of this information could have been "obtained personally by Mr Nelson from the Administrator and so have avoided this unnecessary publication of matters of no importance to the European community of this Territory."[5]

Ta'isi responded in kind, hoping his letter would appear in the next issue. Rather than publishing the letter, the editor, G. P. Brown, admonished him: "Your letter in part is an attempt to befog the clear replies which the Official Statement made to the allegations in your letter of last week" and "in parts it is couched offensively. Declined." George Westbrook was also given similar treatment from Brown. This public rebuke of Ta'isi was followed by a report penned by the editor showing "the high esteem in which the Administrator is held by those in highest authority in the British Empire." It highlighted Richardson's appointment by the Imperial Conference to sit on the commission to inquire into the Condominium Administration of the New Hebrides by Great Britain and France.[6] The implication was perfectly clear: Richardson was without fault. All fault lay at Ta'isi's feet. In New Zealand, different parts of the government fed stories to the press, augmenting the media image of the Sāmoa administration—which was of paramount importance in the unfolding public relations battle.[7]

Richardson thought he had the agitators surrounded and he set about moving in to finish them off. There would be no hearing from the minister from the appointed delegation even though the committee appealed to him multiple times via letter, telegram, and then legal representation.[8] S. H. Meredith went alone to Wellington and was seen by Prime Minister Coates. Coates referred the matter to the minister, who Meredith did not see.[9] Instead of the six Sāmoan committee members, four *faipule* (Malietoa, Toelupe, Malupo, and Tu'u'u) made their way to New Zealand to represent Sāmoa for the upcoming visit of the Duke and Duchess of York.[10] A *Samoa Times* report about the latest *fono* of *faipule* agenda checked off every complaint made about them or the administration. The paper was clearly trying to create an appearance of caucusing issues and findings in favor of Richardson by the "legitimate" representatives of Sāmoans, in an attempt to defuse all of the arguments Ta'isi and his cohort had made.[11] The *faipule* complained about the price of copra and requested that the administration commence purchasing the commodity to drive up prices. Richardson expressed due reticence to become involved, but if the *faipule* wanted to improve the quality of Sāmoan copra and export it themselves, he could help them. It was pure noblesse oblige. In every regard, the administrator and the *faipule* were in lockstep. So was the minister for external affairs and the *Samoa Times,* which had become, in Ta'isi's estimation, "a servile organ of the administration."[12] Richardson's maneuvers were choking the agitation of its oxygen, he thought. He also thought he had Ta'isi beaten; he "is afraid and ashamed," Richardson wrote in late January.[13]

Richardson continued to turn the screws. Legal representatives for the Citizens' Committee warned the government that if the minister did not receive committee members, they would petition parliament, a tactic Sāmoans had used before with New Zealand and before that with Germany.[14] This new intelligence sent Richardson to his desk to compose a flurry of letters and devise new strategies to prevent an escalation. He wanted government authority to say "any person can appeal to Parliament but that no Native Appeal can be received that has not been considered and recommended . . . by the Fono of Faipules. May I be permitted to say this?" he inquired. Also, he and Judge Woodward had contrived a new ordinance to be called "the Maintenance of Native Authority Ordinance." It was "not a new idea," he conceded, "but is based on an Ordinance in African Colonies."[15] Its aim was to shut down political activity between Europeans and Sāmoans as the latter were "very susceptible to political propaganda."[16] So much so that Richardson commenced a blatant propaganda. In the July *Savali,* Richardson appealed to the "people of Samoa" to recognize that "in October last a false prophet suddenly appeared in Samoa." This "false prophet collected a few Samoan

Chiefs around him . . . and said unto them 'Go ye and spread . . . the Gospel of hate against the Government—and I will reward you.'" There was no mistaking who Richardson's "false prophet" was or that the administrator was now resorting to new levels of highly charged rhetoric.[17]

While Richardson was casting Ta'isi in some biblical epic, he maintained Sāmoan history had shown "epidemics of political unrest and serious trouble [had] occurred almost annually" since the 1860s; Sāmoans were therefore highly susceptible to agitation he reasoned. He cited Ta'isi's father-in-law, H. J. Moors, as an agitator in 1889 and E. W. Gurr, an active member of the Citizens' Committee, was also marked as a man who caused trouble in German Sāmoa, as well as in American Sāmoa. Richardson insisted this legislation was necessary to the interests of native welfare. But, he cautioned the minister, "such legislation as is proposed in this Ordinance would probably not be tolerated in New Zealand." "Legislation of every country is an index of the psychology and advancement of the people."[18] The argument that New Zealand legal standards should be applied in Sāmoa was not relevant, Richardson argued to Nosworthy. "It is not easy for the New Zealand Government to appreciate that Natives here are very different in some ways from the Maories [*sic*]; wars, political dissensions and widespread agitations amongst them occurred far more recently."[19] To his confidant, J. D. Gray, Richardson was more candid on this point. Sāmoans were in fact "children and should not be legislated for as if they were a modern people. They are still less than 100 years from the stone age and yet Nelson talks about democracy and British justice," Richardson railed. "Such rhetoric is a menace to these people who are not able to understand the arguments arising out of party politics," and so Richardson wanted legislation to be able to punish the Europeans who engaged politically with Sāmoans as he had the powers to punish Sāmoans who defied his edict.[20]

Ta'isi was the main target of this ordinance. Richardson had it on good authority that Ta'isi continued to hold meetings at Tuaefu into 1927 despite Richardson's express orders for this activity to cease. Ta'isi delivered "orations to Samoans in the most dramatic manner" in his home "explaining that he is doing this for his great love of Samoa and his people." "He is not a Samoan as you know," Richardson wrote to Nosworthy in February. He does not admit to Sāmoans that "the British Flag and New Zealand occupation of this Territory made him a rich man" and that he "does not pay a penny of income tax"

(Ta'isi always argued how much he contributed to government coffers through the many taxes on his businesses).[21] Sāmoans did not trust him, Richardson assured Wellington, but Ta'isi was able to generate political gatherings by supplying kegs of beef and other nominal offerings, he revealed.[22] Added to this "crooked" form of political activity were the accusations of German collusion with the Citizens' Committee—especially with Ta'isi—that Richardson was ramping up in early 1927.[23]

Petitioning higher powers to draw attention to a cause was a well-established practice used previously by Sāmoans and many other groups spread wide over geographic and temporal periods: it was the resort of the disenfranchised. Yet in the context of the League of Nations Permanent Mandates Commission (PMC), the question of petitioning tied up a great deal of time in the latter months of 1926. Commissioners thought this might be useful to open a line of communication to people living under these mandatory regimes themselves rather than just hearing from the mandatory powers. In September the PMC proposed to increase the level of detail in annual reports (a requirement already resented by mandatory powers) through a questionnaire.

The most controversial aspect of the questionnaire, apart from its 230 questions, was that it sought to make a provision for people living within mandates so they could petition the League and appear in person before the commission. These developments were rendered even more suspicious, particularly to the British bloc of powers, by Germany's entry into the League in September 1926. Mandatory powers feared that Germany was intensifying a propaganda campaign in efforts to regain their lost colonies. This paranoia about Germany affected New Zealand's initial reactions to the Sāmoan political agitation, as we have seen, but proof of connections between Germany and the agitating Sāmoans were elusive. The mandatory powers argued that the questionnaire was "inquisitorial" and way too detailed; the burden of producing such a report annually would be too great.[24]

To the "radical" notion that those living in mandates should have an opportunity to not only petition the League but appear and give their side of the story, the mandatory powers objected in the strongest terms. Not only would this bring about unrest and embolden malcontents with grievances of questionable validity; it was assumed that people living in mandates were not to be trusted. Their evidence would be inherently dishonest. Such representations would undermine the authority of the mandatory power and, most importantly, the prestige of the European mandatory powers (and Japan) would suffer, threatening the entire colonial system. The unified and fervent objections to both proposals resulted in neither being adopted. Petitioners could not directly address the commission, except in "only rare and exceptional cases" and with the support of the mandatory power. Instead petitioners had to be content to make written submissions.[25]

This line of thinking that closed the door to political agitators to be fully heard by the PMC, with the exception of the tiny chink left open only to the petitioners who had the blessing of the power they were criticizing, was being replicated by New Zealand in 1927. Nosworthy wrote to Richardson about it in March. Nosworthy outlined the PMC's decision of late in 1926 and knew this policy was at odds with the way things worked in New Zealand. "I do not think it would be wise or expedient, having regard to the conditions existing in this Dominion under democratic government, for a responsible Minister to deny . . . the right of an audience to a bona fide citizen of any of New Zealand's territories," Nosworthy told Richardson. However, given the decision of the PMC, which was fully supported by the secretary of state for foreign affairs, "I am of the opinion that the procedure" of not granting an audience to Sāmoan petitioners "is the correct one."[26]

Emboldened by Wellington's support and knowing the wider context of the League of Nations stance, Richardson delivered a provocative speech to the legislative council on March 15. He leveled the speech at the three elected members, even blaming their conduct for the grave illness that afflicted Harry Griffin, the secretary of the Native Department, whose professional duties and recent worries had led to a "serious break down in his health"[27] (Griffin died in May 1927). Richardson repeated the list of arguments about the achievements of the Sāmoan administration, how well-represented everyone was in Sāmoa compared with other mandates and Fiji, and what the restricted role of the elected members was. The legislative council was not a parliament, and the elected members were there to voice opinions relative only to the 230 constituents on the electoral roll. Among all the competing Sāmoan interests Richardson was uniquely placed; he had "no personal interests whatever to serve." This was diametrically opposed to Ta'isi, who he accused, without naming him, of the "evil practice" of stirring up the natives, undermining their confidence in the government that not only protects them but also contributes so much to their "true welfare." Ta'isi, along with the small group of Europeans and "Europeanized Natives," were only interested in their own "ulterior motives." He referred to the "seditious" statements they had recently circulated for their commercial and political gain. Sāmoan history did not reflect well on political agitators who claimed to be "champions" of the native race. Instead, Richardson claimed, "New Zealand's record in dealing with Native races, and I hope my record also, should be sufficient to show who are the real champions of the Native race."[28]

Richardson's speech did not articulate many new criticisms that had not been already publicly aired in newspapers. Yet in making this speech in that forum, he crossed a line. He publicly insulted all those politically involved and every Sāmoan to boot, emphasizing their gullibility and the need for an impartial man like himself to preside over the fray. He knew his speech would be incendiary: "it will make me very unpopular," he warned Nosworthy, "but it has to be done."[29] To Gray, he said, "my statement . . . will be a bombshell but it will do good."[30] "After my statement Nelson and his half caste clique will of course treat me as an enemy," he continued, confirming that Ta'isi was his main target. "He would have liked to avoid me being drawn into this," Richardson explained, "but he had not brains enough to see that his vanity was leading him into a conflict he could not extricate himself from without clashing with me." "He is going to get a terrible exposure, and for that reason will say any unscrupulous thing to clear himself," Richardson predicted. "Rumour has it," he revealed, "that he is in frequent communication with Sir Maui Pomare but he is not fit to lace the boots of Sir Maui although he would like to ape him." Richardson hoped that "Sir Maui will not allow himself to be drawn into this matter as Nelson . . . would use anyones [*sic*] name to save himself."[31]

Richardson lobbed his grenade, but it did not eliminate his opponents as he thought it would. Rather than dissipate the protest through his public shaming of all Sāmoan parties, excepting the *fono* of *faipule,* it galvanized the opposition. A crowd of five hundred met at Tuaefu the Saturday following Richardson's speech to participate in a Citizens' Committee meeting to hammer out the objectives of the Samoan League that became known colloquially as the Mau. Their four-point declaration was imbued with sentiments from America's Declaration of Independence with a modern twist—"all men are equal in the sight of God . . . irrespective of station, race, colour or creed." It also stated that it was an "inherited privilege of a person living under the British Flag . . . to assist members of a subject race in advancements towards civilization, good morals and a Government of the people in accordance with the will of the people." All constitutional authority must be maintained and respect shown for all authority figures, from the administrator to the village policeman. Finally the declaration stated that with this authority and respect in place "it is a privilege and a duty" for "every person to endeavour to procure by lawful means the alteration of any matter affecting the Laws, Government or Constitution of the Territory which may be considered prejudicial to the welfare and best interests of the people." Overall the objectives of the league were "the advancement of Samoa" and "the promotion of the Peace, Order, Good Government and the general welfare of the Territory."[32] Rather than treat this development with the gravity it deserved, Richardson wrote back to Wellington that the reason so many people gathered at Tuaefu "is obvious." "In Apia the local Natives can always be assembled where free food is likely to be obtainable," he claimed. They also wanted to hear "how their money was spent and what Mr Meredith had to say about his trip" to New Zealand.[33]

Despite Richardson's deep cynicism about the movement, the pace and expanse of the protest-related developments increased markedly. Some of these developments were driven by legislative changes sought by Richardson, like an amendment to the *Samoa Act* to make exile without trial from Sāmoa legal. This change in particular precipitated extensive debates in the New Zealand parliament in June. Other developments were driven by protestors, like the fallout from the petition signed by 150 chiefs and orators sent to the New Zealand parliament.[34] Given all this activity, it was misleading for Gray to write to the governor-general's secretary on March 30 to tell him "from recent advices from General Richardson it would appear that the political agitation in Western Samoa has about run its course."[35] All these developments were accompanied by media coverage for or against the New Zealand government. Publicity and the support of prominent people, especially leader of the opposition Harry Holland, bolstered the Mau case, drawing attention to what was happening while undermining the government line put out in the dominant conservative press.

In order to combat the hostile *Samoa Times,* and hopefully influence opinion beyond Sāmoa, too, Ta'isi, along with E. W. Gurr and Percy Andrews, began to organize his own newspaper. This paper would be "a real newspaper" and not a "party organ" presenting precisely what the administrator and New Zealand government wanted in print. The *Samoa Guardian* was launched on May 26, just ahead of the minister's visit. It was printed in English and Sāmoan and covered a scope of topics from within Sāmoa and around the globe with one dominant theme—it was always opposed to colonial enterprise and championed Indigenous views and causes. The first issue of the paper claimed its neutrality: "we do not desire to be an organ of any institution or faction, but shall represent the people and get down to 'grass roots.'"[36] Partially bankrolled by Ta'isi's money and staffed by key Mau and Citizens' Committee people, the *Samoa Guardian* was not impartial. Instead it encapsulated the protest movement's agenda seeking to tackle tangible issues. It published key documents and as the protest movement ground on, it documented that, too. As well as incendiary words, the paper circulated cartoons from New Zealand sources that mocked leading political figures, showing a complete disregard for white prestige. It aimed to be an open source, to legitimize the anticolonial movement, to keep the Mau personal, and to connect Sāmoans to one another.

The *Samoa Guardian*'s other purpose was to connect Sāmoa's protest to comparable situations elsewhere in the world. It highlighted consistently that Sāmoans were not alone in their struggles by covering "Mau" movements from Indonesia to India and tracking the fate of others in League of Nations Mandates, particularly those in "Irak," who gained considerable concessions toward self-government in the 1920s and were self-governing by 1932. These revelations prompted the obvious question—"why not Sāmoa, too?" American Sāmoa was also a constant comparison to the mandated territory. Unsurprisingly, the comparisons were not flattering to New Zealand's rule. The *Samoa Guardian* was never sympathetic of course to the administration. It hectored and derided men who considered themselves unassailable owing to their positions. It was monitored, analyzed, and resented from the outset.[37] The government studied it to build cases against agitators, and it would be consistently cited for its violation of arbitrary ordinances. Production moved to New Zealand in 1929, and it was renamed the *NZ Samoa Guardian* and stayed in print until 1934.[38] This iteration of the paper embraced high production values. It published photographs and continued to glean political cartoons from left-wing New Zealand papers that ridiculed individual politicians and the egregious situation to great effect.

Figure 7.1. Lampooning Sir General George Richardson's militaristic tactics with Ta'isi representing the Citizens' Committee. *Samoa Guardian,* September 1, 1927, 4. Courtesy of the National Library of Australia.

Figure 7.2. William Nosworthy, minister for external affairs, is ridiculed along with the various government explanations for the Mau—"agitator, half-truths, German propaganda, native credulity, liquor, political interests and lies." *Samoa Guardian,* January 19, 1928, 3. Courtesy of the National Library of Australia.

The administration tried to prevent it reaching Sāmoa once it was published in Auckland by tampering with mail arriving in the mandate. Its circulation elsewhere is difficult to gauge, but copies of it can be found in the Library of Congress, Washington, DC, the British Library, and the National Library of Australia, which hints at how far it traveled. As far as the New Zealand government was concerned, any circulation of it was objectionable. In Richardson's estimation, the *Samoa Guardian* did "incalculable" harm to "the Natives."[39]

Despite these new dynamics, Minister Nosworthy continued to treat the situation with nonchalance. He delayed his visit more times until he finally arrived in Sāmoa in June. Even then, he rubbed further salt into the wounds. With Richardson orchestrating the schedule, Nosworthy held a meeting with the Citizens' Committee on the tenth day of his visit, his last day. The point of making the Citizens' Committee the lowest priority on his agenda was not lost. The June 11 meeting began with Nosworthy making a long, stern speech where he recounted Richardson's case against the agitators, likening them to a "festering wound on the body politic of Samoa." Their conduct was "nothing less than criminal and deserving only to be dealt with as a crime."[40]

As chairman of the Citizens' Committee, it was Ta'isi's role to respond first to the minister. Though others in the committee chimed in with comments, what followed Nosworthy's incendiary speech was a testy exchange between the two men, where Ta'isi forcefully put forward the case of the protest movement. He raised the governor-general's recent politicized public remarks about the price of copra, for instance. Nosworthy reacted as if Ta'isi blasphemed; "you must not pass comment on the Governor General," he ordered. Ta'isi pointed out Fergusson had overstepped his duties by going "into the political arena in New Zealand." Ta'isi chastised Nosworthy for waiting until the eve of his departure to meet with the delegation all the while trying to point out to him that "Savai'i belongs to the Mau" and the same "is true of Upolu." The minister had not seen the true picture of what was happening as Richardson had led him around. Ta'isi emphatically told Nosworthy that "the New Zealand Government continues to send glowing reports to the League of Nations, thus soliciting world praise, when the people of Samoa are crying out for deliverance." Nosworthy was unmoved.

The exchange between Ta'isi and the minister plumbed comical depths when Nosworthy accused Ta'isi of assuming the status of the administrator for having an "opposition ball and opposition sports" event to mark the recent king's birthday. Nosworthy had attended the official version of events a few days earlier as Richardson's honored guest. Ta'isi and other members of the committee were not invited to Vailima, but that was no excuse for competing with official events, Nosworthy argued. Ta'isi claimed that committee members were just as loyal to the British king and wished to demonstrate this with a consequential event. To Nosworthy, holding rival events was tantamount to "taking on the function of the government." The politics of parties notwithstanding, Ta'isi was getting the better of the minister in this exchange. The Sāmoan members of the committee—Alipia, Tuisila, Afamasaga, and Faumuina—all presented their view to the increasingly exasperated minister before he ended the meeting by confirming he was deaf to all pleas for negotiation. He warned the Citizens' Committee again that they would be held responsible if there was "any further agitation amongst the Natives in Samoa." The following day the minister sent the committee a detailed reply to their demands that must have been prepared in advance, being eleven pages long. Again, it confirmed the government policy that no negotiation would be considered.[41]

The war of words then moved to Wellington. Ta'isi planned to travel to Wellington on July 1 to engage in talks as the aftermath of the petition played out. Ahead of his departure, Richardson sent him a letter telling him that if he undertook the trip, upon his return he might "suffer immediate deportation under clause 6 of the Samoa Immigration Consolidation Order."[42] A. G. Smyth received a similar letter. Ta'isi took his chances and traveled to New Zealand. He expected justice would prevail in the parliament, and Richardson's threats would be deemed illegal. What he witnessed in parliament was intensely personal. Many times he was the topic of discussion. Nosworthy articulated the most extreme line that Ta'isi preached "revolution" and "bloodshed" in Sāmoa. Labour MPs defended him vigorously against this charge, pointing out that this was the *opposite* of what Ta'isi advocated. Instead these supporters put on record Ta'isi was warning Sāmoa would go down this path if reforms were not rapidly introduced.[43]

As well as hearing discussions questioning his own character and conduct, Ta'isi listened to other speeches relating to the proposed amendments to the *Samoa Act* that would further empower Richardson to deport people from the mandate without trial. These speeches evoked a range of routine subjects, administrative procedure, orders in council, as well as stirring and passionate ones—British Empire, race, and New Zealand history.[44] Most conservative members rubber-stamped the changes, expressing mawkish admiration for Richardson and his work in Sāmoa. They clung to the government line, encapsulated by Minister for External Affairs, William Nosworthy's statement, "I can stand in this house and say confidently that there is nothing wrong with the Samoa Administration."[45] Prime Minister Coates argued that exile and banishment without trial were standard powers in "the United States of America, France, Germany, Spain and then the British countries of South Africa, Australia, India and Egypt."[46] Empowering New Zealand to do likewise was nothing out of the ordinary. Labour politicians begged to differ, and did so strenuously. Opposition leader, ardent supporter of the Sāmoan cause, and correspondent with Ta'isi, Harry Holland, described the situation:

> Has it come to this: that whoever dares to criticize the Administration of Samoa is to be met with a sentence of deportation? This is not to the credit of New Zealand: it constitutes an outrage upon every principle of British liberty, and is the reason to-day why there is so much resentment throughout New Zealand and other countries because of what we are doing in Samoa.[47]

Holland promised that if Labour were elected, "Samoans would be able to run the country under the British flag." As well as this outrage against British justice, Holland looked back at history and warned parliament that Ngāti Maru leader "Te Kooti was deported and trouble followed"—a prescient observation. He was referring to the turbulent and violent history surrounding Te Kooti Arikirangi Te Turuki's exile without trial to the Chatham Islands in 1866—as well as his escape back to New Zealand in 1868, and his prosecution of a draining war that lasted four years. Holland was not alone in seeing New Zealand history repeating itself. Holland's fellow Labour members William Lysnar, Edwin Howard, and Peter Fraser also evoked New Zealand's troubled colonial history, puncturing the myth milked by Richardson and his supporters that New Zealand was a racial paradise. Howard cited that exile without trial also had bloody consequences for Taranaki Māori resistance.[48] "Looking back right through history to the Native wars we have had . . . especially the trouble at the foot of Mount Egmont [Taranaki], we can trace it all back to bad mistakes in administration," Howard told parliament on July 19, 1927.[49]

Howard was likely referring to the November 1881 military attack on the nonviolent community of Parihaka in Taranaki, which resulted in the capture of the community's leaders, Te Whiti O Rongomai and Tohu Kakahi, their exile to the South Island, and then the extensive confiscation of Māori lands. Te Whiti is credited with developing a bloodless form of resistance derived from Christian principles that he described as "a fighting peace."[50] The Parihaka community did not take up arms to combat the rapid confiscation of Māori lands that were transformed into Pākehā-owned dairy farms; they were breaking the cycle of violence that had gripped the region for decades. What they did do was sabotage the farms on occupied lands by plowing up fields, removing fencing, and scattering precious livestock into the night. They also undertook to repair damage to their own infrastructure caused by Pākehā activities (such as repairing their own fencing torn down) under cover of night. The newcomers were not going to surrender the spoils of Taranaki's extraordinarily rich volcanic soils, regularly soaked with rains. With legislation and military force, the Parihaka community's nonviolent campaign was ostensibly stopped.[51]

Edwin Howard recalled this past for parliament. For another parliamentarian, this history was particularly acute. That man was Sir Māui Pōmare. As a five-year-old boy, Sir Māui witnessed the infamous invasion of the community where he lived with his parents, who were followers of Te Whiti. Legend has it that the horse ridden by John Bryce, the leader of the military expedition, trampled Sir Māui's foot during the pandemonium of the morning of November 5, 1881, severing one of his toes. Once the community had been overrun, Tohu and Te Whiti were arrested and, without trial, exiled to the South Island to serve out their sentences.[52]

The past was also very much on Sir Māui's mind at this time as he had been the driving force behind the *Royal Commission to Inquire into Confiscations of Native Lands and Other Grievances Alleged by Natives* (known popularly as the "Sim Commission" after Sir William Sim, who headed the inquiry) that heard about nineteenth-century Māori land confiscations from February 9 to May 12, 1927.[53] Sir Māui told Ta'isi in late 1926 that he was very much occupied with setting up the Royal Commission charged with inquiring "into some of our old grievances caused by the confiscation of large tracts of land consequent upon the Maori War." "Succeeding Governments have always been diffident about giving us a hearing," he explained, because "they knew that some dirty linen would have to be washed and hung up to the public view." Sir Māui informed Ta'isi that "a great many of us were termed rebels, but in the confiscations, the lands of the rebels, as well as the lands of the neutrals and the so-called loyalists were likewise confiscated." Sir Māui felt the inquest would "clear matters up."[54]

The tight entanglement of the Māori past and the Sāmoan present in 1927 was also felt in other ways. Through their close friendship, Sir Māui influenced Ta'isi and then others in Sāmoa to adopt a nonviolent path. Nonviolent resistance was, of course, most prominently being pursued in India at this time, but Sir Māui's friendship with Ta'isi directly linked the Sāmoan Mau to a deeper and more proximate history of resistance in the British Empire, to Parihaka in Taranaki. Parihaka was a historical precedent to what was now happening in Sāmoa, where Pākehā New Zealand had to again confront nonviolent resistance.[55] Too few parliamentarians were cognizant of this.

Sir Māui's initial response to the debates on the *Samoa Act* surprised Ta'isi. As Ta'isi sat in the gallery, he could not understand why his friend sat in silence as the debates raged around him, seemingly unmoved. The Labour members railed on the behalf of the Mau cause, but Sir Māui did not.[56] Until July 26. Then Sir Māui rose to address the parliament. "I have been especially interested in the present debate because the Samoans are akin to my own race," he began. He concurred that the "history of one country may be repeated in another" if the government set Sāmoa on the course it proposed. There was no question that the "episode of Te Kooti [was] due to banishment without trial. No one can doubt that that was so; it is a matter of history," he said. Sir Māui's own homelands of Taranaki were similarly racked by war "because trial was refused; and thus we lost thousands of lives and millions of money." Sir Māui challenged the view that Sāmoans were "thriftless," "easily led," and "are children." The same has been said of Māori, he argued. He also noted that Sāmoa "is a conquered territory, and is different in that respect from New Zealand" because "[the] Maoris, of their own volition, elected to come into the British Empire." Article 22 of the League of Nations Charter was about ensuring "Samoa for the Samoans," but, he asked, when would Sāmoans be allowed "to walk on their own feet?" Tongans could. So why not Sāmoans?

Sir Māui then waded into very controversial waters when he began addressing New Zealand's record in Sāmoa. Yes, there were many benefits from the building of infrastructure and curing of hookworm, "but that is part of our job and we need not pat ourselves so very much for what we have done." This drew Sir Māui's own prime minister to feet. Coates noted that "every individual in this country" is helping Sāmoa to which Sir Māui responded that "every individual in the country helped to spread influenza to those islands wiping out upwards of a fourth of the population." "That is nonsense," Coates shot back. "It is not nonsense," Sir Māui countered. The two men went back and forth over New Zealand's impact on Sāmoa and the need for Sāmoans to feel "gratitude," as Coates put it. Sir Māui then raised the problems with the self-governing structures—the *fono* of *faipule* and the legislative council—and pleaded to give "the Samoan a little more responsibility in the government of himself." Sir Māui eloquently concluded his contribution to the debate with a Shakespearian speech delivered by Portia in *The Merchant of Venice* about justice and mercy: "and so we must be careful when we extract our pound of flesh that we do not shed one drop of Samoan blood."[57]

The *Auckland Star* reported Māui Pōmare's speech was so "sensational" that it "thrilled the house."[58] Ta'isi's admiration for his friend grew as he watched his performance. Later he wrote him a letter showing how close the two men had become:

> My Dear Pomare, Often did I want to rush up to your Ministry Room for a chat but knowing how busy you were with the Parliament in Session I refrained from doing so. Then again, knowing your sentiments towards your Samoan Cousins in our hour of trial and the wrong impression which may be created on your own position in the Cabinet by my hanging around you, I thought it better to keep away until you needed me or required any information.[59]

Sir Māui berated Ta'isi for breaching Polynesian etiquette and not calling on him despite Ta'isi's explanation for keeping his distance: "Ta'isi . . . do you really think that I would prostitute my honour or forfeit the heritage of our people for a seat in Cabinet or a portfolio in a pakeha government?" "It is yet my sincere hope in life," he continued, "to maintain and restore to my Polynesian kinsmen" what has been lost for all time to Māori, governing themselves in "Maoriland."[60]

Despite Sir Māui's daring rebuke of his own government's policy and the tenacious arguments put forward by the Labour Party, the government prevailed; the amendments were passed. After the *Samoa Act* was amended, the government launched an inquiry called the Joint Samoan Petition Inquiry Committee. Sparked by the petition and the Citizens' Committee's protest, this inquiry was deemed "strictly confidential." Chaired by Sir James Parr, a range of parliamentarians (including the main players in Sāmoan affairs like Harry Holland, Sir Francis Bell, Sir Āpirana Ngata, and Minister Nosworthy), counsel for the petitioners and government hammered out the events that led to the unrest. Not only was the strict secrecy of this inquiry unusual, and questioned by nongovernment ministers and counsel, it was also anomalous because it called only one witness.[61] Despite the initial appearances of legitimacy, the inquiry turned out to be little more than an inquisition of the sole witness who gave exhaustive testimony over eleven days of hearings (including Saturdays).[62] Who was the one witness? Ta'isi O. F. Nelson.[63]

The Citizens' Committee had been calling for an inquiry for some time, but Richardson had always refused. Why did he allow one to happen in August 1927? The government and the administrator were determined to control any investigation, a difficult feat when the inquiry was being conducted in Wellington and Labour politicians were also asking the questions. Harry Holland, who never retreated from his causes, wanted Richardson called before the inquiry; the government did not want Richardson demeaned and exposed in that way. As it proceeded, it became clear how government control over the inquiry would be achieved.

Running from August 5 to 26, the inquiry generated nearly two hundred pages of testimony and documentation. The press reported on the existence of the "Samoan inquiry" but little detail found its way into the public arena. The hostile counsel for the government, Michael Myers, sternly noted that it was reported in Sāmoa that Ta'isi had "gained a point" over the government by it consenting "to set up a Select Parliamentary Committee" in the first place.[64] Ta'isi was rebuked and told that under no circumstances was he to feed stories to the press about what was going on. After the hearings were concluded, no findings or report were generated and the transcripts of the hearings were suppressed. What was buried was a trove of information and the most sustained record of Ta'isi speaking, interacting with both hostile and supportive parliamentarians while giving his version not only of what immediately preceded the unrest, but also of the deeper histories of Sāmoa, including autobiographical information.

The inquiry commenced with discussions about the terms of the investigation and outlining the history of the unrest. On Tuesday August 16 it was time for Ta'isi to take the stand.[65] In his extensive testimony, Ta'isi constructed a timeline for the rapid deterioration of relations with Richardson that defied sense. The two men had been friends, confidants. Richardson sought Ta'isi's advice regularly, they socialized together, and Richardson's kind letters to Ta'isi during his absence in Sydney in 1926 were submitted as evidence. The text of the effusive welcome-back speech of September 1926 was also offered as testimony to show the dramatic changes in Richardson's conduct. As the committee was privy to government correspondence of the time that traduced Ta'isi's character, they could see the inconsistencies in Richardson's conduct, prompting Ta'isi's counsel to ask if Richardson was a "lying hypocrite."[66] With Holland's support, Ta'isi's counsel was determined to offer a counternarrative of the "very vicious" recent attacks on Ta'isi's character in parliament, in the papers, and especially from Richardson himself. Even Sir Francis Bell described the attacks on Ta'isi as more than "vicious" but "violent," to which Holland agreed that they were "violent and vicious, if that will suit Sir Francis Bell."[67]

Ta'isi's testimony showed that he was not the only one who had experienced a sudden and seismic shift in Richardson's good opinion. Richardson turned on Afamasaga (referred to as Lago Lago since his title was stripped from him) shortly after he attended a party at Afamasaga's house, delivering speeches and encouraging guests to give Afamasaga three cheers. Within a short space of time, Richardson had banished Afamasaga. His offense was brewing beer in excess of 3 percent alcohol by volume and selling it. In addition to this offense, Richardson always mentioned a dated financial matter stemming from a failed Sāmoan-led business enterprise (started with Logan's approval) in order to consolidate Afamasaga's "crime," hoping to offset the anger felt by many about what they saw as an outrageous overreaction by the administrator.[68] Other banishments were also discussed, particularly that of Tupua Tamasese Lea'lofi and Richardson's inexcusable insult of walking by an *ifoga*, a public demonstration of contrition asking forgiveness for Tupua Tamasese after he was banished to Savai'i.[69]

Over his time in the stand, Ta'isi was relentlessly questioned by his counsel, Dudley R. Hoggard, various parliamentarians, and the government legal representative. In his testimony Ta'isi answered crisply, explaining events and how he tried to raise increasing concerns with the administrator. The minutiae of Sāmoan events and the growing dissatisfaction with Richardson were raked over, as well as larger underlying issues like the dangerous ideas Sāmoans were receiving about their equality with Europeans. Ta'isi referred to a schoolbook in the Sāmoan language that stated, "The Samoan is in every respect the equal of a European." He testified that this stance was "different to what it had been under previous Governments." Such ideas of equality justified many things, not least was the notion that Sāmoans and Europeans could mix politically because they had shared rights, interests and concerns.[70]

From Saturday, August 20, the inquiry got to the crux of accusations against Ta'isi. Was he an exploiter of Sāmoan copra growers who deliberately suppressed prices? Was he fanning discontent to enhance his own wealth and power? Ta'isi explained the December 1926 encounter he had with Chief Judge Woodward at Johnnie Ah Mu's garage as he stopped en route to work. He revealed the judge told him that he felt "sorry" for him as he was being "mislead" by Arthur Williams and George Westbrook, who had "nothing to lose." In contrast, Woodward told Ta'isi, he had "everything to lose." Ta'isi responded that he was "very pleased . . . that you tell me that others are misleading me, because there has been such a lot of talk about me being the chief offender in this, and that I am misleading others." The judge reportedly repeated to Ta'isi that "you have all to lose." Woodward then told him, "as a friend," that the administrator would now buy copra "and you will be the loser." Ta'isi questioned why the administrator's "feelings for me [should] influence him in this matter at all one way or the other."[71]

Ta'isi then described the nature of the copra industry to the inquiry, explaining that the market price of copra hinged on quality, quantity, shrinkage rates of the dried copra, and shipping costs determined by the distance from the Apia market and also the costs of shipping the copra to distant foreign markets.[72] Fifteen thousand to sixteen thousand tons of copra were exported from Sāmoa per annum. Of this, Sāmoan growers produced twelve thousand tons. O. F. Nelson and Co. handled about half of this "native grown copra."[73] Yes, his company dominated the copra trade in Sāmoa; he had "about one hundred" copra sheds and "about forty-five" trading stores.[74] Money flowed into government coffers through taxing copra sheds and trading licenses rather than income taxes. A current trading license was fifteen pounds; combined with other taxes, O. F. Nelson and Co. contributed more than two thousand pounds per year to the Sāmoan treasury.[75]

Richardson's punitive copra-buying scheme was to purchase copra at four pounds, ten shillings above what other traders (like Ta'isi) were paying. The traders' price was calibrated to the per ton London value, Ta'isi explained. Ta'isi calculated that Richardson's inflated purchase price meant Sāmoans got more for their copra but that the government then sold it on to Burns Philp at a loss, meaning that the government coffers would lose about one thousand pounds that year. This was, Ta'isi argued, an indirect deficit to the Sāmoan people because any profits from the Crown Estates were to be paid to the Sāmoan treasury, and any loss was also borne by the treasury, too. Ta'isi assured the committee that an administration official—H. P. Ritchie, who was the director of agriculture—told him the scheme of inflating prices had no effect of raising the price of copra.[76]

Ta'isi conceded Richardson was right in asserting that copra growers in American Sāmoa had got higher prices than their counterparts in the mandate over the "last three or four years," but there was a good reason for this. In American Sāmoa US warships carried copra for free; the terrain also meant copra was more easily accessed and transported, keeping costs down. Ta'isi explained Western Sāmoa was divided into four districts according to the difficulty of collecting copra by boat and the distance from Apia. In the mandate, "New Zealand warships do not carry our copra free" and this cost, which was not negligible, was reflected in the prices paid. Added to this, American Sāmoans worked at different rates and received one payment (whereas growers in the mandate got several), so the comparison of prices for copra that appeared at first glance to be straightforward was, in fact, not.[77] The price of copra in the two jurisdictions did not differ because Ta'isi and his firm drove prices down in the mandate, he maintained.

From a business perspective, Ta'isi argued, Richardson's copra-buying scheme was not only unsustainable, it came at a significant cost to the Sāmoan people.[78] The scheme was financially disastrous and, it was strongly implied, a cynical exercise to curry favor with Sāmoans who saw an immediate appreciation of their returns. Yet parliamentarians' questioning was less about Richardson's motives and more about whether Ta'isi was an exploiter of Sāmoan copra growers. Ta'isi kept to the argument that his firm was paying fair prices in accordance with global markets, explaining at length how the copra industry operated as he was questioned repeatedly about it. He submitted detailed calculations of the on-costs of copra and invited "anybody" to "see our books if they like."[79]

So what of Ta'isi's supposed political ambition and lust for power? How did Ta'isi answer this charge? Sympathetic Labour MP, Edwin Howard, drilled Ta'isi about this, giving Ta'isi the opportunity to categorically refute all the charges made against him by Richardson in a damning report he wrote on July 25, 1927. Howard asked Ta'isi if he considered himself "an authority on the psychology of the Samoan people," to which Ta'isi responded, "Yes, I do." Richardson however, was not an authority, Ta'isi said (despite his claims to the contrary), otherwise "the present trouble would not have arisen." Quoting from Richardson, Howard again set out the administrator's explanation for the trouble. It was "not initiated by the Natives, as they were not then dissatisfied." He went on:

> One person, with one object only, was the originator of the present trouble—viz. Mr Nelson, the wealthy half-caste merchant, whose aim was apparently to increase his power, and influence, particularly in Native matters, and so materially enhance his commercial interests.[80]

To this Ta'isi countered that the "dissatisfaction among the Natives was long before" October 1926 and had been "growing all the time." As to accusation of increasing his political power he responded, "There is no truth whatever in that." He had "the respect of the people in Samoa, the Samoans and the Europeans, and even the Administrator, right up till then." "There was no attempt on my part to increase my power and influence—in fact, I do not see how it was possible," he continued. He insisted that he had "always avoided, or assisted to prevent, any unrest, because that was opposed to my own ordinary interests." "Dissatisfaction amongst the Samoans must be detrimental to the interests of the traders and the merchants," he asserted.[81]

The hostile government barrister, Myers, then had his turn to question Ta'isi from the afternoon session on August 20. Myers wanted to know how long Sāmoans had been discontented and what the current connection was between the Citizens' Committee and the Welfare League. Ta'isi explained there was no protest organization in place in late 1926 and so there was no continuity from the Welfare League that had formed to protest against Tate's administration. Myers was not convinced and went back further, to the 1910 petition to the German parliament, arguing that this petition "bears a strong family likeness . . . to the grievances of Mr Nelson today." Ta'isi disagreed. An increasingly aggressive Myers continued to paint Ta'isi as a constant and leading troublemaker from 1910 to the present. "Coming down to the bed rock," Myers insisted, the current agitation was "merely a feud between you and the administrator." Ta'isi insisted his personal relationship with Richardson was irrelevant; instead "we would like to see New Zealand redress the people's grievances."[82]

As their exchange continued, it became increasingly tense. Ta'isi refused to answer a number of Myers' questions, possibly an indication he thought them inappropriate. Myers, frustrated at being outclassed in his understanding of the copra market, turned to anthropological and historical assessments of Sāmoan customs by referencing a 1880s diary of the British consul to Tokelau. Myer assumed Tokelauans were Sāmoan, which Ta'isi corrected. Myers was not convinced. "Are not the people of the Tokelaus Samoan," he asked, "do they not speak the same language as the Samoans?" "No," replied Ta'isi. "What are they?" Myers inquired. "They are no more Samoans than Maoris are. They are Tokelau people," Ta'isi answered. Myers quickly changed the topic to specific cultural practices and points of translation. He made an enormous amount out of a wish by one Sāmoan published in the *Samoa Guardian* before Ta'isi left Sāmoa for New Zealand. The wish was that Ta'isi would return to Sāmoa with Richardson's kava title. Myers tried to make the case that this was evidence of Ta'isi's ambition to overthrow the administrator, even though he had nothing to do with the letter. Myers was making mountains out of molehills. The more he got out of his depth, the more aggressive his tone became, to the point where he shot back, "I did not ask you that. Do you not understand English, Mr Nelson?" Myers' questioning continued to descend into an attack on Ta'isi. It got so hostile that other parliamentarians called him to order for "browbeating" the witness and bringing "heat" to his questioning.[83]

As the inquiry dragged on, the purpose of investing so much time, effort, and energy from so many people on these secret hearings became clear. On the last day of hearings—August 26—the nongovernment MPs and the petitioners' counsel found out through unofficial Apia channels that Richardson had completely reversed his decision (stated on August 12) that an inquiry would not be held. No one from the government side would confirm to the Joint Samoan Petition Inquiry Committee if a Royal Commission was now going to be held in Sāmoa and when. This resulted in farcical exchanges. The government was asked directly on August 26 if Richardson had asked for a Royal Commission to be set up. The government gave vague responses. When Myers was asked, he replied, "How can I answer that? It is an absurd question."[84]

Not only had a Royal Commission been organized; its formation had been "announced" on August 23, according to Prime Minister Coates. This was three days before the hearings in Wellington finished late on August 26, and when the government MPs and their counsel were still denying its existence.[85] John Findlay, also representing the Citizens' Committee along with Hoggard, protested strongly to Prime Minister Coates. Findlay asked that the Sāmoan hearings for the newly announced inquiry be postponed. Given the subterfuge surrounding the inquiry Findlay told Coates that all parties needed adequate time to prepare and get to Sāmoa by the next *Tofua*. This request was denied. Counsel for the petitioners then advised their clients not to appear before this very questionable commission, though many did end up presenting evidence. With this latest development it became clear that the Joint Samoan Petition Inquiry Committee had been conducted to ensure Ta'isi and his elite counsel would have little influence on the Royal Commission. Labour politicians were outraged. The government argued that because there would now be a Royal Commission there was no need for the Joint Samoan Petition Inquiry Committee to make any recommendation. It was superseded and now superfluous. It had all been a ruse.

The Royal Commission Concerning the Administration of Western Samoa began hearings in Sāmoa on September 24.[86] Richardson had told J. D. Gray in late August to not give Ta'isi or any half-castes a platform or they would dominate the Commission.[87] The commissioners were Justice Skerrett, chief justice of New Zealand, and Charles MacCormack, judge of Native Land Court. Three lawyers appeared for the New Zealand administration (McCarthy, Klinkmueller, and Meredith) and two for the Mau (Baxter and Slipper).[88] The terms of reference were narrow and subjective. The commission was to investigate if there was "reasonable cause" for complaints or objections about the way New Zealand governed the mandate, whether the Administrator or officials had "exceeded their duty" or "failed to exercise their respective functions honestly and justly" and finally, it was to investigate if it "was prudent or safe to wholly repeal and abrogate all power" to banish a Sāmoan from "one place on the islands to another."[89] More compromising was that Richardson orchestrated many aspects of the inquiry. He suggested witnesses and arranged itineraries for the judges and arranged other more minor details. His fingerprints were all over the inquiry.[90] The judges went through the motions of due process, interviewing a wide array of Sāmoans associated with the Mau (ninety witnesses) or not (sixty-five witnesses) over twenty-three days of hearings.[91]

On October 11 Ta'isi, back in Apia, was called as a witness before the commission. Unlike his recent performance in Wellington, he was one of many witnesses given the opportunity to present evidence. Ta'isi's evidence covered a lot of the same ground as the Joint Samoan Committee. His evidence delved into his grievances and his advocacy for Sāmoan representation on the legislative council. Not only because Sāmoans were the largest taxpayers and so financial matters concern them, Ta'isi argued, but because the mandate needed Sāmoans to be given responsibility in legislation. "Samoans will make no headway if they are treated as a backward race," he argued, as they were currently.[92] The other line of questioning from counsel for the administration tried to undermine Ta'isi's honesty and his honor. Why had he forgotten to mention a meeting after he returned to Sāmoa in 1926 with Sāmoans and Europeans? How could he have betrayed Richardson by plotting against him and making "charges" against his administration while appearing to be his friend? Ta'isi insisted he always conveyed his views to Richardson, even when the administrator did not like them. Not mentioning the meeting in question was not a sinister act, but merely forgetfulness, Ta'isi explained. Many things happened in quick succession after he returned to Sāmoa in September 1926 after a seven-month absence, he argued.[93]

Importantly, the Royal Commission also generated the most detailed analysis of the Sāmoan copra trade to date. Mau lawyers wanted to confront the damaging accusation that the trade—especially as far as O. F. Nelson and Co. was concerned—was based on the exploitation of Sāmoan growers. The Mau called witnesses representing the three firms who divided up the remaining market share of the copra trade after Nelson's: Burns Philp, Morris Hedstroms (which had only be operating for six months in Sāmoa after having bought out Smyth and Carruthers), and P. C. Fabricius. Walter Voight of Fabricius, who had been in the business for a quarter of a century, testified that the four firms met and decided copra prices for each of the districts when the "European market takes a change." The last meeting about prices took place at the Burns Philp office. Each witness confirmed that the four firms paid the exact same price for copra as agreed beforehand. Voight also testified that this system for determining the price of copra "is a very old one, and as far as I can remember—twenty-five years back—it has always been followed." This would date this system to around 1902 when Ta'isi had just joined his family firm at nineteen years old, and the copra trade was dominated by the DHPG. Voight also explained that copra prices had to be sufficient so growers did not bypass local traders, go to another station, or take the copra to Apia themselves, where the highest price was always received. Each witness of the four firms confirmed there was no way they could pay the advances the government currently was (especially when there were irregularities about how these advances correlated with actual copra deliveries) and that none of them had been notified of Richardson's scheme in advance. Each firm submitted balance sheets that bore out in figures what the witnesses told the commission.[94]

Once the hearings were concluded, the judges returned to New Zealand to compile their report. Their report was written quickly (by November 29) and its key findings drip-fed to the press from December 10.[95] (The full report was withheld until January 1928.) The commission's findings were no surprise. Richardson and the administration were exonerated on every count. The culprits for unrest were Europeans stirring up trouble and making arguments based on bogus evidence. The worst offender in this was Ta'isi, accompanied by A. G. Smyth and E. W. Gurr. Like Robert Tate before them, the judges reinforced the narrative that no fault lay with the New Zealand government in carrying out its colonial duties. Yet it altered the narrative by erasing the persistent troubles that plagued Tate's administration. The commission found that until the public meeting of October 15, "there was no real dissatisfaction amongst Samoans with the Administration," that is, until Ta'isi returned from Sydney.[96] It also found Ta'isi was dishonest, misleading, and that he had engaged in "animadversion" toward Richardson; in short, the report could not have been more damning.

What affect did all the detail about the copra business aired during testimony have on the stinging and enduring accusation that Ta'isi exploited Sāmoans? The commissioners let the accusation fester. They stated there was no competition between traders and little incentive for growers to improve their crops but they side-stepped all the evidence that pointed away from Ta'isi as a malicious exploiter. They found the administrator's buying scheme was "a pure measure of policy and does not come within the scope of our inquiry." Despite being beyond the inquiry's terms, the commissioners "observed" that the scheme was experimental, any losses sustained will be borne by the New Zealand government so "it is a pure act of generosity."[97] The scheme did not work; within three years pro-administration Sāmoans were complaining about the price of copra.[98] The commissioners did not solve the problem, address traders' concerns, or answer the biggest question. If Ta'isi and his firm were exploiters, why did so many Sāmoans sell their copra through his stores when the competitors offered the same price? There were two distinguishing features of O. F. Nelson and Co. from the other three firms—they were the largest operation and so had the most trading stations and they employed Sāmoans, afakasis, and Europeans without discrimination and so were more connected into communities. Trading stations extended credit, acting like banks, and sold a range of goods. Having favorable operations on this front may also explain why so many Sāmoans opted to sell copra through O. F. Nelson and Co.—a fact that no one in the administration could explain without resorting to crude racial stereotypes.

With these findings in place, Richardson then made his next move, the dramatic climax to the year filled with tensions. On December 15 he ordered Ta'isi, Gurr, and Smyth to appear before him the following morning to show cause why they should not be deported. With F. D. Baxter, Ta'isi appeared before the administrator at Vailima on December 16. Ta'isi had to disprove Richardson's charge that he was "the recognized and active head of an organization called the 'Mau' or League of Samoa, the purpose of which to secure self-government for Samoa and in furtherance of such purpose, by unlawful means to frustrate and render ineffective . . . the function of the Administration of the Territory."[99] Ta'isi refuted all charges.[100] Richardson was unmoved. He found Ta'isi's "answers to my questions . . . evasive and I am satisfied that the charge has not been disproved."[101]

On December 21 deportation orders were signed. Ta'isi, Gurr, and Smyth were charged with "hindering the due performance by New Zealand of its functions and duties under the Mandate." Ta'isi and Gurr were ordered to leave Sāmoa for five years, Smyth for two.[102] News of these orders spread like wildfire around Sāmoa. Sāmoans who had abided by pleas to remain calm and peaceful in the face of the administration's provocations were dangerously enraged. As Christmas 1927 approached, Sāmoa was again like a volcano about to erupt.

Chapter Eight

Exile and the Road to Geneva (1928)

Sāmoa was in uproar over Christmas in 1927. Ta'isi had been ordered to leave Sāmoa, along with A. G. Smyth and E. W. Gurr. Vague charges had been laid against them—"preventing and hindering the due performance by the New Zealand government of its functions and duties under the Mandate and the due administration of the Executive Government of the Territory of Western Samoa." The men protested that such imprecise indictments had not been proved nor could they be disproved. Whatever "due performance" and "due administration" meant, it was clear that the due legal process of a trial and all attendant rights were being set aside.[1] An order authorized by the governor-general and issued by the administrator, General Richardson, was all that was required for these men, presumed guilty, to be exiled.[2] Mau supporters converged on Apia, incensed by the conduct of Richardson and the New Zealand government encapsulated in the findings of the 1927 *Royal Commission Concerning the Administration of Western Samoa,* by then only partially released, that completely exonerated the administrator of accusations of misrule.

Ta'isi's alleged criminality was based on consorting politically with Sāmoans as chairman of the Mau or the League of Samoa.[3] Richardson had deemed this act illegal from the public meetings with Europeans and Sāmoans in late 1926, though Ta'isi maintained he ceased this activity after Minister Nosworthy's visit to Sāmoa in mid-1927. Yet in late 1927 Richardson asked Ta'isi to do what he had previously judged illegal and again consort politically with Sāmoans. Richardson wanted Ta'isi to defuse the rising tensions in Apia by issuing orders to restive Sāmoans who had traveled to the capital. Richardson wanted them to return to their villages and homes, so much so that he undertook to end most of the previous banishments he had ordered if there was rapid cooperation.

Ta'isi must have flinched. Why should he do the administrator's bidding? Was this a trap set by Richardson to compromise him before the Mau? If he told them to return to their villages in exchange for Richardson's promise, and then it was reneged, only he stood to lose face. Ta'isi asked for a meeting with Richardson so they could come to an agreement. On December 23, Ta'isi met with Richardson for the last time on Sāmoan soil. Again Ta'isi's lawyer, F. D. Baxter, accompanied him to Vailima for this meeting. Ta'isi wanted to ensure that if he spoke to Mau supporters that he would do so with the latest secretary of native affairs, Australian Methodist Reverend F. G. Lewis, present. Lewis' presence would be a guarantee that the reversal of banishments was a genuine offer from the administrator.[4] His other purpose in calling the meeting was to clarify what Richardson had asked him to do in the presence of counsel: he was being asked to break the decree made by the administrator, and then backed by the minister, that Europeans and Sāmoans must not engage in political activity together. Also, he wanted to raise the possibility that if Sāmoan members of the Mau did not listen to him, he would not be left to shoulder the blame for any subsequent affray. He was not the Mau puppet master but Richardson did not recognize this. Ta'isi tried to make his "difficulties" apparent to the administrator. Richardson was both frustrated and dismissive of Ta'isi throughout the tense meeting. Any sense that Ta'isi was telling Richardson how to proceed fired the administrator up. Yet ultimately Richardson confirmed he would reverse previous banishments in a pragmatic act of clemency. Ta'isi's own predicament of imminent deportation was not raised.[5]

Ta'isi made the descent from New Zealand's seat of power on Mount Vaea on December 23 with small concessions; the peace of Sāmoa and his own fate still hung in the balance. He would not return to Vailima, where he had regularly been a guest of all three New Zealand administrators and probably the two German ones before them, for many years.

On Christmas Eve, he did as he promised and addressed Mau supporters. Reverend Lewis was on hand to endorse Ta'isi's claim about the administrator's offer of clemency. The meetings did not proceed as Ta'isi had anticipated. Mau supporters were still seething at the deportation orders; they were not in a cooperative mood. Even though Ta'isi played down the deportations, there were many "hot speeches" in response to his entreaties.[6] He was not able to quell the menacing anger.

On Christmas Day Ta'isi penned a letter to Reverend Lewis in a continued effort to make peace. He wrote that if "His Excellency could be persuaded to release the banished chiefs now, I feel confident our hands would be strengthened in working up a basis for negotiations which would lead to a settlement." He was also "pleased to advise you when I think the time is ripe" to hold another meeting with the Mau committee.[7] The letter also illuminated the pressure Ta'isi was experiencing as the day of his exile loomed. He would leave on the next *Tofua,* he told Lewis, "so I will be rushed to breaking point to complete all my business and family arrangements." He wanted to let Lewis know he was trying to broker a "settlement of the political controversy . . . solely in the interests of the Samoan people which I have always been happy to serve." "It does not devolve on me to do this, more especially in the position the Administrator has placed me," he insisted. He did "not approve of the methods now adopted by the Mau Committee" but he remained "fully in sympathy with the sentiments and aspirations of the Samoan people." He hoped "the day will soon come when the 'powers that be' will also appreciate" the Sāmoan people, "to the extent of granting such concessions as will restore the full confidence of the Samoans and thus establish lasting goodwill and tranquility."[8] The letter shows that Ta'isi still possessed his deep resolve to fight on, regardless of the personal penalties. Being a religious man, Ta'isi no doubt offered prayers at the Christmas Day service in the Tuaefu chapel for the protection of his large family, for peace to come to Sāmoa, for justice to be done, and for his exile to be short-lived.

His Christmas Day letter to Lewis went unanswered by the secretary of native affairs. Ta'isi wrote to him again on December 29, explaining the Mau committee had just met again, but as Lewis had not responded to his Christmas Day letter in any form (and as a consequence Ta'isi was not able to act), a vital opportunity was lost in making headway on a settlement with them.[9]

As 1927 turned into 1928, the grand celebrations of one year earlier were not repeated. A funereal atmosphere pervaded as Ta'isi prepared for his exile. Perhaps one bright spot for Ta'isi was that his racehorse, Loyal Irish, won both the Christmas Handicap and the

President's Handicap at the Apia Turf Club's annual race meeting on Boxing Day.[10]

After Ta'isi was served with Richardson's deportation order, he sought legal opinion in New Zealand and also from H. V. Evatt—the leading legal mind and future political figure—in Australia. Evatt advised Ta'isi not to submit to the order and instead wait to be arrested and then issue a writ of habeas corpus. For Ta'isi's legal protection, Evatt advocated a standoff with the administration. The situation was so volatile Ta'isi feared taking this course of action would trigger a violent confrontation. Instead, on January 5, he formally assented to his deportation order. He did so in a damning letter to Richardson that set the battle lines for the fight he would continue outside Sāmoa. Ta'isi "strongly protested" against the order (as did Smyth and Gurr) for numerous reasons. There were "no definite charge . . . laid against me" and there was also no evidence given in support of Richardson's decision "except the statements—written and verbal—of myself which were entirely in my favour. I was not confronted with any witness to enable any cross-examination" and "no oath was administered." "I have committed no offence against the laws of the land," he asserted. "Your order is based on the fact . . . that the Government cannot function . . . I desire to point out that such [a] situation cannot be attributed to any action on my part." Most damning, he said, was the fact that "I have not been given the opportunity of having my case dealt with under the ordinary rules of law and procedure—rules that have taken centuries to perfect—rules that protect an accused person under the laws of England and should not be set aside by any Act of the New Zealand Parliament, or the newly granted prerogative of the Administrator." "I and others have been subjected by Your Excellency, without proper trial, to a most grievous punishment for allegedly disturbing the country," yet "you have requested me in effect to 'pull the country together.'" Ta'isi concluded by reiterating the following:

> I will depart Western Samoa under this Protest, and in so doing I call Your Excellency's attention to the fact that I do so for the sake of preserving the peace of the Territory and avoiding a possibility of a more violent protest . . . by those who recognize the unjust treatment meted out to myself and others.

He vowed to pursue "redress for your wrongful order" and seek "full compensation for any financial loss sustained by me" as well as "refute the unfounded attacks on my loyalty to the British Flag and to assure my return to my beloved country."[11]

Richardson's reaction to Ta'isi's emboldened letter was encapsulated in his letter to Minister Nosworthy the following day. Sāmoans remained restless. Richardson was surprised the royal commission did not have the salutary effect on the Mau he hoped it would, although its findings were only partially reported in the press; the commission's full report was still not generally available (Harry Holland complained as late as January 27 that he had still not seen the report).[12] Sāmoans "have the minds of children and are only influenced by tangible evidence which deportation will provide," he wrote.[13] Ta'isi was due to leave Sāmoa January 13. Richardson had a week to wait out, to see if this prediction was correct. Once Ta'isi left Sāmoa, Richardson felt certain, the Mau would dissipate.

The day before he was due to leave Sāmoa, Ta'isi made detailed arrangements for his varied business and personal interests. His attorney would be held by "W. M Burnett and R. Kruse jointly and severally. All my personal and private affairs will be conducted by them." As for Tuaefu, "my residence will be closed during my absence." He would entrust the house and grounds to the care of his cousin, Masoe Tulele, who lived at Tuaefu with his extended family.[14] "Masoe will open the house every morning and close it every afternoon" and "send girls in to the House to sweep and dust once a week." Ta'isi made provision for wages, food, kerosene, and benzene for the Masoe family use. He also wanted fuels used to "keep the Lighting Plant going" that was on the Tuaefu grounds. Brother-in-law Harry W. Moors would also oversee the upkeep of Tuaefu and assist with payment of Masoe and others. Moors was to sell "car no. 36" while "van no. 82 will be propped up on blocks in the Tuaefu garage" and his cousin Tauvao "should visit Tuaefu once in a while to see to the engine." Regarding the Mau, he instructed that he was "responsible for certain unpaid expenses of the 'Mau' such as lawyers fees etc.," but he had "contributed my share" and the "Samoan 'Mau' members must pay the rest." He also entrusted his financial stake in the *Samoa Guardian* to Harry W. Moors, and he instructed that "I would like every effort made to keep" the paper "going without a break." A new editor, Mr. Tarr, was due from Suva to replace Gurr. Ta'isi wanted to ensure the "paper is carried on efficiently and the same policy is kept up." He stressed, "There must be no letting down on the policy of the paper," and Mr. Tarr would be "well versed" with that policy before he got there.[15]

Regarding O. F. Nelson and Company, Ta'isi wanted "the business of the Company . . . conducted in the usual way, the same policy will be followed." He felt "confident all faithful and loyal members of staff will co-operate with the management to maintain the position we hold in the Trade and Commerce of the Territory." The board of management would consist of W. M. Burnett (secretary), R. Kruse (branch manager), and J. Helg (merchandise manager), and Harry W. Moors "remains a director of the Company and will sign with the Secretary such documents which require the signature of a director." Ta'isi put stress on "punctuality" that "should be observed by every member of the Staff and it is due to the company that the staff devote their attention and service during Office Hours." Ta'isi wanted extensive reports on the various aspects of his business by "every mail." He noted that there may be a "native boycott of stores" (as part of the Mau protest against New Zealand goods) and "when this comes about and the pinch is severely felt, the stations with the lowest turnovers must be temporarily closed, though traders who had nowhere else to go could remain on the premise and be paid half their salaries to upkeep the stations." He wanted to ensure good staff were kept and the assets of the company looked after. The complexities of his business would be left in numerous hands to weather whatever lay ahead after he left Sāmoa the next day.[16]

On the same day—January 12—the *Samoa Guardian* editorial stoked the already tense situation. Its editorial vigorously defended Ta'isi, Gurr, and Smyth, as expected, saying "the Administrator has gone as far as the law will permit him and he has fired his last bomb."[17] The paper optimistically predicted that in twelve months "nearly all, if not all, the changes for reform in the Administration submitted by the 'Mau' [will] have been put into practice." The Mau, which Richardson had dismissed as an "insignificant body . . . is now of such force and weight that General Richardson's Administration cannot function successfully." Instead of adopting a conciliatory policy to achieve "peace and contentment . . . we have an administrator heaping on acts towards the accomplishment of his own hidden policy which look toward a general uprising with violence." The *Samoa Guardian* went so far as to claim, "It appears at times as if the Administrator desires a condition of open revolt so as to bring out his military experience 'to save his face.'"[18]

The day Ta'isi was due to leave, Richardson reported to Nosworthy that "several hundred natives have assembled here from Savai'i and are displaying a foolish attitude and talking wildly about resisting

Mr. Nelson's departure, capturing Mulinu'u [the seat of government] & c."[19] Sworn reports from witnesses sympathetic to the administrator—"the Administrator's Intelligence Department," according to the *Samoa Guardian*—described the scene to Richardson who stayed well away from the waterfront.[20] "Mau police" dressed in uniforms supposedly supplied by O. F. Nelson and Co. were visible in the streets and "some of these bogus policemen" accompanied Ta'isi as he went on board the *Tofua,* Richardson reported back to Wellington. Richardson's *papālagi* spies reported that Ta'isi addressed "Mau natives," telling them, "I ask you to stick to the Mau stick to it stick to it." As this firsthand report was passed along the line, Ta'isi's words were altered to "rely on me . . . I am going to win a victory for Samoa . . . I ask you to stick to the Mau stick to it stick to it."[21] This quote was duly reproduced in the press, aiding the government version of events that maintained Ta'isi was the *éminence grise* of the Mau.[22]

The *Samoa Guardian* offered a different view than Richardson's of Ta'isi's departure. There was no menacing crowd gathered at the waterfront. Instead relatives and friends gathered at the Customs Wharf at two thirty that afternoon to see off the deportees. The *Samoa Guardian* reported Ta'isi thanked the gathering for "making no demonstration and for their resolution for peace." The deportations were "steps towards victory for the people who desire changes in the policy of the New Zealand Government," the paper reported Ta'isi as saying. "The Mau can be strong without using force and without disobeying laws." His final words to the crowd before he stepped onto the launch that would convey his party to the *Tofua* were "act peacefully and victory will be theirs."[23]

The rival *Samoa Times* was jubilant at the departure of Ta'isi and Smyth. (Gurr would leave for American Sāmoa at a later date. He was denied entry there, so he traveled to New Zealand.[24]) Western Sāmoa would soon have a brighter outlook than it has had in months, the paper triumphed, because some "arch disturbers" were leaving today. It described "Nelsonian propaganda grievances" they predicted would dissipate now Mr. Nelson was exiled from Sāmoa for five years.[25] Press reports in New Zealand were divided in favor of the government or for the Mau cause, as was the established pattern of coverage on Sāmoa troubles. The volume of stories (more than one hundred New Zealand press stories in January 1928 alone) about the deportations showed how much the story interested New Zealanders.[26] The *Auckland Star* ran a letter to the editor that argued deportations without trial were "contrary to British law and sentiment" and New Zealand was reversing the Magna Carta's protections that underpinned justice.[27] Other articles followed this line, arguing the deportations were an outrage against centuries of established British law. In other pieces, fact and rumor often got equal billing. While Ta'isi was en route to New Zealand, a number of papers falsely reported that he was selling his Sāmoan businesses.[28] The *Evening Post* had him retiring to the South of France, where, they claimed, he owned a property.[29] As Ta'isi's business arrangements before his departure show, he had no intention of selling and wanted to maintain a "business as usual" approach in his absence.

Intense public interest in the deportations finally compelled Prime Minister Coates to give an official explanation. He chose January 23, the day the *Tofua* was due to dock in Auckland in the late afternoon, to issue a lengthy statement. His admissions were quite extraordinary. He began by noting that "there seems to be some misapprehension throughout the country as to the reasons underlying the Government's action in approving the deportation from Samoa of Messers Nelson, Gurr and Smyth." Coates claimed, "It is not generally recognized . . . that our administration of Samoa has for many months past been very largely ineffective." Sāmoans were "seriously disunited," a "large section of them are in a state of passive resistance to constituted authority," and the "King's writ is not running." The rebels were refusing orders of the court and to pay their taxes. They neglected their plantations and kept their children from government schools. Civil disobedience had gone so far as to become a matter of life and death, Coates argued. Mau supporters were "rejecting medical help and neglecting sanitary precautions." So dangerous was the rebellion that mothers "subject to Mau influence" refused to bring their babies to child welfare officers and so avert infant mortality. Some Mau villages were now "no better than cesspits" and an outbreak of disease was expected as a result. The Mau had derided the medical department, Coates argued, and so "destroyed the confidence of the natives in our health administration." As a result "many innocent lives must be lost in Samoa."[30]

How did Coates account for this catastrophic situation? He reiterated that a handful of Europeans were stirring up trouble because of prohibition and the administration's intervention in the copra business that, he noted, directly impacted Ta'isi's extensive business interests.

The recently concluded royal commission had confirmed the causes of the Mau and so, as far as Coates was concerned, "I am no longer called upon to prove the facts of this sorry business." New Zealand's duty, vested in it by the League of Nations, was to govern Sāmoa, but Ta'isi was constructing an alternative government complete with a Mau police force some of whom, Coates explained, "actually accompanied Mr Nelson on board the *Tofua* prior to his departure from Samoa." New Zealand had a duty to reinstate "law and order" in Sāmoa. "We had ample power, if we chose, to enforce the law" in the same way "we would in New Zealand—by force." But New Zealand shied away from this as "it would have involved inflicting grave hardship on many natives who have been, in our opinion, merely dupes of others more responsible. It might have even led to bloodshed and the loss of innocent lives." But New Zealand had an alternative, which was to amend the *Samoa Act* in 1927 so the administration could remove "three persons" from Sāmoa. Coates argued, "There is nothing unprecedented or unconstitutional in this course," nor does it infringe "in any degree the fundamental principles of British administration." Deportation without trial "is possessed and exercised by the Pacific administrations around us," in American Sāmoa (he cited the governor's harsh response to the 1920 Mau in American Sāmoa) and British-ruled Fiji. This power was "contemplated even by the Magna Carta" he went so far as to claim. New Zealand had only three courses of action at their disposal, said Coates: let the situation alone, bloodshed, or to remove the three people responsible. Given all the evidence Coates presented he "found it hard to understand the solicitude that has been shown for Mr Nelson and his colleagues by the leader of the Labour Party and by a section of the press and public." Rather than directing their sympathy at a "handful of Europeans," the government had opted to "prefer the interests of the large number of natives" and so "we are satisfied that the course we have adopted is correct and that it will be justified by the event."[31]

It should not have been surprising to Coates that New Zealanders were confused about the scale and depth of discontent in Sāmoa. The government had delivered mixed messages to the New Zealand public. On the one hand, it had downplayed the significance and pervasiveness of the Mau from the outset. On the other, it had acknowledged discontent but refused to accept this discontent—so widespread and catastrophic, according to the prime minister—had anything to do with the administrator, but instead was solely due to the influence of a handful of Europeans, led by Ta'isi. Sāmoans were so easily led, this argument ran, that they did as they were directed. Without this direction, they would resume their normal lives, and Richardson would return to his position of high esteem and power.

Reactions in the press to Coates' statement were forceful. The *Auckland Star* ran a story that argued, "The Prime Minister, who thought that there was nothing to explain before, has almost now explained too much." Coates' "suggestion that those who have asked questions about the deportations are more solicitous for the welfare of Mr Nelson that for 'the health, welfare and prosperity of the Samoan people' . . . is offensive and foolish to an almost unbelievable degree."[32] Harry Holland was only too pleased to weigh in on the prime minister's explanation for the deportations. He charged Coates with "wholly evading any reference to the real reasons why the Samoans are in revolt." It is "not the work done by agitators, either European or Samoan, but our own maladministration" that is the "cause of the grave unrest which exists to-day."[33] Needless to say, the antigovernment sectors in New Zealand and Sāmoa remained unsatisfied with the government's deeds and justification for them.

The *Tofua* steamed into this maelstrom and Auckland Harbor on Friday afternoon, January 23. Ta'isi was confronted by press at the wharf asking for his response to the prime minister's statement that he had not yet seen. He remained tight-lipped and said he would consult his legal counsel before making any statement. He did refute the rumors he was selling his businesses and retiring to his property in southern France. Both rumors were fabricated, he said, and were "part of the propaganda against himself and the Mau."[34] Ta'isi mustered his legal defense in the first weeks of his exile, while making arrangements for where he and his family would live while they were in New Zealand. Ta'isi was certain his exile would be short-lived, and so looked for temporary accommodation but in one of the most salubrious of Auckland's suburbs, Remuera.

Meanwhile, in Sāmoa, the deportations were not having the effect Richardson assured the government they would. Tensions escalated. Mau from Savai'i paraded along the main street of Apia "singing defiant and obscene songs against the government," Richardson reported.[35] Mau police uniforms were still being worn (one informant reported his eighteen-year-old daughter had seen one—an indication of the quality of the administration's intelligence). Richardson admitted there were no laws to prevent Samoans "dressing themselves in any way they desire" as existed in other jurisdictions, like Australia's Papua colony.[36] Richardson would soon fix that. The boycott of New Zealand goods came into effect, and a small police force was dispatched to Apia.[37]

Richardson also started to move to have other troublesome Europeans removed from Sāmoa. This time he targeted S. H. Meredith, George Westbrook, and Arthur Williams. The New Zealand government was not of the same mind. Nosworthy told Richardson, "I think you will appreciate the fact that if you desire to punish any of these offenders for the trouble they have caused action must be taken through the Courts."[38] The solicitor general, Arthur Fair, was also of the opinion Richardson did not have the legal powers to deport other Europeans on the basis he wished to. Fair's letter reveals the sensitivity within the government for Richardson's stature and reputation. He made a point of saying, "Without intending any criticism of the Administrator's action."[39] The regard the government had for Richardson was blinding. However, by the end of January, as Richardson's predictions did not eventuate, they began to question his judgment, albeit in small ways. The government still tried to salvage their case: a "mild outbreak" of "bacillary dysentery" was reported on Savai'i—right on cue—and so Coates claimed "my fears on the subject" have been "justified." No one was to blame for this, but the Mau, he said.[40] Sir James Parr, the high commissioner in London, reported back to Wellington that the prime minister's statement along with the "publication of findings of the Royal Commission" had led to "sympathetic leaders in 'Scotsmen' and 'Manchester Guardian' whilst 'London dailies silent.'" The all-important views from the mother country seemed to support New Zealand, and Parr predicted the League of Nations "will be satisfied with outcome of enquiry" due in June.[41]

In early February, Ta'isi gave his defiant reply to Coates' justification for the deportations. The *Evening Post* reported Ta'isi as challenging "facts used by Mr. Coates and declares the Mau is not responsible for the reported outbreak of dysentery." He restated that the administrator had a case to answer for the discontent and "submits that he and his colleagues have been banished for no other reason than that they have presented complaints to the Government concerning the Administration." No charge was laid against him and no trial held. The prime minister "took over four weeks after the deportation orders were made 'to think out for publication excuses for the outrage.'" Also the prime minister released his statement when Ta'isi was due to arrive, depriving him once again of adequate time to respond, until now. He still had not been given the royal commission's report, and this was after the government had sent out multiple copies to parties they wished to influence.[42] High Commissioner Parr had received full reports one month earlier, on December 22, and he had distributed them to papers in Europe and Britain where the government wanted to maximize favorable publicity of its findings.[43] Yet the leader of the opposition and Ta'isi—who rated considerable mention in the report—had not yet been given access to it one month later. For Ta'isi, not having the report meant his legal recourse was stalled until his legal counsel had the report in hand.

Ta'isi's rejoinder launched a searing attack on the prime minister. He chastened Coates for his "amusing" position that the New Zealand people were somehow at fault for not realizing the situation in Sāmoa. Ta'isi asked, "Who but Mr Coates is responsible for hitherto suppressing information? He has been pretending for long enough that the trouble in Samoa is not serious, and now he has the nerve to speak as though the public ought to be aware that the trouble is serious." The situation *was* serious, Ta'isi stressed, "and the position is wholly due to maladministration, tyranny and other causes for which the Administrator and the Government are responsible." Added to this, Coates was not accurate in his representation of what was happening, Ta'isi argued. Coates' claim, for instance, that children were being kept from government schools was false. The director of education in Sāmoa contradicted the prime minister on this point. Ta'isi also punctured Coates' accusation the Mau were responsible for the latest outbreak of dysentery. There had been outbreaks before during Richardson's time as administrator. In 1926, Richardson wrote to Ta'isi in Sydney about an outbreak and claimed it was "endemic" to Sāmoa (which Ta'isi challenged at the time). Now "the Mau is the present excuse. Neither excuse is true," he asserted.

Ta'isi and the Mau were not responsible for the spread of disease. Nor would he accept he was attempting to fashion an alternate government evident in the Mau police. On this accusation, he said, "I did my best to stop the formation of the Mau police. The Administrator knows that I have used the utmost efforts and have not hesitated even to sacrifice my own dignity to preserve peace at all costs." Yet the peacemakers, himself and Smyth and Gurr, were deported. Why? Because they dared to criticize Richardson's shift in governing style from 1926. "He shed his ingratiating ways . . . when he began to feel his feet and realised he had a free hand from the New Zealand Government. He became a petty tyrant and dictator." The legislative council was reduced to a "farce," and he banished fifty-six chiefs before the Mau was formed and fifty after. Ta'isi's intense criticisms touched on the long-standing *faipule* grievance, and again he dismissed prohibition or copra trading as the cause of the discontent. On recent administration attempts to combat tensions he said:

> I protest the sending of extra police to Samoa. I protest against the demonstration with Maxim guns, made at the rifle range, and the silly talk about the bomber and his Mills' bombs and the fleet hovering within call. My protest will not affect the Government, I am sure, but I want to put it on record because I believe that now, not only the Administrator but also the New Zealand Government wants to provoke trouble.

The truth will come out, Ta'isi believed. When it does "what a sorry spectacle New Zealand must cut before the world unless it repudiates the acts of its Government and the Samoan Administration."[44] Ta'isi might be in exile, but he was not cowed.

Ta'isi poured his energy into fighting his deportation. With the paralysis in the New Zealand government, the only hope for justice for Ta'isi and the Mau lay overseas in Geneva, at the League of Nations, and at the Privy Council in London. He prepared for decisions in both forums that would take place mid-1928. Before he left New Zealand in March to take the fight to Europe, Ta'isi became actively involved in a grassroots movement based in Auckland, where he aligned himself closely with the Labour Party—especially its leader, Harry Holland, who continued to champion the cause—and other liberals. Regular meetings were held over the country, speeches were made, and New Zealand voters heard unfiltered accounts of what was happening in Sāmoa. On February 12 the Empress Theatre in Wellington was filled with people who came to hear Holland deliver a fiery address on New Zealand's maladministration of Sāmoa. Ta'isi was there, too, and reported "the place was packed, there being over 1,000 of a mixed audience." More than half the audience "were not members of the Labour Party," he reckoned. The pleasing presence of "expensively dressed and bejeweled ladies" indicated to Ta'isi that the demography of Sāmoa's supporters extended beyond the working class: they included voters for Coates' Reform Party or the other conservative party, the United Party, led by Sir Joseph Ward. Ta'isi was impressed by Holland and his performance. "I was surprised at his eloquence and mastery of the subject. He is a very well read man and a student of Samoan affairs being a great admirer of Stevenson and his works," he wrote. A resolution protesting against the drastic laws was "carried unanimously." Another meeting in Wellington, where Holland would also speak, was scheduled in a week.[45] Sir Māui Pōmare, still a senior minister in the Coates government, continued his support for Ta'isi and the Mau, though in less public forms than Holland. Ta'isi and Sir Māui, thanks to Ta'isi's New Zealand exile, would spend a lot more time together. The two men and their families became very close.[46]

Ta'isi was committed to a peaceful course for the Mau. His devotion to "passive resistance" was unwavering, but what he did fight—in earnest and with sophistication from 1928—was a paper war. In Sāmoa the *Samoa Guardian* continued to publish, though Richardson issued an *Order in Council* on January 23 preventing anyone from publishing in the Sāmoan language without his permission (missionaries were excepted). He was trying to prevent the publication of the *O Le Matua Tausi Samoa*—the Sāmoan-language supplement of the paper. This paper nevertheless continued its fearless protest against the administration, tracking the fate of the deportees outside Sāmoa and disseminating cartoons of New Zealand origin that mocked Richardson and other government officials. In May 1929 the paper moved operations to Auckland and published as the *NZ Samoa Guardian,* though the *Samoa Guardian* continued, in challenging circumstances, to appear until February 1930. In both forms it served as the main means of communication for the Mau and was the newspaper of record for the protest movement.

In addition to the *Samoa Guardian,* Ta'isi wrote letters, many of them. He wrote to former administrator Robert Logan (who lent his support to Ta'isi) and even his old adversary Robert Tate, who did not respond.[47] As well as these administration figures, he wrote to contacts all over the globe: business contacts, friends, acquaintances, foreign politicians, or those interested in Sāmoa, from anthropologists to fans of Robert Louis Stevenson. Stevenson put Sāmoa on the map for an international community of readers, and his enduring popularity meant Sāmoa remained a place of sympathetic interest for his many fans scattered around the globe. Sāmoa featured in his later fiction writing as well as his nonfiction account of the political situation circa 1880s and 1890s (*A Footnote to History*) before his death at Vailima in 1894. Stevenson was loved by Sāmoans and given the name Tusitala in recognition of their high regard. Colonial agents were less enamored. The governor of Fiji and consul general for the Western Pacific (that took in Sāmoa at the time), Sir John Thurston, wanted to deport Stevenson for his interfering ways in Sāmoan politics. This deportation did not come to pass as Thurston's quest was not supported by the British government. The fact that even the revered Stevenson was considered fit for deportation at one time was not lost on Ta'isi, who raised this uncomfortable fact often during his own deportation travails.[48]

The Stevenson connection was particularly concentrated in the United States. Stevenson's stepdaughter, Isobel Field, who used her Sāmoan name, Teuila, in her correspondence with Ta'isi, spearheaded an American-based campaign of publicity about the Sāmoan troubles from New York.[49] Clem Yore, a noted man of letters from Colorado, had spent time in Sāmoa and was an enthusiastic supporter of the Mau and was no fan of Richardson. The feeling was apparently mutual; "Richardson hates me like poison," Yore wrote.[50] When Ta'isi and Yore began corresponding in 1928, Yore encouraged Ta'isi to make contact with the Stevenson Club of England and Scotland. They "ought to be importuned . . . to side with the Mau and you." (Incidentally, Richardson—though he lived in the famous house Stevenson built—was not a fan of "RLS," telling Yore that Stevenson was "a muchly overestimated man."[51]) Yore was not a man of great political influence, but other correspondents were. Ta'isi had the support of Quincy Roberts, who was US consul in Fiji during Ta'isi's exile and had previously been posted to Western Sāmoa when he presumably developed his close friendship with Ta'isi and his family. Roberts was sympathetic, but had to tread carefully. When he was writing a history of the Sāmoan islands, he sent Ta'isi the unpublished manuscript for comment. During exchanges about this book Roberts told Ta'isi that although he knew the New Zealand period of Sāmoan history better than any other because he was there for eight years of it, "I am more or less restricted in my comments upon recent happenings in Samoa by reason of the official position I now hold."[52] The book, *A History of the Samoan Islands*, was published in 1929. Their correspondence continued after this, with Roberts adhering to his sympathetic stance for the Mau and his friendship with Ta'isi.

The US attitude to the Mau was interesting. In early 1928, the governor of American Sāmoa had to contend with the flare-up of a

Mau movement there, too. The New Zealand government characterized this as a direct result of the Mau in Western Sāmoa, as if political protest in the two Sāmoas was a contagious disease ("the 'Mau' Committee here are in communication with the agitators in Tutuila").[53] Unlike himself, the new governor, Captain Graham, immediately acted in a conciliatory manner with "a self constituted body of Samoans," Richardson notified Wellington. Sāmoans there had announced—"so I am informed"—they would not pay taxes. Richardson feared Captain Graham's actions "will create great difficulties for himself and re-act on the 'Mau' in this Territory." "Like the 'Mau' Natives here," Richardson went on, they "have no clear objective other than to give themselves power and prestige in the eyes of their people and gratify their vanity." Predictably, Richardson could not perceive any legitimate grievance, but "half-castes" were to blame for "disturbing the Natives." The *Samoa Guardian* had duly reported these happenings as "a way to discredit me in the eyes of Samoans," Richardson wrote with bitterness.[54] The situation in American Sāmoa did not deteriorate, and their 1920 "Mau" troubles were not repeated.[55]

Like the damning comparison to the handling of the 1918 influenza epidemic in the two Sāmoas, New Zealand's administration suffered when American Sāmoa was brought into view and it was upheld (rightly or wrongly) as best practice for colonial governance by the *Samoa Guardian* and Ta'isi. US correspondents were a central part of Ta'isi's letter-writing campaign and would increasingly be so, as the Mau campaign from 1930 focused on treaties with the United States, Britain, and Germany over the Sāmoan islands. Ta'isi was also in contact with networks of pacifist organizations like "War Resisters International."[56] Like the US connections, these organizational links would grow in importance as the campaign dragged on, though in 1928 Ta'isi could not have conceived of this course of events.

In late February 1928 Ta'isi was preparing to leave Auckland for Sydney. Sir John Findlay K. C., his counsel in Wellington, was at the time "preparing a Petition to the League of Nations for me to sign."[57] Also, he wrote, "I have just despatched [*sic*] to Samoa a monster petition for the Samoans to sign for the League of Nations."[58] This monster petition comprised 140 facsimiles of the petition that was disbursed to villages across Sāmoa. On March 9 more than seven thousand men "from the highest degrees to the humblest" signed it, giving their rank and village as well as their name.[59] Ta'isi was sure this petition would "inform the world the Samoans will not be satisfied to stay under

New Zealand rule." They would be submitted to the New Zealand government first, and "I will be in Europe when they reach the League of Nations in Geneva and [I] will be prepared to give further particulars if required."[60] Ta'isi continued his contact with H. V. Evatt, who remained both sympathetic to the Sāmoan cause and a legal adviser on the multipronged actions Ta'isi and the Mau were involved in. (Evatt later wrote a pamphlet when he was a justice of the high court of Australia, *The British Dominions and Mandatories,* demonstrating the expertise he developed in cases involving the ample legal "grey areas" in New Guinea, South West Africa and Sāmoa.[61]) Ta'isi was also getting considerable advice and assistance from the former New South Wales premier and elder statesman, Sir Joseph Carruthers, a staunchly conservative imperialist (he put Ta'isi in touch with Evatt in the first instance).[62] This relationship further demonstrated the unlikely but extremely important networks Ta'isi fostered that underpinned the Mau campaign. The Joseph Carruthers connection also gave the Mau more substantive Australian dimensions that included a direct link to Charles Brunsdon Fletcher at the *Sydney Morning Herald,* who gave the Mau cause publicity that aggravated New Zealand officials greatly. Ta'isi supplied photographs of himself and his family to Carruthers and another New South Wales politician who he befriended (E. H. Farrar) that might "come in handy for publication in Australia."[63]

From Sydney, Ta'isi left to do battle in Europe. His trans-Pacific voyage avoided Apia but took him to Pago Pago on April 6. New Zealand requested that he be refused landing rights. Instead His Excellency, Governor Graham, and "his good lady" greeted Ta'isi on board.[64] On land he met briefly with friends who traveled to Pago Pago for the occasion, like George Westbrook. He then sailed on to Honolulu. Here he was welcomed by Lorrin Thurston, the owner of the *Honolulu Advertiser,* who also gave the Mau cause his support at this time through fostering publicity; this was a curious position for Thurston given his leading role in eroding the Hawaiian monarchy during the 1887 Bayonet Constitution.[65] Thurston spent the day with Ta'isi, driving him, his oldest daughter, Viopapa, and the secretary of Ta'isi's Auckland office, Rex Pleasants, around Honolulu and taking them to lunch. Ta'isi was thankful to Thurston. He wrote to him expressing his gratitude for his "very kind hospitality" and for giving Ta'isi the opportunity to "pay my respects to His Excellency Governor Farrington—thanks to you." Ta'isi also told him "the interest you have

Figure 8.1. Ta'isi and all his daughters circa 1927. From left, Salafai Masoe (cousin), Viopapa, Piliopo, Taufau, Malienafau behind Ta'isi shoulder, Sina, and Noue. This image was probably supplied by Ta'isi for publication in Australia. With permission Fairfax Syndication.

taken in the cause of the Samoan people is also greatly appreciated."[66] Thurston not only shaped the content of his own newspaper—the *Honolulu Advertiser*—he also sent on information to counterparts placed at the helm of other great papers in the United States. After Honolulu Ta'isi traveled to San Francisco, then overland by train through Chicago to New York, where he boarded a ship for London.[67] All along the way, Ta'isi "left a trail behind him" of press articles illuminating the Mau cause.[68]

Two days after Ta'isi passed through Pago Pago, Richardson left Sāmoa. As Ta'isi prepared for the David-and-Goliath battle that lay ahead, Richardson's fortunes as administrator sank. Ta'isi described the situation in late February 1928 as "the Samoans are leading poor Richardson a merry life. They have made a joke of the New Zealand Fleet. The whole situation is beginning more than ever comical. It beats anything Gilbert & Sullivan ever put up."[69] Ta'isi took a lighthearted view on this occasion of a deteriorating situation that was equal parts serious—and potentially deadly—drama and farce. Richardson had predicted the Mau would disappear once New Zealand cut off the movement's European leadership, but the very opposite happened. The Mau swelled in size and visibility in the weeks after Ta'isi departed on the *Tofua*. The administration tried everything—new legislation and military muscle flexing on land and sea—but it did little to quell the dissent. The warships, HMS *Dunedin* and HMS *Diomede,* were sent to intimidate the Mau—now led by a very defiant Tupua Tamasese Lea'lofi III, a development that should have destroyed the notion the Mau was only a European political intrigue. Richardson issued a new version of the *Maintenance of Authority in Native Affairs Ordinance* forbidding Mau members from congregating in Apia, holding meetings, wearing Mau uniforms (a purple *lava-lava* with a white band around the bottom), or collecting funds.[70] It also deemed that a Sāmoan carrying a stone or a stick was criminal. Offenses committed under this ordinance carried jail terms of up to six months.[71]

On February 23, an armed force of four hundred New Zealand troops landed and set about arresting Mau members, who had gathered in such large numbers that 250 were arrested and sent to Vaimea Gaol. The next day, another two hundred Mau were arrested but could not be accommodated at the jail, so they were driven out of town and released. On February 25, between two hundred and three hundred Mau attempted to enter Apia but were stopped at the Fugalei Bridge by troops. The next day, another two hundred protesters were arrested but with so many imprisoned, the prison system was utterly overwhelmed. These increasingly absurd clashes continued until March 10, when repeated attempts to capture Tupua Tamasese Lea'lofi failed, and the HMS *Dunedin* retreated to New Zealand. The HMS *Diomede* left for Suva seven days later, around the time Richardson's replacement, Colonel Stephen Allen, was announced. Wild reports were published in New Zealand, not least by the *Auckland Herald,* claiming things had become so bad that white women were being molested and insulted on the streets of Apia by the Mau. This suggestion, Ta'isi responded, was "wicked and malicious," not to mention untrue. "A white woman at Samoa is safer than she is in Queen St. Auckland."[72] When Colonel Allen left New Zealand in April to take up his post, he was accompanied by a contingent of police; the Sāmoa administration now had the capacity to bring the Mau into line using force.

During this month of high drama, Prime Minister Coates was blatantly urged by the New Zealand governor-general Charles Fergusson

Figure 8.2. Colonel Stephen Allen leaves New Zealand to take up his post as the new administrator of Sāmoa in April 1928 accompanied by police reinforcements attired in Great War uniforms. Sir George Grey Collections, Auckland Libraries, AWNS—19280426-38-3.

(going well beyond his constitutional role) to use violence against the Mau. Fergusson was enraged that the "moral effect of our armed forces has been lost owing to the natives having become alive to the fact that they have been forbidden to use force . . . our bluff has been called and exposed . . . Imperial troops have been publicly derided and brought into contempt." Fergusson wanted New Zealand to act with "firmness and decision." He told Coates in mid-March that "the immediate arrest of Tamasese and the dispersal of the Mau from Apia at all costs are essential steps to be taken."[73]

Coates balked at using violence, though it was certainly discussed.[74] He told Fergusson the intelligence received from Apia was that the "arrest of Tamasese by force of arms" could not have been effected by the navy without the "possibility of injuring and perhaps killing a large number of natives." The commodore in command was "deeply impressed with the difficulty of applying naval force to ignorant and childlike natives who have offered no violence on any occasion." Coates acknowledged, like Fergusson, that he feared "our prestige has suffered" and that while "we are determined to remedy the position by force if this is the only way," the government felt they had acted appropriately against the Mau who had stuck to their "pacific course."[75] What Coates did not admit to Fergusson in this letter—although Richardson would reveal it to the Permanent Mandates

Commission in June, asking them not to "record [it] in the minutes"—was that New Zealand had taken care not to "prejudice" the Permanent Mandates Commission's opinion of New Zealand ahead of the June meetings by using force against Sāmoans when tensions ran so high in March.[76]

Ta'isi arrived in London on May 10 with Viopapa and Rex Pleasants. As well as throwing himself into business affairs, he was hard at work preparing for the leave to appeal to the Privy Council and the League hearings. Initially the Privy Council was due to hear the leave to appeal on June 29, but the case was rescheduled to July 9. The legal groundwork for this hearing and the Permanent Mandates Commission hearings on Sāmoa, due to commence on June 20, began long before Ta'isi arrived in London. Ta'isi's lawyer, John Roberts of Jacques and Company, with offices in Holborn Circus, did the lion's share of the work on both legal fronts and would become Ta'isi's friend during the time they spent together in London and traveling to Geneva to the League of Nations. To represent him at the Privy Council, and to get legal advice on the petitions to the League, Ta'isi engaged the services of Stafford Cripps, then a leading King's Counsel and soon to be leading Labour Party politician.[77] Like Harry Holland in New Zealand and H. V. Evatt in Australia, Ta'isi gravitated to Labour Party figures in London to pursue Sāmoan interests as the party's ethos about draconian colonial rule were shared across the three interconnected countries. Regardless of the prestigious people he had representing him, Ta'isi was experiencing great difficulties communicating with Sāmoa from London as he prepared the cases. Censorship prevented his telegrams being received in Apia or ones being sent to him from there. Despite this great frustration, he did manage to receive a cablegram from Sāmoa with Tupua Tamasese Lea'lofi's signed power of attorney "reciting his authority and giving you [Ta'isi] full power to act for Sāmoan petitioners at Geneva or elsewhere."[78]

Following closely in Ta'isi's wake on this long journey was Richardson. Traveling with his daughter Rona, Richardson took the same route to San Francisco, Chicago, New York, and then on to London and the Continent. One passenger who greeted his ship, *Tahiti,* when it arrived at San Francisco thought Sir George "the most amiable gentleman in the British Empire." The British consul in San Francisco entertained Sir George. When the press interviewed the general, he tried to undo the impressions of the Sāmoan situation given recently by Ta'isi. Richardson kept to the well-worn government script about the Mau and argued he had no need to further refute Ta'isi's claims as the royal commission had put all the Mau accusations to rest.[79] Once Richardson had made the journey "home" to England, he was invited to the Royal Box at the Olympia, but could not go as his luggage had not yet arrived. In the following days, he met with many men involved in colonial affairs and with knowledge of the League, planning his forthcoming appearance in Geneva with Sir James Parr. He also marveled at the great changes in London since the war and enjoyed London's attractions and society.[80] A highlight was that his daughter Rona was presented at "the second Court at Buckingham Palace" with several other New Zealand "ladies."[81] He left for the continent on June 13.[82]

Ta'isi arrived in Geneva first on June 14 and checked into the best rooms in one of Geneva's finest hotels (the Grand Hôtel Beau Rivage) with "a suite of lawyers."[83] Richardson arrived soon after and, it was reported, he checked into more economical accommodation, the Ward Hotel. This was not accurate: Richardson would stay at the equally luxurious Bergues Hotel, adjacent to Pont du Mont Blanc, and inhabit the same Geneva precinct as Ta'isi. Richardson caught sight of Ta'isi in a restaurant "in evening dress" as he strolled around after dinner on his first night. Seeing Ta'isi in this place made Richardson's bitterness rise. He had heard gossip that "Nelson has a very nice villa in the Rivieria—this has been his scheme for years," he wrote.[84]

Appearances might suggest these two men inhabited similar worlds in Geneva; they did not. Beneath the elegance of Geneva a raft of ideological clashes converged on this world city because of these two men. Both represented a form of governance diametrically opposed to the other. Richardson staunchly supported the old imperial order of complete European dominance over "less evolved" races. Ta'isi wanted the self-rule colonized peoples had demanded since 1776 with varying degrees of success. The body that functioned as a world government, the League of Nations, would adjudicate who was right and who was wrong. It was a showdown.

Chapter Nine

"If There Is Any Justice at All" (1928)

Ta'isi was feeling hopeful on June 19, 1928. He wrote to Sir Māui Pōmare from Geneva, telling him the Permanent Mandates Commission (PMC) would begin its three-day hearings on Sāmoa later that day. "I have had very interesting and courteous interviews" with "several" delegates to the commission, he reported.[1] "I know they are fully alive to the situation, and would take the first opportunity, if such be possible, of giving me a hearing." He had prepared statements for circulation (that he was also sending to Sir Māui). There was a "voluminous" amount of other documentation the commission needed in order to assess the situation, which Ta'isi feared would mean "the matter will be postponed until the September Session." If that happens, "I will be here again to stand by in case I am needed." A potential delay was not ideal as the PMC "must recognise that an early settlement is necessary as the Samoan situation cannot remain much longer as it is."[2]

Ta'isi knew this was a pivotal moment; and he was anticipating a profound shift in the power balance in Sāmoa that would have international repercussions. He told friend and US diplomat, Quincy Roberts, that he felt "confident that some important developments may shortly take place" in Geneva.[3] To his mind, any member of the PMC imbued with the League's proclaimed intention to protect people in the mandates and guide them toward self-rule would see the merit of the Mau case. For Ta'isi, it was obvious what had to happen. "If there is any justice at all," he told Sir Māui, "I cannot help but feel that in a very short while the cause of the Samoan people will be viewed in a very different light from that expounded by the New Zealand authorities."[4]

Ta'isi possessed this optimism despite the fact he had been denied the opportunity to appear before the PMC himself and officially present the Mau case. All the mandatory powers strenuously protested the proposed change that would allow "malcontents" such a voice, but the PMC could make exceptions in the "most exceptional of circumstances."[5] The PMC did not deem the Sāmoan case exceptional so Ta'isi would have to be content to make representations in writing and informally, where he could.[6]

While Ta'isi was hopeful, Sir George Richardson had been very apprehensive. "In the face of the lies—malice—abuse and underhand scheming to injure me," he felt he could not "hold [his] head up very high" in Geneva. "The press of the World has attacked me," Richardson complained to Sir Francis Bell, as they feed off the "cunning, malicious and lying propaganda spread" by the Mau.[7] Ta'isi "got the *Journal Geneve* to publish an article which did not flatter me," so the mandate commissioners could not have missed the criticism of Richardson Ta'isi had spread through the international media.[8] Not only had Richardson's name and reputation been traduced; he was also nervous about how the German member of the commission, Dr. Ludwig Kastl, would treat him.[9] The enemy of the Great War might still be marking Richardson as these newer, Sāmoan ones were. Richardson knew Ta'isi had met with several commissioners, but "that was just what I wanted him to do." "He has a pleasant manner & is able to deceive many at first sight," but the PMC was "comprised of men who have . . . seen agitators before, &, who know their methods," and so, Richardson felt certain, they would be inured to Ta'isi's personal charisma.[10]

Richardson's impression of the PMC was not conjecture, he had gained these insights first hand since his arrival in Geneva. Richardson spent a lot of time in the company of "the guardians," the eminent members of the League, especially those on the PMC before the formal hearings began on June 20.[11] On his first day in Geneva, Richardson lunched with Joseph Vivian Wilson, a New Zealander and Great War veteran who was now secretary to Sir Eric Drummond, the League's secretary-general—a critical connection.[12] After lunch Richardson headed to the League headquarters, the Palais Wilson, where he interviewed Vito Catastini, secretary of the PMC, Mr. Briss from Denmark, and Huntington Gilchrist, the American member of the mandates section who had met with New Zealand officials in London about this matter in March.[13] All of these men, Richardson recorded, "understand Samoa." After this meeting Richardson began his acquaintance with Lord Lugard and "all the distinguished members" of the PMC when he joined them for tea. Lord Lugard told Richardson, "Nelson has his lawyer here and has tried to interview him but he won't see him."[14]

Over the next six days before the hearings commenced, Richardson dined with Lord Lugard, having "a very pleasant evening" with this "recognized authority on Native administration," as Richardson phrased it. Joseph Wilson also attended this dinner. Richardson also saw Gilchrist again, at his home, along with other notable people in the Geneva expatriate set in the week before the hearings. On the day the hearings commenced, June 20, Richardson met William Rappard again, director of the mandates section, and other members over lunch, before heading to the Palais Wilson at five for the hearings to commence.[15]

Before his warm reception in Geneva, Richardson's anxiety about Ta'isi and the Mau petitions led him to draw up comprehensive notes to refute "the bogus and lying petitions worked up by Nelson and his associates" as he traveled "home" to the United Kingdom, answering every paragraph.[16] He had these comments (running to fifty pages) typed and on hand when he and Sir James Parr fronted the hearings at six o'clock in the evening.[17] The chairman of the committee, the Marquis Theodoli, opened with flattering comments about Sir James and his "competence and tact" that was "appreciated" at the previous session. Sir James thanked the chairman for "his kind remarks" and set about introducing Sir George, describing him as an "old friend of many years standing" and a man "who enjoyed the respect of everyone in New Zealand." Richardson had been "a very distinguished soldier" who other soldiers not only saw as "a commander but as a personal friend" for he "possessed humanity and sympathy" in abundance. Sir James "ventured to think that a perusal of the records would show" a consistency in Richardson's conduct in his latest role as Sāmoa's administrator. The records give "proof" of his "qualities of humanity, sympathy and patience in dealing with the great problem in Samoa," Sir James suggested.[18]

Richardson was very pleasantly surprised with the reception he received, though he characterized the whole experience as having been "a great war in Geneva." He told Carl Berendsen, the secretary of the Department of External Affairs, that the secretary of the commission (Catastini) read his notes and "advised copies be issued to every member." "That was good business as it shortened our work." "We were not asked one question about either Nelson or the Native petition. The Commission dealt with those without reference to us," he stated, with palpable relief, even surprise.[19] Rather than admonishing him for harsh treatment of Sāmoans, the committee "seemed inclined to blame me for weakness in not punishing European agitators for embroiling the natives in the early stages." Richardson impressed them with the "mild and courteous" warning he issued in November 1926 requesting that the second of the joint meetings with Europeans and Sāmoans cease. The PMC "were apparently astounded that Mr Nelson should disregard it, & refer to it as Intimidation," Richardson further explained. He went on to let Berendsen know that "they were surprised at my not punishing the Natives severely after the warships arrived" and "in this matter," Richardson confided. "I found it difficult to explain so I did what was unusual—I asked them not to record in the Minutes what I wished to say," he continued. "I then informed them of the gaol difficulty—the deportation difficulty and the changed minds of many Natives after they had heard me explain matters to them." Richardson also told Berendsen that he let the PMC know that "the Govt. were most anxious that I should not do anything which would or might prejudice the position at the forthcoming Mandates Commission—in view of the widespread misrepresentation of the True position." Richardson's candor and deference to the PMC "did a lot of good" and it brought home to the PMC that they had a great responsibility.[20]

As far as Ludwig Kastl was concerned, Richardson was equally pleased with how he dealt with him. Kastl had been told by Germans in Sāmoa to "back Richardson" for he is "a good man and has been fair and just to us all." The Germans and New Zealanders shared a common cause, according to these Sāmoan-based Germans, Richardson revealed. They told Kastl, "If Nelson is backed it will be the end of the white man's prestige in Samoa." Richardson was also surprised by the support he received from Harold Grimshaw, the International Labour Organization (ILO) representative with whom the general had "become friendly." The British Labour Party had written to Grimshaw "to give him information re Samoa" (presumably in favor of Ta'isi), but "he had supported me and the Govt." Unlike the other Labour figures who populate the story of the Mau in several national contexts, Grimshaw "had no time for Nelson." Richardson was so confident of the commissioners' view of his conduct after all his interaction with them, he concluded his letter to Berendsen with the directive "don't worry any more about Samoa."[21]

Ta'isi and Richardson both met at the Geneva train station the evening the hearings concluded. The former was saying good-bye to lawyer John Roberts and the latter, Sir James Parr, both of whom were returning to London. Richardson reported Ta'isi "smiled and sniggered," but "we ignored him."[22] Richardson was feeling triumphant. He told Prime Minister Coates that he "got to know, and be intimate with a number of them [mandates commissioners]." These new "intimates" conveyed their "private views" to him. These views included that the system of government in Sāmoa is "ideal" and in the "best interests of the natives," "that every endeavour should be made to prevent the 'beach' having any political power over the natives," "that NZ has done most splendid work in Samoa," that "Nelson and his associates should have been dealt with earlier," and "the natives should have been dealt with more firmly."[23] Richardson's "intimates" were Lord Lugard, William Rappard, Joseph Wilson, and Harold Grimshaw, who Richardson hosted at dinner the Saturday after the hearings concluded. Richardson recorded, "We talked until five minutes to twelve—the time passed so quickly."[24] This gathering left Richardson very pleased; "I have had a very useful evening," he privately wrote.[25]

Richardson did not have to wait long to get confirmation about his impressions of proceedings at Geneva. Just over a week later, the PMC's report on Sāmoa was sent exclusively and confidentially to the New Zealand High Commission in London, two months before it was made available to Sāmoan legal representatives or the press. "It is a stinger for Nelson and a great victory for me," Richardson wrote.[26] After this, Richardson advised Coates to issue a strongly worded announcement that conveyed the League's attitude and entreat Sāmoans to look to "their Administrator who will help & guide them to work out their own destiny and prosperity." Richardson signed off by reassuring Coates—like some imperial superman—that his work in Geneva was done but he would "always remain in readiness to fight for Truth and good Govt in Samoa."[27]

Without knowing all the backroom machinations that took place, Ta'isi left Geneva still hopeful the PMC would find in favor of the Mau. He was also hopeful the Privy Council would allow him to contest his exile in that court in the case known as *The King ats Nelson.* He traveled to Innsbruck and Zurich and was in Munich when he got a telegram from his London lawyers conveying bad news: "leave to appeal refused."[28] Despite Stafford Cripps putting "his points most cogently and ably, after he had been on his legs for about an hour, the court decided against him."[29] New Zealand's King's Counsel, Mr. Jowitt, was not even called to present the government's case. Jowitt spoke four sentences at the end of the proceedings, asking about the awarding of costs. For this work he charged a "heavy" fee, Parr complained to Coates, of over four hundred pounds.[30] This was the only win Ta'isi would have: the New Zealand government's costs were not awarded.[31] "The Court held that the act of the Administrator was an executive act against which there was no appeal to the Courts," while Cripps countered that "it was a judicial act." One of the "Law Lords" suggested that Ta'isi should have allowed himself to be arrested and issue a habeas corpus. Several other of the "Law Lords suggested that proceedings could be taken in Samoa" against the administrator's decision. Cripps tried to explain the difficulty for Ta'isi of launching proceedings in Sāmoa. He would not be able to present evidence or give instruction because he was exiled; the Privy Council were unmoved by this argument. Cripps strenuously argued Ta'isi had "no remedy" to appeal the administrator's action and so natural justice was denied.[32] In conveying details of the hearing Ta'isi's lawyer, John Roberts, told him that launching an appeal in Sāmoa "would appear very sharp proceedings if there were any other remedies for you."[33] Richardson could barely contain his glee when he learned of the Privy Council decision. He told Sir Francis Bell: Nelson's "last appeal you know has been refused so he has only one appeal left, vis. To the Devil."[34]

The PMC kept the New Zealand government confidentially informed about its findings. On August 10, Sir James Parr obtained, in the "strictest confidence," the report, yet to be published, reiterated the summation of the PMC decision sent in early July.[35] As before, the PMC accepted Richardson's version of events in their entirety but challenged the New Zealand administration to more actively exercise their authority and maintain law and order. Though they did not specify how to do this in their official report, Sir James had told Prime Minister Coates, "it is safe to say that a stiffer attitude to the Mau will not be disapproved at Geneva," suggesting that in all-important private meetings members supported the future use of force.[36]

Ta'isi's lawyer knew in late June that a decision had been made by the PMC and details of it disseminated to the press; "our friend Jennings" from the *Daily News* had seen the report, John Roberts told Ta'isi.[37] A month later, Roberts wrote to Vito Catastini, saying, "The Press have purported to give a summary of the finding of the Commission and to quote statements therefrom." If the press already had access to the PMC findings, Roberts reasoned, he wanted to attain a report for his clients immediately.[38] The *Samoa Times*, for instance, ran a story July 27 that quoted the forthcoming League report very accurately.[39] Vito Catastini responded that the report "will probably be available to the public from the middle of August" and Mr. Nelson would receive a copy then.[40]

Sir James Parr tried to dampen any suspicion there was anything other than a rigorous investigation conducted by the PMC. He went to the press describing the three-day PMC hearings as "almost as bad as the third degree" and a "searching examination"—a gross distortion if ever there was one. The "15 members" represented different countries and were all "extraordinarily able and experienced men" he opined.[41] Sir James contrasted the noble and thorough work of the commissioners, Sir George and himself with Ta'isi's extravagance—he was "established in a suite in the leading hotel . . . with three English lawyers and two secretaries." Ta'isi was not there "to fight the tyranny of General Richardson" but was mired in self-pity, Sir James said. His "immediate occupation" was to "pour his tale of woe into the ears of all and sundry at Geneva"; that is, he was "busily engaged" in the lowly task of "lobbying."[42]

Vito Catastini's letter to John Roberts also indicated the League would take action on the PMC's report in September, so Ta'isi kept to his plan to be on hand in the UK.[43] He signed a lease on a furnished apartment on Upper Baker Street in Marylebone in July to last until late September.[44] Based in London again after his time in Europe, Ta'isi continued to consult with his lawyers about the ongoing proceedings. In late July, he received their account for all the legal work dating from mid-March that involved the League and Privy Council matters. It totaled £718 17s. 5d., or more than £30,000 in contemporary monetary value.[45] After the decision of the Privy Council, Ta'isi pursued the possibility of challenging his exile in Sāmoan courts; the only course left he could pursue. John Roberts had been trying to contact Thomas Slipper and Ta'isi's Apia office about this, but no reply had come. If no word came soon Ta'isi was "thinking of sending the proposed telegram to Dr. Evatt in Sydney asking him to proceed to Samoa to take the matter up there." He "would have preferred an appeal to New Zealand to be handled by Sir John Findlay, but the censorship ruling in Samoa seems to make it impossible for me to communicate with Mr Slipper" and Findlay would not institute the initial proceedings. This is why he was thinking of approaching Dr. Evatt from Australia.[46] The Privy Council's suggestion of an appeal to the Sāmoan courts was an action supported by Stafford Cripps despite the logistical difficulties of rigid censorship that hampered Ta'isi's communications with people in Sāmoa as well as his inability to appear and instruct. Even with these immense challenges, Ta'isi wanted to pursue this avenue to challenge his exile: it was the last legal option he had left.[47] As well as this legal redress, Ta'isi took up the pen and began writing up comments for use by the press. He sent remarks "I have prepared as a lead" to John Roberts so he "or some other friend might be able to influence [a journalist] to write an article on Samoa." "It is much longer than I intended, but as it is not to appear in my name, I only set down the leading points, which a proper journalist can cut down into probably two small paragraphs," he told Roberts. He sent the remarks to Cripps as well, and his business broker, Mr. Daniels, in the hope he could get the *Daily News* interested.[48]

The attention Sāmoa was getting in the UK press attracted the attention of those in very high places. When Richardson, accompanied by Rona, attended a garden party at Buckingham Palace on July 26, he realized His Majesty, King George V, also took an interest in the troubled Pacific islands within his realm. Richardson was presented to their majesties and the king then "kept me a long time talking about Samoa and enjoyed the conversation apparently." King George "knew all about the Mau" but asked "why did the half caste agitators get so many of the natives to join the Mau"? Richardson explained, "If I gave the natives a tin of salmon and His Majesty gave them a keg of beef they would follow him." The king was amused by the "joke" and also told Richardson: "my opinion is the Govt did not support you as they should but of course I cannot officially express my opinion." Richardson was pleased by this revelation. "How nice for me to have the backing of the King—I appreciated the Kings [*sic*] sentiments very much," he wrote, "and wish the natives could really know and understand this."[49] Richardson immediately wrote to Catastini so the PMC could know this important development.[50]

Ta'isi also spent his time in the UK and Europe in 1928 doing business. This included working on importing goods, especially copra, from Sāmoa.[51] He also sourced products in Europe for sale in his stores. He applied to be the sole agent for Aston Martin cars for Sāmoa and Tonga, for example. He also ordered a variety of other goods. His quest for suitable products included finding a "palatable" low-alcohol beer that complied with Sāmoan prohibition regulations. He found a German beer, though the supplier told him it had to be 3.2 percent alcohol by volume in order to be "imperishable." The supplier feared it therefore might not be permitted into Sāmoa (prohibition regulations stipulated that beverages could be no greater than 3 percent alcohol as a volume percentage).[52] A shipment was arranged nonetheless, but Ta'isi had full financial liability if the beer was rejected in Apia. For his own purposes, Ta'isi spruced up his wardrobe with tailored suits and shirts.[53] He also became associated with London's Royal Colonial Institute in August, an organization that had a busy round of information sessions on site in Northumberland Street as well as "interesting outings." The secretary of the institute asked Ta'isi if he would like to attend fortnightly lectures in the "Smoking Room of the Institute" and whether he would deliver an address on Sāmoa on one of these occasions.[54]

News of the PMC findings again hit the papers on August 18 when their report was officially released. Headlines in New Zealand ran "Mr Nelson condemned" and "Nelson Blamed." The PMC report declared, just like the 1927 royal commission, it could not "too strongly condemn" Ta'isi. It claimed he was motivated by personal interest rather than the welfare of Sāmoans in whipping up the political activity of an "impressionable people." General Richardson had not acted with sufficient firmness against the Mau but in all other regards the New Zealand administration "seems to have made every effort to improve the natives" conditions, notably in public health, education, agriculture, and commerce.[55]

Ta'isi was crushed by this latest news. He documented this in a letter to the secretary-general of the League of Nations—Sir Eric Drummond—desiring to "place on record my grave disappointment at the Findings of the Commission." He went on:

> It was a matter of deep regret that although present at Geneva during the sittings of the Commission, my request for an opportunity to appear before the Mandates Commission, to defend my honour and personal character and to support the petition presented by me, was refused.

Ta'isi told Sir Drummond, "I feel certain that if such an opportunity had been given me, I should have been able to substantiate the points raised in my petition and to refute the statements made at the hearing by the representatives of the Mandatory." If he had been allowed a voice "the strong pronouncements against me by the Mandates Commission" would not have been made. Ta'isi asked him to "kindly note my earnest protest against the findings of the Commission, replying upon time to vindicate my character and actions in respect to the troubles in Samoa."[56]

With a heavy heart, Ta'isi took a road trip to Scotland with Viopapa and Rex Pleasants (his secretary). In early September they visited Wales before heading back to London.[57] Traveling near Rugby, Ta'isi's car was struck by an oncoming car as it crossed a narrow canal bridge. Ta'isi, Viopapa, Mr. Pleasants, and the chauffeur were thrown onto the road, as were the four occupants of the other car. Ta'isi suffered a cut eyelid and forehead that required surgery; he also sustained a leg injury that would manifest itself later. Both Viopapa and Mr. Pleasants apparently suffered from shock, and the chauffeur was taken to hospital with head injuries.[58] For Viopapa, the car crash sparked serious mental health complications that would become apparent in coming months. Ta'isi's run of misfortune continued—although, considering the potential tragedy of the car crash, his luck could be considered to have been in. He received insurance payouts and consulted doctors for his injuries during his last month in London.[59] On October 11 he left, traveling back to Sydney stopping in Monte Carlo on the way, where he stayed at the Grand Hotel for a few days.[60] Arriving in Sydney November 23, he was interviewed by the *Sydney Morning Herald*. He reportedly stated, "I would not go back to Samoa unless on my own terms."[61] He stayed in Australia for a number of weeks before heading to Auckland for his first Christmas in exile where he would reunite with all his daughters.[62]

With the PMC's emphatic condemnation of Ta'isi, the New Zealand government expected that now (surely) the Mau would lose their faith in Ta'isi and fall into line with Colonel Allen's administration.

The government feared publicity boosting Ta'isi would circulate in Sāmoa, but the paper in lockstep with it—the *Samoa Times*—ensured a steady stream of negative publicity against Ta'isi was printed. On July 27 it opined, "It would be wrong to say Mr Nelson has got nothing by going to Geneva. He has got a reproof." But the negative publicity and cutting Ta'isi's lines of communication into Sāmoa did not kill the Mau. Administrator Colonel Stephen Allen, who did not have a chance to ease into his role, had to combat a very tense situation from the outset. On his appointment in April, Allen was presented to the public in one newspaper profile as a "disciplinarian" who excelled in the New Zealand Expeditionary Force and had developed an "enigmatic" reputation for his wartime feats. The report warned the "recalcitrant natives to abandon their present attitude," for it "would be a thousand pities if the necessity to use force should arise." "Law rests upon force and duty is still duty however unpleasant it may be . . . should further clemency fail, the regrettable alternative must be faced."[63] To reinforce this warning, a new military police force of seventy-four, to be made up, ideally, of "unemployed returned soldiers," supported Allen's administration as previously noted.[64]

In May New Zealand forces were involved in scuffles trying to arrest the Mau agitator Leota. Allen billed this incident as the "battle of Malautu" and reported to Prime Minister Coates that the incident "shook them up badly" and nearly sparked a defection of supporters from the Mau.[65] Allen ominously predicted that if another similar incident occurred, the Mau would dissolve quickly: "if by chance they resist arrest and there is some bloodshed I believe it [the Mau] will go quickly, especially if we find any good chance to arrest the leaders." Coates should "expect something of this sort to happen."[66]

These episodes of menacing violence stood in glaring opposition to the continuing nonviolent stance of the Mau. Now that Ta'isi's efforts in Europe on their behalf had failed, the Mau's chief weapon was continuing to inflict economic pain on the administration. The *Samoa Times,* though it ran stories claiming the Mau was now finished (yet again), had to admit that their campaign was biting. In August, amid congratulatory coverage of the PMC findings, the paper acknowledged that revenues from collected taxes had fallen by a drastic 86 percent.[67] The cost of providing services to Sāmoans was more than £58,000 but they contributed just over £4,000 to these costs. The New Zealand government made substantial loans to the Sāmoan Treasury to make up the shortfall. Even the most zealous colonial advocates—like those who wrote for the *Samoa Times*—could see that the economics of the Mau was dire. To make matters worse Sāmoans were not attending to plantations and the collection of the destructive rhinoceros beetle. The financial squeeze prompted Allen to make "painful" staff cutbacks in October telling Coates he was trying to reduce "expenditure to proper dimensions." "Retrenchment is always unpopular but to put it mildly there is [a] certain air of extravagance about previous estimates here and some action is essential" Allen admitted. Here was Richardson's successor acknowledging one of the Mau's long-standing criticisms.[68]

Allen talked hard against the Mau, but he also reported to Coates that Tuimalealiifano and Tupua Tamasese Lea'lofi came to see him during a lull in the administration's combat of the Mau. They told him they were still waiting for the League of Nations report and for "a report from Nelson who had gone to Geneva as their ambassador." Allen told them the PMC report was released (copies had been sent to them) and that Ta'isi would not be returning to Sāmoa for five years—but neither man would accept this. Tupua Tamasese said the report from the League was "not signed or sealed" (so they treated it with skepticism) and that "Nelson had not written or reported" (because all his communications into Sāmoa were blocked), so they refused to accept the information given by the administration was correct. There was no trust or faith toward the New Zealand government at all.[69]

Allen was frustrated the word from Geneva seemingly had no impact on the Mau leadership let alone the lower ranks. On the one hand, Allen acknowledged Mau criticisms had a basis ("our troubles here mainly arise from losing touch with native opinion") but also told Coates he ought to take action against the Mau now in "the nest in Vaimoso." To this end he needed to "reenact the 1922 *Samoan Offenders Ordinance* which is now a dead letter in the view of the Solicitor General's opinion."[70] He was reluctant to "bring up again the question of so called banishments" but "a few of the die hards" needed to be "out of the way." And he asked Coates' advice about how to proceed. Allen read all the cables sent from Sāmoa intended for Ta'isi. He reported that "Nelson's friends have been urging him in repeated cables to intervene and advise the natives to a conference with me to get what concessions they can." Ta'isi's friends "evidently . . . realize the game is up, and want to get themselves and Nelson into better favour," though Allen stressed he would not be entering into any negotiations with Ta'isi or this group of Europeans who were in touch with him.[71]

Though Ta'isi was still being monitored constantly by the New Zealand government wherever he went and in all his correspondence, the administration increasingly focused on Tupua Tamasese Lea'lofi as the next Mau leader to punish. Lea'lofi complicated the well-worn argument about the Mau being a movement started by Europeans and "half-castes"—namely, Ta'isi—to further their own economic and political interests. (The *Samoa Times* quoted a visiting member of the New South Wales Legislative Assembly, Sir Thomas Henley, who reframed the Mau catch-cry "Samoa for Samoans" as "Samoa for the half-castes and slavery for the Natives."[72]) Tupua Tamasese Lea'lofi did not fit the narrow profile of Mau leadership the New Zealand government had been propounding since 1926 at all. As time marched on, the dismissive reasoning that he was the "dupe" of Ta'isi wore very thin. He consistently defied and outwitted authorities when they sought to arrest him. He gained an increasingly enigmatic presence. He was young and photogenic, as were his family, his beautiful wife, Ala, and their young children. He continually turned the other cheek in face of great provocation. His noble *tama aiga* rank blended with being a prince of peace. But what *was* his ulterior motive in leading the Mau? The New Zealand government, as much as they tried, could not come up with a satisfactory answer to this question. His political activism was a direct result of the capricious and harsh administration of Sāmoa starting with his 1924 banishment by Richardson, along with the many others who suffered a similar fate.

Despite the supposed effect of May's "Battle of Malautu"—to frighten the Mau and weaken their resolve as Allen saw it—Tupua Tamasese Lea'lofi stood firm. At the Vailima meeting with Allen in October, Tupua Tamasese Lea'lofi would not accept the defeat of the Mau's international efforts to get justice. At this meeting, Allen had thought that the young Mau leader "was not very sure of himself," but events proved Allen wrong. Tupua Tamasese proved he was an obdurate opponent. With the PMC's June directive to maintain law and order, Allen sought orders in council from the governor-general to exercise his powers under the amended *Samoa Act*. He wanted to force a list of ten Mau leaders (Tupua Tamasese was at the top of the list) to return to their villages in late October. The "psychological moment has now arrived for breaking up the 'Mau' Committee," he told the minister for external affairs.[73]

Another boost to this scheme to ramp up the administration's attack on the Mau again came from PMC in early November. James Parr wrote to Coates having just returned again to London from Geneva, where he traveled with General Richardson, for the presentation of the last annual report to the PMC. Parr told Coates the PMC asked "many questions as to the present position and confessed disappointment in view of Royal Commission's report and Mandates Commission's own report last June that disaffection still very serious, taxes unpaid and plantations neglected." The PMC were fully aware that the Mau was "seriously imperiling [the] economic position of [the] territory." Parr explained it was hoped the policy of toleration "might gradually wear down and exhaust opposition." The chairman of the PMC, "while refraining [from] direct criticism" of New Zealand's present policy, "clearly indicated Commission would be sympathetic to a more vigorous handling of situation should N.Z. Government consider such a course advisable."[74] Armed with this information and Allen's conviction the time had come to act on the Mau, the government and Allen worked together on what form it would take. Coates told Allen that "some slight show of force . . . showing we mean business will not I think be amiss."[75]

Tupua Tamasese was again in New Zealand sights for arrest in November. Allen alerted the government that in "executing [the] warrant now some bloodshed will almost certainly occur."[76] Prime Minister Coates, who was "up to [his] ears in General Election work" (which was to be held on November 14), replied that "any action to be taken is left to your discretion."[77]

Coates' government suffered a devastating loss at the general election, losing twenty-seven seats. Joseph Ward and his United Party gained sixteen, and Coates' government tenuously clung to power by one seat. Harry Holland's Labour Party gained seven seats, consolidating its place as the third most powerful party in parliament. Holland's vocal position on Sāmoa policy was strengthened. Allen admitted to being in "considerable shock" at this news. Allen also told Coates he made a "blunder over Tamasese yesterday" that he similarly classified as a "shock." Allen set out to arrest him for nonpayment of taxes "in the ordinary way." He wanted the arrest to be done quietly when Tupua Tamasese was alone and off guard. This did not happen. Six police went to arrest Tupua Tamasese "and on a shout being raised a mob collected, stoned the six police who went out pretty heavily and drove them off." Allen admitted he was now "in a quandary." Would he let the matter slide, "which I don't think I can do"? Or would he "go in with all the available force and effect the arrest, which will probably mean bloodshed"? Allen revealed to Coates, "I do not object to a slaughter on principle at all, but I did want to avoid fighting on this particular ground." "Now my hand seems to be forced." Allen was resigned to the use of violence so he could reassert the authority of the administration driven off by stone-throwing Mau, but Allen assured Coates he would wait to discuss his course of action with Carl Berendsen, who was due to arrive in Apia the next day.[78] Berendsen presumably agreed with Allen's view of matters because on November 17 Allen informed Wellington, "I intend to proceed with the arrest of Tamasese with all the force available."[79]

Despite Allen's bravado, he sought assurance that cabinet endorsed his course of action to end the "farcical state of affairs in Samoa." Unless Tupua Tamasese submitted to arrest peacefully, the "numerical superiority of his followers" meant force of arms would have to be used, an administration official told the minister for external affairs. "History has an unhappy way of repeating itself," the official reminded the minister. He recalled the "incident of 1899 when Samoans routed a British and American Naval detachment of 110 men" as well as the monument at Mulinu'u "to the memory of a considerable number of British, American and German sailors killed in various sections of the Territory." He omitted the fact many of these men perished in the legendary hurricane of 1889 during the naval buildup of the three nations, and many more their sailors would have died if it were not for Sāmoan assistance in treacherous conditions.[80] Allen also wanted warships to support land forces, though later retracted the request.[81] Allen waited for the chance to arrest Tupua Tamasese whose movements were closely watched.

On November 27 Tupua Tamasese was finally arrested.[82] Accusations flew that Ala Tamasese was injured in the fracas that erupted while military and civil police arrested her husband at their Vaimoso home.[83] Allen reported some police injured by thrown stones. Tupua Tamasese was brought before Judge Woodward December 5 on charges of "resisting police" and "contempt of Court." He got over seven months. Allen was pleased with what seemed like immediate results; "believe result of arrest and sentence good and will materially weaken Mau," he radioed through to Wellington.[84] This was the last involvement of Gordon Coates in the Sāmoan affair, though he did sign off to Allen noting that the arrest of Tupua Tamasese and his sentence "is very welcome news."[85] He was replaced as Prime Minister on December 10.

Allen wrote to the new prime minister, Sir Joseph Ward, with the news that he intended to send Tupua Tamasese to New Zealand to serve out his sentence, "which I think will have a good effect both on him and others." The Mau leader was "a big overgrown boy with too good opinion of himself and a good stint [of] prison discipline would do him much good." After his sentence was up, Allen suggested Tupua Tamasese be "shown some of the more impressive things in New Zealand." Of the Mau, Allen informed Ward that as there were no "aim and objects" it makes it "difficult to deal with—there is nothing definite to cope with, no tangible points to discuss." Some "white people (real or so called) probably have definite aims in view," but the native Mau leaders "have no ideas at all." Allen assured Ward the situation was under control and as the "rank-and-file" Mau were "utterly sick of the thing long ago," there was "no enthusiasm for it among any of them" and it was now likely to disappear.[86]

Tupua Tamasese Lea'lofi shipped out of Sāmoa on December 15 aboard the *Tofua.* Also aboard was Chief Judge Woodward, who had not only sentenced him but had been a forceful administration activist against the Mau beyond the courtroom (even being convicted of striking a Mau member). Woodward traveled with his wife and children for a four-month furlough. Carl Berendsen, the secretary of external affairs, sailed on the *Tofua,* too. He was heading home having wrapped up the joint investigation into the Sāmoan administration with Alexander Park and Paul Verschaffelt that would appear as the "VPB report" in 1929 and cause considerable waves.[87]

Two days after the *Tofua* left Sāmoan waters, Ta'isi arrived back in Auckland with his six daughters. Press met the boat, the *Niagara,* seeking comment from Ta'isi about the latest Sāmoan developments and his future plans to contest his deportation. Ta'isi was circumspect. "It would very unwise for me to say anything regarding my intentions at this juncture, especially when a new government is taking over affairs," he said. Though "I shall be very busy attending to my business," his first priority was to travel to Wellington to consult with his counsel, John Findlay. When asked about his mission to Geneva he replied, "I am not disappointed and have no regrets." "It is just as well to know where I stand."[88] Despite his mission not having gone as he would have liked, Ta'isi gave the impression he viewed the fluid situation with optimism; "everything is in the melting pot as far as Samoa is concerned," he said.[89]

Ta'isi put on a brave, even nonchalant front to the press, but was proceeding with a challenge to his exile in the High Court of Sāmoa, as he was directed to do by the Privy Council, his last legal recourse. He also consulted John Findlay about a legal remedy for Tupua Tamasese during his trip to Wellington now he was back on New Zealand soil.

Ta'isi's caution about what he said to the press received a blistering attack from the *Evening Post.* In an article entitled "Mr Nelson's Silence," the paper likened Ta'isi to "a lady who, 'whispering I will ne'er consent' consented" by supposedly saying he would give no comment but then giving the press "comments he prefers not to make." The article further assailed Ta'isi for weakening "law and order in Samoa" and Tupua Tamasese Lea'lofi, as well, describing him as "not merely Mr Nelson's fellow-sufferer but also his dupe." Nelson "created the Mau" because of his "personal vendetta" against Richardson, and it was the Mau that got Tupua Tamasese Lea'lofi into "trouble." The Mau was "evil" and "spread strife, idleness, disease, and poverty among the Samoans." It cited Ta'isi's "crushing defeat" in Geneva as "almost comical for its thoroughness because it not only acquitted the New Zealand Government and the Administration . . . [but] censured the mischievous activities of Mr Nelson in scathing terms."[90]

Ta'isi was back at the Auckland wharf ten days after he arrived to see the passengers from the *Tofua* disembark. It was a cool, drizzling evening when the most noted passenger was escorted down the gang-plank by police, being photographed as he went. Observers were impressed by the "fine looking Samoan chief" who was only "about twenty-four though he looks less" and a "splendid specimen of his finely-made race." Reports also noted he was sentenced for not paying his taxes, "like thousands of his fellow countrymen had done." Friends had gathered to greet him. Some shouted out to him in Sāmoan, but he did not respond. As Tamasese caught sight of Ta'isi, he raised his hat before he was bundled into a waiting Black Maria and driven to Mount Eden to start his prison sentence. Although he smiled on his arrival, passengers reported "he often gave way to tears in his cabin during the trip."[91]

Ta'isi wanted to see Tupua Tamasese immediately. He wrote to the Honorable T. M. Wilford, the new minister for justice and prisons, the next day on December 28, requesting permission to visit him. His request was refused because "high Chief Tamasese . . . is in hospital suffering from influenza." This was alarming news, given the devastating impact of this disease on Sāmoa nine years earlier. Ta'isi wrote again on December 29, asking, "May I visit him in hospital?" "I am more than ever anxious to visit him now," Ta'isi wrote. He wanted "to ascertain whether I can help him in any way, more particularly in respect to Samoan native foods which, with the doctor's permission, may assist in his recovery." The minister responded he "had no power to grant permission for you to visit High Chief Tamasese while in the prison hospital," though he was "referring your suggestion re food to the Medical Officer who decides all questions of diet."[92]

The government's refusal to allow Ta'isi to see Tupua Tamasese, even on humane grounds, was his last bitter lesson of 1928 about justice. Justice, which Ta'isi had felt so certain was within his grasp throughout the year, had proven to be a scarce commodity. It was not blind or even-handed. It was capricious and only accessible if you happened to be on the right side of the colonial equation. Ta'isi, like his fellow Sāmoans, was not. The year 1928 was full of setbacks, but harsh lessons about colonialism and its withering impact on justice were still to come.

Chapter Ten

Slander, Abuse, and Calumny (1929)

In 1928 Ta'isi and his family spent their first Christmas in Auckland. It must have been a far more modest affair than the customary festivities held at Tuaefu. The day was overshadowed by the impending arrival of the prisoner Tupua Tamasese Lea'lofi, who spent Christmas Day on the *Tofua* heading for his prison term. Ta'isi and Tupua Tamasese would have to make their way in a country where the Sāmoan community was small; possibly fewer than two hundred Sāmoans lived in all of New Zealand at the time.[1] Though Ta'isi still hoped in early 1929—in spite of all the setbacks of 1928—that his exile would be of short duration, he began to put down Sāmoan roots in his newly enforced home of Auckland. The sentimental idea that New Zealand was a racial paradise where equality between Pākehā and Māori reigned was one that had a lot of currency at this time, particularly among conservative politicians who liked to tout that fantasy. Both Ta'isi and Tupua Tamasese Lea'lofi would see New Zealand's "racial paradise" quite differently.

Since arriving in Auckland on December 15, Ta'isi and his family had been staying at the Hotel Cargen. He was "anxious to get out of hotel life before Christmas," so sought furnished accommodation. He did not think it worthwhile to invest in real estate, furnishings, or even bed linens for his family, so certain was he that they would soon be home. The Auckland manager of O. F. Nelson and Co., Mr. Bentley, was tasked with locating suitable furnished accommodation. A house at 41 Mount Hobson Road, Remuera (where the Southern Motorway now runs), named "Bingley," seemed the most appropriate. Ta'isi went to meet the owner, Mrs. Wilson-Smith. At first Mrs. Wilson-Smith impressed him. "She was very courteous and expressed her wish that I would rent her house as she felt sure that my 'charming daughters,' as she called them, would . . . be most suitable tenants and would keep the place in order." Ta'isi had his doubts because "The house was on the small side, the furniture was old, poor and scanty for my large family who were always used to a large and well-furnished home." His daughters were won over by the "handy tennis court" and as Christmas was fast approaching Ta'isi's doubts were overruled by his children; he would rent the house.[2]

Mrs. Wilson-Smith offered, for a price, to add to the inventory of "furniture, linen, crockery and cutlery." Ta'isi did not think he would need the house for "more than two or three months at most," so he agreed to pay extra for the option to give two weeks' notice to vacate. The total rent was raised to nine pounds, nine shillings per week. There was no inventory of furnishings, though Ta'isi asked to see it. Mrs. Wilson-Smith "felt sure all would be well" as "she had every faith in my daughters and myself keeping the place in order." Contrary to how Ta'isi thought events would play out, the family would stay at Bingley for fifteen months, much longer than Ta'isi anticipated. During this time, the relationship between Ta'isi's family and their Auckland landlady would sour. She did not keep up her end of the bargain to augment the furnishings, and she refused to undertake necessary repairs or to reimburse Ta'isi when he resorted to paying for repairs himself. Mrs. Wilson-Smith cried (literally) poor and also often visited the family, bringing friends with her, which the Nelsons found increasingly tedious and burdensome. Ta'isi and Mrs. Wilson-Smith would end up in court. This experience would teach Ta'isi another bitter lesson, this time about racism that operated on a quotidian and "slanderous" level.[3] Mrs. Wilson-Smith's legal action was full of personal and racial invective toward the Nelson family. The case was also suspiciously well timed to humiliate Ta'isi and his family while they assisted the Labour Party during a by-election for the seat of Parnell in May 1930. For Christmas 1928 the Nelsons were ensconced in reduced circumstances in "Bingley," ironically just a few streets from General Richardson, who resided at 20 Omahu Road. The two rivals who last met in Geneva were now neighbors, a situation that no doubt irked Richardson no end.

When he took the lease of "Bingley," Ta'isi was hoping for a rapid restitution of his right to return to Sāmoa. Now that the Privy Council and the PMC failed to reverse his plight, he turned in earnest to publicity. He wrote *Samoa at Geneva,* his often-quoted pamphlet that detailed Sāmoan aims and how they were rebuffed by the PMC in mid-1928. Five thousand copies of *Samoa at Geneva* were published in Auckland in December, and he then disseminated this tract as far and wide as he could.[4] He also continued to pursue the few legal avenues left to him. The first was an appeal to the high court in Sāmoa as some privy councilors had suggested. He was also trying to secure Tupua Tamasese's release by adopting the method some privy councilors and legal counsel suggested he should have deployed to resist Richardson's deportation order one year earlier: issue a writ of habeas corpus.

Would justice now prevail given that the highest legal authorities in the British Empire suggested these remedies? The first answer came in early January. On January 9, Acting-Judge Alfred McCarthy refused the application made by Thomas Slipper to Sāmoa's high court appealing Ta'isi's deportation (*Nelson v. Richardson*). The reasoning: "order refused for reason both parties now in New Zealand where there is concurrent jurisdiction with High Court." It would be more cost-effective and convenient to "both parties" if the action was launched in the High Court of New Zealand instead.[5] Once again the judiciary was in lockstep with the government line.

The legal fight would drag on in other forms; so would Ta'isi's ongoing fight with New Zealand's conservative press. He wrote a lengthy response to the blistering attack on him in the editorial, "Mr Nelson's Silence," which had been published in Wellington's *Evening Post* in late December just after he had arrived back in New Zealand. Ta'isi took the paper to task for resuming "its offensive operations against me" and for the editor's "glaring inaccuracies which call for attention." The claim that Ta'isi's aim was to "weaken the cause of law and order" was a gross misrepresentation. He recounted how he agreed to Richardson's request in late 1927 to ask Sāmoans to return to their homes, but they refused to comply because they lacked confidence in the administrator. Ta'isi assailed the editor for suggesting Tamasese was his "dupe": "Tamasese was never a member of the Citizens' Committee and did not even take an active part in the Mau until the warships arrived in Samoa which was some time after I was deported." If Tamasese "is a flagrant violator of the law so are nearly 8,000 other Samoan men," he argued. Ta'isi also attacked the idea that "I conducted a personal vendetta against the late Administrator": it was "absurd" to say so. New Zealand politicians "attack each other with heat and vehemence without being charged with personal vendettas," but similar behavior in Sāmoa was deemed criminal. If "there has been a personal vendetta it was the Administrator who conducted it," Ta'isi wrote. On the charges that the Mau was "spreading strife idleness, disease and poverty": this was "pure hysteria." There was no substance to the claim that poverty and disease were on the rise or that the Mau had any impact on them. If Sāmoans "chose to indulge in the luxury of being 'idle' who has the right to deny them?" Ta'isi asked. "I have noticed that there are a lot of idle people, rich and poor, in New Zealand, and some blame the Government for it," but "unemployment," with "all the poverty and misery it brings in its wake," had never been a problem for Sāmoa. And finally, on the depiction of Ta'isi's Geneva campaign as a "crushing defeat," he instead described it as a "walkover" for "I was never heard." Even though he was not aware of the full extent of Richardson's access to the PMC Ta'isi dismissed the institution:

> Sir George Richardson and Sir James Parr were permitted to make elaborate ex parte statements behind locked doors. I was excluded. What else could one expect from such a Star Chamber proceeding but a verdict for the defendants?

Ta'isi finished by asking the paper "on a sense of fairness and sportsmanship to allow this reply to appear." The *Evening Post* editor complied, though not without taking further swipes. The editor insisted the accusation that Ta'isi intended to undermine Sāmoan law and order was made on solid grounds. Both the royal commission and the PMC held this view—although their views, as we have seen, were self-referential and profoundly shaped by Richardson.[6]

The *Evening Post*'s attack on Ta'isi and its furiously loyal defense of the administration, the 1927 Royal Commission, and the PMC's 1928 decision on Sāmoan petitions would all be shaken in mid-January 1929 by the findings of *The Samoan Public Service and Finance Report,* which also became known as the "VPB Report." Dubbed "VPB" after its authors—Paul Verschaffelt, Alexander Park, and Carl Berendsen, who were the public service commissioner, assistant secretary of the treasury, and the secretary of external affairs, respectively—the report should have drastically altered the government's course and ended the Mau standoff and the deportations. What was so sensational about this report was that after all the deflection of Mau criticism of the administration, here were three mandarins of New Zealand government concurring with the Mau's view. The report stated, in no uncertain terms, that the Sāmoan administration was rife with mismanagement and inefficiencies. It was at pains to point out Colonel Allen was "in no way responsible for the various matters to which we have felt it our duty to call attention."[7] So, without saying it directly, the fingers all pointed at Richardson as the architect of this situation.

Commissioned by Prime Minister Coates, the VPB Report directly contradicted the 1927 Royal Commission findings and all the government assertions to date that steadfastly declared there was no fault—*at all*—with the Sāmoan administration. Verschaffelt, Park, and Berendsen found plenty. In their fifty-page report, they meticulously analyzed all aspects of the administration. They cited multiple issues: from individuals whose work was unsatisfactory to areas where the cost of services exceeded what they should to the rents paid on various reparation estates. From the minutiae of their six-week study in late 1928, Verschaffelt, Park, and Berendsen drew a picture of the Sāmoan administration "placing an annual burden on New Zealand" that both Coates and Allen felt was unjustifiable, hence the need for the investigation. The report did not mince words: "we find the Service is overstaffed, and that the officers, with few exceptions, are incompetent and inefficient."[8] The VPB Report was careful where it assigned blame; no doubt in deference to the general, who was still held in revered status. Even when the questioned expenditure was the extravagant use of funds on the administrator's residence (to bring Vailima up to the standard of Tuaefu) for the precise dates of Richardson's tenure, which amounted to £7,500, the report avoided referencing him and deemed this spending as "necessarily high" owing to the age of the building.[9] Overall the report hedged around Richardson. It stated, "Whatever the causes may have been" for the problem, and it then damned him implicitly by following with "we are entirely satisfied that the Samoan Service as it exists today is by no means creditable to New Zealand, and that urgent and drastic action is necessary to improve the position."[10] These were points Ta'isi had been making in the legislative council since he was elected to it in 1924. He made them again—as did other Sāmoans—from 1927 onward as part of the Mau campaign. Making these very points was deemed by Richardson, and seconded by the Coates government (excepting Sir

Māui Pōmare), as illegal political agitation and was the cause of Ta'isi's deportation and the slew of banishments within Sāmoa. The VPB Report made thirty-six general recommendations and many more specific ones, such as recommendations to improve the Chinese Department (abolish it), to impose a "horse tax," and to "show the New Zealand Ensign" more as a means to bolster the nation's "prestige" in Sāmoa (the Union Jack would retain its pride of place as Sāmoa was "British" first and foremost).[11]

Comprehensive though the report was, along with omission of Richardson's name there was also little reference to the Mau. Verschaffelt, Park, and Berendsen would not acknowledge that their findings aligned with the Mau critique in any way. They only made passing reference to the fiscal consequences of the nonpayment of taxes and suggested that if the movement continues all schools should be closed excepting the "white" school at Ifi Ifi.[12] In another major break with the Royal Commission Report (which was not much more than one year old at this point), the VPB Report made no mention of Ta'isi, nor did it attempt to assign blame to him or the Mau for administrative shortcomings. Though Ta'isi was not mentioned, the report cited numerous individuals described as "half-castes" as the culprits for administrative failings. The report argued that poor work performances by a number of these men, who were inherently "inefficient" because of their racial makeup, dragged down the whole system.[13]

The Ward government received this damning report in mid-January. It was clearly a rebuke of Richardson and deeply embarrassing. No amount of linguistic gymnastics could square these findings with the positions taken before. What would the Ward government do with such explosive findings? The answer was to release a censored and partial version of the report. The government acknowledged they were releasing an extract for the reason they were protecting the identity of named public servants, but they were protecting a lot more than that. Prime Minister Ward made an early bland statement that a reorganization of the Sāmoa service would be implemented to reduce expenditure.[14] The conservative press duly reported this toned-down version of the report, but once the report itself was released more than a week later—even in its sanitized state—it made electrifying reading.[15] Imagine the reaction for Ta'isi, other Sāmoans, and those dedicated to their cause when they read the papers after the report's release. Papers quoted the most incendiary finding verbatim "The Samoan

Public Service as it exists to-day is by no means creditable to New Zealand, and that urgent and drastic action is necessary to improve the position."[16] Critics had been saying this for months at great personal cost.

As word spread about the report, Mau supporters began to sense this was a watershed moment. The *Samoa Guardian* reported the "Mau is naturally jubilant" about the report's disclosures that "have to a considerable extent supported their claims for an inquiry into local affairs." The report had "vindicated the Mau and its sympathisers." Sir Māui Pōmare used these new circumstances to write an opinion piece in the *Auckland Star* calling for a "fresh start." "Let's bury the hatchet," Sir Māui advised Prime Minister Ward; it would take "a strong man to do it," and Sāmoans would see that.[17] The *Auckland Star* sought Ta'isi's views. He stated unequivocally that he gave his full support to Sir Māui's views. Given Sir Māui's experience and "knowledge . . . of the native mind," Ta'isi continued, his views should shape the new government's policies even though they did not impact the former one.[18] As far as the League was concerned, this contradiction would expose New Zealand to its due scrutiny. Had the PMC "not banged, barred and bolted the door against the Hon. O. F. Nelson in June 1928," the *NZ Samoa Guardian* wrote, "the League of Nations would have heard the truth about Samoa." Instead it was "fooled and bluffed by the utterly unreliable statements and half truths of the General and the High Commissioner for New Zealand."[19] The paper was also clear about what should now happen as a result of this changed circumstance. It should "leave the way clear for the opening up of negotiations towards a satisfactory settlement of differences."[20]

American Consul to Fiji, Quincy Roberts, wrote to Ta'isi once he had received a copy of the *New Zealand Herald* containing information about the VPB Report. He told his friend "my first impression is that the report of the Civil Service Commission is a complete vindication of the Mau and the deportees." Roberts went on: "the report must make rather bitter reading for General Richardson, Nosworthy, and the members of the Royal Commission."[21] Two months later he wrote to Ta'isi again, expressing his "hope that the Ward Government has called you in to a conference and that some arrangement has been made for the recall of deportees."[22] Nothing of the sort happened. Despite the unequivocal and harsh findings, precious little changed as a result of the report. Back in February Berendsen complained to Colonel Allen that "one difficultly in having the Prime Minister as

Minister of External Affairs must necessarily be that he is so immersed in other matters that personal attention to the problems of Samoa is difficult to obtain." Even though this explosive report was on his desk and the situation in Sāmoa was at a critical juncture, Berendsen told Allen that Ward's lack of attention "is certainly very pronounced at the present time." He hoped that "as things settle down the Minister will be able to devote more time to the Territory."[23] This did not come to pass. Ward remained both prime minister and minister for external affairs throughout and his attention to Sāmoa only continued to dwindle as matters of higher national priority took hold as 1929 progressed. Ward had made hopeful statements dating back to February that he intended to enter a new era in relations, but this offer of negotiation came with the caveat that there would be no negotiation "with any movement that is openly subversive of good government in the Territory."[24] Even when the VPB Report found the Sāmoan administration could not be equated with "good government," Ward would not negotiate.

The mandate was in dire financial straits: all parties seemed to agree on this in February 1929. Allen's solution to this situation was the imposition of a new personal tax in March 1929. The big dilemma was how to make Sāmoans pay it. Allen's tactic of first resort was threats of violent punishment if the taxes were unpaid. Villages would burn; lives might be lost. This situation infuriated Governor-General Charles Fergusson, who wrote a strongly worded letter to Ward on March 17, 1929 that he again prefaced with the disclaimer "not of course in any sense as advice to you." In his eyes, the Mau were acting as they always had done "in carrying out Nelson's parting advice to stick to their passive resistance . . . and all would come right in their favour." He told Ward that "in dealing with natives . . . you must look on them and treat them as children—be kind, be just, be tactful; but above all be strict, never allow rules to be broken with impunity . . . never threaten without carrying out the threat, if cause is given." Fergusson recounted his days in the Sudan service where the nonpayment of taxes was frequent.[25] The resistance was dealt with by descending on a village and "seizing the headman" and "distraining on the inhabitants," Fergusson explained. "Payment was taken in kind, in corn or cattle or produce and a fine inflicted." The "headman remained in custody till the fine was paid . . . if there was active resistance, then heads would get broken and possibly then the village was burnt." Fergusson reminded Ward that the League of Nations "has expressed its opinion pretty strongly that the fault of New Zealand in the past has been its want of firmness . . . and it has practically called upon New Zealand to carry out its task of enforcing law and order." "The opinion by men who are one and all experts in dealing with native races" was "ample justification in the eyes of public opinion for standing no more nonsense in Samoa."[26] Fergusson urged Ward to authorize punitive action against Sāmoans.

To Fergusson's even greater frustration, New Zealand revoked the tax after Allen was recalled to Wellington for meetings mid-March. The Ward government concluded that, given the size of the population and the opposition to the tax, even loyal Sāmoans would not pay up without the use of "hard and stern means."[27] The government was also still unsure how the PMC felt about the use of force to break the impasse and would directly solicit their views on this in the meetings scheduled for June. Britain's representative, Fergusson, was clear on this; he was an unstinting advocate for force. The New Zealand government wanted an additional green light from the PMC, too.[28]

The impact of the VPB Report in Apia, like Wellington, was minimal. Allen only fully engaged with the exacting report in September, eight months after he first received it.[29] The lethargy and lack of a substantive and positive impact on the situation angered Ta'isi. The *Samoa Guardian,* and from May 1929 the *NZ Samoa Guardian,* continued to dedicate much space to the report as a way to highlight the increasingly absurd government stance. The *NZ Samoa Guardian* published the released version of the VPB Report in a special supplement in late October to ensure that its contents were as widely circulated as possible and in an effort to push the government into action.[30]

While the VPB Report was reverberating, Tupua Tamasese Lea'lofi's travails with the New Zealand legal system continued. His wife, Ala, and their three children followed him to New Zealand. Like her husband, Ala Tamasese was young, photogenic, and captured the attention of the press. She was also no stranger to New Zealand, having gone to school there for three years. She spoke English fluently (her children did not), but as an act of nationalistic defiance, she opted to speak to the press in Sāmoan via an interpreter. She told the press (as she did Samoa Defence League meetings during her six-month stay) of the excessive force used to capture her husband, the scale of the civil disobedience at the present time, and that she was forced to converse in "a foreign language" (English) when she visited her husband in jail.[31] This edict prevented her three young children from communicating with their father as they only spoke Sāmoan. She questioned these measures, especially since New Zealand authorities insisted her husband was not a political prisoner.[32]

For Tupua Tamasese Lea'lofi, everything hinged on the hearing of his habeas corpus case. Ta'isi was deeply involved in this behind the scenes, as his January correspondence to Alfred Hall Skelton shows.[33] The first hearing of the application was delayed well beyond the usual expeditious twenty-four-hour window for such a matter. On February 9 Tupua Tamasese finally had his time in court before Justice Blair. The judge promptly dismissed the case. He argued habeas corpus did not apply in Sāmoa and shielded behind the League of Nations jurisdiction over the mandated territory; a factor previous legal and governmental decisions had deemed subordinate to New Zealand's position.[34] Tupua Tamasese's initial sentence of six months hard labor for nonpayment of taxes (a "crime" committed by more than eight thousand other Sāmoans at the time) would stand.[35]

As 1929 ground to a "stalemate" in the view of the *NZ Samoa Guardian,* Ward clearly showed he would not deviate from the course set by his predecessor.[36] The great bulwark of political conservatism in New Zealand would remain firmly intact under his government. Indeed he went further than Coates as he increasingly entertained force as the solution to the Sāmoan impasse. The PMC seemed to indicate in 1928 the use of force was necessary but doubts prevailed. Governor-General Fergusson was unambiguous. As far as Fergusson was concerned, force had the dual benefit of crushing colonial opposition and assuring the bedrock of the imperial system—the prestige of the white race—was maintained. The opinion of the PMC was more difficult to decipher. Sir James Parr would once again front hearings in Geneva in June. As in 1928, he was briefed to inquire directly about the PMC's attitude to the use of force. This time New Zealand sought a more specific statement on it that would go further than the ambiguous response previously received that "authority must be enforced." Parr was to ask about "the manner in which, and the degree to which [the PMC] consider force should be applied." He was also to highlight the Mau had "never been threatening and . . . the movement, unfortunate and mischievous as it undoubtedly is, has been conducted . . . with some dignity and restraint." As instructed, Parr asked, and got a similar response to what he had received in 1928 in the public meetings, though in private audiences with commissioners the sentiment in favor of violence was likely to have been more unequivocal, as it had been the previous year.[37]

As the charismatic Mau leader's jail term was coming to its conclusion in June, Colonel Allen wrote anxiously to Wellington in mid-May that he feared Tupua Tamasese Lea'lofi would make a "propaganda tour of New Zealand for the Samoa Defence League."[38] He wanted him released from prison early and taken on a tour of New Zealand "in an endeavor to broaden his mind" and hopefully soften his attitude to his colonial rulers.[39] The shipping schedules were such (and perhaps the realization that a midwinter tour might not endear New Zealand to a Sāmoan) that Berendsen instead suggested that once the prisoner was released he be driven around the city where he had been held prisoner for half a year. In the time available, "it will be possible to show Tamasese . . . the size of Auckland, the principal buildings and streets and a panoramic view of the town shortly before the sailing," he wrote.[40]

Before Tupua Tamasese was released, Sir Māui Pōmare, whose worsening health (he had tuberculosis) had kept him making public appearances in support of the Mau for some months, paid him a visit.[41] Sir Māui wrote emotionally of this encounter. He told Tupua Tamasese of what his "elder relative Te Whiti" said, that the "tongue is greater than the gun." Sir Māui railed against the "blind, bungling" that had put this man in prison but mostly he focused on describing Tupua Tamsese's face. When he finally could look at this man, Sir Māui wrote, "I looked into the countenance of a Tama—an Ariki—a Prince." He said he saw the face of a "patriot" and, presciently, a "martyr."[42]

When Tupua Tamasese Lea'lofi finally walked free from Mount Eden Prison on June 4, dressed in his now-iconic white clothes, he was met by Ta'isi, who finally got his meeting with his young friend on New Zealand soil. They were photographed outside the prison shaking hands and smiling broadly, with the activist minister of Auckland's Saint Albans Church, Reverend John Greenwood, looking on.[43] The *NZ Samoa Guardian* ran the photograph on the front page of their June 6 edition under the banner "Tamasese Free."

Quite a crowd also awaited the celebrity prisoner. The *Dominion* reported a "long string of motor cars," containing his family, members of the New Zealand Samoa Defence League, and "many supporters of the Mau movement from Samoa and in New Zealand," were there to greet him. "Residents in the neighborhood of the gaol turned out in

Figure 10.1. Ta'isi shaking hands with Tupua Tamasese Lea'lofi on his release from Mount Eden Prison. From Percy Andrews, ed., *Samoa in the Shadows: A Pictorial Record of Recent Events in Western Samoa under a Mandate from the League of Nations to the Dominion of New Zealand* (Auckland: NZ Samoa Guardian, 1931). Courtesy of the State Library of New South Wales.

strong force," too, and "there were continual bursts of cheering and much enthusiasm" that were echoed by prisoners within Mount Eden's walls. Once greetings were done, a procession of cars flying the "Mau purple . . . prominently" made their way down Queen Street to deliver Tupua Tamasese Lea'lofi to Ta'isi's offices in the Endean's Buildings.[44] He was then brought to Ta'isi's Remuera home of Bingley. Ta'isi's cousin Tauvao performed a kava ceremony in Tupua Tamasese's honor on the tennis court.[45] The reunion of the two leaders was short. Tupua Tamasese Lea'lofi left New Zealand for home shortly after. Ta'isi never saw him again.

The chief's arrival in Apia on June 27 was an even grander affair than supporters had mustered in Auckland. A flotilla of *fautasi* awaited the arrival of the *Tofua* and then accompanied Tupua Tamasese and his family to shore. Inspector Arthur Braisby marred this ceremonious return. When the *Tofua* anchored in Apia Harbor, the police inspector boarded the vessel and served Tupua Tamasese Lea'lofi with a summons for the nonpayment of taxes for two years, in the sum of roughly two pounds per year. This provoked an angry reaction from the Mau camp. As adamant as the government was that Tupua Tamasese would pay his dues, their pursuit of unpaid taxes petered out in August; Tupua Tamasese refused to pay up and the government's only redress was to repeat the previous punishment. This happened at the time when Tamasese's pursuit of £2,000 in compensation "for alleged illegal imprisonment, illegal arrest and illegal banishment," a case launched in New Zealand while he was still imprisoned, also appeared to fall by the wayside.[46] The coincidence of these dueling legal cases (as well as the direct linkage of them in government correspondence) shows how the government continued to use the courts as a punitive tool.[47]

The release of Tupua Tamasese Lea'lofi prompted the outspoken Methodist minister Reverend J. F. Goldie to advocate for a "clean slate" and for the government to have open talks with Mau leaders, as Sir Māui Pōmare had done earlier in the year.[48] The conservative press pilloried the suggestion. An editorial in the *New Zealand Herald* depicted Goldie as well intended but "unable to deal with scientific or commercial or political questions" requisite for any informed view on Sāmoa. While deriding Goldie, the editorial took aim at Ta'isi, too. Goldie noted the trouble had not abated since Ta'isi exile. To this the paper responded, "As far as that is true, the blame is demonstrably due to Mr Nelson's maintained incitement of resistance." Ta'isi was "the sinner" who had shown no "repentance" for inciting the resistance for his own financial and political gain.[49]

Ta'isi was incensed by this latest attack on his character and conduct. Coupled with similar sentiments made in *New Zealand Herald* editorial comments in January 1928 following his deportation, Ta'isi considered this libel. He launched proceedings against the owners and publishers of the paper, Wilson and Horton Ltd. and Mr. W. R. Wilson, seeking £10,000 in damages on June 25. This proceeding, Ta'isi hoped, would expose the Sāmoan administration and the New Zealand government once and for all via their media advocates at the *New Zealand Herald*. The stakes for both sides were high; Ta'isi could not then anticipate the lengths the government would go to protect itself from further embarrassing revelations. When the matter was set down for a February 1930 hearing Howard Richmond, the lawyer for the defendants, worked closely with the government in preparing the case. Richmond pointed out the interests of his clients and the government were one and the same. He wanted administration witnesses released from duty in Sāmoa and brought to New Zealand to testify; Carl Berendsen for External Affairs willingly complied. Richmond was careful to try to avoid perceptions of impropriety or collusion on the part of the government. He noted, "We are aware, of course, your Department [External Affairs] must and will remain entirely aloof from the present litigation," meaning that all public dealings were to appear as if arrangements were made with individual officers and not the government itself.[50] As the case preparation proceeded, the extent of government involvement in preventing Ta'isi's witnesses from similarly appearing in court was extraordinary: indeed, events precipitated by this case drastically altered the course of history.

Ta'isi did not stop at challenging the *New Zealand Herald* in its slanderous representations. When Sir Francis Bell made attacks on Ta'isi in the upper house of parliament on August 29, accusing him of "rousing the natives to what amounts to a rebellion" after the government's orchestration of elevated copra prices, Ta'isi did not turn the other cheek. He challenged the conservative powerbroker to prove his accusation "to the satisfaction of an independent and impartial tribunal." If the tribunal deemed Bell had proved his case, Ta'isi would donate £100 "to any charity he selects and also all expenses of the tribunal." But if Bell was found wanting, he was to donate £100 to the Auckland City Mission and pick up costs. Bell never responded to the challenge. The *NZ Samoa Guardian* delighted in reporting on Sir Francis' stony silence.[51]

Ta'isi was proving not only litigious but also increasingly audacious and provocative. New Zealand's political kingpins must have been longing more than ever to cut him down to size. Being exiled to New Zealand meant Ta'isi could express himself with greater freedom and he took full advantage of this legal environment's liberties. But conservative criticism that Ta'isi was inciting rebellion with the strong inference this included violence was way off the mark, and the government knew it. The Sāmoa administration was reading and keeping records of Ta'isi's private and candid correspondence back to the Citizens' Committee in Apia. In his reports back to the Citizens' Committee, Ta'isi did not waver from the position he had held throughout the troubles, despite all the aggravation. He wrote in February 1929, for instance, "I solemnly pray and firmly believe the Samoans will maintain the peace at all costs and suffer further punishments and humiliation to attain their justified ends along constitutional and peaceful lines."[52] In March 1929 he railed, "I have been slandered, abused and calumniated by the New Zealand Government and its agents throughout the four ends of the earth." But, he made clear, "if they offer even now a bona fide solution of the Samoa trouble . . . acceptable to the people of Samoa as a whole I should be only too willing to forget my personal resentment." He would "join in with them to bring about the best results of such a solution for the common weal."[53] There is no evidence that Ta'isi was anything but genuine in this pledge. But Ta'isi's conviction to work for the "common weal" regardless of the personal cost was muddied by seemingly egocentric statements—"my faith in the justice of the cause remains unshaken and I will struggle along—alone, if need be, to the end." The government was more than privy to Ta'isi's thinking but no amount of evidence to the contrary would alter their prejudiced view of him and his intentions. The government did not want criticism from any quarter; particularly from someone they perceived to be an uppity zealot who pursued them at every turn.

Ta'isi's pursuit of the government went beyond litigation and public challenges in late 1929. He also wrote to William Rappard, the Permanent Mandates Commissioner based at the Geneva University, drawing his and the other commissioners' attention to the VPB Report. Ta'isi had tried to obtain the original uncensored version of the report. He wrote to Harry Holland requesting three copies of this report to assist in the preparation of his case against the *Herald.*[54] Holland had been pushing to have the full VPB Report released to parliament and the public for months and duly approached Prime Minister Ward with a request for copies. Ward refused; but allowed Holland to read the original version *"in confidence."* Holland did so without delay hoping it contained references to General Richardson. Holland wrote back to Ta'isi, telling him there were no references to the former administrator. "The portions which have been omitted from the printed report are references to individuals [designated 'half-castes' in the report] in subordinate positions," Holland wrote, "and recommendations for their dismissals."[55] Holland's quick reading did not catch deletion of the most incendiary language from the original version and other omissions of fact. The day after Holland penned this letter, Ta'isi wrote to Professor Rappard. Ta'isi let Rappard know of the VPB Report's existence, that three experts from the New Zealand public service compiled it, and that "many important paragraphs are said to have been censored by the Government . . . on the excuse that it contains only references to individuals." Ta'isi told Rappard:

> As the published portion contains scathing indictments on the inefficiency of the Public Service in Western Samoa and on the misuse of Finances of the Territory, the censored parts naturally give rise to the idea that they contain references which are too bad to print.

Ta'isi continued that "as the Samoan unrest continues unabated . . . it seems more than ever surprising that the report of the three experts will not be submitted to the Permanent Mandates Commission." He finished by saying, "I take the liberty to respectfully draw your attention to the text of the three experts' report, a copy of which I enclose herewith."[56]

Sir James Parr had been instructed to deliver a bland account of the VPB Report to the PMC. He was to state that the report's findings did not substantiate any of the Mau complaints about the Sāmoa administration and that "any burden of want of economy has been borne, not by Western Samoa, but by New Zealand."[57] When Parr returned to Geneva in November 1929 for subsequent PMC meetings, he was once again to press the point about the commission's view on the use of violence and prepare them for the possibility of bloodshed occurring in Sāmoa.[58] Instead he reported back to the government "have had a most difficult time" in Geneva. He suspected Ta'isi had a hand in this: "believe Nelson has been active in some quarters here." Unlike Parr's previous PMC meetings that oozed with mutual admiration, this time "commission disconcerted and irritated by V.P.B. report and found it impossible to understand changed attitude re staff and finance after previous Annual Reports and Richardson's evidence last year." Parr tried to "correct impression of conflict" and still hoped "for fair report from Commission."[59]

The Mau took the initiative, given New Zealand's damaged international image from their accumulated missteps, and issued another petition to King George in mid-November 1929, requesting the administration of Sāmoa be transferred to the British Colonial Office (this is highly ironic given the views of Governor-General Fergusson on the use of violence, as well as those of the monarch himself).[60] Britain and the League of Nations both rebuffed this appeal. Ta'isi received a letter informing him the chairman of the PMC "does not consider it necessary to communicate your petition to the Mandatory Power and to the members" of the PMC.[61] Sir James Parr's attempt to repair matters in the government's favor worked. Nevertheless, New Zealand was left with a lot to prove to the PMC about its imperial capabilities. The empty political verbiage and lack of constructive action that characterized the Ward government's response to Sāmoa to date was about to change. The government would not negotiate with the Mau. The Mau was as strong a force as ever but had not deviated from its nonviolent path. The New Zealand government was now ready to abandon its stance of tolerance; it had been given approval by Britain (explicitly) and the PMC (tacitly) to alter its course and deploy violence.

The pressures stemming from Sāmoa were palpable, but another fundamentally important factor in shifting Sāmoa policy in late 1929 was far larger than either New Zealand or Sāmoa. It was the Great Depression. In November 1929 the New Zealand government, like governments across the world, was reeling from the cascading and unprecedented effects of global economic free fall. The crisis was immediate, stunning, and all consuming. If parliamentary debates were an indication of the focus of politicians—which they invariably have to be—after October 1929 there was a steep decline in time given to Sāmoan issues. The high-water mark of interest and devotion of parliamentary attention to Sāmoa reached with debates over the *Samoa Amendment Act* in mid-1927 was not attained again. So, as the New Zealand government moved toward what it thought would be the final act in breaking Sāmoan resistance, New Zealanders and their representatives were preoccupied with the unraveling crisis at home.

Another embarrassing petition had been sent to London, and Ta'isi was readying himself for his libel case. He could not travel to Sāmoa, and few witnesses could make the journey to New Zealand (as well as the issue of cost, the administration had to grant passports, which they were reluctant to do). The exceptions were Mau leaders and revered chiefs Tuimalealiifano and Faumuina Fiame, who were granted permission to travel to New Zealand in September to be witnesses in *Nelson vs N.Z. Herald*.[62] To get around these considerable impediments, Ta'isi instructed Alfred Hall Skelton to travel to Sāmoa to gather witness testimony. He would travel with A. G. Smyth, whose two-year exile from Sāmoa was due to expire in late December 1929; Smyth wished to return immediately.

Ta'isi wrote to Smyth before his return, entrusting him with a speech to read at the reception in honor of his arrival. Ta'isi also warned him to take care and "trust nobody" except Tupua Tamasese and Faumuina.[63] Ta'isi also wrote to Hall Skelton. The letter was due to arrive in Apia after Hall Skelton had, and it followed on from prior discussions about preparing for their case in the *Herald* dispute. It shows how hard Ta'isi was working in preparing for the case. He was busily corresponding with various parties and trying to organize witnesses—Sir Māui Pōmare might be available and Sir Joseph Carruthers, the former premier of New South Wales, would "come in a hurry." However Ta'isi feared a New Zealand jury might "resent an Australian appearing only to lay down the fundamental principles of British justice" and so thought better of asking Sir Joseph to appear. He had also prepared "in Samoan a long statement of events which our Samoan witnesses can consider and add to if required in preparation for the case." Ta'isi also reported to Hall Skelton that three Sāmoan chiefs arrived unexpectedly in Auckland the previous day, Afamasaga, Ainu'u, and Asiata, as well as Crown Solicitor, Alfred McCarthy, who Ta'isi joked was "probably decorated with the Samoan Order of the D.C.B. (Don't Come Back)." All up, "the Herald are determined to give their witnesses a good schooling beforehand." Given how the Herald were arming themselves with ample and prepared witnesses, Ta'isi asked Hall Skelton to select witnesses he deemed "essential" but also to "use . . . discretion so as to have the approval of the Mau to those who are being called." The Mau had paid the fares of Tuimalealiifano and Faumuina last time, and might do so again, but if not, "I will have to pay." Two men were coming from O. F. Nelson and Co. at the firm's expense. Ta'isi wanted Father Diehl to come but "would sooner go without his assistance than risk alienation of the sympathy of the Roman Catholics in Samoa." Ta'isi worried that Inspector Braisby had gotten hold of two reports Ta'isi had sent back to the Mau and would use the contents against him.[64] These were the things that preoccupied Ta'isi over the Christmas period until Saturday, December 28, 1929.

Chapter Eleven

Sāmoa's Gethsemane (1930)

The shocking news came through to Auckland on Monday morning.[1] Ta'isi read the *New Zealand Herald* in disbelief. "Riot in Samoa." "Mau and Police." "Loss of three lives." "One constable killed." "Numerous casualties." "Telephones wrecked." Prime Minister Ward broke the news to the media that Sunday night. He stated, "A large number of Mau" came into Apia "to welcome Messers Smyth and Hall Skelton, and paraded with a number of men wanted by the police who tried to arrest some of the men wanted." "The arresting party was armed with batons only, and was attacked immediately by some 200 of the Mau with sticks and stones." Additional police armed with "revolvers, moved up to the rescue and got the police clear, with the exception of Constable Abraham, who was struck with an axe and beaten to death." The police withdrew to the police station, using their revolvers for cover, but the Mau attacked the building and were driven off only "by a Lewis gun being fired over their heads into the sea." Two Sāmoans—Leota and Migao—were dead (though Ward did not give their names). The Sāmoan casualties figure was soon raised to eight.[2] The Mau party was then driven from town, wrecking Apia's telephone lines along the way, Ward informed the New Zealand people. Sir George Richardson also commented. He was positioned as the voice of authority about the political situation and the setting for the "riot." He described how the wrecked telephone lines cut all wireless communications out of Apia. He also noted that the "whole of the disturbance" took place on the highly symbolic Beach Road that faced the Tivoli Wharf where the *Lady Roberts*, with A. G. Smyth and Alfred

Hall Skelton aboard, was waiting to dock and where they saw machine-gunned bullets hitting the sea. It was also on this road "that the New Zealand troops landed in 1914," Sir George added, overtly linking this incident with New Zealand's first action of the Great War when it occupied Sāmoa.[3]

The news reports that Monday morning were bad enough. Then Ta'isi received a phone call from the *Auckland Star* with even more devastating news: "Tamasese had succumbed to wounds received in the fracas between the police and the Mau." Ta'isi was stunned by the news that the young chief who embodied the nonviolent ethos of the Mau had died in these circumstances. He wrote that "this has cast a spell on the whole of the friends of Samoa here." After hearing the news he wrote to Hall Skelton, saying, "I really did not know what to do . . . and can write nothing at all . . . but to you . . . condolence and expressions of sympathy seem to me in such an eventuality mere mockery."[4]

Though Ta'isi was reeling from the day's news—"my heart is too full of sorrow"—he was very clear about a number of things. First, he was struck by the great tragedy of the death of Tupua Tamasese Lea'lofi, who, he said, "lived a noble life and died a noble death."[5] Ta'isi was also immediately suspicious of Ward's official account blaming the Mau for defying orders by letting wanted men march in the parade and then attacking the police who went to arrest the wanted men. There had been previous parades and similar orders about wanted men, but the authorities had not tried to execute arrests as they did on that day.[6] This was unusual; even J. H. Luxford, the chief justice who conducted the coronial inquest noted it as such.[7] Ta'isi told Hall Skelton he thought the "riot" was "provoked by the police not only as a gesture to Mr Smyth." He also suspected it was "also as a means to give the Administrator the excuse to restrict you in your movements and activities on your mission to brief witnesses and secure evidence for us in our pending libel suit." Ta'isi was not the only one thinking this.[8] There were too many strange coincidences and threats that something of this nature was going to happen. In the words of the *Evening Post* (and as correspondence from the New Zealand government, the League, and the governor-general's office corroborate) the government sentiment was "there had to be a showdown."[9]

While officials talked tough and acted accordingly, an image of the dead Tupua Tamasese Lea'lofi lying in state, wearing his trademark white and surrounded by Ala (who was four months pregnant), his

Figure 11.1. Tupua Tamasese Lea'lofi lying in state, December 1929. Sitting next to him are Ala Tamasese, Alfred Hall Skelton, and A. G. Smyth. Tama Aiga, Tuimale-aliifano wears a sling, and Faumuina Fiame sits in front. Tattersall, Alfred James, 1866–1951. The lying in state of Tupua Tamasese Lealofi III, Samoa. Ref: PAColl-0691–1. Alexander Turnbull Library, Wellington, New Zealand, http://natlib.govt.nz/records/22865150.

children, and Mau supporters (including Smyth and Hall Skelton), also began appearing in newspapers. Even in this tragic event, the Mau understood the necessity of publicizing what happened with poignant photographic documentation. The vignette would become an iconic representation of New Zealand's rule over the mandate. Other photos of Ala weeping over the coffin and the grand funeral procession in Vaimoso also illustrated for the world the ugly and oppressive events that had taken place.

Ta'isi knew from the first instance the libel case "has fallen very badly into the shade in view of the tragedy which has befallen Samoa." This "disaster to Samoa" has "upset me so much that I really do not care very much what happens now," he wrote.[10] Like the bullets fired by the sharpshooters and machine gunners positioned on the police station veranda, news of the shootings ricocheted through the network of Sāmoan supporters. Sir Māui Pōmare was utterly distraught. He had worked tirelessly to bring about a just and peaceful resolution in Sāmoa and, like Ta'isi, almost religiously believed in nonviolent resistance, a view forged in Taranaki's nonviolent community of Parihaka in the 1870s and 1880s. He had formed a friendship with the young Sāmoan chief he had likened to the Māori prophet and nonviolent community leader of Parihaka, Te Whiti O Rongomai.[11] For this young man to perish so violently was unthinkable. From his sickbed Sir Māui sent Ta'isi a telegram that read:

> HEART BLEEDS FOR YOUR PEOPLE SICK UNTO DEATH I SENT TAMASESES WIDOW MESSAGE OF CONDOLENCE NO NEED TO TELL YOU TO KEEP STEADFAST AND ABOVE ALL TO KEEP CALM AM WRITING AROHA GALUMALEMANA.[12]

Sir Māui was so devastated by this news his health took a serious turn. Ta'isi wrote to Lady Pōmare a few days later, informing her of developments in Sāmoa, though he asked her to read out only the portions of the letter she thought appropriate so as not to upset her husband further. Ta'isi also sent Sir Māui a Sāmoan Bible, which Lady Pōmare told Ta'isi "gave him great comfort last night in his very trying hours."[13]

The small Sāmoan community in Auckland and its supporters gathered at Saint Alban's Church on January 2 to remember Tupua Tamasese Lea'lofi, a man the *NZ Samoa Guardian* began referring to as the "Martyred Mau Leader" and Sāmoa's "Martyred Prince." A picture of the Auckland gathering of mourners whose grim facial expressions said it all, with Ta'isi front and center, also appeared in the press.[14] While Ta'isi was filled "with horror" and reeled from daily reports of what followed with news of more deaths, killings, and brutalization of Sāmoan people, he was being blamed.[15]

"Disgracing" Ta'isi had been a government tactic since the Mau began, but now the accusations moved beyond the arguments that he incited the Mau because of his opposition to prohibition and his continuing desire to economically exploit Sāmoans through depressing the price of copra.[16] In the wake of the massacre, both Governor-General Fergusson and his good friend General Richardson laid the blame for the deaths on December 28 at Ta'isi's feet. In his final report as Governor-General, Fergusson wrote approvingly to the secretary of state for the Dominions, Lord Passfield. The massacre—a tactic he had been pushing for months and wanted to see continued "with the utmost

Figure 11.2. Ta'isi leads mourners at a service at St Albans Church, Auckland. *NZ Samoa Guardian,* January 9, 1930, 3. Courtesy of the National Library of Australia.

vigour"—had broken the stalemate.[17] But it was Ta'isi, in Fergusson's determined view, who had to accept responsibility for the deaths incurred; "upon him justly falls the odium of misguiding . . . this backward though lovable Samoan people," he wrote.[18]

Echoing Fergusson's sentiments, Richardson wrote to the prime minister, suggesting he make a statement to buoy loyal Sāmoans and express "deep regret at loss of life—the *responsibility for which rests on those who have misled the natives.*" Richardson reiterated that "the difficulties in Samoa are entirely due to the influence of one or two persons in N.Z. who have kept the movement going solely to 'save their own face.'" "These people were deported," Richardson went on but "are doing now what they were doing before deportation." "It was impossible to maintain peace order and good Government while they were in the country—and it is impossible now because these persons are still at work," he argued. "In a larger British Colony," Richardson reasoned, "they would have been gaoled" for sedition, but in Sāmoa there was the problem of witnesses who would have been swayed by intimidation and fear, and so that path would not have worked.

The "evil" culprits for the Sāmoan trouble were those who had "misled" those in the Mau, but there could be only one person Richardson was referring to despite his animus toward the two other exiles, Smyth and Gurr. Richardson concluded by congratulating Ward on the forceful tack he had taken—it was *"absolutely the correct course"*—so much so that Richardson wished Ward "may live long and go down to posterity as the man who saved Samoa."[19] Neither of these wishes came to pass.

As more details of the massacre filtered through once lines of communication from Apia were restored, Ta'isi had renewed interest in the libel case. Perhaps he saw it as another means to hold an inquiry into the shootings. Given the record to date, he was right to be skeptical that the Sāmoan administration would conduct a searching inquiry. Despite the horror of machine gunning a peaceful parade, Justice J. H. Luxford found the machine-gun fire to have only been used for its "moral effect" and aimed over the heads of the Mau.[20] Indeed Luxford supported the machine gun's use by citing his own expertise in ballistics learned from his war service in the New Zealand Machine Gun Corps (he even wrote the official history of this corps, *With the Machine Gunners in France and Palestine* of 1923).[21] Despite a number of questionable circumstances, Luxford absolved the administration of any wrongdoing. Even with his great determination, reviving the libel case was going to be difficult, or, as Ta'isi would find out, impossible. He asked Hall Skelton in a January 6 telegram, "How many [of] our witnesses shot?"[22] The answer was two witnesses were killed; the three sharpshooters wounded others.

As the aftermath of the shootings played out, Ta'isi realized the opportunity to expose the government and administration via this libel case could not happen. He had no witnesses. The ones who survived the shooting were at large; they fled into Apia's heavily vegetated hills to escape the police, who were raiding homes in search of them. Administrator Allen had laid new charges against them after the shootings and ordered them to surrender.[23] Some witnesses, like Faumuina (who was grazed by bullets on December 28), "had been walking at large for 7 weeks" but was charged with using abusive language in his speeches and so was now too a fugitive.[24] There was no way he or any of the other witnesses would be granted passports to travel to New Zealand to give evidence, let alone by the February 20 hearing date. Ta'isi was defeated; his "hands were tied" by being deprived of all his "vital" Sāmoan witnesses.[25] He had no choice; he withdrew the case on February 5. The final sting came when the judge used special discretionary powers to award additional costs to the defendants (the owners and publishers of the *New Zealand Herald*). Ta'isi was ordered to pay them more than £500 for discontinuing the case.[26]

The demise of the libel case paled into insignificance in light of the "atrocities" committed by New Zealand forces.[27] The Mau had been using the "mailed fist" metaphor to evoke an image of New Zealand rule for some time. The Black Saturday Massacre, as it became known, was a gruesome start to a pincer movement of even harsher rule. The government's stated policy in January 1930 was to "stamp out the Mau once and for all as speedily as possible." The government left the means to effect this end up to Administrator Allen. If he needed it, the warship HMS *Dunedin* and a new force of 250 men would be sent in three weeks' time.[28] The Mau countered in the *NZ Samoa Guardian* by depicting New Zealand rule as now akin to "black and tan terrorism" and its eager recruits as "terrorists."[29] The Mau was drawing a comparison with the infamous force recruited into the Royal Irish Constabulary to combat Republican forces and activities during Ireland's War of Independence. Like the recruits who signed up in Depression-ravaged New Zealand to be deployed in Sāmoa, many of the Black and Tans were former World War I soldiers. The Black and Tans, to many people then and now, were little more than brutal uniformed thugs fighting for the British Empire. This was a potent metaphor; the Mau milked it from 1930.

The police raids on homes in search of Mau men in the immediate aftermath of the massacre shifted Sāmoan troubles beyond a battle between colonial men and Sāmoan men into one against colonial men against Sāmoan women and children. Gender, an ever-present but muted factor up to that point, became an overt feature of the fight between the Mau and the New Zealand government. Both sides began deploying gender and sexual morality as a tool. The *NZ Samoa Guardian* described the weeks after the massacre as "Samoa's Gethsemane": "a war against women and children."[30] The response from Sāmoan women was to organize politically. Four wives of Mau leaders—the now widowed Ala Tamasese, Faamusami Malietoa (wife of Faumuina Fiame), Paisami Tuimalealiifano (wife of the *tama aiga* and Viopapa Nelson's aunt), and Rosabel Nelson formed the Women's Mau along with significant numbers of other women in January.[31] The administration had enacted so many draconian laws essentially making outlaws of all the Mau men that women moved to the forefront of the movement.

The emergence of Mau women caused a significant public relations problem for the New Zealand administration. As harsh as their conduct now was, even they balked at the suggestion that their "at all costs" crackdown involved brutalizing women and children. Allen began combatting the women's actions in a number of ways. He deployed the punitive use of legislation, especially of seditious libel laws, and the character assassination of Mau women and Mau supporters, like Apia-based lawyer Thomas Slipper. The first blow struck was against Slipper. Slipper had already been alerted to harsh representations of himself being circulated around the administration and its friends in New Zealand and beyond. In April 1929 he was informed that he was described as someone who had "drifted to the islands where he gradually sinks lower and lower." According to this view he had deserted his New Zealand wife, now cohabited with his typist (Flora Horneman, whom he married in late 1930) in Apia, and "is always under the influence of liquor, and is one of those sad cases of a white man with some little natural talent and education, degenerating into a sot, consorting with natives and becoming an outcast."[32] Then on February 11, 1930, he penned a letter with Rosabel Nelson and her younger sister, Priscilla Muench, to the administrator and commodore of the New Zealand navy, Geoffrey Blake. The letter included the passage "it is regrettable that death and bloodshed appear to be of small consequence to Your Excellency as compared with the desire, evidence and expressed, of absolutism." The letter was seen by only a handful of people—"Commodore Blake, four Samoan ladies, Mrs Muench and a person whose name I do not know," Justice Luxford said in his judgment.[33] Nevertheless, Luxford deemed the letter to have been "published" and used it to charge Slipper with "defamatory libel" and for "having used threatening, abusive or insulting words or behaviour towards an officer of the Samoan Public Service and Member of the Legislative Council." Justice Luxford, fresh from his coronial inquest into the Black Saturday Massacre, found Slipper guilty on both counts.[34] When his appeal failed, Slipper was jailed for three months.[35] Sāmoans had pooled a fund together to fight his appeal, but when these funds were exhausted, there was no more money to get him out of prison earlier.[36]

The travails of Thomas Slipper revealed a new insidious front in the New Zealand government's attack on the Mau. The government became intent on the personal ruin of those who opposed its Sāmoa policy. They had been trying to effect this as far as Ta'isi was concerned from the outset. They continued to pursue him with vigor but they also had others in their sights, especially the lawyers hired by Ta'isi and the Mau. New legislation and the courts were deployed to great effect. Authorities seized confidential Mau communications, some of which contained unflattering portrayals of people, and their contents were disseminated. The effect was that backstabbing and rumors within the Mau, some of a very personal and bitter nature, became rife. Mau ranks began to break.

For Slipper, the price for aiding the Mau was extremely high. Not only was he jailed; he was prevented from practicing law for a period. Once he was released and was permitted to practice again, he told Faumuina in mid-1931, there was no work to be had; the Depression had dried up that economy, too.[37] For everyone, including Ta'isi, the Depression hit hard. Without funds, the Mau as it had operated would collapse. Coupled with the problems within the Mau, the deeply conservative and politically connected New Zealand legal establishment shunned Slipper. Outrageous as the legal case against him was, few of his colleagues were moved by his plight. Ta'isi's long-term barrister, Sir John Findlay, had earlier complained to Ta'isi "that his [Findlay's] loyalty to me and the cause of Samoa has meant great sacrifices and pecuniary losses to him."[38] The pressures had become too great; Findlay and Ta'isi severed their professional ties in April 1929.[39] Before this official end to their business relationship, Findlay betrayed Ta'isi by forwarding legal documents (letters from Ta'isi) to Prime Minister Ward. Findlay knew precisely how unethical his sharing of legally privileged documents was: they were sent by service messenger, were for Ward's eyes only, and were to be returned immediately. Findlay was possibly attempting to restore his professional standing with the new prime minister with this double-dealing act.[40] New Zealand was a small society; its upper echelons and legal fraternity even more so.

One facet of this campaign of character assassination was inflicting damage on the reputations of Mau women in addition to the use of the criminal code. Rosabel and her younger sister, Priscilla Muench, no doubt because of their relationship with Ta'isi (estranged wife and sister-in-law), were particularly vulnerable to attack coupled with the fact that they were "half-caste women" and subject to all the character defects conservatives believed they possessed.[41] Both women had lived in Germany, a history written by Arthur Braisby claimed, and spoke fluent German. Braisby also described Priscilla as "a very live wire" who had traveled for some years with a US vaudeville troupe as a Hawaiian singer and dancer and was "now (c.1934) believed to be living in Shanghai or Saigon."[42] In April 1930 they were before Justice Luxford on sedition charges. He convicted them but suspended their sentence of jail and exile, for the rather patronizing reason that they did not fully understand the seriousness of what they were doing. In exchange for a suspended sentence, they had to completely disengage with the Mau. Luxford took the opportunity when delivering his judgment on April 22 to lecture the women (and de facto the Mau) from the bench about how misguided the movement was.[43]

Even though Rosabel and Priscilla were let off, the Women's Mau remained active. Mau men were still in hiding, and so it was women who kept the protest active. They continued to hold processions through Apia, as they did on May 14, and gathered for a game of cricket that the administration suspected was a ruse to hide Mau meetings.[44] Rosabel continued to be targeted. On May 15 she was in her bathroom when Inspector Braisby and four other armed police burst in on her, though "fortunately she was clad." Braisby, the man described as "that infamous blackguard," who was reputedly "heavily interested in the opium traffic," had a warrant to search the premises.[45] Finally, in a kerosene tin in her chicken coop, they found a stash of communications from Ta'isi meant for Tupua Tamasese that had been loaned to Rosabel to read out to Women's Mau meetings held in her home.[46] Ta'isi was incensed when he got this news. He had tried to make sure his communications did not fall into government hands; he had received repeated assurances that all his communications were destroyed once they had been read. These instructions had not been followed and everyone, including Ta'isi's company through which these communiqués had been secretly sent, was greatly compromised.[47] The government was now sitting on a lot of very useful evidence they would use in future court actions. Ta'isi decided to no longer send detailed reports but rather letters to family and friends. He wrote a slew of letters after this that the administration again intercepted. They, too, were filed and kept as evidence.[48]

Rosabel was very unsettled by the government action against her. In May she sent an urgent request for either Piliopo—also known by her parents as Billie—or Malienafau to come immediately to Apia to be with her. Patrick Fitzherbert told Ta'isi Rosabel was in "a state near a breakdown" and needed at least one of her daughters with her. Ta'isi discussed the matter "fully with the girls and left them free to decide." All agreed "that if their mother is seriously ill, one or all of them would be prepared to go," but their preference was to stay with him. Ta'isi was concerned about letting them return. "Samoa at the present time is not the place for young girls who have just left school and least of all for any of my daughters on whom the Administration would not hesitate to vent their wrath on the slightest provocation or excuse."[49] Noue and Billie (Piliopo) had finished their schooling in Sydney. Malienafau, the most stellar student among her sisters, was completing her studies in law at Auckland University College. The prize-winning student would both graduate and become only the twelfth woman admitted as a solicitor in New Zealand in 1931.[50] Billie was now also at university. Sina and Taufau were attending Remuera Ladies College (and from 1932 they attended the Diocesan High School of Girls in Epsom).[51] As matters continued to worsen for her mother, Billie decided to return to Sāmoa to be with her in March 1931, an act that hurt Ta'isi and caused a rift between them for some time.[52]

Administrator Allen's way of combatting the grotesque image of New Zealand soldiers brutalizing women, used to great effect by the *NZ Samoa Guardian,* was to accuse them of being "dissolute" and without their usual "work" once Mau men headed into the hills to escape New Zealand forces after the massacre. Allen was falling back on the tried-and-true argument against women's political activism that such women were "public women" or "prostitutes" that was here compounded by racial inferences of ingrained sexual "immorality."[53] The very recent publication of anthropologist Margaret Mead's momentous work, *The Coming of Age in Samoa: A Psychological Study of Primitive Youth for Western Civilization,* in 1928 no doubt bolstered Allen's view that Sāmoan women lacked sexual morality and a culture of free love prevailed in the islands (a pervasive but debunked view).[54] Allen kept his thinking about the lack of virtue of Mau women out of the public realm for some months, but accusations were made privately. When New Zealand's annual report to the League was released in August, it contained passages by Allen about Mau women. "This movement," he wrote, "originated by two half-caste women, both of who are actively opposed to the Administration." Allen described the women involved in the Mau as dissolute and exhibiting "loose behavior."[55] A flurry of protest erupted. The women fired back, writing to Allen that their cause was a response to "frightening . . . us and our children in our houses in the middle of the night . . . you have called us HARLOTS and you state that we have no WORK SINCE THE DISPERSAL OF THE MEN OF THE MAU."[56] The women demanded a retraction; it never came. The Women's Mau then submitted a petition; Allen responded by accusing them of using "indecent" and "impertinent expressions" instead of supplying the names of genuine supporters of their cause.[57] The accusations of dissolution enraged Ta'isi and other Sāmoan nationalists. Ta'isi wrote another petition to the New Zealand parliament in late August where he lodged a number of complaints about the tenth report to the League on Western Sāmoa. Among a lengthy list of complaints he asked that the whole offending passage about Mau women be erased "as it is an attack on the good morals and chastity of the womanhood of Samoa."[58] Of Ta'isi's own intimate life, there were relatively few comments in official correspondence, though Allen would describe Viopapa as "illegitimate" with all the attendant smears on her, her mother, Leata, and, most particularly in this case, her father.[59]

Ta'isi publicly defended the all-important reputation of these women, whom he emphasized were respectable wives of leading men (excepting Ala, who was now a widow). As he was backing Rosabel and other women, he was also trying to avoid a worse "scandal." The police were still watching her, an embittered Slipper let Ta'isi know in August. Rosabel was not only drinking excessively; she also had a "married man" sleep over at her home in Papaloloa.[60] Slipper named the man as "Tamasese," who presumably was Tupua Tamasese Mea'ole, the unmarried younger brother of Tupua Tamasese Lea'lofi, who would become Rosabel's son-in-law when he married Noue (Rosabel and Ta'isi's oldest daughter) in 1934.[61] Allen had informed Wellington earlier that "Tamasese appears now to be well in the clutches of Mrs Nelson and Mrs Muench and drives about in their cars. He is a young fellow very susceptible to flattery and his head has been turned by their attentions."[62] Ta'isi talked to his daughters about Slipper's revelations. Rosabel had proudly told Ta'isi earlier that she was now a woman in the fashion of the flappers of the time; she now drank, smoked, enjoyed men's company, and laughed at their jokes. "Whatever may be my opinions of what you describe as 'a woman of the world,'" Ta'isi tactfully wrote, he did not think his daughters should be exposed to this at their current ages when they were all bridling against his paternal authority.[63] Yet Rosabel's ideas of personal freedoms in the context of the Mau were another weapon to disparage her and the movement, indeed to disparage all Sāmoan women. Wishing to avoid a "scandal," his daughters agreed that Ta'isi should write a carefully worded letter to Rosabel. He did, revealing the accusations and allowing her the chance to get a withdrawal from her accuser, so casting doubt on the veracity of the rumors. Yet he implored her, "for the sake of Samoa and the Cause," to take it no further than that. I leave it to your "wise discretion," Ta'isi told Rosabel. As well as this diplomatic letter, Ta'isi also wrote to family in Apia to make cautious inquiries. While maintaining all propriety, Ta'isi let Slipper know that in spite of the rumors "my family and I have been quite interested in the part she played in the inauguration of the Women's Mau movement."[64] Ta'isi seemed to question Slipper's rumor. Ta'isi found out from his brother-in law, Harry, that "Rosie is very disturbed about some scandalous rumours about her." Harry had "not enquired into it but she is taking is very seriously."[65]

Police were also watching Rosabel's sister, Priscilla, and reporting on who visited her house, and, more important, stayed overnight. The target of these police inquiries was not only the lady herself but also the Apia-based Mau barrister Patrick Brekley (P. B.) Fitzherbert. He was a married man whose family lived in New Zealand. Fitzherbert shared a good rapport with Ta'isi, who called him "Fisipate." Fitzherbert's daughter visited Ta'isi's home, and the Nelson girls reciprocated, visiting "your good family," who, Ta'isi let Fitzherbert know, were all in good health.[66] Fitzherbert also requested Ta'isi pay his wife directly for his professional services.[67] Police reports on Fitzherbert's supposed sexual misconduct remained out of the public domain, but Allen conveyed their details back to Wellington. He told of the salacious relations with Mrs. Muench, that servant girls had seen Fitzherbert lying on his bed "masturbating," and that he had attempted to rape someone, though Allen admitted "this story could not be confirmed" (unlike the others).[68] Fitzherbert had told Ta'isi "very early after my arrival here" Priscilla "volunteered to come into the office and do typing and interpreting." Fitzherbert was paying her "a small salary," but he hoped the business would grow enough for her to receive a "decent salary" as "she is absolutely invaluable and a very talented woman."[69] Fitzherbert's aspirations for his Apia practice did not materialize. As well as compiling this dossier of sexual dissolution, Allen also canceled Fitzherbert's license to practice law in June 1930. Allen's reasoning was that "he is becoming a centre of the Mau agitation. I consider in the present improved state of feeling it is too risky to allow him to continue to practice."[70] Fitzherbert then continued to work for Ta'isi and the Mau from Wellington.

While Sāmoans were dealing with the multifaceted effects of New Zealand's iron rule, Ta'isi had his own problems to contend with. Few of these problems were far removed from the Mau and were substantially compounded by the unfolding pressures of the Great Depression. Like other countries, the extremity of the Great Depression sent shock waves through the country at all levels. At the political level, differences within New Zealand's three-party system—two viable conservative parties (United led by Joseph Ward and Reform led by Gordon Coates) and Labour (headed by Harry Holland)—opened up. This was evident in various communities including in Ta'isi's local Auckland electorate of Parnell. Here, party politics, the Black Saturday Massacre, the effects of the Great Depression, and the concerted campaign against Ta'isi collided.

In March 1930 H. R. Jenkins, the sitting member for Parnell resigned from the United Party, the party under whose banner he won the seat in the November 1928 general election that put Ward into power. Jenkins' dramatic act was a response to being snubbed for a cabinet position, the press reported, saying Jenkins had expressed keen interest to Prime Minister Ward in the portfolio of "Tourist and Health Resorts."[71] In 1928 Jenkins won the seat of Parnell in 1928 by 849 votes; the Reform candidate got 4,793 votes, and the Labour candidate got 1,661.[72] Jenkins' resignation triggered a by-election to be held on May 7. Jenkins was one of four United MPs who stepped away from the party, causing political instability at a most critical time. Jenkins was initially going to run as an independent, but then he withdrew; the three parties fielded candidates in the solidly conservative constituency. Nevertheless, Labour launched an enthusiastic campaign they tried to make into a referendum on Ward's Sāmoa policy along with other pressing issues stemming from the Depression. Harry Holland campaigned for Thomas Bloodworth and tried to fire up the Parnell community about Sāmoa, as well as unemployment, infrastructure, commodity prices, and tariffs. When asked about Sāmoa, Bloodworth stated that if Labour gained power, it would adopt "more suitable methods of dealing with natives," and he did not "agree with a military dictatorship and the use of machine guns."[73] In contrast, both the Reform and United candidates dismissed Sāmoa as an issue. Bill Endean for Coates' Reform Party considered that "both the Reform and United Governments had discharged their duty to Samoa in a very fine way." All "the talk about 'Samoa for the Samoans' was about as ridiculous as advocating that a kindergarten should be governed by the children in it," Endean remarked.[74]

Ta'isi stepped into this highly volatile situation by swinging behind the Labour candidate, dedicating use of his car and other material support to Bloodworth's campaign. Jenkins triggered the by-election around March 22, having announced his resignation from the United Party on March 6. Then an uncanny coincidence happened. Ta'isi's disgruntled landlady from "Bingley" in Remuera, Josephine Wilson-Smith, launched a public suit against him. As described before, Mrs. Wilson-Smith and her rental property left a lot to be desired from the beginning. On March 14 Ta'isi and his daughters moved out of Mrs. Wilson-Smith's house after long negotiations about payment for major renovations where she would only bear a fraction of the costs involved. According to Ta'isi, this all occurred amicably and according the terms set out from December 1928, where he had been paying additional money to vacate at short notice. Ta'isi had discussed the situation with Mrs. Wilson-Smith, who continued to frequent "Bingley," as was her unwelcome habit, right up until the Nelsons vacated. She brought a prospective tenant through the house that the Nelsons had thoroughly scrubbed for the purpose. All the family, including Ta'isi, were present at this inspection, and "she expressed no displeasure with the appearance of the property and there were no grounds for complaint."

As the family was moving out on March 14 to more "roomy" accommodations at 44 Ranui Road, Remuera, in a house called "Kuranui," Mrs. Wilson-Smith returned. She met with Viopapa and gave the first hint that she "was out to make trouble for us." She accused the Nelsons of extensive damage to furnishings and breakages, despite Ta'isi coughing up considerable sums for repairs that Mrs. Wilson-Smith never undertook as she always had an "oft repeated" and "monotonous" "hard luck story." She threatened Viopapa with Ta'isi's public exposure for "cheating her" out of two weeks' rent, as "she knew many business men in Auckland." Ta'isi then found out she had been "very reckless in her remarks about my family and myself stating that if twenty horses were let loose in her house they could not have done more damage than we did" and similar comments at ladies' morning teas attended by friends of the Nelson family. Rather than refunding Ta'isi for his out-of-pocket expenses made in addition to a hefty rent (that included additional monies to pay for the use of furnishings) and taking into account the costs of cleaning and replacements for some breakages, Mrs. Wilson-Smith presented Ta'isi with an outrageous bill for more than £300. He refused to pay despite his wish to "avoid publicity." Not only was the claim unjustifiable; she had "slandered" him and his daughters. "I consider that she has done me serious injury many times the amount of her claim" from her repeated comments about his family.[75]

Mrs. Wilson-Smith then sued Ta'isi. This time the hearing date was set expeditiously; it was to take place in the final week of the Parnell by-election campaign. The papers lapped up the sensational details from the courtroom. The plaintiff's lawyer said the house was "vandalized"; it "was really incredible that human beings could live in a place and reduce it to the state it is in at the present time." The magistrate, W. R. McKean, inspected the property five weeks after Ta'isi vacated, during which time the house was locked up and susceptible to mold during a wet Auckland autumn. He described it as being in a "shocking state." Valuable items were found discarded under the house, carpets seemed to have been left out in the rain, and the backyard was full of shells and coconut husks. Witnesses testified the house had a "peculiar smell" never before experienced in Remuera that was so bad the house had to be fumigated. Alfred Hall Skelton, once again appearing for Ta'isi, questioned witnesses and Magistrate McKean about the offending odor, which the latter also claimed to have observed. "I suppose you suggest that Samoans smell differently from Europeans?" Hall Skelton asked. McKean demurred that it was Hall Skelton who was "bringing that out."[76] Hall Skelton countered that Ta'isi's "home in Samoa . . . compared with any in New Zealand" and it "contained furniture worth thousands of pounds." His "daughters were educated at the best of schools in Australasia," and the family "had stayed in various parts of the world and had never had a complaint." Mr. Nelson, Hall Skelton continued, "had a reputation for cleanliness . . . was spotless in his attire and in the keeping of his home." The family had been attacked, and it was a "matter vital to their well-being" to defend themselves.[77] When Viopapa testified later in the weeklong proceedings, she was grilled about how much they entertained ("only on Saturdays and Sundays when people would call for tennis"). Did they have evening entertainments? Where was alcohol served? Did they dance in the living room? How large were these gatherings? Viopapa claimed forty or fifty maximum, whereas Mrs. Wilson-Smith alleged that there were regular parties with more than one hundred guests. Viopapa was also asked if "during your occupancy of the place it was really the headquarters of all visiting Samoans." No, Viopapa insisted, and she also denied that Tupua Tamasese Lea'lofi had stayed at the house after his release from prison.[78]

Hall Skelton maintained the proceedings were politically motivated and were designed to "damage his client." This was of course denied, but it is hard to see the proceedings as anything but politically motivated given how the case played out.[79] Once the mud had been flung in the courtroom and duly reported in detail by the press, Magistrate McKean took ill. This happened to be the day of the Parnell by-election, May 7. Proceedings were suspended. When the magistrate was well enough to continue, he ordered Ta'isi to pay Mrs. Wilson-Smith. In a small concession, the magistrate found her claim exaggerated, and so Ta'isi was ordered to pay her sixty-six pounds.[80] Labour also resoundingly lost the Parnell by-election, receiving the lowest number of votes of the three parties. Bill Endean for the Reform Party won handsomely, strengthening Coates' party against the faltering Ward government.

As personally humiliating as the suit by his former landlady was, Ta'isi was most concerned after the court proceedings ended with traveling to Wellington. He was anxious to see Sir Māui Pōmare before he left for California; it was hoped this trip might restore the ailing statesman to better health. The two dear friends did see each other, and they talked about the Sāmoan cause and how it would fare in the current political climate. After seeing Ta'isi, Sir Māui also saw Gordon Coates. On his way across the Pacific Sir Māui related, in confidence, the gist of their conversation to Ta'isi. "I told him there was only one thing between him and myself and that was the Samoa Question," Sir Māui wrote. He informed Ta'isi that Coates had promised him autonomy for Sāmoans in a limited number of years, repeal of the banishment orders, and full representation of Sāmoans in a house of elected representatives. Sir Māui told Ta'isi, "Now draw your tigers off Coates because he is the coming man and if I live to come back to you I am certain what Gordon Coates has promised me will be faithfully carried out."[81]

Sir Māui did not come back to him. He died in Los Angeles on June 30, eliciting great outpourings of grief and expressions of admiration for his work over his long period of public service. In the many expressions of condolence made in parliament, only Harry Holland recalled Sir Māui's stance on Sāmoa: "those of us who listened to his speech on the third reading of the Samoa Amendment Bill in 1927 know that it was one the greatest efforts ever made in this House."[82] But no one expressed sorrow and gratitude with more passion than Ta'isi. "The clouds of heaven disperse," he wrote, "the titles are scattered—there is death—the moon has fallen in the Council of Chiefs and Kings of Aotearoa. POMARE IS DEAD." He wrote of the great personal loss as well as the loss to Sāmoa: "Pomare you have left us, but on whom shall Samoa lean? Who shall be the fortress of our little country? You have been the main pillar of our faith," and he pledged that "your name and your love for Samoa will never be forgotten."[83]

Pōmare's ashes were returned to New Zealand, via Rarotonga. As he had been the long-serving minister for the Cook Islands and was held in high esteem, there he was afforded full honors. In New Zealand his *tangi* (funeral), held at the Ōwae Marae in Waitara on August 25 and paid for by the government, was an enormous affair attended by thousands, including many members of parliament and the judiciary. Ta'isi sent his cousin Tauvao Talese, Viopapa, and Piliopo to represent him and Sāmoa. After the three had arrived in New Plymouth, Sir Māui's family insisted on Ta'isi's presence, too. Ta'isi made a last-minute dash from Auckland along winding and rough roads, arriving the morning of commemorations.

Amid Māori burial rites and before politicians who had both supported and persecuted Sāmoans, Ta'isi and his family stepped forward. Ta'isi made a "speech according to Samoan custom" and then presented an *'ie toga* (fine mat) that "was spread by Viopapa the elder daughter of Taisi on one side, by Piliopo on the other side and Tauvao at the rear all wearing lavalavas of siapo [mulberry barkcloth]." Ta'isi explained:

> This mat was one of the principal mats in the *lagi* (burial ceremony) of Tamasese, the father of the late Tamasese Lealofi and the present Tamasese. On that occasion this mat was presented to Mr Williams, the then Deputy Administrator of Savaii. From Mr Williams the mat passed to Petia LeSavaiinaea (Mr P A Jenson). It has now been released to be presented this day as a *mavaega* (parting gift) between Ta'isi and his dear friend Pomare.[84]

The loss of Sir Māui Pōmare was incalculable. Ta'isi had lost his cherished friend. The Mau had lost their most prominent and respected supporter. Coates' commitment to Sir Māui never came about. The United government did not fall after Joseph Ward resigned the prime ministership on grounds of ill health on May 28, 1930. (Ward died July 8, 1930.) George Forbes assumed the prime ministership and led the United government for another fifteen months; he did not deviate from his predecessor's Sāmoa policy at all.

Administrator Allen reported to his new prime minister in October that he had undertaken a *malaga* (tour of villages) around Sāmoa and that everything had returned to a state of normalcy. The men were "back in their own villages working on their plantations," and "even in former Mau villages" there was a state of cooperation and order. "The general situation in my opinion is highly satisfactory," Allen let his minister know. This news was sent onto Forbes in London for dissemination to the League and Dominions Office.[85] The Mau was now a spent force, Allen assured Wellington. The leadership was ineffectual, and in the case of Faumuina, he was unsure of "which side he should be on." "The Women's Mau was negligible though a nuisance." Rosabel had quarreled with Priscilla, and Rosabel "now takes no active part," Allen wrote. Like other small trouble spots Allen identified in October, the continuing nuisance of the Women's Mau was due to "half-caste" influence. There was now only "one danger," which was "from New Zealand where the agitation is carried on by Nelson through his paper" and the respected people that Ta'isi had brought into the protest. Allen was deeply frustrated that Ta'isi still seemed to be shaping elements of public opinion; "the New Zealand public generally still fails to understand what the cause of the Mau was and what its promoters desired." "The whole issue was and still is whether the white man or the half-caste should control the islands," Allen reasoned. Should the islands be "administered on behalf of the natives, the Samoan race preserved and gradually fitted for its own government" or should "the half-castes . . . gain control of the government, exploit the natives for their own benefit and reduce the islands to a half-caste community"? "This," Allen stated, "is the cause of all the political trouble here and cannot be made too plain."[86] General Richardson could not have put it better himself.

Ta'isi feared "there are very few true friends of Samoa among our people left."[87] This revelation pleased Allen; he highlighted this statement when sending a copy of this letter back to Wellington after it had been intercepted, as all of Ta'isi's communications with Sāmoa now were.[88] It was true that 1930 had been punishing for the Mau; the grinding challenges of the Great Depression, exacerbating every tension, coupled with new levels of authoritarian rule. Everyone's resolve was being tested. The time in the "Garden of Gethsemane" was far from over for Sāmoa and Ta'isi.

Yet there were still friends to the cause. Ta'isi received a letter from Isobel Field, the stepdaughter of Robert Louis Stevenson and daughter of Fanny, who had lived "many years" in Sāmoa. She expressed her shock at "the tragic death of the High chief Tamasese." She told Ta'isi that she had "sent what details I could find to England where Samoa has powerful friends." These powerful friends "have asked for 'facts' and assure me that if I can get them the matter will be placed before the King and taken before the League of Nations." She evoked her mother's and Louis Stevenson's graves atop Mount Vaea and the words on their tombs: "Thy country shall be my country and thy God my God." She remembered the kindness shown to her and her husband by Tupua Tamasese Lea'lofi I when they last visited Sāmoa in 1915 (Tupua Tamasese had died not long after this visit, and his son assumed the title). Field came to lay her mother's remains with those of her renowned husband, who had been a quiet sentinel overlooking Apia since 1894. The chief's kindnesses make us "consider ourselves as belonging to his aiga," she said. That his son "should be killed by New Zealand soldiers when he was unarmed and on a peaceful errand is so appalling that I beg you to send me facts and details that I may demand justice."[89]

No matter how much New Zealand authorities reiterated their distorted line about the causes of the Mau and why it needed to be stopped, the "facts" of recent Sāmoan history struck a deep chord with many people across the world. These same authorities knew that the major conduit of information about Sāmoa was Ta'isi. Exile and a campaign of humiliation had not silenced him. They would have to use a different tactic.

Chapter Twelve

Breaking Mr. Nelson in the Great Depression (1931–1932)

Public humiliation and exile had evidently not worked on Ta'isi. He continued to fight using every means available to him. As Ta'isi was based in New Zealand, he lay outside the reach of the sweeping Sāmoan sedition legislation that had brought numerous people before the courts, into jail, and exile by 1930. His company, however, was not beyond the reach of these laws. Armed with the Ta'isi's correspondence found in the raid on Rosabel's chicken coop or intercepted by postal officials and police when it arrived in mail bags, the administration was able to establish how money for the Mau—for the payment of legal fees and for the *NZ Samoa Guardian* costs—was moving between Sāmoa and New Zealand.

From August 1930 the administration began tracking financial transactions between the Mau and Ta'isi that went through O. F. Nelson and Co. As well as dominating the Sāmoan copra trade, shipping, and retail around the islands, "it has always been one of the commercial functions of my Company to accept and make monetary transfers between Samoa and other parts of the world," Ta'isi told Prime Minister Forbes and others.[1] The administration tracked twenty-eight transfers between August and late November 1930, amounting to £214 19s.[2]

The transfers were a response to Ta'isi's increasingly frequent requests for the reimbursements for costs Ta'isi had covered on the Mau's behalf.[3] The costs of running the legal actions and the newspaper were becoming too much for Ta'isi to shoulder alone. Not only because "I am not a millionaire," as he told Ale Malu in a July 1930 letter, but because a financial investment from as wide a group of people as possible offset the long-standing accusation that the Mau was Ta'isi's one-man campaign. Ta'isi revealed that £20,000 had been spent, but the Mau had sent only £5,000. The *NZ Samoa Guardian,* which he wanted to keep running as "I see its usefulness in letting the world know the cruelty of the Government in Samoa," was in substantial debt and costing £1,500 a year to run.[4] The rest of the money was spent on accumulating legal costs and to offset the cost of Ta'isi's Geneva trip. That Ta'isi had funded 75 percent of the Mau's costs "would not matter to me if I had plenty of money left, but now it is all gone and I still have my children to keep."[5] In a letter to Ala Tamasese, also from July, Ta'isi discussed the disappearance of some Mau levies. He revealed he was keeping track of all monies sent to him and how it had been expended.[6] All of this intelligence was music to the New Zealand government's ears. No doubt it was pleasing for officials to read Ta'isi was hurting financially but he was also explaining how the Mau—seditious organization—operated.

Ta'isi's financial woes were very real. The combined effects of personal, national, and global events had hurt business—a lot. He had been away from Sāmoa approaching three years in the later part of 1930. In his absence a culture of slackness pervaded the company's employees, according to Rosabel and others. Rosabel wrote a forcefully worded letter on this to Ta'isi in May 1930 that left no doubt about the state of the firm he had always kept in peak running order. Rosabel told him when she called into the offices and store she found employees talking and not "doing a stroke of work." Not only was no work being done; Rosabel visited two open bars on Nelson premises and had a drink in each, to prove alcohol was being served during business hours. In addition to this, her ire was raised when no representative from the firm, including her brother, Harry W. Moors (the company's secretary), attended her court hearing in April. Afterward she went to the store and abused the staff for not showing support for the Mau cause in which she and Ta'isi were so heavily invested. "I called your staff cowards and every dirty name I could think of," Rosabel told Ta'isi, who was also very familiar with her hot temper. On a business level, big customers, like the Marist brothers, had become so tired of the "awful service they have lately received at Nelson's that they have been forced to transfer more of their business to B.P.'s [Burns Philp]." Rosabel wanted to "save you in your business" because "where will we all be," as well as all those Sāmoans who relied on the firm for their livelihoods, if the company went under?[7] Rosabel's interest in these matters was also personal; she was the second-largest shareholder in the firm. With Ta'isi she held 75 percent of the shares in O. F. Nelson and Co. Things were so dire, Rosabel said, she thought Ta'isi should appoint her to a managerial position. With that authority she could then appear at the company and bring some discipline to bear. Ta'isi tactfully declined to do this; her shareholder position should be sufficient to make the staff listen to her, he reasoned.[8]

Ta'isi was also deeply concerned about the company. He told Rosabel "the financial position of the Nelson Company has caused me some concern for quite a long time." When he was on the spot in Apia, the company never needed advances from the bank, but since he left, hefty advances and overdrafts were becoming routine. The political unrest in Sāmoa "made for abnormal conditions," but copra purchases had increased over recent years. It did not compute.[9]

"My financial position is very embarrassing indeed," Ta'isi told Rosabel in May 1930. He was letting her know he could not buy one thousand of her company shares to boost her own liquidity. Things had gotten so tight that he would need to borrow in the near future. His financial burdens were various. *NZ Samoa Guardian* costs and Mau legal fees—Thomas Slipper requested that Ta'isi either settle his bills or give him credit from O. F. Nelson and Co.—were too much. He told Rosabel, "I have not and I cannot yet think that it is my duty to meet all these obligations myself." The *Herald* libel case had cost him, too. Other financial burdens were admittedly of his own making: "I blame myself for the heavy expenditures of my house and family as in my foolish fatherly love for the girls I have brought them up rather extravagantly, providing for their every want and whim." Despite the financial stress he wanted the girls to "feel the pinch as little as it is possible for me to make it." Their three eldest daughters being out of school "now require complete new outfits having discarded their school tunics." He did not mention the additional expenses generated by Viopapa (being the stepdaughter Rosabel intensely disliked), though Viopapa also had a taste for fine clothes like her sisters. "With careful manipulation and self-denial . . . we can pull through," Ta'isi assured Rosabel with his characteristic optimism. The girls were "very reasonable" in this regard, which Ta'isi found "very gratifying."[10]

In these exchanges, Ta'isi expressed his intense love and devotion to his daughters. He talked to them about all manner of things, as though they were adults, but spoiled them too. Ta'isi knew they resented some of his advice (how could six young daughters not?) and hoped they all could come to an understanding "without a serious breach." Ta'isi was absolutely "adored" by his daughters.[11] The girls may have resented how their conduct would reflect on the family, the Mau, and Sāmoa, but Ta'isi was more than aware they were subject to additional scrutiny. The very recent Remuera landlady suit had unpleasantly demonstrated the public scrutiny all the Nelson family was under.

The other factor in Ta'isi's financial stress was, of course, the Great Depression. He told Rosabel that "the rest of the world" was going through "stressing times" like they were.[12] Ta'isi did not divulge much of the company's woes to Rosabel, but other business letters reveal the extent of the problems. The price of copra had plummeted in London, having a great impact on the Sāmoan economy, which was pegged to that commodity price. The dividend paid to O. F. Nelson and Co. shareholders accordingly dropped in 1930 (though Ta'isi said this was also due to an auditor insisting substantial monies be moved to cover bad debts).[13] Ta'isi told Harry W. Moors in September 1930, "I think the time had come when we must seriously consider retrenching staff and stocks and even closing down departments and trading stations which do not pay."[14] In October there were "great retrenchments ordered in Head Office." Those who retained their positions "had to accept a cut in salary from 10% to 20%." Ta'isi took a pay cut of 25 percent.[15]

In the second half of 1930, as Ta'isi fretted over company finances from Auckland, New Zealand sent the minister for defense, John Cobbe, to Sāmoa. In August 1930 Cobbe was party to talks with Mau men who had been coaxed out of hiding in the mountains by LMS missionaries (so Reverend Bartlett claimed).[16] Cobbe witnessed Colonel Allen broker a rapprochement with the men leading to the administrator's August declaration the Mau was "quite dead among the Samoans." Allen qualified his declaration of the Mau's death (the latest in a series of such pronouncements) by acknowledging the "little group of half-caste agitators in Apia continues in its activity."[17] Ta'isi was also cited for fanning the flames of discontent. To put a stop to Ta'isi's activities and frustrate these Apia-based agitators (as many of them were supposedly connected to O. F. Nelson and Co.), the administration monitored monetary transfers and continued to closely scrutinize Ta'isi's communications with family, the company and the Mau in preparation for a legal case against his firm.

Allen's picture of the Sāmoan situation was strenuously combatted in heated parliamentary debates sparked by Harry Holland on October 7. Harry Holland brought the latest contentious report to the League up for discussion as a way of reviewing the longer history of Sāmoan policy. Parliamentary wrangling sparked another round in the war of words outside parliament. It was stoked by the public appeal by seventy-nine eminent New Zealanders for an investigation into Sāmoan affairs and more petitions to parliament. Ta'isi also stoked it.[18] Allen was quite correct in his assessment of Ta'isi's role in fanning the Mau, as Ta'isi's activities in late 1930 bear out. The mainstream press was tiring of the story, exemplified by the *Evening Post* headline "Samoa Again" reporting on the parliamentary debates.[19] The dwindling number of reports also attest to the declining attention being paid to Sāmoa. Yet Ta'isi kept putting the issues forward. In late October 1930 he authored another pamphlet, *What Samoans Want,* which was reprinted from the *NZ Samoa Guardian.* In it, Ta'isi reiterated the history of New Zealand's rule and the causes of the Mau up to the "scandalous" assailing of "the chastity of the womanhood of Samoa" in the latest annual report to the League. He strenuously countered the administration line "Samoans are beginning to realise they have been misled by 'agitators' and matters are settling down," a picture Allen further justified after his recent *malaga.*

What *did* Sāmoans want—according to Ta'isi—in late October after there was an easing of military pressure that the Mau took as a defeat of the administration (though Allen saw it as the opposite)? Ta'isi summarized it in five points. First, tell the truth about Sāmoa and withdraw the latest annual report. Second, apologize sincerely to the women of Sāmoa for slanderous statements. Third, make full reparations to Sāmoans for all the valuable lives and property destroyed during the crackdown. Four, "mete out proper punishment to all those responsible for the shooting, killing and ill-treatment of the Samoans." Five, discuss with "properly accredited representatives of the Samoan people the best means of transferring" the mandate to a "Power with sufficient experience and sympathy with the aspirations of the Samoans to conduct the Protectorate in the terms of the solemn treaty concluded in 1889 between Samoa and the Powers"—in other words, the United States.[20]

At that same time Ta'isi's pamphlet was circulating, the US Congress had conducted an "epoch-marking event": the American Samoan Commission.[21] Three Sāmoan representatives met with four from

Congress, and on October 7 agreed to the terms by which the status of American Samoa and American Sāmoans would be formalized with the United States. During the hearings, High Chief Tuitele of Tutuila asked why the United States could not "take over the Western Samoa mandate from New Zealand" which "allowed her white policemen to shoot down the natives." This was excruciating for New Zealand on all levels, made worse by the fact Ta'isi and the *NZ Samoa Guardian* amplified these developments as much as possible.[22] In September the paper ran two contrasting images; one of Tupua Tamasese Lea'lofi's freshly dug grave, captioned "The Ever Open Grave," and another of an idyllic Pago Pago Harbor, noting that this was where the commission was sitting and the accompanying caption "Where Samoans are Happy."[23] The contrast could not be plainer. When the official government report was issued in March 1931, the *NZ Samoa Guardian* reported, "America Frees Samoans."[24] Ta'isi ordered five hundred copies of the US government report for distribution to New Zealand members of parliament (and to many others, too, given the size of the order).[25] The story also gained some coverage in the mainstream New Zealand press.[26]

In November 1930 Ta'isi publicly challenged the acting prime minister. Describing himself as the "accredited representative of the Samoan people," Ta'isi took issue with statements by, E. A. Ransom, who voiced the government line responding to these latest developments.[27] Many aspects of Ransom's response to the latest criticism angered Ta'isi. The worst was Ransom's written response to the seventy-nine signatories Ta'isi described as "the intelligentsia of New Zealand." Ransom told these men "the government have persistently and determinedly endeavoured to ascertain just what were the grievances of the disaffected natives."[28]

Ta'isi also wrote a long and impassioned letter to Ransom in December on commercial concerns. "I wish to place on record my urgent protest against the export duty on all bananas shipped from Samoa."[29] With copra prices depressed, Ta'isi pinned a lot of hope on a healthy banana export trade to sustain the Sāmoan economy.[30] He tried to separate business from Mau politics in his direct communications with the New Zealand government in late 1930, but the government was in the advanced stages of conflating the two in its legal action.

While the administration was still amassing evidence and planning its next move, the first anniversary of the Black Saturday Massacre came. The administration was nervous and deployed a considerable number of armed constables around Apia on December 28. Mau leaders, like Faumuina, as well as rank-and-file men, were told they could not participate in public commemorations.[31] Allen reported secondhand about a "muster of Women's Mau" who proceeded from Apia to Tupua Tamasese Lea'lofi's grave in Lepea; there were "454 women in the procession when it passed central offices and in all 613 in last stages."[32] To Allen, this was a sign the Mau was indeed a spent force.[33] However, for an eyewitness, the procession he saw signaled the opposite. "The Mau as strong as ever," reported George Westbrook to Ta'isi. He estimated more than double the numbers of women paraded (he said fifteen hundred) and they did so dressed in mourning with white trim—the uniform of the Women's Mau. They carried wreaths and other floral offerings to the grave, where a service was held and hymns sung.[34]

Ta'isi thought of Black Saturday when he watched a riot on Queen Street from his office window a few weeks after the first anniversary of the massacre. Like the tragic events on Ifi Ifi Street, the riot erupted with a clash of a procession and police. But here on the streets of Auckland it was a procession of the unemployed who threw bricks at police. Police responded with batons. Injuries were sustained on both sides. Things "looked very ugly for a while," Ta'isi said. He was struck by how differently law enforcement operated here in New Zealand and in Apia. "Had this riot occurred in Samoa," he reasoned, "there would have been a number of Samoans killed by 'unnecessary' rifle fire, but in New Zealand the Police would not dare carry arms, least of all use them on the mob if they had them."[35] He was probably right in this assessment.

By the time Ta'isi saw this violent episode that captured the trauma inflicted on New Zealanders by the Great Depression, his own fortunes had taken an unwelcome turn, though he was unaware of it at the time. On January 10, 1931, the offices of O. F. Nelson and Co. were searched. Administrator Allen had called Harry W. Moors to Government House (Vailima) and "invited him to assist" in the search. Moors submitted to the request. After the search was carried out, Allen reported it was successfully conducted "on very courteous lines." Allen knew what they were looking for: books that documented monies transferred. They got them—and with clearly set-out amounts, names, and details showing money transferred to Ta'isi from Mau supporters via O. F. Nelson and Co. There was no concealment of these books or the activities they recorded by Moors or other employees.

Ta'isi found out—more than two weeks after the fact—when a letter informing him of the developments made it to Auckland on the *Tofua*. Censors had blocked an earlier radio message.[36]

Within days of Ta'isi becoming aware of what was happening, proceedings began before Chief Judge Luxford. O. F. Nelson and Co. faced twenty-eight charges under the *Samoa Seditious Organizations Regulations* enacted one year earlier in January 1930. Principals in the company, like Rudolph Kruse and Moors, gave evidence that monies paid to Ta'isi represented legitimate debts owing to him for legal costs incurred for various Mau actions. Ta'isi was owed these monies as part of the arrangement of being the Mau's representative in Geneva and New Zealand. The debts were incurred prior to the Mau being declared a seditious organization in January 1930. Kruse and Moors, like the books seized in the search of the company office, openly stated what had happened.[37] Similar payments were made to Ta'isi to settle these debts via the post office ("in fact over £100 has been sent through the Post Office since the raid," he told his friend and business associate in San Francisco D. B. Crane).[38] Though Ta'isi was fully alive to the "tragical aspect of the situation" he nonetheless thought "this case would supply material for another Gilbert & Sullivan Comic Opera." As "farcical" as New Zealand's "bungling" of Western Sāmoa was, it "provides more material for a drama than a comedy" Ta'isi realized.[39] As the case played out, Ta'isi's observation became increasingly accurate.

Administrator Allen wrote to Wellington: "case is simple and conviction seems beyond doubt."[40] Judge Luxford thought so, too, but he did think it was prudent to adjourn proceedings so Ta'isi could give evidence in Auckland. Allen assured Wellington, "I cannot discuss with the Chief Judge the reasons prompting him to suggest the obtaining of Nelson's evidence," yet "I have the strong impression he is considering the imposition of a heavy penalty and he wishes to disarm criticism in advance such as might attribute a conviction to Nelson being unable to give evidence and explain the matter." Allen again assured Wellington there was no untoward collusion between himself and the chief judge: "I am merely guessing in forming this opinion."[41] Prime Minister George Forbes (who had taken over from Ransom in May 1930) was miffed at Luxford's decision because it gave Ta'isi another opportunity to gain publicity in New Zealand.[42] Luxford's decision highlighted one major problem with the case: Who was the defendant? Was it a company or the company's main shareholder and director after whom the company was named? Ta'isi acted on legal advice and did not give evidence so as to distance himself from proceedings and the perception he was on trial.[43] Luxford (as Allen so accurately predicted he would) convicted O. F. Nelson and Co. on all charges on April 21. He also imposed the heavy penalty Allen "guessed" he might, a fine of £200 for each charge, £5,600 total. He also wanted to "cancel the defendant's license to trade" but did not have the power to do so; he hoped executive authority would impose this penalty.[44] After the judgment was handed down, Harry Moors heard "prominent Government officials" say as they left the courtroom "we made Nelson, now we're going to break him."[45]

Ta'isi's reaction to the decision and the size of the penalty was one of astonished realization of what the government really intended to achieve with this case. He wrote to D. B. Crane in San Francisco that "this excessive penalty has astounded the New Zealand people and will cause a temporary reaction but such will only be shortlived as in former cases." He told Crane there would be an appeal as it "will be seen . . . that I am not only deprived of means to collect what is owing to me" but the "huge fine is meant as the knockout blow to me." "It is hoped," he continued, "that when I am reduced to penury all opposition to the Administration will be removed and New Zealand will again pose as the 'Model' Mandatory."

When Ta'isi wrote to Prime Minister Forbes some days after Luxford's decision, he did not sound like a man broken by the courts. His tone was more emotional (exasperated or agitated would be closer descriptions) than usual, but it nonetheless stayed within his measured and eloquent style. His prompt for writing was the *Western Samoa Gazette* he had received that week. It gave notice there was a new arduous system of procedure and paperwork for any fruit exporter. This new law added another layer of "excessive legislation" to the lives of Sāmoans who would have to meticulously account for the provenance of any fruit bound for export; any failure to meet these rigorous requirements was subject to a fifty-pound fine. Fruit from the New Zealand government-owned reparation estates were exempted from these laws. Coupled with the export tax on bananas of "50% on the purchase price," Ta'isi saw these new provisions would cripple small-scale communal producers and so their economic viability would be further jeopardized. This was the latest in now a long line of "laws imposed . . . restricting [Sāmoans] free movement and action in keeping with their social life and old political system of local government." Ta'isi pointed out (again) that this was "one of the fundamental grounds of the original complaints." A Sāmoan was now not free to move "from one village to another or perform hardly any one of his formerly lawful pursuits without a police permit." Ta'isi also raised Luxford's recent decision in the prosecution of his company. While noting there would be an appeal ("I do not propose to discuss the finding of the High Court at the present juncture"), he told Forbes both the prosecution and the defense gave evidence that the payments were for "an old debt to me." In pursing this case, Ta'isi said, "the Government is only making a rod for its own back in encouraging the Samoans by law to repudiate their acknowledged lawful debts." Teaching Sāmoans to repudiate their debts along with the other restrictive laws discussed "can only produce a demoralizing influence on the formerly clean Samoan mind."[46]

Ta'isi also noted that a new opportunity presented itself to broker a real solution to the problem with the new administrator Brigadier General Herbert Ernest Hart. If this solution was to come about, New Zealand had to cease denying Sāmoans "the constitutional rights and privileges of free speech of a freeborn citizen of a free born country." He mentioned his own exile and that "I have yet to be convinced that I have in any way, in any of my actions, infringed or exceeded" any rights and privileges of free speech enjoyed by those in New Zealand. "In my humble opinion," he went on, "it ill becomes a country like New Zealand, professing democratic principles to withhold from anyone in this native country those rights of free speech and action which your own laws allow him to enjoy in New Zealand." The justification for imposing this grossly inconsistent suite of rights between the home country and its colony also needed to be abandoned. Ta'isi argued:

> The claim that the Samoans are too backward in education, intelligence and culture to be given in their own country the privileges extended to the Maoris here, is based on a fallacy which, unless withdrawn, will remain a stumbling block to an honourable settlement.

Ta'isi stressed this letter was "prompted by the desire to promote to the utmost the gesture towards friendly negotiations" that was also contained in a letter from the chiefs to Administrator Hart upon taking up his new appointment.[47] Ta'isi wanted a negotiated solution on respectful terms as he warned, "You can never wear the Samoan down by attrition."[48]

The decision of what to do about O. F. Nelson and Co.'s trading license was left up to the new administrator, who was making his way to his new posting as Judge Luxford delivered his decision. This timing was one piece of good fortune for Ta'isi, as the new administrator did not proceed with canceling the license. This decision was probably not unrelated to the fact Hart met with Ta'isi before he left Auckland. Ta'isi reported, "I had a very cordial interview lasting nearly an hour before he left here."[49] H. E. Hart hailed from the Wairarapa, and he was a man of character; action and courage, attested his friend from Masterton, H. H. Daniel.[50] During the war, Hart had distinguished himself at some of the great battles: Gallipoli (he landed there on April 25 but was wounded two days later, recuperated in England, and returned in September); Armentières; and the third battle of Ypres.[51] Like his predecessor, he returned to civilian life and legal practice (in Masterton and Carterton) after the war's end only to be called up to serve as the fourth administrator of the mandated territory in 1931.

Despite all the claims the Mau no longer existed, Hart could have been under no illusions about the difficulties he faced as the mandate's new ruler given all the local, national, and international pressures bearing down on the Sāmoan territory at that time. As Ta'isi characterized the situation, "Hundreds of leading Samoans are even now in gaol and being arrested daily because they will not ask for police permits to move from one part of the village of district to another." Nor were many Sāmoans seeking police permission to carry the knives, axes, and hardwood staves they needed for the agricultural pursuits and were being arrested accordingly. "I greatly fear," he wrote, "Samoans will be goaded by these barbarous tactics to violent retaliations in sheer desperation." Yet he hoped "that the patience and dignity of the Samoans will hold out to the end and will continue to urge the Samoans to maintain peace at all costs."[52] Ta'isi also conveyed this view of the situation to Prime Minister Forbes, and it is likely he discussed it with General Hart, too, before he left New Zealand for Apia.[53]

Despite the one reprieve Ta'isi got from the New Zealand administration—that his trading license was not revoked—his economic situation worsened. In 1931 he took another substantial cut in pay and, with no income from dividends, he estimated his income was now down 40 percent. His Sydney and Auckland offices were going to have to follow the retrenchment and reduced-pay regime already undertaken in Apia.[54] Ta'isi's papers tell the story of other businesses collapsing, selling assets, requests for bank credit, and other accommodations and pressures. Ta'isi received an anguished letter, for example, from a man in Suva whose mortgage with O. F. Nelson and Co. in Apia would be foreclosed if he did not promptly settle his outstanding account. Ta'isi replied saying that while he did not have personal knowledge of this man's circumstances his company was "forced by pressures brought upon us by our own creditors to take measures to ensure early collection of . . . debts which in better times we might have been pleased to hold over."[55] To his Sydney manager, Donald Stewart, Ta'isi said, "We must all reef our sails to the lowest possible security so as to weather the storm."[56] The stress for the company was widespread and exacerbated by the administration's campaign and Ta'isi's absence from the company's helm. Like Rosabel in May 1930, A. G. Smyth gave Ta'isi a bleak appraisal of O. F. Nelson and Co. one year later. Smyth wanted to know, "Why is it that you have had to close so many of your stations?" He had only closed one of his and Burns Philp none of theirs. Smyth said:

> We see members of your Apia staff hanging around gossiping at all hours. No one seems to me to have your interests at heart, wholly, they seem to think that their job is an everlasting one, yet if any of them lost their job with you they would find it most difficult at the present time to find another job half as good.[57]

An exemplary work ethic had to be set by the company's heads, Smyth said. They should arrive on time each morning and be back from lunch promptly, and they should have no "outside interests." The sloppy work and attitude at O. F. Nelson and Co. meant the competitors were getting ahead.[58] Ta'isi's bankers, the Bank of New Zealand, found other causes for the financial problems besetting O. F. Nelson and Co. The general manager of the bank, H. Buckleton, wrote to Ta'isi: "In your absence from Samoa the bank would like a first class business man—a European—in charge of the business down there."[59]

O. F. Nelson and Co. was still the largest of the three trading companies operating in Sāmoa. It differed, however, from the competing interests of Burns Philp and Morris Hedstroms as "it is purely a Samoan business and is owned and managed almost entirely by Samoan half-castes and Samoan employees." The company was "a family affair" with shareholders being predominantly members of the Moors and Nelson families, and Ta'isi owning 57 percent of the shares.[60] Like Harry Moors and Rudolph Kruse, family filled many of the upper ranks of the company. This structure had benefits, but also downsides. From mid-1931 Ta'isi regretted a venture initiated by Moors to build a picture theater in Apia. From 1929 Island Tifaga, a business connected with Hollywood juggernaut MGM, was given a huge credit to finance the venture. Harry Moors had personally given the security. The building itself consumed huge expense, and then there was the costly projection equipment and hopefully new-fangled and expensive equipment for "talkie" films (though MGM said in 1932 they were only going to send silent films to Apia). Island Tifaga's special accommodation was a great drain—they owed more than £6,000—and Ta'isi blamed it and Moors for jeopardizing the financial position of O. F. Nelson and Co.[61]

In April 1932 Ta'isi wrote to his nephew and trusted company manager, Rudolph Kruse (with whom he usually had an affectionate relationship), "It was most shocking to me to find that even you seem to have taken little notice of my continuous warning against the rising accounts of Harry Moors and the Island Tifaga Ltd until now the position is more than serious."[62] The problem with Island Tifaga was replicated, albeit on a smaller scale, throughout the Nelson account books. Many people, churches, and organizations like the Apia Turf Club and the Masonic Lodge, as well as government departments (like the Police and Prisons Department) had credit accounts with O. F. Nelson and Co. The list of creditors even included Arthur Braisby, the inspector of police, and Judge Luxford—the man who aimed to put O. F. Nelson and Co. out of business entirely. Braisby did not owe much (four pounds) and neither did the judge (a little over one pound). Others did. As money got tighter, so did the resort to credit. Some of the worst offenders owing the company were family members like Nimo Moors (Ta'isi's mother-in-law), Gustava Wetzell (his sister), and A. Wetzell (brother-in-law).[63] Getting these people to settle their debts was a complicated process entangled with family, position, and money. As the latter got tighter—for everyone—the company had to resort to canceling shares as a means to recover debt.[64] Coupled with the administration's campaign against the company, calling in debts combined to make it rough sailing for O. F. Nelson and Co. Ta'isi also worried that the "white population" was boycotting his stores as a mark of solidarity with the New Zealand government once his business was directly targeted.[65]

Sāmoans still kept sending Ta'isi money (via the post office) despite the constant threat of prosecution and their economic straits. Ta'isi wrote a letter in October 1931: "I am very happy and thankful that you are helping me with the money being sent forward. I am not squandering it as I know the extreme poverty of these days." "We all share in this poverty," he said, "yet we should not weaken at this time, Samoa still has breakers ahead and should still strive until the voyage is satisfactorily ended." He also told of the new tactic to combat New Zealand. "The Moon is nearly at the full, no more spearing [of fish] is to be done, the coconut is concealed, we cannot reverse oars in the objective of the Mau," he wrote, "petitions are going forward now to the Three Great Powers."[66] His notion was to return to the 1889 Berlin Treaty between Britain, Germany, and the United States that guaranteed "the neutrality, autonomy and independence of Samoa."[67] "There was some opinion that such distant matters could not be revived," Ta'isi warned, but this process circumvented the League's whole mandate structure and also New Zealand. The League had given nothing but a tin ear to a recent succession of Sāmoan petitions.[68] It might be "futile to revive old pledges between Samoa and the Great Powers," he conceded. But, he wrote presciently, even "if results are not seen by the present generation, yet no doubt they will serve as a resting-place for all the generations of Samoa to come."[69] The petition was disseminated.[70] The New Zealand government was irritated and embarrassed by this latest attempt to draw international attention to Sāmoa. Sāmoans waited (and waited) for a response.

Luxford's decision against O. F. Nelson and Co. was appealed to the full bench of the Court of Appeal in Wellington, which began hearing the case in mid-October 1931. The *Seditious Organizations Ordinance* stated:

> No person shall participate in activities of, or aid, abet, or encourage in any way whatsoever the continuance, activities or object of any seditious organization or by any badge, symbol, uniform, flag, banner or any other means whatsoever, identify himself with or express his approval of any seditious organization.[71]

Lawyers for O. F. Nelson and Co. argued that Luxford's decision be overturned on the grounds that the "appellant is an incorporated company" and that the regulations do not "apply to such a company." If the word "person" in the regulations did include a company, the existence of *mens rea*—a guilty mind—was necessary before there could be a conviction. Although the prosecution presented all the evidence of Ta'isi's association with the Mau and its members it had been collecting from the mail and raids, this was not brought into evidence. The court determined it was not Ta'isi but the company on trial. The court of appeals delivered its decision on December 16. A majority of three judges upheld the convictions; two judges dissented.[72] The penalties were significantly reduced; a maximum of £200 on one charge and £10 each in respect to each of the others. Chief Justice Michael Myers represented the majority judges. Four years before he was King's Counsel for the government during the confidential Joint Samoan Petition Committee hearings in August 1927 and had sparred repeatedly with Ta'isi while he gave extensive evidence. Now Myers sat in judgment over his firm. In the majority judgment, Myers used "very strong words in laying the blame on me even though it was not an action against me," Ta'isi wrote. He wondered if Myers "may still have some irritation against me on account of those happenings when he was unable to confuse me, and the questions that were put to me were turned against him and his side." Only one of the two dissenting judgments was published, which Ta'isi also thought irregular along with Myers' intemperate and personal remarks. Despite feeling there was justification for taking this matter further, Ta'isi would not appeal to the Privy Council as it would "waste further money." "Therefore this matter will be finished but one cannot tell whence some other matter may come against me at any time," he wrote with foreboding. His faith and optimism would see him through this uncertainty; "let us rely on God in all things" he wrote, as well as "there is no use in becoming disheartened by such things."[73]

Many people were digging deep into their spiritual reserves to see them through the *sturm und drang* of 1931 and 1932. The unprecedented social and economic turmoil of the Great Depression was at its nadir. 1932 saw more riots on New Zealand streets as despairing citizens vented their angst in direct action. Ta'isi was shocked by the aftermath of the riot in Auckland in April 14 when shop windows were smashed on Queen Street, goods looted, and mounted police attacked. The next day as he made his way to his Queen Street office, it was as if the "city had been struck by a great earthquake or a violent storm," so great was the damage. "The people of New Zealand are now all savagely accusing each other," he wrote. The implications for Sāmoa were clear: "the name of Samoa has not been heard in the present session of the New Zealand Parliament," Ta'isi reported.[74] Even though Sāmoa was low or virtually off the political agenda, Ta'isi's work in shaping New Zealand public opinion remained a factor; there was sufficient sympathy for the Mau cause to impact future political decisions. On the international front, Sāmoans still awaited a response on the petition to the three powers.

Sāmoa may have been dropping from the political agenda, but Ta'isi was not; he was at the center of the thoughts of Administrator Hart, the prime minister, and External Affairs. From the beginning of 1932, officials discussed what would happen if Ta'isi returned to Sāmoa when his term of exile was due to expire at the end of the year.[75] The solicitor F. D. Baxter, who had represented both Ta'isi and opposing parties, wrote to Forbes in March 1932 offering his services to broker a deal with Ta'isi. Baxter pointed out that although their professional relationship had been mixed, Ta'isi had always been "courteous" and, Baxter believed, Ta'isi wanted a genuine peaceful solution. The alternative to not negotiating with Ta'isi, Baxter argued, was the reawakening of the Mau that his return would inevitably bring about. Officials debated this offer, which even had the backing of General Richardson's previous lieutenant, former Chief Justice of Sāmoa W. H. Woodward.[76]

By April Forbes rejected Baxter's offer outright.[77] Instead the debate among officials turned to whether Ta'isi should be permitted to return to Sāmoa at all. Prime Minister Forbes asked the solicitor general for an opinion about whether it would be legally possible to prevent Ta'isi's (and Gurr's) return. Forbes was "convinced" Ta'isi's activities in New Zealand "during the last few years are amply sufficient to warrant an extension of his period of deportation if this should be considered the proper course to adopt *in our own interests.*" After thinking about it, however, Forbes came to the conclusion "it would not be advisable to prevent the return of the deportees . . . unless of course you should hold a contrary opinion."[78]

Hart notified the prime minister that Sāmoans were already planning lavish welcoming ceremonies for "Ta'isi Nelisoni." He also conveyed the contents of letters Ta'isi had written in which he told Mau supporters, "New Zealand is getting very weak and there are very many poor people whom the government of New Zealand have to care for and feed or they would die." Because of this, he went on, "the Government is also very poor and weak, so be strong and steadfast and we will soon be successful in getting all our demands granted if you all remain true to the cause of the Mau."[79] Watching the effect that the anticipation of Ta'isi's return was already having on many Sāmoans, Hart dropped his sympathetic stance. He told Forbes:

> I am of the emphatic opinion that Nelson should not be permitted to return in December next nor for a period of two years from the time he ceases his present activities, and even then subject only to his giving satisfactory guarantees for this future conduct.

Unfortunately, there was no existing legal power to prevent Ta'isi or Gurr returning. So, Hart said, "I therefore urge that the necessary steps be taken to obtain such power as early as possible."[80]

Forbes responded to Hart that "we entirely recognize the force of your representations" and "the return of Nelson and Gurr may well lead to a position of considerable difficulty and perhaps to the recrudescence of political troubles." Nevertheless, the government did not believe they could enact legislation to prevent the exiles' return. The main reason being the "impossibility of carrying public opinion with us" if they passed the necessary legislation, and, if they did, Ta'isi would become more of a martyr than he already was. As consolation Forbes promised Hart he could have more police and also a cruiser "at your disposal," though it would "of course be highly undesirable for the ship to be in Apia at the time of Nelson's arrival." Forbes reasoned, "This would I think be damaging to our prestige and would be a great encouragement to Nelson and his followers as indicating the importance that we obviously attached to their movements."[81]

While New Zealand officials talked police and military reinforcements to quell an uprising upon Ta'isi's return, Sāmoans talked about continuing their nonviolent resistance. A group of six Mau chiefs wrote again to Hart in May 1932, as they had done one year earlier when he took up his office. Hart had not even replied to the first letter. They expressed their grave disappointment there was no respite from the oppressive laws they identified. The chiefs affirmed their faith in the three powers petition and that it would eventually deliver Sāmoans from their oppression. It had already put them on an improved footing with the League as far as they were concerned. Regardless of all these great discontents the chiefs told Hart, "We shall ever continue passively to resist with all the constitutional and peaceful means available to us that vicious system" that permits "arbitrary banishment, degradation, deportation, imprisonment and persecution of our people and permanent citizens of our country by a foreign authority."[82]

Ta'isi's explanation of his devotion to nonviolence at this time was not prompted by New Zealand's latest misstep but by the Marist brothers of Sacred Heart College Ponsonby. Ta'isi was "sore grieved when my nephew August came home today with a full-sized modern rifle" and proceeded to give the school's principal a lesson in history, current affairs, and Christian values. It was the king's birthday the following day, and the weapons were handed out "for use at a military parade" in his honor. Ta'isi approved "of all honour and respect being paid to the King," but "I most decidedly object to the military training of school-boys and their being taught at such an early age the use of deadly weapons." This engendered "a warlike spirit" and was responsible for all the "attendant suffering and miseries" of the late war. "It is rather significant," Ta'isi told the principal, "that while the Great Powers are holding conferences towards general disarmament, militarism is being instilled into the youth of New Zealand." "The old idea that peace can be maintained only by preparedness for war has been proved to be the notion of bullies who aim to suppress weaker people by intimidation," he continued. Ta'isi pointed out New Zealand's militarism had serious implications for his nephew's native country. "You are not unaware" of the situation in Sāmoa, Ta'isi ventured. "Only recently" military contingents have "been recruited here to send to Samoa where the use of fire-arms has proved fatal to the Samoans and the relations between the Dominion and her mandated ward." In contrast to the encouragement of militarism in New Zealand, Sāmoans had "since the surrender of their fire-arms to the Great Powers some 30 years ago . . . developed the really true Christian spirit of despising all tendency to warfare and have consistently practiced peace by disarmament." Black Saturday again loomed for Ta'isi, "but for this, the tragedy of Christmas week 1929 might have been a totally different story." Ta'isi finished his missive by saying that "unless the carrying of fire-arms by school-boys is compulsory by law on such occasions, I should be obliged if you will excuse August from future military training, armed parades and demonstrations."[83]

Since 1931 the family lived in Takapuna (first on the corner of Campbell Road and Killarney Street, and then later at "Buona Vista" on Anzac Street), enjoying the greater space the location gave them on Auckland's northern shore. "We are very happy at Takapuna,"

Ta'isi wrote on November 19, 1931—which he also noted was Sina's birthday—adding that the family "may stay there even after the Summer or probably for the rest of my term away from Samoa."[84] And although the location had its downsides, that is what they did. Ta'isi worried about the longer hours it took Sina and Taufau, as well as his nephew—August or "Gussie"—to get to their schools and, in the case of Malienafau, university. He wrote notes asking for them to be excused for being a little late now their commutes involved ferry, bus, and tram trips.[85] He organized piano lessons, uniforms, supplies, special English tuition for Gussie, homework, pocket money, and school holiday trips.[86] Ta'isi was upset with Piliopo after she left Auckland to be with Rosabel in Apia as she would not accept her father's discipline and did not (it seems) accept much from her mother, either.[87] He also looked out for members of the wider Sāmoan community evident when he took a close interest in the welfare of Queenie, the daughter of his Apia friend (and architect of Tuaefu) F. E. Syddall, when she was ill in an Auckland hospital.[88] Ta'isi organized and paid a large part of the costs for a monument unveiled in Auckland in 1932 for Brother Philippe Leonard Charay, who taught him as a child at Saint Joseph's Apia.[89] With all the worries bearing down on him, Ta'isi remained attendant to his obligations and duties. He was a paterfamilias, ran a tight domestic ship but also fostered a very affectionate home for his many charges.

Some serious family problems surfaced in 1932, however. Frank Nelson, Ta'isi's nephew, for whom Ta'isi was also a legal guardian, changed his name to "Nelson Meredith"; a move that outraged Ta'isi. Frank then took legal action to remove Ta'isi's legal and financial oversight over his life and affairs, in favor of his maternal grandfather, S. H. Meredith. He took Ta'isi to the high court in Sāmoa regarding the investment of his trust monies (that were invested in the Nelson Company). On top of the administration's campaign against Ta'isi, this family matter, made very public, and which cast doubts on Ta'isi's abilities in his most revered role as the family *matai,* was most unwelcome. In March Justice Luxford in the high court found against Ta'isi (yet again) and ordered that the funds—£4,000—be withdrawn from O. F. Nelson and Co.'s coffers, producing another financial drain that could only be met by raising the company's credit with the Bank of New Zealand.[90] The legal case and Frank's rebellion against his uncle sparked tension between the two, and Frank was no longer welcome for holidays with Ta'isi's family, which suited all parties.[91]

Frank's younger half brother Gussie, however, continued to live with Ta'isi and was the source of a lot of his attention. Ta'isi felt duty bound to ensure he had a good education with Auckland's Marist brothers.

The other family matter concerned Viopapa. She suffered from a form of mental illness, probably what would be diagnosed today as an eating disorder. Viopapa was usually a person with a "sweet temperament . . . a most loving and dutiful daughter to me and looked up to by all her sisters with great respect and admiration."[92] Of late, she had stopped eating, took very long walks when she was not locked away in her room, and exhibited other signs of mental distress. Ta'isi suggested she go to Sydney and stay with her cousin Auguste Lembke, who lived in Botany Road, Randwick. Her aunt Gustava Wetzell, who had been staying in Auckland with Ta'isi, was now visiting Sydney; Ta'isi thought the change of scenery would help Viopapa. In December 1932 her condition deteriorated. Ta'isi wrote to her that he was "very distressed to read in your letters about your health and must ask you take good care of yourself." Ta'isi said she could take a trip to the Blue Mountains at his expense with Auntie Gustava, but he would prefer that she came home to Auckland by the next vessel.[93]

Things went from bad to worse. Ta'isi immediately corresponded with Dr. Chisholm Ross of Macquarie Street, expressing his "grave anxiety" about Viopapa's condition. Ta'isi told Dr. Ross that although "she has always been somewhat extreme in her views on things she . . . never [gave] reason for anyone to think she was mentally deranged until this time, when she began to be rather eccentric before she left here for Sydney." To Dr. Allen, Ta'isi laid out Viopapa's medical history in which he cited the 1928 car accident in Rugby as "having seriously affected her nerves ever since."[94] Viopapa was hospitalized, and Ta'isi sent Noue to Sydney immediately. When she saw Viopapa the day she arrived, Noue sent an alarming message to her father:

> Have seen Miss Lucy Nelson [Viopapa]. Absolutely defiant regarding returning. Impossible leave her here in present condition . . . Only alternative in order to control her and restrain her from causing trouble to others is to take drastic action which Dr Ross will do with your sanction.[95]

There were no details given about what "drastic action," in the range of horrific 1930s mental health treatments, was being contemplated. Ta'isi trusted Dr. Ross to make the judgment call on this, but he hoped

Viopapa was in "just the Public Hospital and not the mental asylum which I should wish to avoid my daughter entering." Ta'isi hoped Viopapa would make a full recovery and wished to know what precautions to take in the future to avoid a recurrence. In the midst of the crisis in January 1933, he wanted to stop her hurting herself and others and put an end to her "hallucinations."[96] Viopapa recovered (there are no documents to suggest otherwise), but her sisters remained wary of her, suggesting a lingering change in her demeanor.[97]

It was probably no coincidence that Viopapa's breakdown occurred when it did. The great pressures on Ta'isi undoubtedly affected his family—Viopapa's travails are strong testament to that pressure. The campaign of disgrace and ruin was apparent in many ways, including Ta'isi's association with Freemasonry; he was an active member of Auckland's Manukau Royal Arch Chapter. In 1932 Ta'isi wrote to Mr. Crowther of the chapter, enclosing his subscription dues and the message: "I greatly regret my inability to attend the Chapter for some time, this is due to certain circumstances which I prefer not to discuss here." Ta'isi nevertheless hoped "the time will shortly arrive when I can attend regularly without inconvenience to anybody," an allusion to the campaign of ostracism being waged against him also from within this bastion of British imperial manhood. Crowther was sympathetic, telling Ta'isi, "We shall be delighted to see you whenever you are able to attend." He went on, "Masonry should not take cognisance of politics at least that is my personal opinion and you may be assured that we have a warm feeling of esteem for you, who so kindly helped us in the early stages of the chapter's history." The campaign of humiliation extended to Sydney, too. New South Wales politician Thomas Henley told fellow politician Sir Joseph Carruthers (who lent Ta'isi and the Mau valuable conservative support from Sydney) that Ta'isi was not a man deserving of Carruthers' backing. Henley revealed to Sir Joseph that Ta'isi was a disgraced man who had been 'thrown out of the Tattersall's Club and nearly thrown overboard for his anti-British remarks by a group of young men en route to NZ."[98] Conservative politics and politicians on both sides of the Tasman were intertwined, adding to Ta'isi's burden in Sydney, a city that was so important for him on numerous levels.[99]

As painful as Ta'isi's social exclusion was, there were even greater pressures coming to bear on the family at this time. Ta'isi's exile to New Zealand was up in December 1932: there was no legal impediment to heading back to Sāmoa, but Ta'isi nonetheless decided to delay their return. The reason was that he was "as anxious as ever to avoid any trouble" in Sāmoa.[100] He was desperately afraid New Zealand authorities were going to provoke a violent incident like that seen when A. G. Smyth returned on December 28, 1929 (Black Saturday). Ta'isi went to see Prime Minister Forbes in late November to get a personal guarantee this would not be repeated. Forbes refused to give him any such guarantee, despite making previous conciliatory statements to parliament. Ta'isi knew he "would be blamed for whatever untoward happening might take place." The "Black and Tans" (the military police, as the *NZ Samoa Guardian* referred to them), who had been causing such a disturbance among Sāmoans since Black Saturday, were still in Apia and were an ominous element of the nightmare scenario of a repetition of events of three years ago. If police attempted to arrest someone who had not paid their poll tax (a huge proportion of the population) at any event to welcome back Gurr and Ta'isi, there was no saying what might happen. General Hart was also talking tough to the *fono* of *faipule* following a visit to New Zealand. Hart warned that if Ta'isi engaged in any activity that was not related to his business, "he would be severely dealt with."[101] Given what happened on Black Saturday, Ta'isi had every reason to be in fear of his life, even though he did not articulate fear for his own well-being but for that of others.[102]

Another Christmas passed in Auckland with Viopapa hospitalized in Sydney. One ray of light in what must have been a tense time was that the financial position of O. F. Nelson and Co. "materially improved" by the close of the year.[103] This was fleeting; 1933 would see copra prices fall to their lowest levels by April, taking the company's financial well-being down with it. On February 23 Ta'isi received a telegram from staff, family, and friends in Apia wishing him a happy birthday. He would turn fifty the next day.[104] Ta'isi's fiftieth year would see events that severely tested his fortitude as the campaign against him moved into a new dramatic phase.

Chapter Thirteen

Return to Sāmoa, Trial, and Exile (1933–1934)

In May 1933 Ta'isi telegraphed the head office in Apia asking them to put the phone on and reinstall stoves at Tuaefu: he was finally coming home.[1]

He had delayed this moment five months because of the menace of violence. He did not want more bloodshed nor the blame for it. On April 20 New Zealand's governor-general Lord Bledisloe made a trip to Sāmoa; an event the New Zealand government feared would be disrupted by the Mau energized by a recently returned Ta'isi. The viceregal visit went off without incident, though the reception of Lord Bledisloe's party was underwhelming: the Mau, making up the vast majority of the population (90 percent by government calculations of the time), stayed away from functions arranged to honor the distinguished visitor.[2] Still, New Zealand claimed again that all was quiet on the Western Sāmoa front. The *Times* of London, the *New Zealand Herald* reported, saw Lord Bledisloe's visit to Apia as "a guarantee of the recovery of Samoa from dissension with New Zealand."[3] As tensions subsided, Ta'isi began to think of his safe return to Sāmoa with greater confidence. With optimism in the air and certain eyes of the world averted after Lord Bledisloe's visit, the timing was better for Ta'isi to make his journey home. The *NZ Samoa Guardian* ran a photograph of him, Noue, Taufau, Malienafau, Sina, and a recovered Viopapa standing behind him with Gussie sitting on the tennis court at Takapuna with the caption "going home."[4] He and his daughters were boarding the next boat—the *Mariposa*—to return from exile.

GOING HOME

The Hon. O. F. Nelson and his family are on their way home to Samoa. (Back row: the Misses. Irene, Lucy, and Olive Nelson. Front row: the Misses Sina and Calmar Nelson, with Mr. Gus Nelson.)

Figure 13.1. "Going Home," *NZ Samoa Guardian,* May 11, 1933, 1. Courtesy of National Library of Australia.

Despite this new confidence, Ta'isi was under no illusions about what this journey home might entail. He told his Apia general manager in April that "owing to uncertainty of the length of my stay in Samoa if I do come down in May it will not pay me to bring my cars with me."[5] He was anticipating trouble. He had been warned that any association with "native" Sāmoans or the Mau would trigger a reprisal; the problem for Ta'isi was that the Mau pervaded his family and community as it pervaded Sāmoa. It was impossible to avoid, even if he chose to. The laws were so tight, the slightest misstep would have him running afoul of the *Samoa Seditious Organisations Regulations* or the host of other laws that criminalized so many aspects of Sāmoan lives at the time.

Along with this threat, Ta'isi had to deal with serious and unpleasant business matters upon his return. The improved financial news at the end of 1932 was augmented in March by good news from London. As copra was "the main ingredient in the manufacture of margarine [it] is naturally affected by the market for the other edible fats," Ta'isi wrote. The price of copra was pegged to the price of butter and it had just risen in price by about 10 percent. This was good news for copra and Ta'isi's company; "if this comes about we shall be able to redeem a goodly portion of our prospective loss from this quarter."[6] It did not come about. Copra prices crashed to their lowest levels in April 1933 fetching only ten pounds a ton.[7] Things were bad. In February, O. F. Nelson and Co. had sought legal advice about restructuring the company, including options for liquidation.[8] The company's survival depended on credit from the Bank of New Zealand, the only bank that operated in Sāmoa. In April, the bank began withholding funds.[9] Business-wise, Ta'isi was returning to a crisis.

In the troubling days before he departed New Zealand there was one pleasing turn of events: General Richardson got his comeuppance. Richardson was now chairman of the Returned Serviceman's Association (RSA). On March 30 when Richardson rose to address a meeting of ex-soldiers in Auckland, the meeting erupted into "uproar." Shouting and hostilities lasted for about half an hour before members ousted Richardson and his executive from their positions. One digger shouted out—according to the *New Zealand Herald,* which had used gallons of ink defending Richardson in Sāmoa—that the reason for the commotion was "we want to get rid of the parasites and make this a diggers' show." All this animus against Richardson stemmed from the unfair distribution of government relief funds for ex-soldiers with non-RSA members claiming discrimination. RSA members (the only ones allowed in the fiery meeting) were also outraged. In a desperate country deep in depression, Richardson's position was one of extreme importance for many and his performance fell way short of expectations. It was disclosed by one member that "a long series of maladministration had been levelled against the executive."[10] "Maladministration" by Richardson? Despite Ta'isi's continuous sympathy for the plight of New Zealanders battered by the depression, it must have been satisfying for Ta'isi to read about Richardson's unceremonious and very public rejection. The *NZ Samoa Guardian* duly reported Richardson's shameful demise hoping the news would spread in Sāmoa.[11] The RSA rebellion against Richardson should have prompted questioning of the government stance against the Mau and whether their claims against Richardson had any validity (as the VPB report had also done). Nothing happened to dislodge the mailed fist of New Zealand's rule; it would remain firmly in place. All Ta'isi and the Mau got from this episode was *schadenfreude*. The Richardson name was then again splashed across the gossip pages in August. Sir George's son Kenneth, who had stayed with Ta'isi at Tuaefu for a number of weeks in 1926 when he and the administrator were on good terms, was going through a public and unseemly divorce. Percy Andrews gleefully wrote to Ta'isi from Auckland about the salacious case—there were accusations of affairs and "carrying on" by both Kenneth and his wife, Mona Mary. "Dicky's name is muddier than ever now," Andrews divulged.[12] The European prestige Richardson always felt he embodied to the fullest was in short supply.

Despite the dark clouds hanging over his return, Ta'isi was going to make the journey in style. He hosted a farewell function at his Takapuna home on April 29; eighty people came to bid farewell to him and his family. Ta'isi made a powerful speech to his guests, thanking them for support and also setting the record straight about the battle he had fought so far. "It has been suggested that I return to Samoa a discredited, beaten man," he told them. "That is not so." He admitted his personal failings: "I have sinned exceedingly in thought, word and deed to my fellowmen and my God." "But to my own little country" he had given everything:

> I have given my substance, my leisure and all that was humanly possible for me to give. I have no regrets for the snubs and scorn directed at me in the past on account of Samoa nor will I shirk what awaits me in the future . . . I return to my country . . . with my head bloody but unbowed.[13]

The family left New Zealand May 9, 1933 and sailed to Pago Pago. During the journey he transformed from an exile into a quasi-statesman. The family stayed in Pago Pago two days and were feted with great ceremony and feasting. Ta'isi also called on Governor Landenberger. They boarded the O. F. Nelson and Co.–owned boat *Calmar,* accompanied by the *Viopapa* with Mau chiefs aboard, for the overnight trip to Apia. A flotilla of other boats and decorated *fautasi* accompanied the *Calmar* to the Custom's Wharf in Apia Harbor.

AN EXILE'S HOME-COMING

PICTURES FROM SAMOA OF MR. NELSON'S RETURN.

Thousands of the Samoan Women's Mau lined the waterfront at Apia in Mau uniform. In the background is the War Memorial Clock presented by Mr. Nelson.

The exile walking through the assembled crowd.

Taisi inspects the Guard of Honour from the Women's Mau. The widow of Tamasese on the right.

Figures 13.2–13.4. Huge crowds gather to welcome Ta'isi and his family back to Sāmoa in June 1933. "An Exile's Homecoming," *NZ Samoa Guardian,* June 30, 1933, 3. Courtesy of the National Library of Australia.

Ta'isi stepped back onto Sāmoan soil on May 16 to an extraordinary welcome. The Women's Mau took precedence in the welcoming committee in order to avoid any confrontation with the police. Three thousand women dressed in Mau uniforms lined the wharf and thousands of others gathered at the waterfront to welcome Ta'isi home.[14] Hundreds formed a guard of honor, and decorated arches had been constructed in the streets. Ta'isi went to the village of Vaimoso, the Mau stronghold. A church service and the king's kava ceremony (an exceptionally high honor) were performed at Tupua Tamasese Mea'ole's home. Speeches were made. Ta'isi then made the pilgrimage to Tupua Tamasese Lea'lofi's grave where he laid a wreath in memory of his young friend and the others who died on Black Saturday. A visibly emotional Ta'isi gave a speech saying "Tamasese and the other favoured sons of Samoa . . . peacefully gave up their lives that Samoa and the Samoans may live and that all generations shall remember their names as the greatest of Samoa's patriots." Afterward a feast was held with more dancing and speeches. Ta'isi asked the crowds to obey the law, to not hold more large gatherings, and to return to their villages. A few days later, an intimate gathering marked Ta'isi's first Sunday at his home. He attended the Methodist Church on the Tuaefu grounds and hosted family and friends. Then the following Friday a larger gathering took place at Tuaefu, where eighteen pigs were roasted and "an infinite variety of fish, fowl, fruit and vegetables" made the tables groan. More dances, fine mat presentations, songs, and speeches were made. Ta'isi was most definitely back in Sāmoa.[15]

As Ta'isi got back to the grim and urgent business of salvaging O. F. Nelson and Co., the authorities watched his every move and kept a daily dossier on his activities. They read his mail, knew whom he met and what was said (most particularly what Ta'isi said) at regular meetings that were taken to be Mau meetings even when very ordinary matters were discussed. Every day Ta'isi was breaking the law by meeting with known Mau members (recall only 10 percent of the population were not involved according the government's own estimate). According to the intelligence dossier, he "prepared" the "whole contents" of the Sāmoan-language supplement for the *NZ Samoa Guardian* from June to August. He also wrote the columns in the English-language section of the paper with the byline "Our Own Correspondent." He enjoyed a constant round of social activities that demonstrated the high esteem in which he was held; a dangerous situation as far as the administration was concerned. On numerous other occasions people came to Ta'isi with an array of problems and complaints.

It was clear the Mau was still a force to be reckoned with and Hart attempted to negotiate with them and suspended the *Samoa Seditious Organisations Regulations* as a gesture of goodwill. The negotiations were stillborn as the Mau committee kept insisting Ta'isi be allowed to attend their meeting. Hart would not consider this; attempts to negotiate ended August 18.[16] Then the legal amnesty ended, without notice. Family and community welcomes for Ta'isi and his family continued, against Ta'isi's wishes, including the men's Mau committee giving their official welcome to Ta'isi and his family at a big *ta'alolo* at Vaimoso on September 13. Seven hundred people (by the administration's conservative count) came.[17] An orator, Fai'fai, welcomed Ta'isi and referred to him as "Prince Tupua Ta'isi."[18] Another "big" *ta'alolo* was held on September 27 in Vaimoso, where other villages feted Ta'isi and his family.[19] On both these occasions Ta'isi spoke briefly in response to welcoming addresses and thanked his hosts for their generosity but steered clear of any controversial topics. His role at these gatherings were no secret; a photograph of him at the September 13 one was published in the *NZ Samoa Guardian*.[20] Yet his two speeches, benign as they were mandatory under Sāmoan custom, would cost him dearly.

The administration operated on the basis a conviction—which was almost certainly guaranteed by Justice Luxford in the High Court, given all the precedents—would be appealed. So even though they knew Ta'isi was breaking the law, the administration bided its time and tried to build a case that was going to stand up to the scrutiny of an appellate court. Ta'isi knew he was being watched and took care with what he said, but he was not careful enough. What he did not know, though he strongly suspected once he became aware of the level of intelligence the administration had gathered, was that there were spies in his midst. In the straightened economic times of 1933, the administration had money, jobs, immunity from prosecution, and even interests in copra plantations to tempt would-be spies.[21] In January 1934 Ta'isi asked in the Sāmoan supplement of the *NZ Samoa Guardian*, "Is a Judas there?"[22] Yes, there was, and there was possibly more than one if New Zealand's records are to be trusted on this question. Ta'isi never knew the identities of the men as far we know—Braisby would later narrow down the possibilities by revealing he had *a* "confidential source" in witness testimony.[23] From his return in May until November Ta'isi acted on the basis that all those around him were true to the cause and loyal to him. This was not the case.

Prime Minister Forbes, armed in early October with the dossier on Ta'isi, was pushing hard to entrap him. He wrote to Administrator Hart, telling him to warn Ta'isi in person or via correspondence that there had been a noticeable rise in Mau activity since his return and that he was being held personally responsible. Even though Forbes wanted Ta'isi warned, he was planning where Ta'isi would be jailed (Sāmoa or New Zealand) upon his conviction. He also thought that, in addition to this jail term, the government should consider legal proceedings against Mau leaders, preventing Mau gatherings at Vaimoso or wherever else they were held. He was also again contemplating the cancellation of O. F. Nelson and Co.'s trading license, though this step would be "drastic" and the prime minister had "great doubt as to its propriety." The *NZ Samoa Guardian* also continued to greatly vex the prime minister, "the last thing we should wish to do is again to make a threat and again . . . find ourselves unable to carry it into effect." Forbes admitted "the facilities for clandestine importation [of the newspaper] are so great that we would I fear find ourselves chasing a shadow throughout the Territory and making ourselves appear ridiculous." Despite Forbes' gung ho attitude, he had advice from the solicitor general, Arthur Fair, that there needed to be evidence against Ta'isi from after August 18, when the period of negotiation with Mau ended.[24]

The government continued to collect more evidence and wait. During this time one of the greatest "defenders" of Sāmoa died unexpectedly: Harry Holland. Holland was attending the funeral of Māori King Te Rata Mahuta, and insisted on climbing up Taupiri Mountain to the burial site. At the summit he suffered a heart attack and died a short time after. Holland was praised in the *NZ Samoa Guardian* for his writings and political action on behalf of the Sāmoan cause; he was a "hard hitter and a keen opponent" in the political game but "he was always a clean fighter who stood on high principals and eschewed personalities."[25] In their tributes, the New Zealand papers did not mention Holland's devotion to the Sāmoan cause except to mention a detail about his final day. When Sir Āpirana Ngata tried to dissuade Holland from climbing Taupiri Mountain, he replied he had climbed Mount Vaea to see Robert Louis Stevenson's grave in Apia; he thought that climb more challenging than the one he now faced. Holland's ascent of Mount Vaea was done thirteen years earlier when Holland came to Apia with the parliamentary delegation, the visit that first brought him into contact with Ta'isi.[26] Together the two men had fought the fight over Sāmoa, but now Ta'isi was without another powerful friend and ally when he arguably needed him the most.

Now that negotiations had broken down between the administrator and the Mau, the next move against the nationalists was planned. Ta'isi continued to write his copy for the *NZ Samoa Guardian,* as well as find a way to keep financing it. Despite the dangers of reengaging with the Mau, Ta'isi had a renewed conviction that was perhaps bolstered by the loss of Holland, who never shrunk from a worthy fight. A special meeting at Tuaefu was arranged for the Mau committee and secretaries for October 20. The meeting's purpose was to organize *malagas* around Upolu and Savai'i. These *malagas* were planned to be substantial affairs, composed of forty men who would be led by Une and Autagavaia on Upolu and Tagaloa and Tuala Tulo on Savai'i. The village tours were to commence on November 13 and "show people how successful the Mau had become, to revive waning spirits and to collect Mau money." They were to also collect data on Mau members, their families, recent deaths, and causes of deaths to generate a demographic profile of their movement.[27]

Administrator Hart knew almost immediately about what had transpired at the Tuaefu meeting. It lasted more than three hours. Whiskey and kava were drunk and Ta'isi made a long speech "praising members for their steadfastness [and] urging perseverance and loyalty to the Mau." He also "presented [a] Mau flag to be flown on important occasions." Hart thought he had Ta'isi cornered. He telegrammed Wellington with the news: "case unassailable . . . intended witnesses are the drivers of the two cars (that had transported men from Vaimoso to Tuaefu) and a Mau Committee member."[28] The solicitor general had a different view once he reviewed the evidence. Fair wrote on November 7 the entire case would rest on the evidence of the committee member and the two drivers—a shaky proposition when they had to front up in court and give evidence. Fair thought it too risky to pursue the case on this basis, so once again Hart had to find the silver bullet that would lead to Ta'isi's conviction.[29]

Things came to a head in November as the Mau moved forward with their plans. On November 11, Armistice Day, Ta'isi wrote to Percy Andrews in Auckland, telling him he had found the poem "Where Is the Flag of England?" in his papers and had translated it into Sāmoan for future use in the *NZ Samoa Guardian* but "certainly not now."[30] Written during the Boer War, the poem by British MP Henry Labouchère was a searing attack on British imperialism. The poem assailed British colonialism with its history of brutality and suffering waged on people across the globe. According to the poem, the Union Jack had

> Floated over scenes of pillage
> It has flaunted o'er deeds of shame
> It has waved o'er the fell marauder
> As he ravished with sword and flame
> It has looked upon ruthless slaughter
> Of massacre dire and grim
> It has heard the shrieks of the victims
> Drown with the jingo hymn.
>
> Where is the Flag of England?
> Seek the land where the natives rot
> Where decay and assured extinction
> Must soon be the natives' lot.
> Go search for the once glad Islands
> Where disease and death are rife
> And the greed of callous commerce
> Now battens on human life.[31]

The poem was clearly "seditious" according to Sāmoan law; could there be a more devastating assessment of British imperialism in verse? Ta'isi also wrote a letter to C. V. Allom at O. F. Nelson and Co. headquarters about acquiring two typewriters for Mau use through company networks.[32] This letter linked the company to Mau activity. On November 15, the strain was getting to Ta'isi. He felt very ill. He had a fever and "felt pains everywhere," so he worked from home. He dictated a letter to friends of Sāmoa in Auckland saying that his "prodigal daughter," Billie (Piliopo), who "just passed her stenography and typewriting lessons . . . is taking my dictation today. If it is not as well typed as my usual style you will know the reason why."[33]

Ta'isi was sick, but he could still joke with his daughter, who accordingly typed up his remarks. Billie also typed up a letter to Percy Andrews: Ta'isi told him the *malagas* had left that day. He also wrote "regarding the silent organizing work of the Mau to run the country, you are quite right in saying that it needs delicate handling and a foolish move might be disastrous."[34] As well as this correspondence, Ta'isi also had many documents relating to the Mau showing how meticulously organized it was. There were statements of purpose, balance sheets, documents generated for collecting demographic information, records of meetings. Some of these documents contained statements like "sharpest weapon of the Mau is the newspaper," but it was not the only one; "all the weapons of the Mau are weapons of peace founded on the laws of God and the wisdom given to men."[35]

Ta'isi was still feeling unwell the following day, November 16, so continued to work at home. He was working in his upstairs office when, at eight fifteen in the morning, Inspector Braisby and five other policemen burst into Tuaefu, almost breaking down its doors. The police raced up the stairs and found Ta'isi at his desk. He calmly asked Braisby, "What is your business?"[36] The appearance of armed police at Ta'isi's home caused great alarm; his daughters and extended family feared Ta'isi would be shot. They had good cause to be terrified: the lorry the police arrived in contained weapons, including "covered by a tarpaulin a machine gun."[37] Ta'isi's daughters leaped to their father's defense and confronted the police, but Ta'isi "restrained his daughters and sent them away."[38] Braisby came bearing a warrant; they were looking for printed matter "in respect of which an offence has been committed" against three ordinances and regulations as well as section 102 of the *Samoa Act*.[39] The police showed Ta'isi the warrant, and he stood by and watched the police rifle through his desk, drawers, shelves, and wastepaper basket to retrieve incriminating documentation. The police left with a cache of evidence, and the New Zealand government now had their silver bullet. In fact, they had thirty-six of them.[40] Ta'isi anxiously waited for what was to come next. Around 1:00 p.m., "troops" returned to Tuaefu, but this time they were not looking for documents. They raided Ta'isi's liquor store, taking everything, including "many distinguished and different kinds which had been there since before the time" of prohibition laws.[41] What became of all this "evidence" is unknown, but perhaps the troops enjoyed dispensing with it.

On the same day Tuaefu was raided, nine men who had set out on the Upolu *malagas* were arrested, and eight who pleaded guilty were swiftly put on trial.[42] Justice Luxford heard three days of evidence. While this trial was proceeding, Ta'isi and his friends worried about what lay ahead for him. Faumuina appears to have been an emissary for Ta'isi to the administration on November 20, though this conversation, like the others he had with officials, was considered to be "Mau intelligence." Faumuina conveyed the contents of correspondence from Ta'isi in which he said he wanted Sāmoans to be "strong and determined and above all trust and pray to the Lord for help and guidance." Ta'isi said he was "prepared for the worst" and even that he "welcomed death in [sic] the hands of the Government . . . so that the natives may see that he is not in the least seeking personal gains."[43] Faumuina also reported that Ta'isi told him on the morning of November 21 he did not want anything done on his behalf and "if it should come to the point that he has to suffer the consequences of the law, he will gladly take his punishment for the freedom and interests of Samoa." If he was exiled again, he wanted Faumuina to take his place and "settle the existing differences" between the Mau and the government.[44]

After "ransacking" Tuaefu twice, as well as other locations in Apia, the police returned to Tuaefu on November 21.[45] This time they were there to arrest Ta'isi on thirteen charges stemming from his association with known Mau members at functions at Vaimoso and from documents found at Tuaefu. Ta'isi was taken to prison but was released on conditional bail after about an hour in custody.[46]

The next day Justice Luxford handed down his judgment in the case of eight Mau men; he found all the men guilty under the *Seditious Organisations Regulations* 1930. Before passing sentence, Luxford gave the courtroom a history lesson delving back into the nineteenth century and the *Mau a Pule* of 1909. "History teaches us many lessons," he sermonized, "and the lesson it teaches me is that when a body of men is formed for the purpose of opposing or upsetting the government then it is a body that must be punished severely." The leader, Autagavaia, was given a twelve-month jail sentence and the others six months each.[47] Six "principals" of the Savai'i *malaga* group were arrested on December 1; four other members of the *malaga* "were not interfered with."[48] The six were tried: four were found guilty and two acquitted because Justice Luxford did not think there was sufficient evidence against them. The *NZ Samoa Guardian* reported that the two who were acquitted "wondered why and were rather reluctant to accept their freedom when their confreres were fined and sentenced."[49]

The High Court of Western Samoa had been busy, but the trial everyone was waiting for was *Braisby v. Nelson.* As both sides prepared, Carl Berendsen wrote to the prime minister, saying that "it was perfectly clear there is more than sufficient evidence to implicate Nelson and his conviction may be expected as a matter of course."[50] So the detailed discussions ahead of the trial among officials were about where to imprison him; there was not even a gesture to a presumption of innocence. The trials of the fourteen Mau men had been conducted with great dispatch. The feeling was that Ta'isi's trial, too, would be dealt with expeditiously, perhaps by Christmas. This turned out to be a considerable miscalculation.

The trial got under way on December 18, after Ta'isi's application for trial by assessors was rejected on the grounds it would "be practically impossible to find four persons in Samoa who are not prejudiced one way or the other in this case."[51] Ta'isi would be tried by just one man, Justice J. H. Luxford, who had found against so many other Sāmoans in Mau-related cases, Ta'isi's company and against Ta'isi himself in other matters. Luxford was a man deeply impaired by prejudice too, though the conceit of his judicial objectivity prevailed, a matter he alone decided. Ta'isi did succeed in having evidence presented in Sāmoan as well as English. The courtroom was filled to capacity and many hundreds gathered outside the courtroom—Apia was "packed" with Sāmoans who had come from far and wide for the trial.[52] German lawyer Gustav Klinkmueller represented Ta'isi. Piliopo assisted in recording proceedings and Malienafau aided the legal preparation for the case.[53] Alfred McCarthy, the crown solicitor, acted for the prosecution.

McCarthy opened proceedings with an overview of the Mau, and Ta'isi's part in it from its beginnings that the crown argued were the two meetings held in late 1926. Starting with a historical argument rather than focusing on Ta'isi's activities over the past months proved to be a considerable tactical error. The first and main prosecution witness was Arthur Braisby. When he began his evidence he affirmed the crown's contention that Ta'isi was the driving force behind the Mau. On the morning of December 20 Braisby began discussing letters Ta'isi had written to friends and family, which Braisby had seized from mailbags aboard the *Tofua* and were now admitted as evidence of Ta'isi's ongoing incitement of the Mau. Ta'isi and Klinkmueller audibly disagreed about how to proceed. Klinkmueller undertook to review English translations of these letters overnight. Ta'isi thought this an impossible task. The court was adjourned. When it returned Klinkmueller stated he was withdrawing from the case. Now the defendant would represent himself with the assistance of E. T. Pleasants. As Braisby himself wrote, Ta'isi "considers that he can cross examine on Samoan matters more clever than any other Lawyer [*sic*]."[54] With this development Luxford had to adjourn proceedings until December 27. Ta'isi's first Christmas back in Sāmoa in six years would be engulfed in a frenzy of preparation for the case.

When hearings resumed, McCarthy finished his cross-examination of Braisby and everything looked like it would be over by the New Year. But when Ta'isi commenced his cross-examination, the trial transformed from an open-and-shut case to one in which New Zealand's entire administration of Sāmoa, indeed British Empire itself, was put on trial. In the assessment of Carl Berendsen, the trial became "a mixture of 'Alice through the Looking Glass' and Gilbert and Sullivan." Berendsen was responding to a horrified Stephen Allen, the former administrator, who could not believe the reports of the trial he got back on his farm in Morrinsville. As ridiculous as the trial had become, Berendsen conceded in dismay there is "nothing we can do about it here."[55]

The defender of the administration became Arthur Braisby. For the greater part of the trial Braisby's "ex tempore evidence" was the administration's "only defence."[56] Like Atlas, Braisby briefly held up the entire world of empire, telescoped into New Zealand's administration of Sāmoa. For twenty-one days, Braisby was in the witness box, most of them being cross-examined by Ta'isi. This turn of events alarmed Luxford "as the reputation of the Administration depended on the accuracy of his answers." Luxford had little faith in Braisby's intellectual capacity. Luxford considered Braisby to be "By nature a slow thinking man." He had a habit of "not answering questions until he understands it properly," which "is apt to create an unfavourable impression." Braisby's increasingly unprepared and comical responses to Ta'isi's questions (the Gilbert and Sullivan and *Alice in Wonderland* moments) nevertheless impressed the judge, contrary to all logic and reasoning; "very few men could have withstood the test—Inspector Braisby did."[57]

Ta'isi spent days of the trial focused on the historical account set out by McCarthy in his opening address, which was, chapter and verse, the line of argument the administration had run since late 1926: that the Mau was masterminded by Ta'isi for his own financial and political aggrandizement. In his questioning of Braisby, Ta'isi demonstrated the absurdity of the laws and that someone like Braisby should hold the powerful position he did. The argument Ta'isi pushed was that, rather than fan discontent in Sāmoa, he had always acted to keep the peace and to pursue Sāmoan grievances through nonviolent means. On this point, Braisby agreed that on numerous occasions Ta'isi and other members of the Mau had acted against their own self-interest to preserve the peace and maintain law and order. Ta'isi also argued that when the Mau flared, it was the result of administration actions; on this point Braisby had more trouble equating this cause with the effect. Where the questions zeroed in on terrain that exposed New Zealand rule (and Braisby) too greatly, Justice Luxford quickly "interposed" to disallow or dismiss that line of questioning. Luxford interposed often.

It was not lost on Ta'isi that the sixth day of his trial was the fourth anniversary of Black Saturday. He spent the anniversary again cross-examining Braisby in an attempt to dismantle McCarthy's timeline for the Mau as beginning with the meetings in 1926. He went back to the Mau of *faipule* of 1919 sparked by the epidemic and noted that it was followed by the enactment of the *Samoan Offenders Ordinance* in 1922. Was not this incontrovertible evidence that considerable unrest existed *before* 1926? The banishments of chiefs under this ordinance amplified grievances. Yet the prosecution was not making Ta'isi the instigator of this unrest (though recall Administrator Tate did cite his interference at the time).[58]

The following day Ta'isi moved on to Richardson's laws that enforced a form of apartheid, tearing at the fabric of Sāmoan society by keeping Sāmoans, Europeans and their affairs separate. Ta'isi asked Braisby how this applied to "the building of roads, of bridges, public works and other utilities for the benefit of all or customs taxes." Luxford stepped in to shut down this line of questioning. Then Ta'isi asked Braisby, "You no doubt have heard of Sir James Carroll, Dr Peter Buck and Maui Pomare and others in New Zealand?" Braisby had heard of them.[59] "They are of part European blood and part Maori blood are they not?" Ta'isi inquired. Braisby could not say. They all "rose to high positions in and out of Parliament" and "there was no question as to their right to represent the natives in matters whatsoever even the law?" Again Braisby could not say. Ta'isi asked if Braisby had any contact with Māori people during his short time living in New Zealand. "No, I saw them about and spoke to some of them," Braisby responded. Braisby could vote in New Zealand but clearly knew very little about the country. Ta'isi told him, "Well then you would not need to know much about the Maoris to know that they were interested in the political question and to know that no one could represent the Maoris unless he was of part blood?" Luxford interposed again.

Ta'isi pressed on, asking Braisby what he knew about his, Ta'isi's, heritage; Braisby replied, "Your mother was a Samoan and father a Swedish subject." Braisby agreed that Ta'isi was elected by Europeans to serve on the legislative council, but he also had "as good a knowledge as any one in the country of the native mind." "And like the men of Maori blood I have quoted," Ta'isi continued, "I also could be instrumental in reconciling the views of both sides?" "I should say you could—if you so desired," Braisby replied. In this circumstance Ta'isi questioned Braisby about how he was supposed to conduct a business when he dealt predominantly with Sāmoans and not discuss import and export duties that effected the "prices of imported merchandise and the export of copra"? Was it a crime for a trader to discuss these matters with Sāmoans? Luxford adjourned the court for lunch. When the trial resumed, Ta'isi moved on to the events from late May that were directly relevant to the thirteen charges against him. He went into the excruciating level of red tape required to not commit offenses in that legal environment. Ta'isi pointed out the inconsistencies in how the law was suspended then reactivated without notice. It was also impossible to stay lawful when a police permit was required for virtually any cultural activity. At this juncture Luxford adjourned the court; it would recommence in the New Year.[60]

Despite the situation he was in, Ta'isi tried to make New Year's Eve at Tuaefu as festive as he could but a heavy atmosphere hung over the house. Sāmoans associated with the Mau had to stay away, though European family and friends were exempted. Despite the gloom, fireworks were let off at midnight as they had been before Ta'isi's exile.[61] As Ta'isi watched the colorful explosions in the night sky, did he wonder if he would ever see in a new year at Tuaefu again? The thought could not have been far from his mind.

When the trial resumed on January 2, McCarthy tried to contain discussion to the thirteen charges and end the embarrassing spectacle.

The tactic did not work. Instead Ta'isi began drilling Braisby on the stated intention of the Mau, (declared in the Constitution of the Samoan Welfare League), which was in evidence. No, Braisby never had any reason to disbelieve the statement that the intention of the organization was to promote "the peace, order and good govt. [sic] and general welfare of the people of the Territory." So, Ta'isi asked, why were leaders banished for being part of the Mau? "They were not banished for being part of the Mau exactly, they were banished on account of orders against the Mau," Braisby responded. Gilbert and Sullivan could not have improved such an explanation.

Ta'isi then focused on Braisby's powers and his status. Was he an administration official? No. Was he a New Zealander? No. Did Braisby know that in the last report to the League sixteen Sāmoans had become British subjects (illustrating the elasticity of these racial categories)? Luxford interposed. Ta'isi then went back to his role as chairman of the Citizens' Committee and who he was representing in this role: Europeans. Given that it had been established earlier that Ta'isi was part Sāmoan, Ta'isi returned to the example of Sir James Carroll. "It is a well known fact that Sir James Carroll was elected as Maori representative first and afterwards for many terms as a 'Pakeha.'" Braisby was "not sufficiently acquainted with this history." "Would you say," Ta'isi continued, "he set himself up as a leader of the Maori or Pakeha or both?" Luxford could see where this was going. Ta'isi proposed that accepting election gave members of parliament "many privileges in discussing problems." "I believe so," Braisby responded. It was established that Ta'isi had been elected by Europeans, but he was Sāmoan. Then Ta'isi asked Braisby if he had learned of the "recent settlement of the Maori claims for land taken in the Maori wars" (the 1927 Sim Commission). Luxford had had enough. "I must ask you to justify that Question—how can that have any relation to the present case?" he demanded. Luxford then thought better of offering Ta'isi an opportunity to explain the very pertinent connection between the treatment of political rights and race in New Zealand with what prevailed in Sāmoa under New Zealand rule. "I must disallow any further questions about Maoris and their settlements," he ordered. "I cannot see that they can help the court. Witness knows very little about the Maoris" and then he adjourned the court.[62]

For seven more days of cross-examination, Ta'isi meticulously took Braisby through the history of the Mau. He probed inconsistencies in the application of the law, the introduction of new laws, and the reasoning behind them all with the point of demonstrating that the Mau did not diminish with his exile. Braisby tried very hard to maintain the line the Mau was defunct on numerous occasions. But why did it revive? Were Ta'isi and the *NZ Samoa Guardian* solely responsible for this? Could new draconian legislation and its enforcement have more to do with the resurgence of the Mau on numerous occasions? Ta'isi kept scrutinizing Braisby's conduct. He began his cross-examination on January 5 with the question: "Mr Braisby, is it part of the duties of your office or of your Department to irritate and aggravate the Samoans as much as possible?" No, Braisby responded. Was it part of his role to show respect and civility to Sāmoans despite his scant knowledge of their Sāmoan customs? "It could be considered such," Braisby answered. Why then did he leave Tupua Tamasese Lea'lofi handcuffed to a bed aboard the *Tofua* when he was about to make his journey to Mount Eden Prison? Why did Braisby describe these actions, as he had in testimony the previous day, as "I left him alive and secure on board and when I got a receipt for his body I came ashore"?[63] Why did he have to treat Sāmoans with such indignity and then compound the offense by describing a now-deceased man as a "body" like he was inanimate cargo? Braisby responded, "I described the facts." Then both Luxford and McCarthy stepped in to befuddle the salient point Ta'isi was making about Braisby's provocative and adversarial conduct with legal argument. Braisby admitted that after Tupua Tamasese Lea'lofi returned, the Mau became more active.[64] Was this Ta'isi's fault or that of the administration?

Ta'isi spun a tale of more uncomfortable truths over the next four days, until January 11, when the strain got too much for him. Just after a heated exchange with Braisby and Luxford about the intensity of feeling among Sāmoans the day before his deportation (almost six years earlier to the day), Ta'isi was overcome by a "sudden seizure" in the courtroom. Luxford adjourned proceedings and a doctor was called. Dr. Dawson announced the trial "had been a great strain on the defendant's health and that his present condition made it imperative that he rest for some days before continuing."[65] The trial was adjourned to allow for Ta'isi's recovery until January 15, but in the meantime Justice Luxford suffered from an infection in his foot after lacerating it on coral. The trial would not resume until February 12.

When Ta'isi's cross-examination of Braisby resumed, it was Ta'isi's turn to reckon with uncomfortable truths. The testimony moved on to the events after Ta'isi's return from exile: the most relevant to the trial. The activities at Tuaefu—the alleged Mau meetings—were raised for questioning. Braisby reported in detail what had supposedly occurred. Ta'isi kept wanting to know, "What proof have you of all what you have said; were you present?" Braisby evaded, so Ta'isi asked more directly: "Who was present who gave you the information?" Braisby responded, "That is confidential and I decline to disclose his name." Ta'isi "pressed for an answer," but, as the transcript notation states, "the Chief Judge upholds witness' objection." McCarthy could perhaps sense that maintaining this confidentiality was highly problematic—this was sworn testimony no less—so he interjected by stating "that while not willing to divulge the name of the informant witnesses will be called who were present." Judas' identity was to remain unclear. Ta'isi managed to carry on as the extent of his betrayal became apparent. As the courtroom battleground on the strain got to Braisby too, he lost his composure and became exasperated at Ta'isi's intricate interrogations.[66]

No doubt Braisby felt great relief when Ta'isi finished his cross-examination on February 16. Then a succession of Sāmoan witnesses—Une, Leleua, Tai'ili'ili, and Tuala Tulo—all testified that Ta'isi was not the leader of the Mau and that he had advised against the *malagas* being sent around Upolu and Savai'i and so they had been greatly reduced in size. McCarthy wanted to know all kinds of details of these witnesses even asking each of them whether a meal was served at Tuaefu at the Mau meeting. All agreed they were fed, as is mandatory in Sāmoan custom, with Leleua responding that "we had a very good afternoon tea prepared by the defendant's daughters," which took the trial back to Wonderland. Alex Macdonald, who was the accountant for Gold Star Transport, testified about taxis taking Mau members to Tuaefu, as did the two drivers. Seiuli, sergeant in the Native Police, testified about the police work he undertook to gather evidence against Ta'isi after his return.[67]

Subinspector Fell, a leading figure in the Black Saturday massacre who showed Braisby's intellect off to advantage, then gave extraordinary evidence. Fell insisted, in response to Ta'isi's cross-examination, that "your general reputation in N.Z. and Samoa is . . . that you are the leader of the Mau." "Whom by in N.Z.?" Ta'isi asked. "A general reputation comes from the general public," Fell responded. "Do you think you are competent to express such an opinion?" Ta'isi asked. Fell thought so. Luxford then asked if he thought "Samoans have reached a state of development to be trusted with the vote." "No," said Fell. Ta'isi asked, "Is that your opinion as a white man?" "That is my opinion," Fell insisted. "On what do you base your opinion?" Ta'isi inquired. Fell answered that if Sāmoans were given government of the country, "it would throw them back into the period before they were governed by Europeans and wars between themselves would follow." No, he did not have much to support his assertion. What about the recent riots in New Zealand, sparked by communists? Did not these riots show all societies were prone to political disagreements that sometimes spilled into confrontation? Were police not attacked and stoned, Ta'isi asked. Why were people in New Zealand free to protest even when violence had erupted? Luxford interposed again. "The position in NZ is different," the chief judge said. "Here we have a law which prohibits seditious organisation—which the Government in its wisdom thinks necessary for the purpose of maintaining authority." Such a law was not necessary in New Zealand, he reasoned, "for the great majority of the people cannot be affected by such people [communists and other discontents]—but the position is different in Samoa." Ta'isi persisted in drawing attention to the Depression-driven restiveness, "the people who rioted in New Zealand were hungry in the midst of a land of plenty." Luxford disallowed the question. The New Zealand comparison was not to be pursued.[68]

Faumuina was the final witness. He testified again that Ta'isi was not the leader of the Mau; he was. Ta'isi gave advice and was kept informed of Mau decisions. Faumuina also corroborated the evidence of other Mau witnesses that they had gone against Ta'isi's advice to not pursue the *malagas* or to refuse a *fono* with the administrator if he was not present. Faumuina said Ta'isi has specifically requested there not be large receptions for him when he returned, nor did he seek the titles he was given.[69] On February 26 evidence was concluded.

Ta'isi had not brought any witnesses in his defense, nor did he opt to take the stand himself. E. T. Pleasants then presented the essence of Ta'isi's case. He argued the whole proceedings were invalid and the charges should be dismissed on the basis that the *Samoan Seditious Organisations Regulations* was ultra vires (beyond the powers) of New Zealand; it conferred excessive powers that interfered with the liberty of the individual.[70] These arguments did not sway Luxford.

The trial then moved into its penultimate phase; the closing arguments. The "facts are plainly before the court," so it was therefore unnecessary to make a long speech, said McCarthy, as the trial was now in its twenty-ninth day. He told the court that the prosecution sought to substantiate three things: the 1927 royal commission finding that Ta'isi was the leader of the Mau; that Richardson was then justified in ordering his deportation and exile for five years; and "to prove to the Court that the accused was not only the head of the Mau then but that he continued as nominal head while he was in exile and that today he is still head of the Mau."[71] He rested the prosecution's case. McCarthy had spoken for fifteen minutes.

It was then Ta'isi's turn. He told the court that the prosecution opened with that "glamour which has characterised most if not all of the cases brought by the police against representatives of the large majority of Samoans who are discontented with the methods put upon them by the Administration, and those who sympathise with [them] including those of part Samoan blood, and that are called Mau offences." He went on that the prosecution "opened by telling the court that this was probably the biggest and in its way, the most important case that has ever been brought to court in Samoa." Throughout the prosecutor's narrative, Ta'isi continued, he "has pointed to me as the author and instigator of all the complaints of the Samoans . . . that I incited and encouraged their grievances and consequent dissatisfaction with the New Zealand mandatory administration." McCarthy had read out "much private correspondence, newspapers articles, and other typed and written matter to the court" that gave "spectacular and sensational features" to the prosecution's case Ta'isi argued. Instead, he submitted:

> The conditions which have been allowed to prevail for many years past [and the] policies . . . of which the people have complained are which no white people could tolerate and which the Samoans resist because they are the very opposite of what they have been taught by the British missionaries of the fundamental basis of British justice, and are repugnant to their own sense of justice and freedom.[72]

He then read from a prepared statement and proceeded to give a sweeping account of Sāmoan grievances, their cause, and his role in them. He pointed out this was the first occasion where he was permitted to appear in court and answer the "many charges against him." He told the court he had always acted in good faith and since his return to Sāmoa he believed the laws relating to sedition had been suspended owing to the attempt to convene a meeting with the administrator. The Mau "felt it had a duty to strive for the welfare and liberty of

Samoans"; there was no intentional guilt. He considered himself a "scapegoat" for wrongs committed by the New Zealand administration, but "the Mau would never rest until their grievances were redressed; where legitimate wrongs existed, no amount of suppression would ever crush the Mau."[73] When he finished his address on the afternoon of Friday, March 2, Ta'isi had spoken for seven hours over three days of hearing. He then rested his case.

The following day, Luxford delivered an interim verdict. This was a twelve-page, carefully crafted document that could not have been the product of one night's labor: he wrote it before the case concluded. Luxford's opening remarks must have been devastating, though not unexpected: "Seldom have the facts of a case which has occupied a Court for 30 days been so simple." "There is ample proof of the guilt of the defendant in respect of three of the charges," he declared. It was clear to him that the importance of the case to the defendant "went far beyond a verdict of conviction or acquittal . . . it was manifest that

Figure 13.5. Ta'isi gives a customary reply of thanks at a *ta'alolo* at Vaimoso held on September 13, 1933. For this act he would be sentenced to a prison term and ten years exile. *NZ Samoa Guardian,* March 9, 1934, 1. Courtesy of the National Library of Australia.

the defendant's intention and desire was to justify his course of conduct throughout the last seven years in the eyes of the Samoan people and to show them that he has not betrayed them." He explained, "Because Samoan matters political have been so involved in this case I am taking the unusual course of delivering" both an interim judgment and a final judgment. He did this because "in my opinion the verdict of guilty or not guilty should be determined without regard to such matters."

Luxford proceeded to go through the relevant evidence that led him to find Ta'isi guilty of charges two, three, and six. These charges were that the accused

> Did on divers other dates between the 18th August 1933 and the 16th November 1933 at Apia and elsewhere identify himself with a seditious organization, to wit, the Mau by meeting and associating with members of the Mau [charge 2];
> On the 13th September 1933 at Vaimoso did address a meeting held by/or for the purposes of a seditious organization, to wit, the Mau [charge 3] . . .
> On the 27th September 1933 at Vaimoso did address a meeting held by/or for the purposes of a seditious organization [charge 6].

For these crimes Luxford sentenced Ta'isi to eight months imprisonment and ten years exile for each charge; each sentence to be served concurrently. He remanded Ta'isi in custody and ordered him to reappear before him the next Wednesday morning at nine o'clock, when he would deliver his final judgment.[74] As Ta'isi was led away to Vaimea Gaol, Faumuina "exhorted . . . Mau onlookers to keep the peace and disperse from the vicinity of the Court."[75] Ta'isi was now a prisoner.

Chapter Fourteen

Sāmoa Evermore (1935–1944)

Seeing their father in prison was heartbreaking for Ta'isi's daughters. Taufau, his "Baby," captured the devastating experience in the poem, "A Daughter's Grief," which she wrote after seeing her father in Vaimea prison the night Luxford had sentenced him. As the door opened, she saw "my dearest, my love, my father" sitting at the rough desk in the corner of his Spartan cell.[1] Despite his circumstances, his eyes lit up at the sight of his family, Taufau wrote. Ta'isi's family and friends swung into action to try to prevent his exile. On Monday morning C. V. Allom and Rudi Kruse, of O. F. Nelson and Co., and E. T. Pleasants asked Administrator Hart if Ta'isi would be sent to New Zealand. Hart (who had been requesting Ta'isi be removed from Sāmoa) hid behind the judicial process; everything rested on Luxford's final sentence, he told them. In the afternoon, a "large deputation of Mau chiefs" made their way up to Vailima to ask that Ta'isi not be sent away.[2] No doubt Hart told them also to wait.

At ten o'clock in the morning on Wednesday, March 7, Ta'isi was back in the courtroom to hear Luxford's final judgment. Ta'isi already knew his fate of eight months imprisonment and ten years of exile. What was left for Luxford to do was to dispense with the legal arguments, as he did in the first part of his judgment, and then to explain "the degree of seriousness with which the proved offences must be regarded" that would decide how he would serve his sentence.[3] The *Samoa Herald* headline reported Luxford's final judgment was "scathing"; it was now his turn to heap scorn on Ta'isi and recover the reputation of New Zealand's administration.[4] In Luxford's assessment,

Ta'isi was a man "obsessed with what he considered the injustice of his deportation for five years." "To me," Luxford explained, "the most painful feature . . . of this long trial was the number of times he used that set expression and the emotion he exhibited each time he made use of it." It "was evident to me and I think to anyone who has any knowledge of human nature, that his grievance has become a deep-rooted obsession, forever present, and which often dominates his thoughts and actions." With this obsession Ta'isi fanned the flames of discontent especially via the *NZ Samoa Guardian* "that waged an incessant campaign of calumny against the Government and those connected with it." When he returned to Sāmoa in May 1933 and tried to step back from the Mau because he feared further punishment, the Mau would not let him be. Luxford "deduced" from evidence and "my knowledge of the Samoan mind" that the Mau leaders were telling Ta'isi "you have led us into this trouble—it is for you to get us out of it." Ta'isi had misled these impressionable people repeatedly, Luxford concluded. Therefore "justice demanded" the release of all the men he recently sentenced for their participation in the Mau *malagas*. Luxford's final words to Ta'isi were severe:

> Your present position can be very briefly described as "a sad tragedy" for the evidence satisfies me, apart altogether from the manner in which you conducted your defence, that your outstanding ability was capable of being, indeed actually was a force of good to this country and to your mother's people, but you have turned the talents wherewith you were blessed into a force of evil.[5]

Luxford reiterated his maximum sentence that would be served from this date. Pleasants immediately applied for leave to appeal to the Supreme Court of New Zealand, which Luxford granted. Pleasants also applied for bail; the police opposed the application. Luxford would decide on this later in the day. At three o'clock that afternoon, Luxford refused bail. At four o'clock, Ta'isi's daughters appeared at Vailima to ask Hart if their father would be sent to New Zealand tomorrow when the *Maui Pomare* sailed. Hart told them "such would be the case." Ta'isi would be exiled from Sāmoa at five o'clock the next afternoon with twenty four hours' notice.[6]

That night many letters and people, including Tupua Tamasese Mea'ole, beat a path to Vailima, imploring Hart to delay Ta'isi's exile. He was unmoved. Beginning at six fifteen in the morning on

March 8, Pleasants called on Hart again asking that Ta'isi be allowed to speak to him and that Ta'isi not be sent away. Hart declined the request. At nine o'clock, Dr. Dawson and Pleasants called and applied for Hart to delay Ta'isi's departure on medical grounds. Hart refused again. At nine thirty, Hart was notified that the Nelsons' Auckland office had been radioed requesting they arrange immediate government representations to prevent Ta'isi's imminent exile. At ten thirty "a big deputation of influential chiefs" met with Hart in the legislative council room. Many more Mau men and women who could not fit inside the room gathered outside. At two forty-five that afternoon, Ta'isi's daughters returned, presenting Hart with a telegram from New Zealand. The prime minister had referred their request to the administrator. Hart would not entertain any changes; the administration believed Ta'isi "inspired" all these representations on his behalf. Fifteen minutes later, a large gathering of Sāmoans arrived at Vailima.[7] Ta'isi's daughters, led by Viopapa and Ta'isi's sister Gustava, Mau chiefs, and, most notably, Malietoa—the great rival of the Mau and the administration's greatest ally—as well as Tuatagaloa appeared on the lawn with a fine mat prominently displayed.[8] They all proceeded to sit with heads bowed in front of the building performing an *ifoga*—a forgiveness ceremony. Hart invited them to come and sit inside on the ballroom floor. They asked Hart to not deport Ta'isi and they presented the fine mat to him as a "mat of settlement . . . between the two great families of Tupua and Malietoa."[9] Hart took the mat but refused their request, telling them "the judgment of the court must take its course." Hart broke strict custom and no doubt many hearts in this one instance.[10]

Ta'isi was already aboard the *Maui Pomare*. When the police had come for him earlier in the day, he was dressed from hat to boots but with no trousers; his daughters had taken them away the night before as a delaying tactic, the administration surmised. When it was clear the police were going to take him aboard regardless, Ta'isi's daughters borrowed some from a friend.[11]

The *Maui Pomare* sailed from Apia Harbor on March 8, on schedule. On this sailing, the vessel would deviate from its usual course and head south to Christchurch. It was here that Ta'isi was to serve his jail time, in Paparua Prison. As Upolu slipped from view, Ta'isi no doubt reflected on the bitter irony that he was being exiled again, this time as a prisoner, aboard the ship named for his great friend and Māori statesman. In the days before his departure he had been thinking about another great man who, like him, was forcibly exiled from Sāmoa. That man was Lauaki, the leader of the *Mau a Pule* who was exiled to Saipan with seventy others in 1909 under German rule. In the *NZ Samoa Guardian* edition that also carried the breaking news that he was a prisoner on the *Maui Pomare,* Ta'isi reflected on having met Lauaki in 1906 when he was on a *malaga* around Savai'i. As readers of that issue of the *NZ Samoa Guardian* reflected on history repeating itself, Ta'isi asked them to consider how Lauaki would have been remembered if he was born in Europe or America. If he had been, "he should no doubt have figured among the greatest of statesmen whose names are beacon lights of history. Because he was Samoan he is still looked upon as a rebel" and not as a "patriot." Ta'isi looked to the first great rebel leader of the Americas for comparison. "If the American Revolution had failed, George Washington and a few more of the now famous Americans would most probably have been sent to the gallows as traitors," but now their names are exalted even by John Bull. The difference was race; being born of the white race as opposed to the ranks of non-European colonized peoples.[12]

Ta'isi's mirroring of Lauaki's fate and his own in the March 9, 1934 issue of the *NZ Samoa Guardian* was the last time his voice was heard in this way. This would be the final issue of the newspaper that had been the "sharpest weapon" of the Mau, the conduit for Ta'isi to communicate to readers in New Zealand, Sāmoa and beyond, and also one of the foremost reasons the New Zealand government was now punishing him as severely as they could under the law. The paper was the specific target of new laws that forbade the distribution of any published material in the Sāmoan language without administration consent; the Sāmoan supplement of the *NZ Samoa Guardian* allegedly penned by Ta'isi was now illegal. The *Samoa Publications Order* that came into effect on January 1, 1934, also targeted "seditious newspapers"; the English version of *NZ Samoa Guardian* was now also illegal. The ordinance also gave the administration additional extensive powers to seize any postal package that contained any illegal material.[13] There was no more will (or money) to push for the paper's continued existence. As Ta'isi told his head office in a memorandum written aboard the *Maui Pomare,* "I have no wish to do other than submit to my defeat."[14]

The conviction and exile of their managing director was not good news for O. F. Nelson and Co. The day after Ta'isi sailed, a number of long-serving managers (H. W. Moors, Jacob Helg, and A. Betham) were let go by the firm but this was done in a face-saving way (that is to say, they "resigned"). Helg understood that dire circumstances underpinned the decision and wanted "my sincere thanks" to be conveyed to Ta'isi "for the treatment accorded me during my 16 years' service with the Firm."[15] More trading stations were closed, too. Ta'isi was "sorry to have to make these drastic changes but everything possible must now be done to save the company from serious embarrassment at all costs," he wrote as he sailed on the *Maui Pomare* toward Christchurch.[16] A. G. Smyth and C. V. Allom were promoted and would steer the firm through the treacherous financial times that lay ahead. Ta'isi would continue to oversee his business by correspondence from prison and then once he was freed, as an exile at large in New Zealand, as he had since 1928.

As the *Maui Pomare* neared Christchurch, Ta'isi was hoping his stay in jail would be short. If Luxford granted him bail, he would be free in a few days' time. His mind was full of troubles, but "I have my dear children at heart now above all else . . . they are the greatest comfort to me."[17] He worried about their schooling and how they would fare in Apia, given what had happened. He wanted Viopapa, Noue, Taufau, and Sina to come to New Zealand by the next steamer; everyone had to be together. The girls would wait in Apia until there was news about Ta'isi's bail application. He was "particularly insistent that they should live together in Tuaefu . . . he does not wish the family to be split up in any way."[18] After Ta'isi was deported, Viopapa suffered another episode of mental illness, prompting her sisters to leave Tuaefu and stay with their mother.[19] Ta'isi worried about the impact a long stay in jail would have on his already poor health, and he hoped for some judicial clemency or a "gracious act" from the government. Malienafau and Piliopo were with him aboard the *Maui Pomare*. They had been permitted "every freedom of the ship which is greatly appreciated"; Corporal Hoggard of the Sāmoa police, who escorted the prisoner, was probably responsible for this benevolence.[20]

When the ship docked in Lyttelton Harbor on March 19, Ta'isi had to be escorted down the steep gangway by Corporal Hoggard and a local policeman. Reporters awaiting Ta'isi's arrival saw this, and reported law enforcement officials were treating Ta'isi roughly. They also reported, incorrectly according to the local police officer, that Ta'isi was horrified by the appearance of a Black Maria waiting to take him to the train station for the twelve-mile journey to Paparua Prison—so much so that Ta'isi tried to hail a taxi. This did not happen, according to the police officer; Ta'isi made "no objection of getting into the van."[21] The papers tried to paint a picture of Ta'isi humiliated but resisting the "first reality of his sentence."[22] The *Christchurch Star* also predicted the famous prisoner was unlikely to get any special concessions in prison.

Ta'isi hired a Wellington-based lawyer, Mr. P. B. Cooke, to represent him. Cooke stayed in Christchurch for the duration of Ta'isi's imprisonment, seeing to the bail application and also being the intermediary between Ta'isi and the firm in Apia. He wrote to C. V. Allom on March 26 and told him how Ta'isi was faring in jail. He was "keeping very well, despite his extreme disappointment on learning on the first day of this stay . . . he would not be allowed to have smokes or drinks." Cooke reported, "The authorities have been very nice and gradually extended several privileges which is making things easier for Mr Nelson." They agreed to "taper him off his liquor supplies and I have been able to send two bottles [probably of whiskey, Ta'isi's favored libation] to the gaol to date." The restrictions on visitors were also very tight—three visitors per fortnight, no physical contact, and only five letters a month. Cooke added, "We have been able to get the chief warder to shut his eyes now and then, but of course is it best not to mention these things." Piliopo and Malienafau were also granted an additional visit per week outside usual visiting hours and Cooke was able to "wedge in" Malienafau with "my visit today on the plea of business and Mr Nelson was very happy to see her." Despite everything, Cooke relayed, Ta'isi showed an incredible spirit. "It is remarkable that Mr Nelson can still make a joke and he is on excellent terms with the warders," Cooke told Allom.

Ta'isi's time in Paparua ended the next day (March 27) when he was granted bail. He had to remain in Christchurch for a period according to his bail conditions, so he could report to Paparua Prison if his bail was revoked. He telegrammed Apia for warm clothes as the chilly autumn weather set in.[23] When the court of appeal heard his case, starting from April 20, he was in Wellington but was advised by his counsel not to attend the hearings.[24]

The night Ta'isi was sent away from Sāmoa, Administrator Hart wrote an impassioned letter to Prime Minister Forbes. The focus of the letter was not Ta'isi and all the desperate pleas on his behalf directed to Hart on that day; these events were almost mentioned in passing. Instead Hart conveyed to the prime minister that the strain of office weighed heavily on him and he needed leave. Braisby and Luxford wanted a break from Sāmoa, too, Hart reported. Forbes would take a dim view of the requests; Hart would have to wait for his trip to New Zealand. In the weeks that followed, Hart was occupied with the business of the reconciliation between the two embittered sides in Sāmoa. A series of *fonos* were held to affect the great rapprochement.[25] It was Ta'isi's wish to see the Mau and the Malo (those who supported the government) come together and dissolve their long-standing feud through the observance of forgiveness rituals. Then the two sides worked toward resolving tensions with Hart. They came to many agreements about how to move forward, but there was one considerable sticking point: they wanted Ta'isi returned to Sāmoa. On this, Hart would not budge: the government of New Zealand had invested too deeply in his prosecution on all fronts. So Hart repeated his previous position that the matter was out of his hands. It became clear to Hart in the weeks after Ta'isi was banished that he had not rid himself of this man; his exile was now a leading grievance that poisoned the gains made between the administration and aggrieved Sāmoans.

The court of appeal handed down its decision on June 29. The four judges were split. Two, Justice Herdman and Justice Reid, fully concurred with Luxford. Myers confirmed the first two convictions but not the third.[26] Justice Blair did not believe there was jurisdiction to "impose a greater penalty than a fine" and so "as a consequence all the convictions entered against the appellant should be quashed."[27] The majority ruled, however, and so the outcome for Ta'isi was bleak. The judges deemed he had served adequate prison time, but the ten-year exile would stand. His only legal redress was now the Privy Council. Ever the optimist, Ta'isi thought Blair's judgment boded well for his prospects with the Privy Council, who would hear the case in January. "I feel certain . . . an appeal to the Privy Council would be successful," he told his cousin-in-law Atoa, but the prohibitive legal costs were biting hard into his depleted finances. As well as a legal victory, Ta'isi hoped the political tide in New Zealand was finally turning to the Labour Party, and he anticipated this would bring about a change in fortune for him and he could return home. He did not think his mind and body could survive ten years of exile but "the spirit is still strong."[28]

As well as having hope for his ongoing appeal, Ta'isi saw another chink of hope from the court of appeal judgments. He wrote to Prime Minister Forbes on July 23, asking for an audience with him. Ta'isi told Forbes that the majority of the court had decided that his offenses were political rather than criminal and therefore "the Governor-General had it in his power to cancel the exile." On July 31 Ta'isi met with the prime minister in the presence of Carl Berendsen in Wellington (Forbes began the meeting with the greeting, "Yes, what is it, Mr Nelson?"). Ta'isi had maintained a buoyant spirit throughout the years of conflict with the government, but now in July 1934 he began to sound like a man breaking. Ta'isi told Forbes that even if the majority decision of the court of appeal had come down in his favor, he would have still wanted the meeting so as to assure the government he wanted "nothing to be done on my behalf which would come into conflict with the Administration" upon his return to Sāmoa. Now the court had reconfirmed his ten-year exile that "at my present age, Mr Forbes, is a prospect which I must accept as exile for life." Ta'isi told Forbes how his family was split up and about the financial burden of maintaining two households, let alone one in New Zealand in the present time. "I am in a very precarious position," Ta'isi said. "My business . . . has been the means of livelihood to many other Samoan-born families besides my own, and that business suffered very severe losses during my [previous] enforced absence." But now his business affairs had reached such a point of "serious crisis . . . that I cannot possibly cope with [it] from this distance if my business is to survive the present depression at all." Ta'isi told Forbes that things had become so bad, if he was to remain "stranded far away from home" where life was cheaper and nature more bountiful, "I shall have to seek other means of sustenance for my family and myself." Ta'isi went through how he was given hours' notice of his deportation and no time to organize his affairs, and all the other factors that amassed hardship and injustice on him. Ta'isi told Forbes that "the high feeling running against me now in official circles . . . will be greatly modified, if not changed altogether, as time goes on" but unless there is "some amelioration . . . shown to me now . . . I shall . . . become ruined in every way." "If I have offended Mr Forbes, I trust you will grant that I have been very severely punished."[29]

Forbes responded at length about how disappointed he was about what happened in Sāmoa after Ta'isi returned last year and that governing Sāmoa was "a difficult task" but was one New Zealand accepted. He spelled out the duties the government had to Sāmoans and that Ta'isi was making that task difficult. "The Government did not want to be in any way vindictive but Mr Nelson must see," he said, "in regard to his hope of amelioration of his exile that he had just come back again to New Zealand after disappointing the Government by his actions in Samoa." If Ta'isi had been "sensible," he would not have opposed the administration again. Given this past, "how could the Government have any confidence that it would not have the same things to do all over again?" Forbes asked. The two men went back and forth, stating their cases with Ta'isi pleading that he in no way wished to "disturb the Administration." Forbes returned to the "intense hostility" leveled at the government through the *NZ Samoa Guardian;* Ta'isi dwelled on the growing resentment in Sāmoa about how he has been treated. Forbes told Ta'isi he would have to consult with the administrator; "a lot would depend on" Ta'isi's "demeanour here" and on the situation in Sāmoa. "The government could not have anyone throwing sand into the bearings when they were trying to get the machine to work smoothly" and Forbes would leave the matter at that.[30] Ta'isi thanked the prime minister for his time and left.

To ascertain the sincerity of Ta'isi's plea that he had ceased his previous activities, the administration continued to read his mail. Ta'isi's letters to family, Faumuina, and Tuimalealiifano, and general messages in late July and August were taken from mailbags, translated (though the originals are not available to evaluate the accuracy of the English versions), and read for any sign of defiant language or intent. Unsurprisingly, Braisby and Administrator Hart found that "Nelson has . . . shown conclusively there has been no change of mind on his part but on the contrary that he is determined to carry on to the upmost of his strength and ability." Hart cautioned: "Under these circumstances it would be folly to authorize his return to Samoa."[31]

Arthur Braisby, refreshed after a long journey to the United States and Canada (where he toured prison facilities), then England (his first visit home in thirty years), wrote to General Richardson at Christmas 1934. He recalled how one year ago everyone was deeply involved in Ta'isi's trial, but now "with Nelson away, this is a changed Samoa. Many people are wiser, and none more so than Nelson." "As we said," he continued, "there was only one man in the Mau—Nelson, and he could only function when he held his principal power—money." Now Braisby recalled, in depth, Ta'isi was near financial ruin, as were his shareholders, and possibly the Bank of New Zealand was about to sustain a big loss, but only Ta'isi was to blame for all of it because of his "activity in the Mau." Braisby enjoyed enclosing a transcript of Ta'isi's interview with Forbes, noting, "It is interesting to compare that with his bombastic talk of 1926." Ta'isi no longer had his source of power, according to Braisby, but the police inspector certainly felt he had his. He recounted for the general how he set the trap to catch Ta'isi when he returned in 1933 and that he was "well satisfied with the result." Most telling was his revelation that "the final chapter is yet to be written and I think that I shall write it."[32]

Ta'isi had to find his way in New Zealand for the foreseeable future. Auckland was again his place of residence, but the family's circumstances were very much reduced. The youngest girls came to live with their father, who took up a place in Depression-ravaged Auckland. Their last years of schooling were greatly disrupted because of their dire financial circumstances.[33] Ta'isi wanted all his children to live together, but his oldest daughters were moving into new phases in their lives. Noue was the first to marry. On October 27, 1934, she married Tupua Tamasese Mea'ole, a union that cemented Ta'isi with Mau leadership and a *tama aiga* and was viewed with suspicion by the administration.[34] Yet Ta'isi did not orchestrate the marriage; at first he strenuously opposed it. Ta'isi worried that Noue was taking on a great deal of hardship by entering into a marriage that would involve living *fa'asamoa* with all the attendant domestic and cultural obligations and the absence of modern conveniences. Not only would domestic duties be more difficult; by marrying someone designated Sāmoan, Noue's own racial status would change. This change would prevent her from inheriting shares in her father's company as being Sāmoan "she may not own shares in a commercial concern."[35] Though he worried at first about all the implications of the marriage, once Ta'isi realized this was a love match, his opposition subsided. Because of his exile he could not be present to perform his paternal duties on her wedding day.[36] He would also not be in Sāmoa to welcome his first grandchild, born to the couple the following October, Fialaui'afualeafi.[37] In 1935 Viopapa married E. J. Grey in Auckland. Grey had been a correspondent with Ta'isi through the Suva trading firm Brown and Joske. He had also been the Suva-based agent of the *NZ Samoa Guardian*.[38] Despite auspicious beginnings through the long-standing family connection, this marriage would end tragically.

Ta'isi's hopes that the Privy Council would deliver justice were dashed in March 1935. Stafford Cripps once again represented him and argued voraciously for over two hours about the merits of the case. The New Zealand government had prepared their case for months that included urgently getting hold of H. V. Evatt's (now an Australian High Court Justice) new study *British Dominions as Mandatories*. Though Evatt had been briefed on Ta'isi's cases from 1928 he did not mention them, although *Tagaloa v. Inspector of Police* was cited for its test of the *ultra vires* argument recently adopted in Ta'isi's trial.[39] New Zealand's expensive and thorough preparation also included engaging a leading King's Counsel, but he was not even called to speak; the court refused to hear the appeal. The government's London solicitors reported "we must confess both Counsel and ourselves were surprised that they did decide in this way." This decision was consistent with other Privy Council cases, apparently. "The only case of an appeal from a mandated territory so far as we are aware is the Palestine case," where the mandatory was Britain and not a dominion.[40] This would have been cold comfort for Ta'isi.

The year 1935 must have been the hardest in the now nine years of Ta'isi's political agitation. The combination of the Great Depression, the series of legal defeats and the obdurate refusal of conservative governments to relent in its punishment, and the frosty atmosphere in Auckland, where many shunned Ta'isi, would have tested him greatly. This exile was much harder than last time, he admitted; before "I had wealth but not so now."[41] To add salt to the wounds, the fourteenth annual report to the League of Nations portrayed him in ways that were inaccurate, and he once again took exception to how the New Zealand government reported matters to the League.[42] In September he wrote another long, detailed letter to Prime Minister Forbes, pointing out that the report's statement that "upon the departure of Mr O. F. Nelson from Western Samoa . . . there was a marked decrease in Mau activities and a complete change in the political situation" was erroneous. He went back through the trial and gave dates for convictions to stress his point that his presence in Sāmoa did not equate to elevated levels of Mau activity. Despite everything he had endured, "I am just as jealous as ever of my character and good name, and rightly wish to correct any misrepresentation of my motives in respect of the welfare of my native country and my people especially in an official document sent to . . . the League of Nations, where most of the leading coutries [*sic*] of the world . . . are represented."[43] Subinspector Fell had found more recent letters posted by Ta'isi to Sāmoa that contained "political" remarks (he discussed recent Sāmoan history), so his "criminality" continued in government eyes and once again, nothing altered.[44]

The long-awaited sea change in New Zealand politics came on November 27, 1935. George Forbes' government was swept from power; Michael Savage was swept in, forming the first Labour Party government in New Zealand history. The Sāmoan cause had been so high on the Labour Party's political agenda when Harry Holland led it, surely Savage would honor Holland's legacy, Sāmoans assumed. Ta'isi waited (very patiently all things considered) until late March to approach Prime Minister Savage, seeking an interview in order to find out where he stood "on Samoan affairs, more especially as it affects my own position."[45] Savage granted the interview, and Ta'isi traveled to Wellington to learn his fate. By April 4 word had spread to the papers that Savage had assured Ta'isi his exile would soon end, perhaps within four months once legal matters had been settled to allow that to happen.[46] On June 19 Prime Minister Savage (who was also the minister for external affairs) requested Governor-General, Viscount Galway, sign warrants remitting Ta'isi's exile. On June 20 this was done. Savage wrote to Ta'isi on June 29, informing him that this would take effect from July 14.[47] On June 24 the acting administrator, Arthur Turnbull, revoked all the most oppressive regulations in Sāmoa.[48] The Mau was no longer illegal; there was great rejoicing at this move.[49] This act was accompanied by the arrival of a ministerial delegation dubbed the "Goodwill Mission." The minister for lands, Frank Langstone, and the member for Westland, John O'Brien, arrived in Apia among the jubilation. Unlike the three previous ministerial delegations since New Zealand's rule commenced, this one came with a tone of conciliation. They declared a new era had begun.

But had it? Before the ministers arrived, officials had gone around the islands informing people of the visit and the changes that were about to take place. They also told Sāmoans that certain things would not change—the administration of Sāmoa would not change nor would white officials be removed, even ones (like Braisby) who had been leading actors in the most egregious moments of the past. Ta'isi was "greatly disturbed" by this news. While he was extremely grateful for all the actions and courtesies extended to him by Savage, which included being given a meeting with Langstone and O'Brien prior to their departure, he noted to the prime minister there was a disconnect.[50] Ta'isi had already written to Faumuina asking him and the Mau to show the delegation "respect and confidence."[51] To Savage he warned that officials' statements that declared there would be no change "can easily undo what good impression might otherwise have been made" by his own entreaties and the delegation itself.[52]

Ta'isi's misgivings about this new era in relations would endure and grow. Yet in the weeks he had left in his exile in New Zealand, he

Figure 14.1. "Returning to Western Samoa—Mr. O. F. Nelson, leader of the Mau, sailed today on the Maui Pomare for Western Samoa, the Government having removed the ban on his return and so ended his exile. He is seen with his three daughters (from left) Misses Calmar [Taufau], Sina and Olive [Malienafau] Nelson—who are also returning to their home in Apia." *Evening Post,* July 15, 1936, 9. Courtesy of the National Library of New Zealand.

had other much happier things to think about. At the end of June Malienafau, who had been a solicitor since 1931, was admitted to the bar as a barrister. This made her one of three women allowed to practice as a solicitor in Auckland and only the second woman to be admitted as a barrister. Justice Ostler of the Supreme Court (who delivered a dissenting judgment in the 1931 O. F. Nelson and Co. appeal) performed the honors on the motion of Mr. Johnstone K. C.[53] On July 15 several papers ran a photograph of Ta'isi on the Auckland wharf with Taufau, Sina, and Malienafau about to board the *Maui Pomare* for Sāmoa alongside photographs of the British royal family in an interesting juxtaposition. A journalist asked Ta'isi for a comment, and he said with a smile "I like New Zealand, I like its people but . . ."[54]

On July 21, the *Maui Pomare* sailed into Apia Harbor. Unlike Ta'isi's previous homecoming three years before, this time the acting administrator, Minister Langstone, and the Hon. John O'Brien went aboard the ship to greet the returning exile before he made his symbolic journey onto Sāmoan soil. Accompanying the government officials on the launch to meet the *Maui Pomare* were family members who reunited with Ta'isi. The ship was surrounded by many craft with more than four hundred people singing and drumming their welcomes. Ta'isi's arrival on land was marked by more music, a parade more than a mile long, ceremonies, and honors. Acting Administrator Turnbull also joined the welcoming committee. The solidarity between Ta'isi and the New Zealand government and the rapprochement between the Mau and Malietoa, brokered in 1934 after Ta'isi's trial, was signified in a photograph taken by Alfred Tattersal. With Ta'isi in the center and three of his daughters (Sina, Taufau, and possibly Malienafau at the end), the acting administrator with his cane, three *tama aiga* stand together—Tupua Tamasese Mea'ole, Tuimalealiifano at the end (dressed in their Mau lava lava), and most notably Malietoa standing next to Turnbull—indicate the state of affairs upon Ta'isi's arrival back in Sāmoa in 1936.

Prime Minister Savage was initially eager to involve Ta'isi in politics again; Ta'isi did not share this enthusiasm, though Savage communicated with him as an equal. When an issue was of enough import, like the Mau resolution in September 1936 to have all Chinese "coolies" removed primarily because Sāmoans now wanted their plantation jobs, Ta'isi communicated this desire (which he shared) to Savage on the Mau's behalf.[55] On his greater political involvement Ta'isi told Savage in October that "my own personal affairs urgently require all the time I can give them . . . so I should be better off outside the political sphere altogether." He went on, "Any office which the Samoans are demanding for me is not at my instigation, but if they believe I can be of service to them and to the successful administration of this little country, I shall always be pleased to do all in my power in that direction."[56] Malienafau's name was also suggested for an administration position. When the *Western Samoa Mail* (formerly the *Samoa Times*) falsely claimed she had accepted a position, Ta'isi wrote an uncharacteristically furious letter to the editor saying "I am quite prepared to take anyone on who attacks me through my daughters" among other passionate remarks on "the long persecution of me."[57]

The euphoria at Ta'isi's homecoming was not universal. The warhorses of the old administration kept a noticeably public silence about the dramatically reversed policy. All except one, who made his sentiments more than clear in a series of letters to the prime minister that ranted and raved as only someone with an unhinged mind could.

Figure 14.2. Ta'isi O. F. Nelson's return from his second exile pictured with three *tama aiga*—Tupua Tamasese Mea'ole, Tuimalealiifano, and Malietoa—and the acting administrator A. C. Turnbull, three of his daughters, and other dignitaries, July 1936. A. J. Tattersal ½-020699-F, Courtesy of the National Library of New Zealand.

Arnold Gozar, the former administration official who had assisted the Crown solicitor in the prosecution of Ta'isi's firm, let fly with invective about the imprudence of putting faith in Ta'isi or releasing him from his due punishment. Gozar thought Ta'isi was the "Napoleon of Samoa," who "will not rest until he has had his fill of REVENGE and POWER." Yet even this most severe of critics had to concede Ta'isi possessed such "phenomenal industry, painstaking attention to detail, organizing ability and tactical skill" that he was "the most extraordinary half-caste that the South Seas Islands will ever produce."[58] Ta'isi's other detractors did not commit their thoughts to paper quite so colorfully as Gozar; but no doubt there was much grinding of teeth. Where did this about face leave former administrators and officials, government ministers, and prime ministers who had invested everything in pursuing Ta'isi and laying all blame at his feet?

The carryover of officials from the conservative political era to the Labour one, however, meant the old patterns of dealing with problems and with Ta'isi persisted. The police (that is, Braisby) kept generating reports on Ta'isi, watching his words and activities closely.[59] Ta'isi was still a problem. He still kept writing letters, now on Tuaefu letterhead with the motto "*E leai se gau mata'u na o le gau alofa*" (*people will submit willingly to love, never to coercion*). His letters raised concerns about the piecemeal reforms where too many vestiges of the past—administration personnel and excessive legal powers—remained in place. Certain important changes had taken place—Ta'isi was reelected and resumed his place as a member of the legislative council, where he joined Tupua Tamasese Mea'ole, who was now also a member of the reformed legislative council as well as president of the Mau. Faumuina Fiame was made inspector of native police and the *fono* of *faipule* would be constituted through election—but these changes still fell short of Sāmoan expectations. There were still palpable tensions that overflowed in early July 1937 when Inspector Braisby's wife, Priscilla, was caught up in an incident and her car "damaged" when she drove through a funeral procession in Apia.[60] For those officials who still feared the Mau (like Arthur Braisby), this incident where the white wife of a leading administration figure was "attacked," encapsulated all their fears of a society trending toward an anarchic state.

The situation reached the point in 1938 that the term the "New Mau" was being used to describe the formation of the latest protest movement that included the traditional Mau base as well as the *fono* of *faipule* who had strenuously opposed the 1926–1936 Mau (although they had led the Mau of 1920–1922). Malietoa still sided with the administration.[61]

The increasing distance between the Mau and the administration left Ta'isi in a predicament. When Ta'isi had to choose between advocating for the administration, which New Zealand officials expected of him, or for Sāmoans, Ta'isi chose the latter, though he never wavered from his stance to pursue grievances through lawful means. Turnbull would write mid-1937, one year after Ta'isi's return, that his unabated habit of letter writing was "not helpful." He could not stop being a political activist and "writing voluminous letters regarding almost every Administration activity," Turnbull complained. His letters were so unwelcomed by Turnbull that he wrote "one cannot help but feel that on certain matters his mental balance has become upset [he had written "deranged" and then opted for the milder term "upset"]."[62] There is no clear increase or change in Ta'isi's style in letters in government files to support Turnbull's searing remark. Turnbull's concerns about Ta'isi were replicated in the *Pacific Islands Monthly* and *Honolulu Star Bulletin* around this time, when articles were published that accused Ta'isi of again being the sole cause of recurring trouble. Ta'isi took legal action. The matter ended with an unreserved apology and the matter being concluded in the high court of Sāmoa in March 1938.[63]

Ta'isi's first year back was marked by frustrations on the political front but, more painfully, it was also marred by personal tragedy. In February 1937 Viopapa died suddenly in Suva, reportedly in childbirth.[64] Her husband, E. J. Grey, being a Rosicrucian, did not believe in medical intervention, and Viopapa perished in questionable circumstances. Her body was brought back to Apia, and great rituals were observed to mark her passing. A funeral party of more than two thousand accompanied her body back to Tuaefu, where Methodist rites were performed, and she was buried in the family cemetery alongside her little half brother, who had been dead nearly twenty years.[65] The loss of a second child, his eldest, was devastating. Though Viopapa had troubled mental health that caused Ta'isi great anguish, the love between father and daughter was intense and not negotiable. Even when it came to Rosabel's wishes and her opposition to bringing Viopapa into the Tuaefu family fold in 1924 (though this was not the sole cause of the marital breakdown), Ta'isi chose his daughter. Viopapa had taken part in the 1928 journey to Geneva with her father, and as the eldest daughter she had assumed a leading role in the family, so was very much a part of the Mau history. Like the loss of his only son, Ta'isi never recovered from the loss of Viopapa.

Despite this event, Ta'isi remained committed (excessively in Turnbull's estimation) to the reform agenda. This included a Sāmoan delegation to Wellington at the beginning of 1938 that Ta'isi led.[66] Ta'isi must have thought about the light years of difference between his previous voyage to New Zealand, when he was a prisoner on the *Maui Pomare,* to this one when he was returning to New Zealand as a statesman of sorts, leading a mission with four other leaders. The other delegates were Tupua Tamasese Mea'ole, the Mau president, Faalava'au 'Au, secretary to the Mau, Alipia Galu, leader of the *fono* of *faipule,* and Leiataua, a member of the *fono* of *faipule*. Malienafau was also part of the mission, acting as the legal adviser.[67] Before the delegation left, Inspector Braisby wrote alarming reports based on information from "a reliable and confidential source" that pictured Ta'isi as up to his old supposed game of inciting agitation to satiate

Figure 14.3. Ta'isi with the delegation to Wellington, January 1938. Also pictured are Tupua Tamasese Mea'ole, Malienafau, Faalava'au 'Au, Alipia Galu, and Leiataua. *Evening Star,* January 24, 1938.

his lust for power.[68] The New Mau had "thirty-six" demands. The leading ones, so Braisby reported, were self-government and the installation of Ta'isi as head of it. He also pushed for lavish spending on things like staying "at the most expensive hotel in Wellington so Europeans can see that Samoans had ample funds in hand for the setting up of a new Government."[69] The funds for the trip were not coming from Ta'isi's coffers but from Mau subscriptions that flowed in (a worrying indication of the extent of Sāmoans' concerns). Braisby also noted that another leading demand was "that all Heads of Departments working in Samoa should be removed," a grievance that cut mighty close to bone for the inspector of police.[70]

In press reports Ta'isi played down the purpose of the delegation. "It is just a friendly visit," he insisted, denying all the troubling aims cited by Braisby that had made their way into the public arena.[71] Instead there was a focus in these press reports on a problem that unified the delegation (though not Sāmoan planters) and New Zealand politicians—the repatriation of Chinese laborers.[72] Overall, the purpose of the delegation, Ta'isi said, was to discuss concerns in person rather than via correspondence, and so achieve the best government of Sāmoa through a partnership with the New Zealand government and Sāmoan leaders. The party arrived in Wellington on January 24 and had a series of meetings with ministers and Prime Minister Savage.[73]

Though a diplomatic welcome was afforded the delegation and they got a "sympathetic hearing," little changed.[74] Soon after they returned, circulars in the Sāmoan language began appearing again, which caused a concerned administration to review laws preventing such activity. Cyril McKay, the secretary of native affairs, wrote that though he had "no proof," he believed all the "cyclostyled circulars are the product of one person—Mr Nelson."[75] Turnbull thought so, too, as he pondered whether to act to stop this circulating literature. "It should be remembered," he wrote back to Wellington in late 1938, "that the trusteeship for the welfare of the Samoans is in the hands of the Mandatory and not of Mr Nelson."[76] Though officials were souring on Ta'isi, voters were not. In November 1938 he was reelected to the legislative council, "topping the polls" with "a very nice majority."[77] The Labour government had also been returned to power in late 1938. On this occasion Ta'isi raised concerns with Minister Langstone, urging him to act. The latter responded that there were many pressing matters occupying the government's time and it would turn to Sāmoan issues "in good time."[78] While the authorship of the circulars was presumed to be Ta'isi, he definitely vented his concerns back to Wellington about dysfunction within administration ranks. He reported public defiance of Turnbull by subordinate officials, business frustrations, and monetary issues (particularly relating to the Controller of Customs) that hampered trading operations. Ta'isi also felt his company was subject to unfair treatment by officials; this generated a lot of written exchanges, too.[79] The political situation may have seemed like history repeating itself: in certain ways it was, and others not. The outbreak of war in September 1939 would essentially suspend developments as the New Zealand government turned its full attention to the war that crept closer and closer to Sāmoan and New Zealand shores.

The years 1938 and 1939 saw challenges for Ta'isi on several fronts, but also brought great joy. On New Year's Eve 1938 Piliopo married Richard Carruthers in a glamorous service that was followed by a reception for over five hundred people at Tuaefu. In March Noue gave birth to a son. At nine months of age, this son came to live at Tuaefu with his grandfather. Little Olaf Fredrick, who became known in his family as Efi (who would go on to become prime minister and

Figure 14.4. Ta'isi holds his eldest grandson, Efi, circa 1939. With permission of Tui Atua Tupua Tamasese Ta'isi Efi.

Sāmoa's third head of state), joined his younger cousin Lelani at Tuaefu. Lelani was Piliopo's first child and, being sickly, she was brought to Tuaefu straight after her birth so she could be near medical care; her grandfather affectionately referred to her as the first "Tuaefu baby."

Their grandfather indulged his grandchildren and delighted in the noise and bustle they created in his expansive house (most of the time). The children of his cousins, Fa'agutu and Atoa, and the Masoes added to the new generations of family that filled the grounds of Tuaefu with the beautiful chaos of young life. In November 1938 Sina married Edward (Ted) Annandale. Taufau married August (Gus) Meyer in April 1939. Malienafau would be the last of her sisters to marry; she wed Fredrick (Fred) Betham in September 1942. Ta'isi was a romantic; he wanted all his daughters to find love and happiness. Since his marriage had collapsed in 1924, his own love life was sparse. When he returned to Sāmoa from exile, he began a romance with famous Apia hotelier Aggie Grey. Things progressed toward marriage, but the relationship ended abruptly.[80] No one would end up replacing Rosabel; though separated for nearly twenty years, they remained married. Perhaps to compensate for his own lack of romance, Ta'isi would read romance stories as well as his more hardheaded works of history and anthropology in his beloved library at Tuaefu.[81]

When the Allies declared war against Germany in September 1939, people of German descent in Sāmoa were again deported to New Zealand for internment. Taufau's new husband was sent to Somes Island in Wellington Harbor; she followed him, hoping to secure his release by using her father's political connections. Despite the fact that Gus had recently been an agricultural student in Germany, he was released after a few months on the condition he did not return to Sāmoa. Taufau and Gus settled in Wellington. When her first child was due, Taufau made the journey back to Sāmoa and gave birth to her daughter Sina there in 1940. Mother and child returned to Wellington, but she came back with toddler Sina and baby Paulele (born in 1942) to see her father in 1943 for what would be the last time.[82]

When war came to the Pacific at the end of 1941, it brought mixed fortunes for the Ta'isi family. The war, especially the basing of troops in Sāmoa, drove up the price of copra and other goods. It pumped money into the economy and revived the economic fortunes of O. F. Nelson and Co. and Ta'isi himself, to some extent. It also made many things scarce, and like most families at the time, there was a constant discussion about acquiring goods and their escalated price.[83]

By 1943 Ta'isi's health was deteriorating, and his life was increasingly confined to Tuaefu. His public appearances became rare and then stopped from June 1943, when he decided he could not make his usual appearance to mark the king's birthday and speak on behalf of his European constituents in the legislative council.[84] Nor could he attend race meetings ("and you know how fond I am of races," he would write to Taufau).[85] As ascending and descending the grand staircase at Tuaefu became too much, he stayed upstairs in his room adjacent to his office. From this part of the house he could command a view of the harbor (which he gazed at through a telescope) and Mauga Folau, and hear the goings-on around Tuaefu, including the music of his beloved choir from the Tuaefu chapel.[86] Business was conducted from this part of the house, and his mind was filled with all kinds of information about commercial and personal events and developments in the firm, the family, and their wide friendship circle. When the New Zealand governor-general, Sir Cyril Newall, visited Apia in September 1943, he wanted to call on Ta'isi at Tuaefu, but Ta'isi's health was so poor he could not receive him.[87]

The gloom of his poor health was lightened by the presence of his grandchildren. By 1943 Piliopo's marriage had ended, and she moved to Tuaefu along with her new son, Tuitautai, who joined his sister Lelani and cousin Efi. Efi's older sister Fialaui'afualeafi was also a regular visitor to the house, and they would be later joined by their siblings Peter (Tusi) and Irene (Piliopo) in frequent visits with their mother. Sina had two daughters, Viopapa and Calmar. Malienafau was pregnant, and Ta'isi fretted about her health (as he also had about Sina), which is not surprising from a devoted father who had already lost a daughter in childbirth.[88] Fortunately, Malienafau delivered a healthy baby boy (Barry) in October 1943. Ta'isi delighted in their antics. "A child should be naughty," he wrote to Taufau, "so long as she is not spoiled and becomes unreasonable."[89] Through the eyes of his grandchildren, Ta'isi was "Grandpa," a loving and larger-than-life man who adored them. They idolized him, too, just as their mothers had.

In early February Ta'isi wrote his last letter to Taufau, who was awaiting the birth of her son, Kurt. Ta'isi discussed numerous things—the costs of goods in Wellington, that Masoe Tulele was going to send her some taro and avocados, that Tuaefu just got a new lick of paint, and Piliopo had made some renovations to the kitchen. Of greatest import was the realization that the next day was seven years since Viopapa had died in Suva; flowers were arranged and Ta'isi could not believe how time had passed so fast. He did not write a long letter as "I feel exceptionally weak this morning."[90] As Ta'isi's health had deteriorated so much, he wanted to see Rosabel. Rosabel's return to Tuaefu was akin to her return to the marriage. When she arrived, a hush came over the house and estate. As she went upstairs to see her estranged husband, everyone in the household held their breath. Then peals of laughter rang out from Ta'isi's room as the two reunited after nearly twenty years apart. Rosabel joined the team of caregivers and tended him; he seemed to be improving. But three weeks later, on February 28, Ta'isi collapsed and died. He had turned sixty-one four days earlier.

Figure 14.5. Nelson women on the day of Ta'isi's funeral in 1944. From the left, Sina, Malienafau, Rosabel, Piliopo, and Noue. Taufau was in Wellington. With permission of Fialaui'afualeafi Tamasese.

Rosabel wrote to a grief-stricken Taufau. The twenty "lonely years he and I had parted seems so foolish," but "the poor darling suffered so much"—it was time for him to go. "It does not seem possible that he has gone forever but now waits for us with Taisi [their son]." Rosabel was racked with "regrets" and "remorse," but, she said, "this teaches us all a lesson to be kind always to the one who has the big heart and forgives."[91] Sina wrote to her sister about their father's last days: "Bops was so good, so patient and so sweet, his only condition was that he wanted us constantly with him."[92] For the rest of her life, Taufau lived with the acute pain of not seeing her father before he passed away. Her sisters were equally devastated by the loss.

Peter Fraser, who had assumed the office of prime minister when Michael Savage died suddenly in 1940, wrote to the family and to Sāmoan leaders telling them of the "deep sympathy . . . felt by the Government and myself." "Mr Nelson," Fraser wrote, "was indeed a great man, and his passing is as deeply and sincerely regretted by the Government as it will be by the Samoan people." A funeral service was held at the Tuaefu chapel, masonic rites were observed at the graveside, and then Ta'isi was buried near his two children in the family plot beneath Mauga Folau.

Epilogue

"Samoans Will Forgive, but Never Forget"

After Ta'isi's burial, his family had to contend with their great loss, the settlement of his estate and his contested legacy.[1] In a final twist to the economic aspect of the story, because Ta'isi died during the war, death duties payable by the family were doubled. The tax on his estate was assessed at £20,000, owing to a questionable valuation of company shares. The family paid almost half (£9,000) and then Malienafau asked on behalf of her sisters and their children for forgiveness for the second half as they had no cash to pay it. They would have to sell their company shares—a move guaranteed to reduce their already doubtful market value. In her letter to Prime Minister Peter Fraser, Malienafau said a study of the accounts "will show the heavy price Father paid for his fight for the Samoans." "It can not be doubted," she went on, "that had he been here during the depression years the Company would have weathered these years successfully." Once he was able to return in 1936 Ta'isi steered the company to better financial health but he still had a £10,000 debt for Mau-related legal expenses, Malienafau explained. With better financial times he made settlement of this hefty debt a priority, and he managed to dispense with it before his death; Ta'isi did end up shouldering the lion's share of Mau costs. Malienafau argued that the company and Ta'isi personally had both contributed amply to government coffers over the years; she went on to argue that, because it was locally owned, his company had been penalized with additional taxation. For all these reasons, Malienafau asked Fraser for special consideration. She also hoped the prime minister would make more trips to Sāmoa and that his name would be associated "with that of the late Mr Holland and Sir Maui Pomare among the sincere and true friends of the Samoans."[2] Fraser was genuinely sympathetic. While the government did not forgive the outstanding debt, they revalued the company share value modestly so the outcome for Ta'isi's family was comparable.[3] Though

Ta'isi had been a wealthy man during his life, he deeply regretted he could not bequeath his children and grandchildren a comfortable inheritance. Instead their inheritance was spent on the Mau.[4]

His daughters no doubt wondered if this investment had been worth it, along with all the other hardships the family endured in the name of the political cause their father championed. At the end of his life, Ta'isi had doubts about this, too. Yet to draw attention to Ta'isi's contribution to his country from 1945, his daughters worked with the administration to construct a memorial of "public value" like a "children's park" or "water fountain."[5] In 1946 O. F. Nelson and Co. dedicated a building in Ta'isi's memory to the Returned Servicemen's Association (RSA) on Beach Road opposite their flagship Matafele store. A plaque noting this bequest was placed out the front. Fate soon intervened to erase the grand O. F. Nelson and Co. store from the Apia landscape. On May 31 the building burned to the ground. The business operated out of the RSA building until a new site on Beach Road was acquired, but it lacked the grandeur of the original.[6] Gradually "Nelesoni" storefronts that were once ubiquitous throughout the islands, along with all the other components of O. F. Nelson and Co., were replaced. The mercantile aspect of Ta'isi's presence in Sāmoan life faded. When it merged with another firm in the late 1980s, O. F. Nelson and Co. finally ceased trading.[7]

In 1960 the family dedicated Apia's Nelson Memorial Public Library to Ta'isi, a fitting tribute given his great love of books and learning. Along with "the Nelson Clock" (World War I memorial) Ta'isi's mark on Apia's public space remained, but over time these monuments aged. The clock started to slow. However, thanks to a recent mechanical refurbishment, it once again tells the right time. Outside the RSA, a building that has seen better days, a rambling garden hid the plaque commemorating Ta'isi. Ironically, in efforts to beautify the RSA ahead of the centennial commemorations of the Gallipoli landing in April 2015, the plaque was revealed again. Remembering those who fought in World War I—many who impacted his life considerably—drew Ta'isi out of the weeds.

Eighteen years after Ta'isi's death Sāmoa was on a course he had played such an instrumental role in charting. It became an independent country on January 1, 1962, the first in the Pacific, making its way in a vastly altered world from that Ta'isi inhabited. As the last vestiges of O. F. Nelson and Co. faded from view, relegated to an era past, so too did Ta'isi, though there were attempts at this time to recall

Figures 15.1–15.2. O. F. Nelson and Co. headquarters in Matafele burns to the ground May 31, 1946. Schaumkell Family Collection/Tony Brunt.

his contributions to Sāmoa's national journey. "The Independence Issue" of *Samoana,* for instance, ran a brief article, "Portrait of the Patriot: Olaf Fredrick Nelson," that reprised his story among those of other historical figures, like New Zealand's administrators.[8] Since Independence his story has continued to appear in histories of Sāmoa and the Mau; yet the story was deficient. His voice, his private worlds, his range of experiences, his passions—both political and personal—were absent. His family remained prominent in Sāmoan life as the next generation rose to take their leading roles. Yet Ta'isi's life and work remained muddied by the campaign of disgrace conducted against him by conservatives in New Zealand and their supporters. Even though the conservative stranglehold over government ended in 1935, the circulation and impact of accusations against Ta'isi continued.

While there has not been a dedicated study of Ta'isi before now, there have been efforts to assess his historical role through a set of circulating images. Ten years before Ta'isi's death, renowned Pacific scholar Felix Keesing articulated, in *Modern Samoa,* questions about Ta'isi that would occupy later researchers. Keesing's book was published at the time of Ta'isi's trial and asked whether Ta'isi "should be regarded as a patriot who pledged his wealth and prestige to a cause of his people and country with sincere motives, if not always with wisdom." Or, Keesing continued, was Ta'isi "an unprincipled exploiter using his sway over Samoan relatives in the cause of personal profit and ambition?"[9] Keesing did not offer a verdict on a story still playing itself out. Keesing had earlier pledged to Ta'isi that he would "study the problems of your people and country in a scientific spirit and . . . keep our minds throughout free of bias of any sort." Ta'isi aided his researches by introducing Keesing to people in Sāmoa that he and his wife, Marie, could interview during their 1930 fact-finding trip to gather material for *Modern Samoa* (the trip did not go so well: Felix contracted dengue fever).[10]

A decade later, upon Ta'isi's death, the *Pacific Islands Monthly* wrote a surprisingly supportive obituary given his long-running battle with the publication over their representation of the Sāmoan political situation and himself. The author (who remained anonymous) again asked the prevailing questions about Ta'isi and his actions through the Sāmoan troubles, and attempted to answer them. Did he love power? Yes, it claimed. What were his aims? The *Pacific Islands Monthly* argued, "There is no real evidence (apart from statements of very prejudiced New Zealand officials) . . . that he had any motive other than a sincere desire to do the best he could for the Samoans under the new regime." It also noted that "everyone liked the big, kindly, hospitable 'Fred' . . . his friends were countless." But he also had many "official enemies." He had "very human faults; but he was an outstanding, able man and if only the New Zealand government had had the wit to enlist his aid in the beginning, instead of ignoring and insulting him, one of the blackest chapters in Samoa's chequered history need not have been written." But did he succeed? No, it argued. "He was doomed to utter failure and complete exasperation," but this "was not his fault." The blame for the "sorry history of Samoa . . . goes primarily to the blundering gentlemen who arranged the League of Nations Mandates, and the greater fools who tried to administer the Mandate," the *Pacific Island Monthly* concluded.[11] Subsequent historians have been divided in their evaluations of Ta'isi that have been based on relatively limited sources.[12] This book has taken the story of Ta'isi in new directions. It brings him, his life, and his political causes into the present and looks at him afresh. Equipped with substantial additional sources, it has restored the fractured picture of Ta'isi that has existed to date. Wherever possible Ta'isi, along with the other central characters in the story, has been given a voice to communicate the history they made.

Following Ta'isi's death, his family continued to expand: Malienafau gave birth to a daughter, Leone; Piliopo had two more sons with her new husband, Hermann Paul Retzlaff, Hermann Theodore (Misa Telefoni) and Erich (who died in infancy); and Sina had three more children, Joseph, Teuila, and Sose. Along with their older cousins, these grandchildren grew up with their mothers carrying a deep reverence and love for their father as well as the acute, painful, and enduring burden of this history. A measure of the family's enduring grief was evident at Tuaefu for decades after Ta'isi died. In his dressing room his suits, hats, canes, and highly polished shoes remained as he had left them until the late 1960s. His library and papers stayed frozen in time, personal monuments his family could not bear to disrupt or discard.[13]

Ta'isi's grandchildren have waited nearly a lifetime for their grandfather's story to be told. Yet this book does not uncritically endorse family memories of Ta'isi; it has weighed up all the evidence to arrive at its conclusions. Though the bulk of evidence about Ta'isi falls into the mandate years, this book has illuminated a longer view of his private life and his experiences before New Zealand's takeover.

This is not only a political history; it has painted a picture of the social worlds Ta'isi navigated. It is also a world history—because of the impressive networks Ta'isi built and maintained to aid the Mau cause and also due to the global layers of British Empire and the League of Nations. In telling his life story, many other people's lives have been illuminated. This is particularly so with the women in Ta'isi's life—his six daughters and Rosabel—who were clearly remarkable historical actors in their own right.

The weight of evidence shows Ta'isi did not seek political power; rather, he wanted to see democratic processes in place for Europeans and Sāmoans as well as a governing system that gave elected officials (like himself *if* he continued to be chosen as an elected representative) a decisive role in governing Sāmoa. He flatly rejected an undemocratic political appointment when Administrator Tate offered it even though the position implicitly came with financial benefits. Instead Ta'isi wanted self-government for Sāmoa in a defined period and he expected preparation for this to materialize rapidly once the mandate was enacted in 1921. When it did not, he began working to achieve it. Though Ta'isi embraced Western political ideas, he also sought quintessentially Sāmoan solutions to disputes. His consistent appeal to New Zealand authorities to caucus problems, to meet and discuss, reflected the bedrock of Sāmoan political processes. He sought expanded democracy—and the refinement of traditional systems of power to accommodate elections—but he did not voice any support for women's enfranchisement. Sources show, however, his consistent support for women's political activity beyond elected office and their enhanced social role through education. He was fiercely devoted to the many women in his family, and he valued women's many social contributions, but adhered to the view that the political realm was a male one. On race, he never countenanced laws premised on notions of Sāmoan racial and cultural inferiority that characterized both the German and New Zealand eras. He rejected concepts of Sāmoan inferiority and European prestige out of hand yet he subscribed to equally problematic ideas of the Chinese menace that had great currency at this time. He had his limitations and contradictions; he was both a conservative and a modernizer. He selected what he saw as beneficial from *fa'asamoa* and the West to move Sāmoa forward in the twentieth century.

Financially he did not benefit from his political activism, nor did he aim to (others, who sided with the administration, did). Ta'isi was a supporter of Sāmoan (European and Indigenous) commercial enterprise and for Sāmoan engagement in financial decision making. He was enriched because of the financial windfall the Great War brought to Sāmoa and the expulsion of Germans. He did not construct the copra buying system in Sāmoa; it preexisted his time at the pinnacle of Sāmoan commerce and was agreed on by the four trading houses. Global markets determined the prices Sāmoan growers received from the four big firms. Despite the years of intense scrutiny of Ta'isi's affairs, the administration could not substantiate their accusation that Ta'isi exploited his fellow Sāmoans. There continues to be a lack of evidence to support the allegation. Ta'isi's success was due to his business acumen as well as the fact his company differed from its competitors by employing people across Sāmoa regardless of race. His firm was bound into communities and this was a critical reason why Sāmoans opted to sell their copra to his traders and continued to do so. Sāmoans supported their own. Despite their strenuous and expensive efforts, the administration could not improve on the system in place to 1926. Global markets worked in Ta'isi's favor and then against him once the Great Depression struck (with the assistance of the New Zealand administration determined to bring about his financial ruin).

This book illustrates for the first time how Ta'isi gained knowledge and ideas from the Māori experience of colonization. His friendship with Sir Māui Pōmare was a conduit of ideas and strategies for diffusing the asymmetrical advantage the British Empire and its forces had over Indigenous peoples it sought to subjugate. The application of nonviolent resistance in Sāmoa connected to the history of nonviolent resistance in nineteenth-century Taranaki and once again profoundly challenged the New Zealand government. Though people perished due to New Zealand's use of force, evidence shows that it was the Mau's consistent restraint that prevented additional force being used. The nonviolent stance Ta'isi insisted that the Mau adhere to limited bloodshed. The Mau stance contrasted diametrically with the New Zealand government's approach that was heavily influenced by the Great War experience and its great myths embodied in the series of administrators who traded on their war experience and military status throughout the Mau episode. This book shows how combatting the nonviolent Mau drew a governor-general and the Permanent Mandates Commission into the fray, revealing how colonial pasts and presents affected one another. It also shows the Mau—specifically through Ta'isi's input—was a global nationalist movement that fought empire on four levels: in Sāmoa, New Zealand, Britain, and Geneva.

Ta'isi consistently cited Māori experience as a means to combat New Zealand policy and practice in Sāmoa by insisting there should be uniform policies in place to govern both peoples. Yet the deployment of multiple and conflicting sets of rights and legal standards from the metropole to external colonies was a classic feature of colonial power. British Empire exemplified this mass of contradictions and hypocrisies as well as any other, but Ta'isi persisted in his call for the same suite of rights for Sāmoans. He also possessed the ideal that British justice and democracy could and would deliver justice for Sāmoans with enough court actions, petitions, soundly reasoned entreaties to government officials and by airing grievances in the media. His consistent citations of the principles of British justice and myths of British superiority were his sharpest weapon. He believed in these virtues initially, but when they failed to materialize, Ta'isi kept holding up the mirror to Sāmoa's colonial rulers as a central component of his political rhetoric.

Evidence does not support the contention Ta'isi was driven by egotism, as some historians have suggested.[14] If Ta'isi's judgment and conduct were colored by this flaw, why then did he not write a memoir after his return from his second exile, or even before it, to set the record straight about who he was and why he acted as he did? No such tract exists, which is curious for a man who wrote so voraciously. There is no question he wanted to be treated with respect—as he wanted all Sāmoans to be treated, whether they agreed with him or not—but this does not amount to vanity. His conduct at the time of his trial, when he was at his most exposed, suggests a man defiant and provocative, acting to his own detriment in order to achieve a greater good for Sāmoa. There is no question he was what would be considered in the parlance of "Jim Crow–era" United States as "uppity"—he did not accept the notion of white racial prestige that was the bedrock of all human interactions for so many of the colonial officials in New Zealand, Britain, and the Permanent Mandates Commission who populate this story—he considered himself their equal, as he considered all Sāmoans to be his. He upset the racial ordering of empire in multiple ways and was punished severely for this stance.

After Ta'isi's death and the end of World War II, New Zealand reset its relationship with Sāmoa owing to the Mau and moved quickly toward self-government. It was achieved in Sāmoa before anywhere else in the island Pacific and many other parts of the colonized world. Yet the history of the Mau sat on the near horizon like the rusting hulk

Figure 15.3. Following her apology speech, New Zealand Prime Minister Helen Clark was hosted at Tuaefu on June 4, 2002 by the Tamasese and Ta'isi families at a dinner in honor of Ta'isi O. F. Nelson and other Mau leaders. With permission of Siuga Paula Masoe.

of SS *Adler* lying in Apia Harbor for decades after the epic storm of 1889. It was an eyesore, an embarrassment, and a constant reminder of New Zealand's (as well as Britain's and the League of Nations') overinvestment in colonial power in Sāmoa. Historians heightened awareness of what happened, but no official recognition for past wrongs was forthcoming—until 2002, when New Zealand Prime Minister Helen Clark made an apology to the Sāmoan people in a speech marking forty years of Sāmoan independence. She apologized unreservedly for the bungling that caused the epidemic, the banishments, and the killings on Black Saturday.[15] After her speech her motorcade stopped at Lepea at the graveside of Tupua Tamasese Lea'lofi. His nephew and Ta'isi's oldest grandson, Tui Atua Tupua Tamasese Ta'isi Efi, presented Prime Minister Clark with an exquisite *'ie tōga* or fine mat—known as Le Ageagea o Tumua, which is on display in the Te Papa Museum in Wellington—as a symbol that past wrongs had been forgiven by the Tamasese family.

Prime Minister Clark was then invited to Tuaefu. On June 4, 2002, the New Zealand prime minister feasted with the Tamasese and Ta'isi families in the house armed police had raided, where illicit meetings were supposedly conducted, where Ta'isi was arrested and exiled from for nearly eight years, and the place where he died fifty-eight years before. Among Ta'isi's gathered grandchildren was a former prime minister (and future head of state), a current deputy prime minister, and other prominent leaders in the Sāmoan community. To have beheld this scene at Tuaefu would have been unimaginable in Ta'isi's lifetime, but Ta'isi's life work and beliefs contributed greatly to this moment.

In this moment lies the answer to the question of what Ta'isi achieved, which was far from failure; in fact, it was a triumph.[16] Throughout his many travails, he faced challenges with forbearance, dignity, and peace. He retained remarkable composure despite the myriad humiliations he and his fellow Sāmoans suffered, and he always urged Sāmoans to do likewise. His Christian faith was a source of enduring strength to him, as was the unwavering conviction that he was always fighting for what was right. Although he could not topple the mighty edifice of colonialism in his lifetime (the list of countries that did is very short), he set a course for Sāmoa's postwar future.

Ta'isi O. F. Nelson was a *tautai,* a navigator. Like his ancestors, he traversed immense and troubled waters. He did not always take the right turn, but his aim was to find a place for his country—with its revered and deep traditions—in the modern world order. It is time to bring Ta'isi's story into the light of the present.

Notes

Prologue

1. With many thanks to Tamasailau Suaalii Sauni for clarifying Sāmoan naming conventions (e-mail correspondence with author, February 18, 2016).

2. Albert Wendt, "'Guardians and Wards': A Study of the Origins, Causes, and the First Two Years of the Mau in Western Samoa" (MA thesis, Victoria University Wellington, 1965); Kilifoti Sisilia Eteuati, "Evaevaga a Samoa: Assertion of Samoan Autonomy 1920–1936" (PhD diss., Australian National University, 1982); Malama Meleisea, *The Making of Modern Samoa: Traditional Authority and Colonial Administration in the History of Western Samoa* (Suva: Institute of Pacific Studies, 1987); Malama Meleisea and Penelope Schoeffel Meleisea, eds., *Lagaga: A Short History of Western Samoa* (Suva: University of South Pacific, 1987); Peter Hempenstall and Noel Rutherford, *Protest and Dissent in the Colonial Pacific* (Suva: Institute of Pacific Studies, 1984); Damon Salesa, "A Pacific Destiny: New Zealand's Overseas Empire 1840–1945," in *Tangata O Le Moana: New Zealand and the People of the Pacific,* ed. Sean Mallon, Kolokesa Māhina-Tuai, and Damon Salesa, 97–122 (Wellington: Te Papa Press, 2012); Nicholas Hoare, "Harry Holland's Samoa Complex," *Journal of Pacific History* 49, no. 2 (2014): 151–169; Nicholas Hoare, "New Zealand's Critics of Empire: Domestic Opposition to New Zealand's Pacific Empire 1883–1948" (MA thesis, Victoria University Wellington, 2014); Susan Pedersen, *The Guardians: The League of Nations and the Crisis of Empire* (Oxford: Oxford University Press, 2015).

3. Mary Boyd, "The Record in Western Samoa to 1945," in *New Zealand's Record in the Pacific Islands in the Twentieth Century,* ed. Angus Ross, 115–188 (London: Longman Paul, 1969); Mary Boyd, "Coping with Samoan Resistance after the 1918 Influenza Epidemic: Colonel Tate's Problems and Perplexities," *Journal of Pacific History* 15, no. 3 (1980): 155–174; Mary Boyd, "Racial Attitudes of New Zealand Officials in Western Samoa," *New Zealand Journal of History* 21, no. 1 (1987): 139–155; I. C. Campbell, "New Zealand and the *Mau* in Samoa: Re-Assessing the Causes of a Colonial Protest Movement," *New Zealand Journal of History* 33, no. 1 (1999): 92–110.

4. J. W. Davidson, *Samoa mo Samoa: The Emergence of the Independent State of Western Samoa* (Oxford: University of Oxford Press, 1967), gave prominence to Ta'isi's voice but lacked clarity about where some of his evidence about Ta'isi came from. Michael J. Field's *Mau: Samoa's Struggle for Freedom* (Auckland: Polynesian Press, 1991) offers the most detailed account of Ta'isi but limits his focus on Ta'isi's story as it related to New Zealand. Tracey Banivanua Mar includes Ta'isi in her study *Decolonisation and the Pacific: Globalisation and the Ends of Empire* (Cambridge: Cambridge University Press, 2016).

5. The *Te Ara* entry on Ta'isi in parts closely resembles a document in Archives New Zealand, penned by police inspector Arthur Braisby. This was a background document prepared to assist lawyers about to contest Ta'isi's appeal to the Privy Council against his conviction in 1934 referred to as "Braisby trial account" in chapter 13 of this volume; see Hugh Laracy, "Nelson, Olaf Frederick," from the *Dictionary of New Zealand Biography. Te Ara—the Encyclopedia of New Zealand,* http://www.TeAra.govt.nz/en/biographies/4n5/nelson-olaf-frederick (accessed April 8, 2014); Archives New Zealand (hereafter ANZ), IT1 44, EX 1/23/20, part 2, R17961384.

6. As Ta'isi's story is an international one, this book is situated within scholarly frames that highlight the importance of international connections, people, ideological movements, and transnationalism. In particular the book has been influenced by the insights of Epeli Hau'ofa, "Our Sea of Islands," *The Contemporary Pacific* 6, no. 1 (1994): 147–161; Alice Te Punga Somerville, *Once Were Pacific: Māori Connections to Oceania* (Minneapolis: University of Minnesota Press, 2012); Antoinette Burton and Tony Ballantyne, eds., *Moving Subjects: Gender, Mobility and Intimacy in an Age of Global Empire* (Urbana-Champaign: University of Illinois Press, 2009); Frances Steel, *Oceania under Steam: Sea Transport and the Cultures of Colonialism, 1870–1914* (Manchester: Manchester University Press, 2011); Fiona Paisley, *The Lone Protester: A. M. Fernando in Australia and Europe* (Canberra: Aboriginal Studies Press, 2012); David Hanlon, *Making Micronesia: A Political Biography of Tosiwo Nakayama* (Honolulu: University of Hawai'i Press, 2014).

7. The new sources utilized by this book are Ta'isi's personal papers, the unpublished papers of Ta'isi O. F. Nelson, Tuaefu, Apia Samoa (hereafter cited as OFN), comprising 101 files housed at Tuaefu, Apia. For further detail of these papers see note 29 in Patricia O'Brien, "Ta'isi O. F. Nelson and Sir Maui Pomare: Samoans and Maori Reunited," *Journal of Pacific History* 49, no. 1 (2014): 1–24. Family letters and testimony are also being used for the first time; the papers of George Spafford Richardson in Frank O. V. Acheson papers incorporating the papers of Sir George Spafford Richardson, MSS & Archives 96/1, Special Collections, University of Auckland Libraries and Learning Services; Ta'isi's testimony to the 1927 Joint Samoa Petition Inquiry Commission, Francis Dillon Bell Papers, MS-Papers-5210–159, Alexander Turnbull Library, Wellington (hereafter cited as JSPIC); the Joseph Carruthers Papers (hereafter cited as Carruthers Papers), Mitchell Library State Library of New South Wales, ML MSS 1638, and Swedish archival material.

8. This book integrates indigenous knowledge with academic scholarship, putting indigenous actors at the center of the narrative and observing respectful protocols and principles that preserve the ownership of indigenous knowledge and evidence. This book is shaped by the work of a range of postcolonial and gender scholars. I have been guided by the scholarship of Tui Atua Tupua Tamasese Ta'isi Efi and his emphasis on the need to centralize the "indigenous reference"; see "Clutter in Indigenous Knowledge, Research and History: A Samoan Perspective," *Social Policy Journal of New Zealand* 25 (2005): 61–69; *Englishing My Samoan: Selected Speeches and Letters* (Suva: University of the South Pacific, 1995); "The Riddle in Samoan History: The Relevance of Language, Names, Honorifics, Genealogy, Ritual and Chant to Historical Analysis," *Journal of Pacific History* 29, no. 1 (1994): 66–79. See also Tamasailau Suaalii Sauni and other Sāmoan scholars who have stressed the need to preserve the "indigenous reference," in this case, the Sāmoan reference: Tamasailau Suaalii Sauni et al., eds., *Su'esu'e Manogi—In Search of Fragrance: Tui Atua Tupua Tamasese Ta'isi and the Samoan Indigenous Reference* (Apia: Centre for Samoan Studies, National University of Samoa, 2008). On historical practice that centers on indigenous perspectives and observes respectful historical practices, aligning with the aims of Indigenous Standpoint Theory, see Linda Tuhiwai Smith, *Decolonizing Methodologies: Research and Indigenous Peoples*, 2nd ed. (Dunedin: University of Otago Press, 2012); Dennis Foley, "Indigenous Standpoint Theory: An Acceptable Academic Research Process for Indigenous Academics," *International Journal of Humanities* 3, no. 8 (2005–2006): 25–36; Karen Martin and Booran Mirraboopa, "Ways of Knowing, Being and Doing: A Theoretical Framework and Methods for Indigenous and Indigenist Re-Search," *Journal of Australian Studies* 27, no. 76 (2009): 203–214; Martin Nakata, *Disciplining the Savages: Savaging the Disciplines* (Canberra: Aboriginal Studies Press, 2007); John Maynard, "Circles in the Sand: An Indigenous Framework of Historical Practice," *Australian Journal of Indigenous Education* 36 (2007): 117–120; Jackie Huggins, *Sister Girl: The Writings of Aboriginal Activist and Historian Jackie Huggins* (St. Lucia: University of Queensland Press, 1998). Like Deborah Bird Rose's *Hidden Histories: Black Stories from Victoria River Downs, Humbert River and Wave Hill Stations* (Canberra: Aboriginal Studies Press, 1991), this book aims to incorporate indigenous accounts in ways that preserve storytellers' voices and, in particular, allow the voice of Ta'isi O. F. Nelson to be heard without scholarly interference. The book's methodology is likewise influenced by the insights of Gayatri C. Spivak, "Can the Subaltern Speak?," in *Colonial Discourse and Post-Colonial Theory: A Reader*, ed. P. Williams and L. Chrisman, 66–112 (Hemel Hempstead: Harvester Wheatsheaf, 1993); Chandra Talpade Mohanty, "Under Western Eyes: Feminist Scholarship and Colonial Discourses," *Feminist Review* 30 (1988): 61–88; Haunani-Kay Trask, *From a Native Daughter: Colonialism and Sovereignty in Hawai'i* (Honolulu: University of Hawai'i Press, 2012). This book is also influenced by the work of Ann Laura Stoler and her focus on intimate worlds in her accounts of colonial histories; see "Tense and Tender Ties: The Politics of

Comparison in North American History and (Post) Colonial Studies," *Journal of American History* 88, no. 3 (2001): 829–865.

Chapter 1: Converging Worlds

1. The author thanks Tugaga Tevesi David of Safune and Seti Sā for sharing their knowledge about Safune and the Nelson family on July 27, 2015.

2. With thanks to Swedish Ambassador Pär Ahlberger for alerting me to additional information on August Nelson's genealogy and to Gullan Olsson, chairman for the Kalmar läns Genealogiska Förening (Kalmar Genealogical Society), who has verified August's family history with parish records.

3. Sylvia Masterman, *The Origins of International Rivalry in Samoa 1845–1884* (London: Allen and Unwin, 1934), 169.

4. Iberian colonialism, which had been active in the Pacific since the sixteenth-century, did not affect the Sāmoan islands. Explorers, especially from France, had pioneered contact relations with Sāmoa from the 1860s. See O. H. K. Spate, *The Pacific since Magellan,* vol. 3, *Paradise Found and Lost* (Canberra: Australian National University Press, 1988); Davidson, *Samoa mo Samoa,* chap. 3; Jocelyn Linnekin, "Ignoble Savages and Other European Visions," *Journal of Pacific History* 26, no. 1 (1991): 3–26.

5. Spate, *Paradise Found and Lost;* Joan Druett, *Petticoat Whalers: Whaling Wives at Sea 1820–1920* (Auckland: Collins, 1991); Lyndall Ryan, *Aboriginal Tasmanians: A History since 1803* (Crows Nest, New South Wales: Allen and Unwin, 2012); Greg Dening, ed., *The Marquesan Journal of Edward Robarts 1797–1824* (Canberra: Australian National University Press, 1974); Deryck Scarr, *The History of the Pacific Islands: Kingdoms of the Reefs* (Melbourne: Macmillan, 1990); Caroline Ralston, *Grasshuts and Warehouses: Pacific Beach Communities of the Nineteenth Century* (Honolulu: University of Hawai'i Press, 1978); Lynette Russell, *Roving Mariners: Australian Aboriginal Whalers and Sealers in the Southern Oceans* (Albany: State University of New York Press, 2012); Ryan Jones, "Environment," in *Pacific Histories: Ocean, Land, People,* ed. David Armitage and Alison Bashford, 121–142 (Basingstoke: Macmillan, 2014).

6. *Report of the Parliamentary Select Committee on Aboriginal Tribes (British Settlements)* (London: William Ball, 1837), https://books.google.com/books?id=JqUNAAAAQAAJ&pg=PR1&dq=Report+of+the+Parliamentary+Select+Committee+on+Aboriginal+Tribes+(British+Settlements)&hl=en&sa=X&ved=0ahUKEwis9_O68aXPAhUHGj4KHeSND4AQ6AEIHjAA#v=onepage&q=Report%20of%20the%20Parliamentary%20Select%20Committee%20on%20Aboriginal%20Tribes%20(British%20Settlements)&f=false (accessed February 2, 2014).

7. British law and Christianity had a significant presence in Sydney from the outset. Yet the working-class and port precincts of the town exhibited similar characteristics of other Pacific port towns.

8. Niel Gunson, *Messengers of Grace: Evangelical Missionaries in the South Seas 1797–1860* (Melbourne: Oxford University Press, 1978).

9. John Williams' son and first US envoy in Sāmoa was John C. Williams. Davidson, *Samoa mo Samoa,* 40; Caroline Ralston points out that the first British consul in Apia was never ratified in London, so officially George Pritchard would be the first British consul in Apia in 1845; see Ralston, *Grasshuts,* 71–72.

10. *Report of the Parliamentary Select Committee on Aboriginal Tribes,* 3–4.

11. Ibid., x, 27.

12. N. J. B. Plomley, *The Baudin Expedition and the Tasmanian Aborigines* (Hobart: Blubber Head Press, 1983); Jacqueline Bonnemains, Elliot Forsyth, and Bernard Smith, eds., *Baudin in Australian Waters: The Artwork of the French Voyage of Discovery to the Southern Lands 1800–1804* (Melbourne: Oxford University Press, 1988); Susan Hunt and Paul Carter, eds., *Terre Napoleon: Australia through French eyes, 1800–1804* (Sydney: Historic Houses Trust, 1999); Nicole Starbuck, *Baudin, Napoleon and the Exploration of Australia* (London: Pickering and Chatto, 2013).

13. James Belich, *Paradise Reforged: A History of the New Zealanders* (Honolulu: Hawai'i University Press, 2001), 194; Judith Binney, *Encircled Lands: Te Urewera 1820–1921* (Wellington: Bridget Williams Books, 2009).

14. Sylvia Masterman dates this New Zealand ambition to annex Sāmoa first to George Grey in 1847, though impetus for this idea came later with the New Zealand Parliament's petition to Queen Victoria of 1871 requesting annexation of Sāmoa. Julius Vogel was the leading figure behind this idea. See Masterman, *Origins of International Rivalry,* chap. 4, 82–104; Ross, *New Zealand's Record;* Salesa, "A Pacific Destiny"; see also Katie Pickles and Catharine Colebourne, eds., *New Zealand's Empire* (Manchester: Manchester University Press, 2016).

15. Paul De Decker, ed., *The Aggressions of the French at Tahiti and Other Islands of the Pacific* (Auckland: Auckland University Press, 1983); Patricia O'Brien, "Think of Me as a Woman: Queen Pomare of Tahiti and Anglo-French Imperial Contest in the 1840s Pacific," *Gender and History* 18, no. 1 (2006): 108–129.

16. Masterman, *Origins of International Rivalry,* 55; Richard Gilson, *Samoa 1830 to 1900: The Politics of a Multicultural Community* (Melbourne: Oxford University Press, 1970), 172–174.

17. Gilson, *Samoa,* 176.

18. Ibid., 179; Ralston (*Grasshuts,* 79) attributes this quote to Captain Home in 1852.

19. Gilson, *Samoa,* 179.

20. John McNeill, "Of Rats and Men: A Synoptic Environmental History of the Island Pacific," *Journal of World History* 5, no. 2 (1994): 299–349.

21. The first of these great new cities were San Francisco and Melbourne. See James Belich, *Replenishing the Earth: The Settler Revolution and the Rise of the Anglo-World 1783–1939* (Oxford: Oxford University Press, 2009).

22. Ralston, *Grasshuts*, 94–96; Masterman, *International Rivalry;* Gilson, *Samoa.*

23. Paul Kennedy, *The Samoan Tangle: A Study in Anglo-American Relations 1878–1900* (Saint Lucia: University of Queensland Press, 2011), 6.

24. Tim Bayliss-Smith and Judith Bennett, eds., *An Otago Storeman in Solomon Islands: The Diary of William Crossan, Copra Trader 1885–86* (Canberra: ANU E Press, 2012), introduction.

25. "The Cocoanut," *NZ Samoa Guardian,* June 6, 1929. There is no byline for this article to confirm Ta'isi's authorship.

26. Lilikalā Kame'eleihiwa, *Native Lands and Foreign Desires* (Honolulu: Bishop Museum Press, 1992); Jonathon Kay Kamakawiwo'ole Osorio, *Dismembering Lāhui: A History of the Hawaiian Nation to 1887* (Honolulu: University of Hawai'i Press, 2002), chap. 3.

27. Gary Okihiro, *Cane Fires: The Anti-Japanese Movement in Hawaii 1865–1945* (Philadelphia: Temple University Press, 1991), 6–7; Brij V. Lal, Doug Munro, and Edward D. Beechert, eds., *Plantation Workers: Resistance and Accommodation* (Honolulu: University of Hawai'i Press, 1993).

28. Romanzo Adams, *Interracial Marriage in Hawaii: A Study of Mutually Conditioned Processes of Acculturation and Amalgamation* (New York: Macmillan, 1937), chaps. 7 and 9; Christine Kirk-Kuwaye and Lori Pierce, "Race and Ethnicity," *Local Sightings/Citings: Teaching and Learning through Local History and Culture*, http://localcite.manoa.hawaii.edu/themerace.html (accessed February 6, 2014).

29. See http://www.kalmarlansmuseum.se/samlingar/vara-samlingar/manadens-foremal/ie-toga-fran-samoa/ (accessed October 26, 2015). Again with thanks to Swedish ambassador Pär Ahlberger. Gullan Olsson, chairman of the Kalmar läns Genealogiska Förening, has verified August's family history with parish records (e-mail communication with author, January 5, 2016).

30. Hugh Laracy gives the birth name of August Nelson as August Nilspiter Gustav Nelson, in line with a document stored in ANZ penned by police inspector Arthur Braisby. See note 5 of Prologue. Family knowledge has the name as Nils Peter Gustafsson, which complies with Kalmar Parish records (Tui Atua Tupua Tamasese Ta'isi Efi, e-mail to author, February 1, 2014). See also *Cyclopedia of Samoa, Tonga, Tahiti and the Cook Islands, 1907* (Papakura, New Zealand: R. McMillan, 1983), 107; "One Hundred Years of Service to Samoa: Nelson's Centenary Supplement," *Samoa Times,* November 29, 1968, 1.

31. Kennedy, *Samoan Tangle,* 6.

32. Gilson, *Samoa,* 162–187; Masterman, *Origins of International Rivalry,* chaps. 3, 4, 5; Ralston, *Grasshuts,* 162–187.

33. "Two Old Firms Amalgamate," *Samoa Times,* November 24, 1922; "One Hundred Years of Service"; William B. Churchward, *My Consulate in Samoa* (London: Richard Bentley and Son, 1887), chap. 17.

34. Tui Atua Tupua Tamasese Ta'isi Efi, interview with author, June 11, 2012.

35. Ibid.; Tui Atua Tupua Tamasese Ta'isi Efi, e-mail to author, April 25, 2013. The dates of birth taken from gravestones in the Apia cemetery. "Death of Mrs. Lucy Kruse," *Samoa Times,* October 17, 1924, 3.

36. "One Hundred Years of Service."

37. Gilson, *Samoa,* 323, 341, 413. The laborers were likely from the Solomon Islands.

38. Ibid., 413.

39. Meleisea, *Making of Modern Samoa,* 22.

40. Malama Meleisea, "Introduction," in *Footnote to Samoan History: Eight Years of Trouble in Samoa,* by Robert Louis Stevenson (Honolulu: University of Hawai'i Press, 1996).

41. Meleisea, *Lagaga,* 76.

42. Kennedy, *Samoan Tangle,* chaps. 3, 4, 5; Davidson, *Samoa mo Samoa,* 51.

43. Davidson, *Samoa mo Samoa,* 46, 47, 49.

44. Meleisea, *Making of Modern Samoa,* 36.

45. Kennedy, *Samoan Tangle,* 9, 12, 19; Meleisea, *Making of Modern Samoa,* 37.

46. Masterman, *Origins of International Rivalry,* 169.

47. By Robert Louis Stevenson, *Treasure Island* (London: Cassell and Co., 1883); *The Strange Case of Dr Jekyll and Mr Hyde* (London: Longmans, Green, 1886); *Kidnapped* (London: Cassell and Co., 1886); *A Footnote to History: Eight Years of Trouble in Samoa,* (London: Cassell and Co., 1892).

48. Masterman, 193.

49. Ta'isi certainly included this event in his brief history of the troubled history of Sāmoa from the 1870s, but does not recount personal memory of it. See O. F. Nelson, *The Truth about Samoa: A Review of Events Leading Up the Present Crisis* (Auckland: n.p., 1928).

50. "Marist Bros' School," *Samoa Weekly Herald,* August 25, 1894, 3.

51. "Marist Brothers' Commercial School," *Samoa Weekly Herald,* August 8, 1896, 2.

52. JSPIC, 119.

53. Ibid., 120.

54. Meleisea, *Making of Modern Samoa,* 41.

55. Kennedy, *Samoan Tangle,* chap. 3.

56. JSPIC, 119.

57. "Confidential Report by O. F. Nelson," March 3, 1932, OFN 23.

58. Tui Atua Tupua Tamasese Ta'isi Efi, interview with author, June 11, 2012.

59. Most of Ta'isi's daughters had a Sāmoan name and an English name: throughout this text, their Sāmoan names are used. Where the English names are used, such as in quotes or text extracts, a note for clarification is included. Viopapa's English name was Lucy.

60. Dates in the company history of A. Nelson and Son do not always match. For instance, *Samoa Times* had the Apia store opening in 1908 ("Two Old Firms Amalgamate," *Samoa Times,* November 24, 1922, 8), while Ta'isi later recalled the Apia store was opened in 1906. See JSPIC, 94.

61. O. F. Nelson to Consul General Count Mörner, June 10, 1908, Swedish Consulate archives from Sydney, series F1:25, the National Archives of Sweden, Arninge. With much thanks to Julia Lindkvist of the National Archives of Sweden and Katarina Prime Linmarker, Embassy of Sweden, Canberra, for their invaluable assistance.

62. Rosabel's siblings were Romana, Harry, Priscilla, Sophia, and her half brothers Mark (whose mother was Epenesa Enari) and Kane (whose mother came from Wallis Island). See Damon Salesa, "Misimoa: An American on the Beach," *Common-Place* 5, no. 2 (2005), http://www.common-place.org/vol-05/no-02/salesa/index.shtml (accessed June 6, 2013).

63. "Two Old Firms Amalgamate," *Samoa Times,* November 24, 1922; *Cyclopedia of Samoa,* 88.

64. I am indebted to Fialaui'afualeafi Tamasese for information about Harry J. Moors, her great-grandfather (interview with author, November 10, 2012).

65. Harry J. Moors, *With Stevenson in Samoa* (London: Collins Clear Type Press, 1910); Moors' love of letter writing is evident in the large file of correspondence between him and the New Zealand administration from 1920 to 1926 (see chapter 3 of this book). He also wrote a series for the *Samoa Times* that was collated and published by his family; see H. J. Moors, *Some Recollections of Early Samoa* (Apia: Western Samoa Historical and Cultural Trust, 1987).

66. Fialaui'afualeafi Tamasese, interview with author, November 10, 2012.

Chapter 2: Kaiser or King?

1. Fialaui'afualeafi Tamasese, interview with author, November 10, 2012.

2. Tui Atua Tupua Tamasese Ta'isi Efi, interview with author, June 11, 2012; Fialaui'afualeafi Tamasese, interview with author, November 10, 2012; Piliopo Maiai, interview with author, July 16, 2014.

3. Evelyn Wareham, *Race and Realpolitik: The Politics of Colonization in German Samoa* (Frankfurt: Peter Lang, 2002), 138.

4. Meleisea, *Making of Modern Samoa,* chap. 7.

5. Damon Salesa, *Racial Crossings: Race, Intermarriage, and the Victorian British Empire* (Oxford: Oxford University Press, 2011); Paul Weindling, "German Eugenics and the Wider World: Beyond the Racial State," in *The Oxford Handbook of the History of Eugenics,* ed. Alison Bashford and Philippa Levine, 315–331 (Oxford: Oxford University Press, 2010).

6. Noue's full name was Irene Gustava Noue, and she was sometimes known as Irene.

7. Ta'isi and Rosabel's other daughters were also sometimes known by the following English names: Olive (Malienafau), Joyce (Piliopo), and Calmar (Taufau).

8. Hermann Hiery and John Mackenzie, eds., *European Impact and Pacific Influence: British and German Colonial Policy in the Pacific Islands and the Indigenous Response* (London: Tauris Academic Studies, 1997); Arthur J. Knoll and Hermann J. Hiery, eds., *The German Colonial Experience: Select Documents on German Rule in Africa, China, and the Pacific, 1884–1914* (Lanham, MD: Universities of America, 2010); John Moses and Paul Kennedy, eds., *Germany in the Pacific and the Far East 1870–1914* (Saint Lucia: University of Queensland Press, 1977); Peter Hempenstall and Paula T. Mochida, *The Lost Man: Wilhelm Solf in German History* (Wiesbaden: Harrassowitz, 2005); Hermann Hiery, *The Neglected War: The German South Pacific and the Influence of World War I* (Honolulu: University of Hawai'i Press, 1995).

9. Sebastian Conrad, *German Colonialism: A Short History* (Cambridge: University of Cambridge Press, 2012), 86.

10. Wareham, *Race and Realpolitik,* 11–22.

11. Hempenstall and Rutherford, *Protest and Dissent,* 26–32 and chap. 1; Meleisea, *Making of Modern Samoa,* 117–121.

12. Peter Hempenstall, *Pacific Islanders under German Rule: A Study in the Meaning of Colonial Resistance* (Canberra: Australian National University Press, 1978), 44.

13. Ibid., 62; Meleisea, *Lagaga,* 117–121.

14. Hempenstall, *Pacific Islanders under German Rule,* 71.

15. "Lauaki: A Samoan Statesman," *NZ Samoa Guardian,* February 9, 1934, 3, and March 9, 1934, 3.

16. "Petition Forwarded by Certain Residents of Western Samoa on the 4th February 1910 to the High President of the German Parliament in Berlin," appended to *1927 Report of visit by Hon. W. Nosworthy, Minister of External Affairs to Mandated Territory of Western Samoa* (Wellington: Government Printer, 1927), 44. *AtoJsOnline,* Te Puna Mātauranga o Aotearoa—National Library of New Zealand, http://atojs.natlib.govt.nz (accessed September 27, 2012).

17. Hempenstall, *Pacific Islanders under German Rule,* 39–43.

18. Nelson Eustis, *Aggie Grey of Samoa* (Adelaide: Hobby Investments, 1979), 48; JSPIC, 120.

19. In 1902 there were twenty-two officials.

20. Wareham, *Race and Realpolitick,* 96–98.

21. "Petition Forwarded by Certain Residents of Western Samoa on the 4th February 1910," 45.

22. Ibid., 44.

23. Secretary of State to Governor of New Zealand, August 6, 1914, in *European War: Occupation of German Samoa by an Expeditionary Force from New*

Zealand, from "Appendix to the Journals of the House of Representatives, 1915 Session I, H-19c," *AtoJsOnline,* Te Puna Mātauranga o Aotearoa—National Library of New Zealand, http://atojs.natlib.govt.nz/cgi-bin/atojs?a=d&d=AJHR1915-I.1.3799&cl=search&srpos=1&e=———-10—1———0Occupation+of+German+Samoa—1915 (accessed March 12, 2014).

24. Erich Schultz quoted in Field, *Mau,* 9.

25. Mary Boyd, "Military Administration of Western Samoa 1914–1919," *New Zealand Journal of History* 2, no. 2 (1968): 148–164.

26. Ibid., 153.

27. Harry J. Moors was forthright in his views about New Zealand. See ANZ, IT 1 443, EX 79/32, parts 1 (R 17962657) and 2 (R17962658).

28. R. W. Tate to J. D. Gray, March 3, 1919, R. W. Tate Papers, Alexander Turnbull Library, Wellington (hereafter Tate Papers), MS-Papers-0264–01, Microfilm- 0082–01.

29. Boyd, "Military Administration," 160.

30. O. F. Nelson to R. Nelson, June 1, 1918; June 4, 1918; June 6, 1918, letters in private collection of Irene Piliopo Maiai.

31. R. Nelson to O. F. Nelson, June 5, 1918, May 30, 1918, letters in private collection of Irene Piliopo Maiai.

32. *Report of the Samoan Epidemic Commission,* in "Appendix to the Journals of the House of Representatives, 1919 Session I, H-31c," *AtoJsOnline,* Te Puna Mātauranga o Aotearoa—National Library of New Zealand, http://atojs.natlib.govt.nz/cgi-bin/atojs?a=d&d=AJHR1919-I.2.2.4.46&e=-10—1-0, 5 (accessed January 10, 2014).

33. Field, *Mau,* 39.

34. *Report of Samoan Epidemic Commission,* 10.

35. O. F. Nelson to Joseph Carruthers, April 4, 1929, Carruthers Papers, Mitchell Library State Library of New South Wales, ML MSS 1638/17.

36. With thanks to Irene Piliopo Maiai for the name of Gussie's mother, e-mail communication to author, March 3, 2015. See the obituary for all four Nelson family members, *Samoanische Zeitung* 18, no. 48 (December 1918): 5.

37. R. W. Tate, February 27, 1919, in "drafts of projected book," Tate Papers, MS-Papers-0264–58, Microfilm-0082–09.

38. *The Petition of Olaf Fredrick Nelson of Apia to the League of Nations,* signed in Sydney, March 29, 1928, 2, League of Nations Archives, Palais des Nations, Geneva (hereafter LONA), box R2322, 1928–1932, series 709, dossiers 801 to 4,000, 6A/875/709.

39. *Report of Samoan Epidemic Commission,* 4.

40. R. W. Tate, "Narrative of Native Unrest c. January 1919," Tate Papers, MS-Papers-0264–32, Microfilm-0082–05; Boyd, "Military Administration," 162–163.

41. R. W. Tate to J. D. Gray, October 20, 1919, Tate Papers, MS-Papers-0264–01, Microfilm-0082–01; Meleisea, *Making of Modern Samoa,* 123; Boyd, "Coping with Samoan Resistance," 155–174.

42. R. W. Tate wrote to J. D. Gray that "we must prove ourselves," November 13, 1920, Tate Papers, MS-Papers-0264–01, Microfilm-0082–01.

43. R. W. Tate, February 27, 1919, in "drafts of projected book," Tate Papers, MS-Papers-0264–58, Microfilm-0082–09; Tate used the term "superlative attributes" in a letter to J. D. Gray, September 12, 1922, Tate Papers, MS-Papers-0264–03, Microfilm-0082–01.

44. O'Brien, "Ta'isi O. F. Nelson and Sir Maui Pomare: Samoans and Māori Reunited."

45. J. F. Cody, *Man of Two Worlds: Sir Maui Pomare* (Wellington: Reed, 1953); Michael King, *Te Puea, a Biography* (Auckland: Hodder and Stoughton, 1977); Dick Scott, *Ask That Mountain: The Story of Parihaka* (Rosedale: Raupo, 2008); Graham Butterworth, "Pomare, Maui Wiremu Piti Naera," *Te Ara—The Encyclopaedia of New Zealand,* http://www.TeAra.govt.nz/en/biographies/3p30/pomare-maui-wiremu-piti-naera (accessed June 8, 2012).

46. O. F. Nelson to Dr. Māui Pōmare, August 13, 1919, and August 27, 1919, ANZ, IT 79/2/1, R17962644.

47. Ta'isi used the term "governor," a title from German rule, rather than "administrator."

48. O. F. Nelson to Dr. Māui Pōmare, August 13, 1919, ANZ, IT 79/2/1, R17962644.

49. O. F. Nelson to Dr. Māui Pōmare, August 29, 1919, ANZ, IT 79/2/1, R17962644.

50. Ibid.

51. Ibid.

52. *The Samoa Constitution Order 1920,* supplement to the *New Zealand Gazette,* May 20, 1920, 1623, via *Samoa Legislation and Law Reports,* http://www.paclii.org/cgi-bin/sinodisp/ws/legis/num_act/sco1920266/index.html?stem=&synonyms=&query=samoa%20and%20constitution%20and%20order%20and%201920#disp2 (accessed March 23, 2014).

53. Davidson, *Samoa mo Samoa,* 100.

54. H. E. Holland, *Samoa: A Story That Teems with Tragedy* (Wellington: Maoriland Worker Printing and Publishing, 1918), 20; H. E. Holland, *Indentured Labour: Is It Slavery?* (Greymouth: Grey River Coy, 1919).

55. *Visit of Parliamentary Party to Pacific Islands February—March 1920, Minutes of Proceedings at Mangaia, Rarotonga, Aitutaki, Niue and Western Samoa,* 25–26, *AtoJsOnline*, Te Puna Mātauranga o Aotearoa—National Library of New Zealand, http://atojs.natlib.govt.nz/cgi-bin/atojs?a=d&cl=search&d=AJHR1920-I.2.1.2.6&srpos=4&e=———-10—1—-byDA—-0+Pacific+Islands+1920-AJHR%5f1920%5fI%5fAZz-D- (accessed March 19, 2014).

56. Ibid., 27–28.

57. Ibid., 29–38.

58. Ibid., 31, 41.

59. In testimony from plantation managers it was revealed that Chinese workers were paid 4s 6d. per day, Sāmoans 3s 11d. per day, and Solomon Islanders £2 per month or roughly 1s 2d per day (ibid., 31, 33, 39).

60. Ibid., 53, 54.

61. Ibid., 45, 46, 47, 49, 56, 57.

62. Ibid., 50.

63. Ibid., 51, 52.

64. Ibid., 64.

Chapter 3: The "Troublesome Garden of Eden"

1. *Visit of Parliamentary Party to Pacific Islands February—March 1920, Minutes of Proceedings at Mangaia, Rarotonga, Aitutaki, Niue and Western Samoa,* 25–26, *AtoJsOnline*, Te Puna Mātauranga o Aotearoa—National Library of New Zealand, http://atojs.natlib.govt.nz/cgi-bin/atojs?a=d&cl=search&d=AJHR1920-I.2.1.2.6&srpos=4&e=———-10—1—-byDA—-0+Pacific+Islands+1920-AJHR%5f1920%5fI%5fAZz-D- (accessed March 19, 2014), 27–28.

2. R. W. Tate to J. D. Gray, October 20, 1919, Tate Papers, MS-Papers-0264–01, MS-Copy-Micro-0082–01.

3. O. F. Nelson to W. F. Massey, January 8, 1921, ANZ, IT 79/2/1, R17962644, 1.

4. Ibid., 2.

5. Ibid., 3–4; *Samoa Constitution Order, 1920,* 261 (1), published in *New Zealand Gazette,* May 21, 1920, 1653.

6. O. F. Nelson to W. F. Massey, January 8, 1921, ANZ, IT 79/2/1, R17962644, 3–4.

7. Ibid., 4.

8. Ibid., 5.

9. Ibid.

10. Ibid.

11. O. F. Nelson to R. W. Tate, September 22, 1921, ANZ, IT 79/2/1, R17962644, 2.

12. Ta'isi details the frustration of trying to get British subject status in London in 1920 in a letter to R. W. Tate, September 22, 1921, ANZ, IT 79/2/1, R17962644.

13. O. F. Nelson to W. F. Massey, January 8, 1921, ANZ, IT 79/2/1, R17962644, 6.

14. O. F. Nelson to R. W. Tate, September 22, 1921, ANZ, IT 79/2/1, R17962644.

15. Ibid.

16. O. F. Nelson to W. F. Massey, January 8, 1921, ANZ, IT 79/2/1, R17962644.

17. O. F. Nelson to W. F. Massey, January 15, 1921, ANZ, IT 79/2/1, R17962644, 1–3.

18. Ibid.

19. W. F. Massey to O. F. Nelson, January 13, 1921, ANZ, IT 79/2/1, R17962644.

20. E. P. Lee to O. F. Nelson, January 15, 1921, ANZ, IT1 EX79/2/1, R17962644, 1–3.

21. Ibid.

22. *Samoa Act* 1921 (New Zealand), section 300, http://www.nzlii.org/nz/legis/hist_act/sa192112gv1921n16137 (accessed June 13, 2013). With thanks to Aisling O'Hagan of the Victoria University Wellington Law Library for her assistance.

23. O. F. Nelson to E. P Lee, January 20, 1921, ANZ, IT1 EX79/2/1, R17962644, 1.

24. W. F. Massey to O. F. Nelson, January 19, 1921, ANZ, IT1 EX79/2/1, R17962644, 1.

25. Massey wanted to consult Sir Francis Bell before sending off such a strongly worded response. Handwritten note following W. F. Massey to O. F. Nelson, January 19, 1921, ANZ, IT1 EX79/2/1, R17962644.

26. He wrote a long letter to native secretary N. H. Macdonald strongly setting out the same grievances he aired in January; O. F. Nelson to N. H. Macdonald, November 21, 1921, ANZ, IT1 EX79/2/1, R17962644.

27. On the issue of land and the administrator's ability to acquire it, see *The Samoa Constitution Order 1920,* supplement to the *New Zealand Gazette,* May 20, 1920, section 261, 1658, via *Samoa Legislation and Law Reports,* http://www.paclii.org/cgi-bin/sinodisp/ws/legis/num_act/sco1920266/index.html?stem=&synonyms=&query=samoa%20and%20constitution%20and%20order%20and%201920#disp2 (accessed March 23, 2014). See the Samoa Act 1921, section 271, 84.

28. Nelson, *Truth about Samoa,* 8.

29. Ta'isi notes that the constitution, for instance, was passed by the New Zealand parliament before it was "even" translated and published in the Samoan language; O. F. Nelson to N. H. Macdonald, November 21, 1921, ANZ, IT1 EX79/2/1, R17962644.

30. Tui Atua Tupua Tamasese Ta'isi Efi, interview with the author, April 9, 2013; Tui Atua Tupua Tamasese Ta'isi Efi, e-mail to author, April 25, 2013; Alesoni to Mr. Harrison, February 2, 1921; Lands and Titles Court case, Savai'i File No. B/S 317/19 (High Court of Western Samoa at Vaisala, Savai'i).

31. "Citizen's Committee Meeting," *Samoa Times,* February 17, 1922, 6–8. Ta'isi's speech to this meeting is reproduced on page 8.

32. "Around the World by Aeroplane," *Samoa Times,* May 28, 1921, 7.

33. Tate cites September 1921 as the point where Ta'isi "took up the cudgels"; R. W. Tate to J. D. Gray, September 21, 1921, Tate Papers, MS-Papers-0264–01, MS-Copy-Micro-0082–01.

34. R. W. Tate to J. D. Gray, September 12, 1922, Tate Papers, MS-Papers-0264–03, MS-Copy-Micro-0082–02.

35. R. W. Tate to J. D. Gray, September 21, 1921, Tate Papers, MS-Papers-0264–01, MS-Copy-Micro-0082–01; R. W. Tate to J. D. Gray, February 7, 1923, Tate Papers, MS-Papers-0264–04, MS-Copy-Micro-0082–02.

36. R. W. Tate to J. D. Gray, February 7, 1923, Tate Papers, MS-Papers-0264–04, MS-Copy-Micro-0082–02.

37. Ta'isi also offered the reason that he was about to embark on his long trip to the United States and Europe with Rosabel; JSPIC, 52.

38. R. W. Tate to J. D. Gray, March 3, 1919, Tate Papers, MS-Papers-0264–01, MS-Copy-Micro-0082–01.

39. Belich, *Paradise Reforged,* 194; Binney, *Encircled Lands.*

40. Tania Cleary, *Poignant Regalia: Nineteenth Century Aboriginal Breastplates and Images* (Glebe, Australia: Historic Houses Trust, 1993); James G. Lergessner, *Chief Bungaree: King of the Broken Bay Tribe* (Woorim, Australia: James G. Lergessner, 2008).

41. From 1975 this situation has been shifting as the Waitangi Tribunal has returned land and natural resources to Māori control.

42. R. W. Tate to E. P. Lee, September 27, 1921, ANZ, IT1 EX79/2/1, R17962644.

43. *First Report of the Government of the Dominion of New Zealand on the Administration of the Mandated Territory of Western Samoa for the Period from 1st May 1920 to 31st March 1921* (Wellington: Government Printer, 1922), 2.

44. J. D. Gray to E. P. Lee, February 8, 1922, ANZ, IT1 EX79/2/1, R17962644.

45. *First Report,* 11.

46. Ibid., 3, 4, 5, 7, 9, 11, 36; the *Samoa Act* 1921, section 300, 88.

47. O. F. Nelson to R. W. Tate, May 15, 1922, ANZ, IT1 EX79/2/1, R17962644.

48. Toelupe was shown favorable treatment as he steered the *faipule* toward the administration. See R. W. Tate to J. D. Gray, February 7, 1923, Tate Papers, MS-Papers-0264–04, MS-Copy-Micro-0082–02.

49. O. F. Nelson to R. W. Tate, May 15, 1922, ANZ, IT1 EX79/2/1, R17962644.

50. R. W. Tate to O. F. Nelson, May 20, 1922, ANZ, IT1 EX79/2/1, R17962644.

51. O. F. Nelson to R. W. Tate, May 25, 1922, ANZ, IT1 EX79/2/1, R17962644.

52. Nelson, *Truth about Samoa,* 10.

53. Ibid., 8–11.

54. Meleisea, *Making of Modern Samoa,* 131.

55. *The Samoan Offenders Ordinance* is reproduced in Nelson, *Truth about Samoa,* 10–11.

56. The formation of the first limited liability company in Sāmoa—the amalgamation of A. Nelson and Son and H. J. Moors' company—followed a 1922 Order in Council "legalizing the formation of limited liability companies in Samoa"; see "Two Old Firms Amalgamate," *Samoa Times,* November 24, 1922, 8.

57. "A Palatial Residence on a Beautiful Site," *Samoa Times,* January 31, 1920, 8.

58. R. W. Tate to J. D. Gray, February 7, 1923, Tate Papers, MS-Papers-0264–04, MS-Copy-Micro-0082–02; George Spafford Richardson, diary entry March 18, 1923, Acheson Papers, 5.2.1.3a.

59. "A Palatial Residence on a Beautiful Site," *Samoa Times,* January 31, 1920, 8.

60. In June 2012 the author and Tenisia Tovio reconstructed the Tuaefu Library. The books had been stored in numerous packing boxes, along with many other family documents during renovations to the house undertaken some years before. Together Tenisia and I searched the boxes over a number of long, hot days for books published before 1944, many of which bore a stamp signifying that it belonged to Ta'isi's library. Tiffany Nelson-Sauni then cataloged the books and restored them to the shelves of Ta'isi's office. This process will be discussed further in my forthcoming article, "Ta'isi O. F. Nelson's Library." I am greatly indebted to Lydia Wevers for her insights into how to "read a library"; see Lydia Wevers, *Reading on the Farm: Victorian Fiction and the Colonial World* (Wellington: Victoria University Press, 2010).

61. See the selected works from Ta'isi's library in this volume's bibliography.

62. These works on English literature came from the library of Gustav Kunst, owner of Vailima until his death in 1905, when the German government bought the house to serve as the governor's residence. See Anthony Brunt, *To Walk under Palm Trees: The Germans in Samoa, Snapshots from Albums* (http://germansinsamoa.net/ebook/ 2016), chap. 5. See the selected works from Ta'isi's library in this volume's bibliography.

63. See the selected works from Ta'isi's library in this volume's bibliography.

64. *First Report on Mandated Territory of Western Samoa 1921,* 9.

65. "Local and General," *Samoa Times,* May 4, 1921, 5.

66. Ta'isi had multiple volumes of Marguerite Wilson, *Dancing: A Complete Instructor and Guide to All the New and Standard Dances* (Philadelphia: Penn Publishing, 1905 and 1924); Cavendish, *The Laws and Principles of Whist Stated and Explained and Its Practice Illustrated on an Original System by Means of Hands Played Completely Through* (London: Thos. De la Rue, 1905). Ta'isi recalled party entertainments at Tuaefu in O. F. Nelson to H. W. Moors, September 10, 1930. OFN 19.

67. Tui Atua Tupua Tamasese Ta'isi Efi, Head of State of Sāmoa, Address to the Methodist Consultative Council of the Pacific, April 12, 2015, Fogaa, Faleula, Sāmoa.

68. See Patricia O'Brien, "Bridging the Pacific: Ta'isi O. F. Nelson, Australia and the Sāmoan Mau," *History Australia*, 14:1, 2017.

69. R. W. Tate to J. D. Gray, February 7, 1923, Tate Papers, MS-Papers-0264–04, MS-Copy-Micro-0082–02.

70. With thanks to Loloma Johnston, the tenth child of Atoa and Fa'agutu, and Siuga Paula Masoe, daughter of Masoe Tulele, for illuminating family life at Tuaefu, where they grew up.

71. Tui Atua Tupua Tamasese Ta'isi Efi, interview with author June 11, 2012.

72. R. W. Tate to J. D. Gray, circa February 6, 1923, Tate Papers, MS-Papers-0264–04, MS-Copy-Micro-0082–02; Newton A. Rowe, *Samoa under the Sailing Gods* (London: Unwin Brothers, 1930), 134.

Chapter 4: A New Era?

1. R. W. Tate to Captain Evans, February 22, 1921, ANZ, IT 1 106, EX2/9, R17961623.

2. D. R. Hoggard (counsel for Sāmoan petitioners) testimony to JSPIC, 29, 30.

3. O. F. Nelson to R. W. Tate, March 16, 1928, OFN 52.

4. The Tate Papers are full of these comments, particularly in his correspondence with J. D. Gray.

5. F. Bell to C. Fergusson, memorandum, June 16, 1921, ANZ, IT 1 106, EX2/9, R17961623, 3.

6. R. W. Tate to J. D. Gray, September 21, 1921, Tate Papers, MS-Papers-0264–01, MS-Copy-Micro-0082–01.

7. "The New Administrator," *New Zealand Herald*, March 2, 1923, 8. Richardson held an array of imperial orders: CMG (Companion of Saint Michael and Saint George), awarded in 1916; CB (Companion of the Order of Bath), awarded in 1917; CBE (Commander of the Most Excellent Order of the British Empire), awarded in 1918; and KBE (Knight of the British Empire), awarded in 1925.

8. "General Richardson," *Northern Advocate*, February 12, 1923, 2; Ian McGibbon, "Richardson, George Spafford," *Te Ara—the Encyclopedia of New Zealand*, http://www.TeAra.govt.nz/en/biographies/3r16/richardson-george-spafford (accessed April 7, 2014).

9. Since 1916, ANZAC Day, April 25, has marked the landing that commenced the Battle of Gallipoli, known as Çanakkale in Turkey. ANZAC has been at the center of the national mythologies of Australia and New Zealand ever since.

10. "Governing Samoa," *New Zealand Herald*, March 2, 1923, 8.

11. "General Richardson Leaving for Samoa," *Auckland Star*, February 28, 1923, 11.

12. "Samoa and Defence," *Evening Post,* February 5, 1923, 6.

13. R. W. Tate to Minister for External Affairs, March 28, 1923, ANZ, IT 1 106, EX2/9, R17961623.

14. JSPIC, 43.

15. "Samoa, Elective Council Demands of the People," *Sydney Morning Herald,* March 21, 1923, 13.

16. "White and Brown," *Evening Post,* March 23, 1923, 6; see also "Samoa an Elective Council Demands of the People," *Northern Advocate,* April 5, 1923, 6; "Samoa Legislative Council Needed," *Auckland Star,* April 5, 1923, 10.

17. "Governing Samoa: The New Administrator. Enthusiastic Welcome. Messages from Dominion," *New Zealand Herald,* April 7, 1923, 11.

18. JSPIC, 43.

19. J. D. Gray to G. S. Richardson, May 24, 1923, ANZ, IT1 445, EX79/78, part 2, R17962677.

20. See chapter 3, note 16 of this volume.

21. G. S. Richardson to Minister for External Affairs, April 21, 1923; also see other correspondence on this topic generated in 1921 and 1922, also in ANZ, IT1 EX79/2/1, R17962644.

22. J. D. Gray to G. S. Richardson, memorandum, April 23, 1923, ANZ, IT1 EX79/2/1, R17962644.

23. "Samoan Mandate Nationality of Natives," *Brisbane Courier,* April 16, 1923, 5.

24. "British Subjects in New Zealand: Acquisition of Status," *Scotsman,* August 29, 1923, 6.

25. Under the British Nationality and Status of Aliens (in New Zealand) Act of 1923 that was "applicable to Western Samoa and the Cook Islands," authority was "given for the granting of certificates of Naturalisation to any approved person who may elect to apply for the privileges of British Citizenship"; see Administrator's Address to Legislative Council of Western Samoa, February 23, 1925, ANZ, IT1 EX1/8/1, part 2, R17961209.

26. G. S. Richardson to J. D. Gray, December 15, 1924, ANZ, IT 1 445, EX 79/78, part 2, R17962677.

27. "Freemasonry: New Grand Office Bearers," *Scotsman,* November 3, 1922. Wellington's *Evening Post* reported, "There was a Masonic service at his graveside" burial in 1944; see "Hon. O. F. Nelson's Funeral," *Evening Post,* March 2, 1944, 6. See also Jessica Harland-Jacobs, *Builders of Empire: Freemasonry and the British Imperialism 1717–1927* (Chapel Hill: University of North Carolina Press, 2007).

28. See chapter 3 of this volume.

29. See comment on the Ta'isi title in Davidson, *Samoa mo Samoa,* 115; Meleisea, *Making of Modern Samoa,* 139 and 247n20.

30. O. F. Nelson and J. C. Andersen, "Legends of Samoa," *Journal of the Polynesian Society* 34, no. 134 (1925): 126.

31. JSPIC, 43.

32. O. F. Nelson to G. S. Richardson, July 6, 1923, ANZ, IT1 EX1/33/1, R17961393.

33. JSPIC, 43.

34. This discussion about the franchise appears without signature and date but probably dates from late 1920 because it refers to "a census [that] will be taken in February 1921." It was written by Tate, we must assume, owing to the use of the first person and other references consistent with Tate's views and position (ANZ, IT1 EX 1/8, R17961230).

35. The Samoan Legislative Council Order 1923, in ANZ, IT1 EX 1/8, R17961230.

36. G. S. Richardson to External Affairs, telegram, January 24, 1924, ANZ, IT1 Ex 1/8, R17961230.

37. O. F. Nelson to F. Bell, February 12, 1924, ANZ, IT1 EX 1/8, R17961230.

38. J. D. Gray to A. C. Day, February 29, 1924, ANZ, IT1 Ex 1/8, R17961230.

39. I am indebted to Ta'isi *aiga* for piecing together this personal history. In particular to Fialaui'afualeafi Tamasese, who had a very close relationship with her grandmother Rosabel (Fialaui'afualeafi Tamasese, interview with the author, November 10, 2012).

40. G. S. Richardson to F. Bell, March 9, 1925, ANZ, IT 1 EX 1/33/1, R17961393.

41. Richardson diary entry, August 6, 1925, Acheson Papers, box 11, 5.2.1.3f.

42. G. S. Richardson to F. Bell, January 8, 1925, ANZ, IT 1 EX 1/33/1, R17961393.

43. The 1925 Minutes of the Legislative Council, n.d., IT1 5 EX1/8/1, part 2, R17961209, 114.

44. See Williams' advertisement in the *Samoa Times,* January 5, 1923, 1.

45. The 1925 Minutes of the Legislative Council, n.d., IT1 5 EX1/8/1, part 2, R17961209.

46. Ibid. For more on these policies, see Field, *Mau.*

47. The 1925 Minutes of the Legislative Council, n.d., IT1 5 EX1/8/1, part 2, R17961209.

48. Ibid.

49. Ibid. See discussion of *Samoan Offenders Ordinance* in chapter 3 and *Mau a Pule* in chapter 2 of this volume.

50. G. S. Richardson to J. D. Gray, April 11, 1924, ANZ, IT1 445, EX79/78, part 2, R17962677.

51. Rowe, *Samoa under the Sailing Gods,* 168–169.

52. For more on Tupua Tamasese Lea'lofi's defiance, see Field, *Mau.*

53. G. S. Richardson diary entry, January 7, 1925, Acheson Papers, box 10, 5.2.1.3e. Malietoa, for instance, wrote to Richardson on January 13, 1934 (when

Ta'isi's trial was in progress), asking him to return and rule Sāmoa. See Acheson Papers, box 9, 5.2.1.1a. Malietoa signed his name "Malietoa O. B. E."

54. The 1925 Minutes of the Legislative Council, n.d., IT1 5 EX1/8/1, part 2, R17961209.

55. Richardson noted during his *malaga* mid-1925 that children no longer seemed afraid of him. This may be another reading of this photograph. See "Message from His Excellency the Kovana to the people of Samoa Concerning His Malaga around Samoa during June and July 1925," 9, in Acheson Papers, box 11, 5.2.1.3f. See "Portrait of General George Spafford Richardson with Samoan children." Rutherford, Alexander Mathieson, 1915– : Photographs of Samoa. Ref: PA1-o-446-61-2. Alexander Turnbull Library, Wellington, New Zealand. View online via http://natlib.govt.nz/records/22777140?search%5Bi%5D%5Bsubject%5D=Richardson%2C+George+Spafford+%28Sir%29%2C+1868-1938&search%5Bpath%5D=items.

Chapter 5: Before the Storm

1. "Samoan Hurricane Damage to Copra Crop Year's Loss of 2000 Tons," *New Zealand Herald,* January 9, 1926, 8.

2. Legislative Council Minutes, March 22, 1926, 11, ANZ, IT 1 EX 1/8/1, part 2, R1761209.

3. When Richardson returned to Sāmoa, Sir Francis Bell, acting as minister for External Affairs, sent him a letter with seventy-nine actionable items with Bell giving his views to Richardson about how to proceed with them. See Acheson Papers, box 11, 5.2.1.3g.

4. G. S. Richardson to F. Bell, October 22, 1925, ANZ, IT 1 EX 1/33/1, R17961393.

5. "Ta'isi's Travels," *Samoan Supplement NZ Samoa Guardian,* April 14, 1932, ANZ, IT 284, EX 37/12, part 1, R17961901.

6. Letters between O. F. Nelson and G. S. Richardson, Exhibit 52, appended to *Report of the Royal Commission Concerning the Administration of Western Samoa* (hereafter *Samoa Royal Commission*) (Wellington: Government Printer, 1928), *AtoJsOnline,* Te Puna Mātauranga o Aotearoa—National Library of New Zealand, http://atojs.natlib.govt.nz/cgi-bin/atojs?a=d&d=AJHR1928-I.2.1.2.7&e=———-10—1———0—(accessed May 13, 2012).

7. O. F. Nelson to G. S. Richardson, April 12, 1926, Exhibit 52, appended to *Samoa Royal Commission,* 464.

8. G. S. Richardson to O. F. Nelson, June 24, 1926, Exhibit 52, appended to *Samoa Royal Commission,* 464.

9. Ibid.

10. O. F. Nelson to G. S. Richardson, June 24, 1926, Exhibit 52, appended to *Samoa Royal Commission,* 464.

11. G. S. Richardson to O. F. Nelson, June 24, 1926, Exhibit 52, appended to *Samoa Royal Commission,* 464.

12. John Wheeler-Bennett, "Fergusson, Sir Charles, of Kilkerran, Seventh Baronet (1865–1951)," rev. Roger T. Stearn, *Oxford Dictionary of National Biography* (Oxford: Oxford University Press, 2004), http://dx.doi.org/10.1093/ref:odnb/33111 (accessed October 3, 2013).

13. See chapter 4, this volume.

14. Patricia O'Brien, "From Sudan to Samoa: Imperial Legacies, Cultures and New Zealand's Rule over the Mandated Territory of Western Sāmoa," in *New Zealand's Empire,* ed. Katie Pickles and Catharine Colebourne, 127–142 (Manchester: Manchester University Press, 2016).

15. G. S. Richardson to F. Bell, March 9, 1925, ANZ, IT1 EX 1/33/1, R17961393.

16. J. D. Gray to A. C. Day, April 9, 1926, ANZ, G48 6 R19162155; J. Stair, *Old Samoa: Flotsam and Jetsam from the Pacific Ocean* (London: Religious Tract Society, 1897); L. Churchill, *Samoa 'Uma: Where Life Is Different* (New York: Forest Stream Publishing, 1902); Robert Watson, *History of Samoa* (Wellington: Whitcombe and Tombs, 1919); George Turner, *Samoa: A Hundred Years Ago and Long Before* (London: Macmillan, 1884); Frederick O'Brien, *White Shadows in the South Seas* (New York: Century,1919); Frederick O'Brien, *Mystic Isles of the South Seas* (London: Hodder and Stoughton, 1921); Robert Keable, *Tahiti Isle of Dreams* (London: Hutchinson, 1925).

17. Patricia O'Brien, *The Pacific Muse: Exotic Femininity and the Colonial Pacific* (Seattle: University of Washington Press, 2006).

18. J. D. Gray to A. C. Day, February 27, 1926, ANZ, G48 6 R19162155.

19. Schedule of Vice-Regal Tour of Cook Islands, Samoa and Other Islands of the South Pacific, April 26–June 8, 1926, ANZ, G48 6 R19162155, 6.

20. O'Brien, *Pacific Muse,* 233.

21. Richardson to Fergusson, March 11, 1925, ANZ, G48 6R19162155.

22. C. Fergusson Report to Lord Amery, June 11, 1926, National Archives, London (hereafter NA), DO 35/4, 7–9.

23. Ibid., 9.

24. Ibid.

25. Ibid., 9–11.

26. Ibid.

27. Ibid., 11.

28. Ibid., 11–12.

29. Unidentified employee of O. F. Nelson and Co. to O. F. Nelson, June 30, 1926, Exhibit 55, appended to *Samoa Royal Commission,* 466. It is unclear if both of these men were in fact imprisoned and for what duration, but Ta'isi was told, and believed, they had been.

30. D. R. Hoggard, address to JSPIC, August 10, 1927, 32.

31. Lyndall Ryan, *Aboriginal Tasmanians: A History since 1803* (Crows Nest, New South Wales: Allen and Unwin, 2012).

32. *Aborigines Protection Act* (NSW) 1909 citations.

33. Commonwealth of Australia, *Naturalization Act 1903,* section 5.

34. See, for example, John Macmillan Brown, *Maori and Polynesian: Their Origin, History and Culture* (London: Hutchinson, 1907).

35. See O'Brien, "Bridging the Pacific."

36. Nelson, *Truth about Samoa,* 3, 44–45.

37. There is substantial literature on 1930s colonial governance and Australia's Indigenous community. See John Maynard, *Fight for Liberty and Freedom: The Origins of Australian Aboriginal Activism* (Canberra: AIATSIS, 2007).

38. Victoria Haskins, *One Bright Spot* (London: Palgrave Macmillan, 2005); Fiona Paisley, *Loving Protection: Australian Feminism and Aboriginal Women's Rights* (Melbourne: Melbourne University Press, 2000).

39. O. F. Nelson to J. D. Gray, June 24, 1926, ANZ, IT1 EX 1 79/2/1, R17962644.

40. J. D. Gray to O. F. Nelson, July 1, 1926, ANZ, IT1 EX 1 79/2/1, R17962644.

41. O. F. Nelson to J. D. Gray, July 7, 1926, ANZ, IT1 EX 1 79/2/1, R17962644.

42. J. D. Gray to O. F. Nelson, July 15, 1926, ANZ, IT1 EX 1 79/2/1, R17962644.

43. O. F. Nelson to J. D. Gray, July 30, 1926, ANZ, IT1 EX 1 79/2/1, R17962644.

44. G. S. Richardson to O. F. Nelson, August 27, 1926, Exhibit 53, appended to *Samoa Royal Commission,* 464; V. R Meredith (counsel's closing address), *Samoa Royal Commission,* 392.

45. G. S. Richardson to O. F. Nelson, August 27, 1926, Exhibit 53, appended to *Samoa Royal Commission,* 464.

46. See other correspondence between G. S. Richardson and O. F. Nelson, Exhibit 53, appended to *Samoa Royal Commission,* 463–465.

47. Administrator's Speech of Welcome, September 28, 1926, Exhibit 54, appended to *Samoa Royal Commission,* 466.

48. O. F. Nelson's opening speech to *First Public Meeting of Citizens Held in the Apia Market Hall 15 October 1926,* Exhibit 52, appended to *Samoa Royal Commission,* 448–453.

49. Ibid. 449.

50. Ibid.

51. Ibid., 450.

52. Faumuina Fiame in ibid., 450.

53. Ibid., 453.

54. Report of Inspector A. L. Braisby in reference to a public meeting held at Market Hall Apia November 12, 1926, in JSPIC, 19–21.

Chapter 6: The Storm

1. J. D. Gray to G. S. Richardson, September 9, 1926, ANZ, IT1 445, EX79/78, part 2, R17962677.

2. Ibid.

3. Ibid.

4. G. S. Richardson to J. D. Gray, September 23, 1926, ANZ, IT1 445, EX79/78, part 2, R17962677.

5. Administrator's Speech of Welcome, September 28, 1926, Exhibit 54, appended to *Samoa Royal Commission,* 466.

6. D. R. Hoggard address to JSPIC, August 11, 1927, 34.

7. "Eulogistic speech" was used to describe Richardson's speech by D. R. Hoggard, address to JSPIC, August 10, 1927, 32.

8. O. F. Nelson, "Conditions in Samoa," *New Zealand Herald,* October 5, 1926, 6.

9. J. D. Gray to G. S. Richardson, October 8, 1926, ANZ, IT1 445, EX79/78, part 2, R17962677.

10. G. S. Richardson to Minister for External Affairs, telegram, October 12, 1926, ANZ, IT1 36, EX1/23/8, part 1, R17961334.

11. Minister for External Affairs to G. S. Richardson, telegram, October 14, 1926, ANZ, IT1 36, EX1/23/8, part 1, R17961334.

12. J. D. Gray to the Minster for External Affairs, memo, October 19, 1926, ANZ, IT1 36, EX1/23/8, part 1, R17961334.

13. Arthur Leslie Braisby, army personal record 1914–1916, ANZ, AABK 18805/W5520, R22278688.

14. Ibid.

15. See the regular reporting on scores from the Apia Rifle Club in the *Samoa Times.*

16. G. S. Richardson to J. D. Gray, October 22, 1926, ANZ, IT1 445, EX79/78, part 2, R17962677.

17. Confidential Report of Inspector A. L. Braisby of Public Meeting Market Hall, Apia, October 15, 1926, JSPIC, 18.

18. Elected Members of the Legislative Council to Minister for External Affairs, telegram, October 16, 1926, ANZ, IT1 36, EX1/23/8, part 1, R17961334.

19. G. S. Richardson telegram to Minister for External Affairs, October 18, 1926, ANZ, IT1 36, EX1/23/8, part 1, R17961334.

20. O. F. Nelson to Minister for External Affairs, October 23, 1926, ANZ, IT1 36, EX1/23/8, part 1, R17961334.

21. Minister for External Affairs to O. F. Nelson, November 12, 1926, ANZ, IT1 36, EX1/23/8, part 1, R17961334.

22. Confidential Report of Inspector A. L. Braisby of Public Meeting Market Hall, Apia, October 15, 1926, JSPIC, 19–21.

23. Ibid.

24. J. D. Gray to G. S. Richardson, November 4, 1926, ANZ, IT1 445, EX79/78, part 2 R17962677.

25. The discussion about tension between Ta'isi and Reverend Maddox was held during a convivial meeting at Tuaefu between the men's descendants, His Highness Tui Atua Tupua Tamasese Ta'isi Efi and Geoff Maddox, and the author during the fiftieth anniversary of the Sāmoan Methodist Church Independence from the Australian conference in Apia, July 13, 2014.

26. W. H. Woodward (Chief Judge of Samoa) to J. D. Gray, November 15, 1926, ANZ, IT1 36, EX1/23/8, part 1, R17961334.

27. G. S. Richardson to Minister for External Affairs, memorandum, November 19, 1926, ANZ, IT1 36, EX1/23/8, part 1, R17961334.

28. D. R. Hoggard address to JSPIC, August 11, 1927, 36.

29. G. S. Richardson to J. D. Gray, December 17, 1926. Richardson uses "free trip" in his secret memorandum, December 6, 1926, ANZ, G48 38 s/17, R19162280.

30. O. F. Nelson, letter to the editor, *Samoa Times,* November 26, 1926, 3.

31. "Elected Members," *Samoa Times,* December 3, 1926, 4.

32. See Richardson to the Minister for External Affairs, memorandum, December 3, 1926, ANZ, IT1 1 EX 1/8, part 1, R17961230.

33. G. S. Richardson to J. D. Gray, December 1, 1926, ANZ, IT1 445, EX79/78, R17962677.

34. G. S. Richardson to J. D. Gray, January 14, 1927, ANZ, IT1 445, EX79/78, R17962677.

35. In his secret memorandum of December 6, 1926, Richardson wrote that "the affair has now ended," ANZ, G48 38 s/17, R19162280.

36. G. S. Richardson to J. D. Gray, October 22, 1926, ANZ, IT1 445, EX79/78, part 2, R17962677.

37. Richardson states his intended audience, which, interestingly, did not include the Prime Minister; G. S. Richardson to C. Fergusson, December 13, 1926, ANZ, G48 38 s/17, R19162280.

38. G. S. Richardson, secret memorandum, December 6, 1926, ANZ, G48 38 s/17, R19162280.

39. G. S. Richardson to C. Fergusson, December 13, 1926, ANZ, G48 38 s/17, R19162280.

40. Translation of the circular has notations of "seditious" written next to sections 4 IV (a) and 4 IV (i). Both the annotated English and the Sāmoan version of the circular are at ANZ, IT1 EX 1/23/8, part 2, R17961335.

41. G. S. Richardson, secret memorandum, December 6, 1926, ANZ, G48 38 s/17, R19162280.

42. Arthur Farr (Solicitor-General) to Attorney-General of New Zealand, March 5, 1927, ANZ, IT1 37, EX1/23/8, part 4, R17961289.

43. G. S. Richardson, secret memorandum, December 6, 1926, ANZ, G48 38 s/17, R19162280.

44. Ibid.

45. "Samoan Affairs: A Strong Protest by Fono of Faipules Warm Support of Administration," *Evening Post,* January 4, 1927.

46. G. S. Richardson to Minister for External Affairs, December 3, 1926, ANZ, EX1/8 R17961230.

47. G. S. Richardson, "Secret Memorandum on German Propaganda," January 13, 1927; J. G. Coates to C. Fergusson, canceled memorandum, July 15, 1927; both at ANZ, G48 35 EX S/3(1), R19162267.

48. See various documents in ANZ, G48 35 EX S/3(1), R19162267, such as J. G. Coates to to C. Fergusson, March 15, 1927.

49. W. Nosworthy to External, June 12, 1927, ANZ, G48 38 s/17, R19162280; draft of W. Nosworthy to Chairman of Citizens' Committee [O. F. Nelson], July 12, 1927, ANZ, IT1 37, EX 1/23/8, part 6, R17961291.

50. G. S. Richardson, "Secret Memorandum on German Propaganda," January 13, 1927, ANZ, G48 35, EX S/3(1), R19162267.

51. G. S. Richardson to C. Fergusson, December 13, 1926, ANZ, G48 38 s/17, R19162280.

52. See chapter 4 for discussion of heated exchanges between Ta'isi and Tate circa May 1922.

53. This evidence was presented on Ta'isi's behalf by his counsel D. R. Hoggard to JSPIC, August 11, 1927, 37.

54. See a summation of Woodward's legal and military career to June 1923 in ANZ, IT1 47, EX1/33/1, part 1, R17961393. Woodward was acting as crown solicitor for the administration when the position of chief judge became vacant in 1923. In his deliberations with Richardson, O. F. Nelson stated that there were not any suitable personnel in Sāmoa to fill the position of chief judge, which included Woodward. See discussion in chapter 5, this volume.

55. D. R. Hoggard address to JSPIC, August 11, 1927, 37. O. F. Nelson also discusses this threat in *Truth about Samoa,* 28. O. F. Nelson evidence to JSPIC, August 20, 1927, 75–76.

56. G. S. Richardson to Minister for External Affairs, July 26, 1927, ANZ, IT1 EX 1/33/1, R17961393.

57. G. S. Richardson to Minister for External Affairs, December 17, 1926, ANZ, IT1 EX 1/33/1, R17961393.

58. W. Nosworthy to G. S. Richardson, January 12, 1927, ANZ, IT1 EX 1/33/1, R17961393.

59. M. Pōmare to O. F. Nelson, November 11, 1926, OFN 58.

60. O. F. Nelson to M. Pōmare, December 17, 1926, OFN 58.

61. "Baby" was one of Ta'isi's nicknames for Taufau.

62. O. F. Nelson to M. Pōmare, December 17, 1926, OFN 58.

Chapter 7: "He Is Not a Samoan"

1. "Ball at Vailima," *Samoa Times,* January 7, 1927, 3.

2. The *Samoa Times* reported on Ta'isi's party on page 5 in the "Local and General" section, as opposed to its page 3 report on the Vailima ball, January 7, 1927.

3. The controlling interest in the *Samoa Times* had been W. H. Woodward, the chief judge of the high court and therefore the deputy administrator, but he sold his shares to G. P. Brown. Ta'isi wanted to divest his shareholdings too to the editor, but Brown refused to enter into the transaction, tying up Ta'isi's funds. Discussion about *Samoa Times* ownership and editorial history was given to the JSPIC, August 20, 1927, 80–81.

4. Hywel Francis, "Cook, Arthur James (1883–1931)," *Oxford Dictionary of National Biography* (Oxford: Oxford University Press, 2004); http://www.oxforddnb.com.virtual.anu.edu.au/view/article/32539 (accessed December 4, 2015).

5. "No Way to Run a Newspaper" and "An Official Statement," *Samoa Times*, January 7, 1927, 3, 6. See also correspondence in ANZ, IT1 37, EX1/23/8, part 3, R17961288, January 1927, for machinations around this visit, particularly O. F. Nelson to Minister for External Affairs, January 14, 1927, and G. S. Richardson to Minister for External Affairs, January 17, 1927.

6. "Sir George Richardson Honoured," *Samoa Times*, January 14, 1927, 4.

7. See correspondence and paper clippings on file at ANZ, IT1 36, EX1/23/8, part 3, R17961288 for early January 1927.

8. W. Vallance (for Wynyard, Wilson, Vallance & Holmden) to Minister for External Affairs, January 25 and 28, 1927, ANZ, IT1 3,7 EX1/23/8, part 3, R17961288.

9. The Citizens' Committee claimed the minister refused to see Meredith, but Nosworthy refuted that charge: Minister for External Affairs to Prime Minister Coates, February 24, 1927, ANZ, IT1 37, EX1/23/8, part 3, R17961288.

10. "Faipule for New Zealand," *Samoa Times*, January 14, 1927, 6.

11. "Fono of Faipules," *Samoa Times*, January 21, 1927, 6.

12. Nelson, *Truth about Samoa*, 17.

13. G. S. Richardson to J. D. Gray, January 26, 1927 (the year is wrongly dated 1926), ANZ, IT1 445, EX 79/78, part 2, R17962677.

14. See chapter 2, this volume.

15. G. S. Richardson to Minister for External Affairs, February 8, 1927, ANZ, IT1 37, EX1/23/8, part 3, R17961288.

16. G. S. Richardson to Minister for External Affairs, February 3, 1927, ANZ, IT1 37, EX1/23/8, part 3, R17961288.

17. The text of Richardson's address to the Sāmoan people is in Acheson Papers, box 11, item 5.2.1.3i. Newton Rowe notes the address was published in July 1927 issue of *Savali;* Rowe, *Samoa under the Sailing Gods*, 224.

18. G. S. Richardson to Minister for External Affairs, 3 February, 1927 ANZ, IT1 37, EX1/23/8, part 3, R17961288.

19. G. S. Richardson to Minister for External Affairs, February 8, 1927, ANZ, IT1 EX1/23/8, part 3, R17961288.

20. G. S. Richardson to J. D. Gray, August 24, 1927, ANZ, IT1 445, EX 79/78, part 2, R17962677.

21. G. S. Richardson to Minister for External Affairs, February 8, 1927, IT1 EX1/23/8, part 3, R17961288. See D. R. Hoggard evidence JSPIC, August 10, 1927, 27–30.

22. G. S. Richardson to J. D. Gray, March 22, 1927, ANZ, IT1 445, EX 79/78, part 2, R17962677.

23. See chapter 6, this volume, for the German dimension of Richardson's campaign.

24. "List of questions which the Permanent Mandates Commission desires should be dealt with in the annual reports of the mandatory powers submitted to Council of League by Östen Unden (Sweden), September 3, 1926," ANZ, IT1 267, EX 25/13, part 1, R17961847. See Pedersen, *Guardians*, 83–91.

25. Report by Östen Unden (Sweden), Work of the Permanent Mandates Commission during Its Ninth Session, September 2, 1926, ANZ, IT1 267, EX 25/13, part 1, R17961847.

26. Minister for External Affairs to G. S. Richardson, March 4, 1927, ANZ, IT1 37, EX1/23/8, part 4, R17961289.

27. Richardson reaffirmed the culpability of the committee with Griffin's death in his summation of native affairs (nine pages circa January 1928) in ANZ, IT1 38, EX 1/23/8, part 9, R17961294.

28. G. S. Richardson to Minister for External Affairs, enclosing remarks he intended to deliver to the legislative council on March 15, March 10, 1927, ANZ, IT1 37, EX1/23/8, part 4, R17961289.

29. Ibid.

30. G. S. Richardson to J. D. Gray, March 11, 1927, ANZ, IT1 445, EX 79/78, part 2, R17962677. In his letter Richardson typed "bombshe," surely a typographical error where the intent was "bombshell."

31. G. S. Richardson to J. D. Gray, March 11, 1927, ANZ, IT1 445, EX 79/78, part 2, R17962677.

32. O. F. Nelson to G. S. Richardson, enclosing objectives of the Samoa Welfare League, March 23, 1927, ANZ, IT1 37, EX 1/23/8, part 4, R17961289.

33. G. S. Richardson to Minister for External Affairs, March 23, 1927, ANZ, IT1 37, EX 1/23/8, part 4, R17961289.

34. One hundred and fifty Sāmoan chiefs and orators signed the document on March 11, 1927; see ANZ, IT1 37, EX 1/23/8, part 4, R17961289.

35. J. D. Gray to A. C. Day, March 30, 1927, ANZ, IT1 37, EX 1/23/8, part 4, R17961289.

36. "The Samoa Guardian," *Samoa Guardian,* May 26, 1927, 2.

37. See the annotated translation of the *Samoan Supplement, O Le Mau a Samoa,* of the *Samoa Guardian* in the Auckland Public Library (NZ11396/NZ072K).

38. The *Samoa Guardian*, later the *NZ Samoa Guardian,* was a weekly until the end of 1930; after that it appeared monthly, though there were irregularities. Davidson, *Samoa mo Samoa,* 437.

39. Richardson's summation of native affairs (nine pages circa January 1928) in ANZ, IT1 38, EX 1/23/8, part 9, R17961294.

40. Minister for External Affairs to Citizens' Committee, June 11, 1927 appended to *Samoa Royal Commission,* 32–43.

41. Minister for External Affairs to Citizens' Committee, June 12, 1927 appended to *Samoa Royal Commission,* 32–43.

42. G. S. Richardson to O. F. Nelson, June 24, 1927, tendered in evidence to JSPIC, 40.

43. William Nosworthy (Ashburton), *New Zealand Legislative Council and House of Representatives Parliamentary Debates* (hereafter NZPD), volume 212, July 22, 1927, 900.

44. Ibid., June 23–July 27, 1927.

45. Ibid., July 19, 1927, 669.

46. Prime Minister Gordon Coates, ibid., July 22, 1927, 831.

47. Harry Holland (Buller), ibid., 839.

48. William Lysnar Holland (Gisborne), Edwin Howard (South Christchurch), Peter Fraser (Wellington Central), and Māui Pōmare (Western Māori), ibid., 897, 676–677, 678, 686, 928.

49. Howard, ibid., 678.

50. Hazel Riseborough, "A New Kind of Resistance: Parihaka and the Struggle for Peace," in *Contested Ground: Te Whenua i Tohea: The Taranaki Wars, 1860–1881,* ed. Kelvin Day, 231 (Wellington: Huia, 2010).

51. With thanks to Rachel Buchanan for additional clarifications about this history.

52. For an account of the Parihaka invasion in 1881, see Hazel Riseborough, *Days of Darkness: Taranaki, 1878–1884* (Wellington: Allen and Unwin, 1989), chap. 6; James Cowan with Maui Pomare, *Legends of the Maori* (Wellington: H. H. Tombs, 1930), x; Cody, *Man of Two Worlds,* 19; James Belich, *I Shall Not Die: Titokowaru's War, New Zealand, 1868–9* (Wellington: Bridget Williams Books, 1989), 285. Dick Scott casts doubt on this story about Sir Māui's toe: see Scott, *Ask That Mountain,* 199; Rachel Buchanan, *The Parihaka Album: Lest We Forget* (Wellington: Huia Publishers, 2009), 145–151.

53. *Report of the Royal Commission to Inquire into Confiscations of Native Lands and Other Grievances Alleged by Natives* (Wellington: New Zealand Government Printer, 1928), *AtoJsOnline,* Te Puna Mātauranga o Aotearoa—National Library of New Zealand, http://atojs.natlib.govt.nz/cgi-bin/atojs?a=d&d=AJHR1928-I.2.2.6.13&e=———10—1———0 (accessed September 15, 2014).

54. M. Pōmare to O. F. Nelson, November 11, 1926, OFN 57–58; Rachel Buchanan, "Te Rā o Māui Pōmare 2013: A Slow Reading," http://rachelbuchanan100.com/2015/05/25/te-ra-o-maui-pomare-2013-a-slow-reading (accessed May 29, 2015).

55. For further discussion of connections between Parihaka and the Sāmoan Mau, see O'Brien, "Ta'isi O. F. Nelson and Sir Māui Pōmare."

56. O. F. Nelson to M. Pōmare, August 8, 1927, ANZ, AAAR W3558 1452, exhibit 66 R23545278.

57. Māui Pōmare (Western Maori), Joseph Coates, NZPD, volume 212, 928–931. Tui Atua Tupua Tamasese Ta'isi Efi (Head of State of Samoa), "Sir Māui Pōmare" (speech given on Pōmare Memorial Day, Waitara Mārae, Taranaki, June 29, 2013).

58. "Sensational Speech," *Auckland Star,* July 27, 1927, 11.

59. O. F. Nelson to M. Pōmare, August 8, 1927, ANZ, AAAR W3558 1452, exhibit 66 R23545278.

60. "Death of Sir Maui Pomare: A Tribute," *NZ Samoa Guardian,* July 3, 1930, 2.

61. Counsel for the petitioners, D. R. Hoggard, protested from the outset. See opening address to JSPIC, August 10 and 11, 1927, 27–36.

62. Ta'isi testified from Tuesday, August 16, to Friday, August 26, 1927, which included a full day of hearings on Saturday, August 20 (JSPIC, 42–161). An abridged version (to page 40) can be found in ANZ, AAEG 950/2/E 311/9/9, R17708883.

63. A. G. Smyth was on standby in Wellington to also deliver testimony, but was not called.

64. Ta'isi had wanted to engage Myers for his counsel. He recognized Myers as a rising star in the legal fraternity who would be appointed chief judge in New Zealand's high court in time to preside over Ta'isi's future high-stakes legal appeals. Their bitter clashes in 1927 likely compounded Myers' already adverse opinion of Ta'isi. O. F. Nelson to L. D. Stewart, July 27, 1927, Carruthers Papers, volume 17.

65. JSPIC, 42

66. Ibid., 34.

67. Ibid., 53. Part of this counternarrative involved recounting Ta'isi's offers of unlimited assistance during the influenza epidemic.

68. Ibid., 46. More details of Afamasaga's failed business venture can be found here.

69. Ibid., 47.

70. Ibid., 61.

71. Ibid., 37.

72. On October 11, 1927, Ta'isi elaborated on the copra industry in his evidence to the *Samoa Royal Commission,* 215–216.

73. JSPIC, 112.

74. Ibid., 94

75. Ta'isi explained that around 1924 the trading license was reduced to a minimum of seven pounds, ten shillings. During subsequent discussions in the legislative council about "unjust and unfair" taxation on those of "small means," Ta'isi agreed to raise the license fee to fifteen pounds again as a way of showing his good citizenship (see ibid., 76–77). The total revenue collected in 1926–1927 was £70,505, according to the *Seventh Report on the Mandated Territory of Western Samoa for the Year Ended 31st March 1927,* 21.

76. JSPIC, 132.
77. Ibid., 122.
78. Ibid., 77, 141.
79. Ibid., 119.
80. Ibid., 77
81. Ibid.
82. Ibid., 96
83. Ibid., 97, 98, 106.
84. Ibid., 146.
85. "Samoan Commission Order of Reference Questioned. Will Inquiry Proceed? Counsel's Strong Protest to Prime Minister," *Evening Post,* September 9, 1927, 10.
86. Harry Holland testimony, August 26, 1927, JSPIC, 146.
87. G. S. Richardson to J. D. Gray, August 24, 1927, ANZ, IT1 445, EX 79/78, part 2, R 17962677.
88. Minutes of Evidence in *Samoa Royal Commission*, 1.
89. *Report of Samoa Royal Commission,* i, ii.
90. For documentation of Richardson's intricate planning for the royal commission, see the restricted file in the ANZ, IT-A5, box 1, AO25/2 R15386146.
91. *Report of Samoa Royal Commission,* v.
92. Minutes of Evidence in *Samoa Royal Commission,* 214–237.
93. Ibid., 217–225.
94. Ibid., 15–27. Exhibits 1, 2,3, 5, and 50 relate to the copra question.
95. "Samoa Inquiry," *Evening Post,* December 10, 1927; "The Samoa Commission," *New Zealand Herald,* December 10, 1927.
96. *Report of the Samoa Royal Commission,* ix, x.
97. Ibid., xx.
98. Legislative Council Debates, January 1930, LONA, R2321 1928–1932, Series 701 to 709 dossiers 800.
99. G. S. Richardson to O. F. Nelson, December 14, 1927, ANZ, IT1 38, EX 1/23/8, part 8, R17961293.
100. O. F. Nelson to G. S. Richardson, December 16, 1927, ANZ, IT1 38, EX 1/23/8, part 8, R17961293.
101. G. S. Richardson to J. D. Gray, December 17, 1927, ANZ, IT1 38, EX 1/23/8, part 8, R17961293.
102. Deportation Orders, December 21, 1927, ANZ, IT1 38, EX 1/23/8, part 9, R17961294.

Chapter 8: Exile and the Road to Geneva

1. O. F. Nelson to G. S. Richardson, December, 1927, ANZ IT1 38 EX 1/23/8 part 8 R17961293.
2. Deportation orders on file at ANZ, IT1 38, EX 1/23/8, part 8, R17961293 and ANZ, IT1 38, EX 1/23/8, part 9, R17961294.

3. G. S. Richardson to O. F. Nelson, December 14, 1927, published in *Samoa Guardian,* 29 December 29, 1927.

4. G. S. Richardson, Draft Report on Native Affairs, January 11, 1928: "Rev. F. G. Lewis, an Australian who had served as a Chaplain with the A.I.F in Gallipoli and France and subsequently as a Missionary in Samoa and was for some years in charge of the Piula Methodist Native College," ANZ, IT1 38, EX 1/23/8, part 9, R17961294; see further O'Brien, "Bridging the Pacific."

5. Transcript of the meeting between O. F. Nelson and G. S. Richardson, December 23, 1928, ANZ, IT1 38, EX 1/23/8, part 9, R17961294. The *Samoa Guardian* also published the transcript: "Hon. O. F. Nelson M.L.C. before the Administrator," December 29, 1927, 2. Richardson also wrote to O. F. Nelson reviewing the meeting and what he agreed to; G. S. Richardson to O. F. Nelson, December 23, 1927, ANZ, IT1 38, EX 1/23/8, part 9, R17961294.

6. O. F. Nelson to F. G. Lewis, December 25, 1927 published in "Correspondence from Hon. O. F. Nelson to Rev. F. G. Lewis, Secretary of Natives Affairs," *Samoa Guardian,* January 5, 1928.

7. Ibid.

8. Ibid.

9. O. F. Nelson to F. G. Lewis, December 25, 1927, published in "Correspondence from Hon. O. F. Nelson to Rev F. G. Lewis, Secretary of Natives Affairs," *Samoa Guardian,* January 5, 1928.

10. "Racing," *New Zealand Herald,* January 27, 1928, 15.

11. O. F. Nelson to G. S. Richardson, January 5, 1928, ANZ, IT1 38, EX 1/23/8, part 9, R17961294. A. G. Smyth and E. W. Gurr submitted similar letters to Richardson on this date.

12. "Samoan Trouble," *Evening Post,* January 27, 1928, 8.

13. G. S. Richardson to W. Nosworthy, January 6, 1928, ANZ, IT1 38, EX 1/23/8, part 9, R17961294.

14. Many thanks to Siuga Paula Masoe for providing me with a detailed family tree for the Masoe family and explaining who lived at Tuaefu.

15. Memorandum by O. F. Nelson (Managing Director), January 12, 1928, OFN 23.

16. Ibid.

17. "Deportations," *Samoa Guardian,* January 12, 1928.

18. Ibid.

19. G. S. Richardson to W. Nosworthy, January 13, 1928, ANZ, IT1 38, EX 1/23/8, part 9, R17961294.

20. "Deportations," *Samoa Guardian,* January 12, 1928.

21. J. D. Gray to W. Nosworthy, January 14, 1928, ANZ, IT1 38, EX 1/23/8, part 9, R17961294. One of Richardson's spies, James Southon, who was an agricultural inspector, declared, "Mr Nelson addressed the assembled Samoans and during the course of the speech used the following words 'well you know I am

going away: All I ask you is to stick to the Mau, stick to it, stick to it.'" Southon added, "These remarks were made in the Samoan language and I understood fully what was said." Declaration of James Southon, January 13, 1928, ANZ, IT1 38, EX 1/23/8, part 9, R17961294.

22. Pro- and antigovernment press reported this speech. See "Stick to It: Nelson's Farewell Words," *Auckland Star,* January 16, 1928, 9.

23. "Departure of Hon O. F. Nelson M.L.C. and Mr A. G. Smyth," *Samoa Guardian,* January 19, 1928.

24. See "Deportation of Mr E. W. Gurr," *Samoa Guardian,* July 25, 1929, for details of Gurr's status in American Sāmoa, and New Zealand's role in him not being allowed to land.

25. "New Zealand Press Opinions on the Mau," *Samoa Times,* January 13, 1928, 5.

26. This assessment of the volume of stories is made from the resources of Papers Past, the digital source for New Zealand papers. Given that not all papers have been digitized or that the search for articles on "Samoa" may not have revealed all the articles, the number of articles on this subject was probably far higher than one hundred in the month of January 1928.

27. "Deportations without Trial," *Auckland Star,* January 7, 1928, 6.

28. "Position at Samoa," *Evening Post,* January 9, 1928, 10.

29. "Retiring to France," *Evening Post,* January 6, 1928, 8.

30. J. G. Coates' statement on deportations, January 23, 1928, ANZ, IT1 38, EX 1/23/8, part 9, R17961294.

31. Ibid.

32. "Explained too much," *Auckland Star,* January 24, 1928, 8.

33. "Unsettled Samoa," *Auckland Star,* January 26, 1928, 8.

34. "Business Not Sold," *Evening Post,* January 24, 1928, 10.

35. G. S. Richardson to External Affairs, January 16, 1928, ANZ, IT1 38, EX 1/23/8, part 9, R17961294.

36. G. S. Richardson to W. Nosworthy, January 23, 1928, ANZ, IT1 38, EX 1/23/8, part 9, R17961294. See also Braisby's letter to the secretary of the administration on Mau police uniforms and how Ta'isi was supposedly implicated, January 17, 1928, ANZ, IT1 38, EX 1/23/8, part 9, R17961294; J. Southon to G. S. Richardson, January 14, 1928, ANZ, IT1 38, EX 1/23/8, part 9, R17961294. Other reports and letters on file at ANZ, IT1 38, EX 1/23/8, part 9, R17961294 tell of the administration's fixation on the lava-lavas being worn and paid for by S. H. Meredith for the Mau.

37. "Mau Boycotts," *Auckland Star,* January 28, 1928, 9.

38. W. Nosworthy to G. S. Richardson, January 26, 1928, ANZ, IT1 38, EX 1/23/8, part 9, R17961294.

39. Arthur Fair to Secretary to the Department of External Affairs, January 28, 1928, ANZ, IT1 38, EX 1/23/8, part 9, R17961294.

40. "Samoan Trouble," *Evening Post,* January 27, 1928, 8.

41. J. Parr to J. G. Coates, January 27, 1928, ANZ IT1 38 EX 1/23/8 part 9 R17961294.

42. J. G. Coates to Secretary-General of the League of Nations, January 30, 1928, ANZ, IT1 38, EX 1/23/8, part 9, R17961294. See the list of intended recipients for the report in ANZ, IT-A5, box 1, R15386146.

43. J. Parr to J. G. Coates, December 22, 1927, ANZ, IT1 38, EX 1/23/8, part 8, R17961293.

44. "Mr Nelson's Case," *Evening Post,* February 4, 1928, 10.

45. O. F. Nelson to Q. Roberts, February 17, 1928, OFN 56.

46. See O'Brien, "Ta'isi O. F. Nelson and Sir Maui Pomare."

47. O. F. Nelson to R. W. Tate, March 16, 1928, OFN 52. Ta'isi told Tate of his happy recollection of their association, though they did not always see eye to eye. He also told Tate that Logan offered his support to Ta'isi. Tate did not respond to Ta'isi but wondered what Logan had said; R. W. Tate to J. D. Gray, March 29, 1928, Tate Papers, MS-Papers-0264–01, MS-Copy-Micro-0082–03, folder 4.

48. "R. L. S. and the Mau," *Samoa Guardian,* April 19, 1928. Ta'isi also raised Stevenson's case in the Joint Samoa Petition Inquiry Committee and in other places.

49. O. F. Nelson to C. Yore, March 8, 1932, OFN 72.

50. C. Yore to O. F. Nelson, February 1, 1932, OFN 72.

51. C. Yore to O. F. Nelson, no date, OFN 72.

52. Q. Roberts to O. F. Nelson, May 6, 1929, OFN 56.

53. G. S. Richardson to Minister for External Affairs, January 16, 1928, ANZ, IT1 38, EX 1/23/8, part 9, R17961294.

54. Ibid.

55. See David Chappell, "The Forgotten Mau: Anti-Navy Protest in American Samoa 1920–1935," *Pacific Historical Review* 69, no. 2 (2000): 217–260.

56. There is an abundance of correspondence between Ta'isi and War Resisters International dating from circa 1930; see OFN 50.

57. This petition is filed at LONA, box R2322, 1928–1932, series 709, dossiers 801 to 4,000, 6A/875/709.

58. O. F. Nelson to C. Yore, February 28, 1928, OFN 72. Davidson, *Samoa mo Samoa,* 133, cited *NZ Samoa Guardian,* June 27, 1929, but supposed this number of petitioners was exaggerated due to Sāmoan custom and as "a matai would consider himself justified in acting for the taulele'a of this family." Other minor *matai* holders would have to accept the more senior *matai*'s commitment, thus diminishing the power of the Mau. The often-quoted figure of 7982 signatories of this petition is inflated, but not for the reason Davidson postulated. Analysis of the 140 folios of this petition indicates the number of signatories to be more in the vicinity of 7,460 because of errors of calculation. The names, ranks, and locations of all signatories are given, showing how pervasive the movement

really was. Additional analysis of this petition is forthcoming. The original petitions are filed in LONA, Col 100, 6A/15281/224–6A/4398/709.

59. This wording comes from the petition's preface.

60. O. F. Nelson to C. Yore, February 28, 1928, OFN 72.

61. H. V. Evatt, *The British Dominions and Mandatories* (Melbourne: University of Melbourne Press, 1935).

62. J. Carruthers to L. D. Stewart, 1 February, 1928, Carruthers Papers, volume 17.

63. See O'Brien, "Bridging the Pacific"; C. Brunsdon Fletcher to J. Carruthers, August 1, 1927; J. Carruthers to C. Brunsdon Fletcher, February 24, 1928, and March 20, 1928; O. F. Nelson to L. D. Stewart, July 27, 1927. Carruthers Papers, volume 17.

64. "Tamasese Returns Home: Government Indulges in Petty Spite," *NZ Samoa Guardian,* June 20, 1929, 3.

65. Osorio, *Dismembering Lāhui,* 193–249.

66. O. F. Nelson to L. Thurston, April 17, 1928, OFN 52; O. F. Nelson to L. Thurston, April 29, 1931, OFN 52.

67. Ta'isi's papers contain numerous correspondence or documents relating to his travels across the United States and Europe in 1928. He stayed in luxury hotels all the way though in London he took a furnished apartment as he was there for such a long duration. Letters written by Ta'isi and Viopapa during their time in New York and when they first reached London, on notepaper supplied by the Biltmore Hotel, New York and the Mayfair Hotel, London, and intended for recipients in Sāmoa, were seized by New Zealand authorities and are now in Archives New Zealand in restricted file ANZ, IT-A3, box 6, R15386131.

68. G. S. Richardson to C. Berendsen, July 3, 1928, ANZ, AAEG W3240 950, box 28, 311/3/7, R17708950.

69. O. F. Nelson to C. Yore, February 28, 1928, OFN 72.

70. Boyd, "The Record in Western Samoa to 1945," 154.

71. *Maintenance of Authority in Native Affairs Ordinance,* February 21, 1928, OFN 74.

72. "New Zealand Press Blast," *Samoa Guardian,* April 12, 1928; "A Foul Canard, New Zealand Herald Hoax, Despicable Propaganda," *Samoa Guardian,* April 19, 1928; "Samoan Matters," *Evening Star,* June 20, 1928.

73. C. Fergusson to J. G. Coates, March 13, 1928, ANZ, AAEG W3240 950, box 29, part 6, R17708952. See O'Brien, "From Sudan to Sāmoa."

74. C. Berendsen to J. G. Coates, February 15, 1928, ANZ, AAEG W3240 950, box 28, part 5, R17708949; see also other documents in this file circa mid-February 1928.

75. J. G. Coates to C. Fergusson, March 21, 1928, ANZ, AAEG W3240 950, box 29, part 6 R17708952.

76. G. S. Richardson to C. Berendsen, July 3, 1928, ANZ, AAEG W3240 950, box 28, part 7, R17708950.

77. See OFN 30, which contains a lot of material relating to the 1928 legal actions.

78. T. Slipper, cablegram, May 20, 1928, OFN 74.

79. "Samoa and the League: Sir G. Richardson's Mission," *Auckland Star,* June 5, 1928.

80. Richardson's diary details his meetings and activities in May and June 1928, Acheson Papers, box 9, item 5.2.1.1a.

81. "Presented at Court—New Zealand Ladies," *New Zealand Herald,* June 14, 1928.

82. Ta'isi claimed to have bumped into Richardson at Versailles when both men were en route to Geneva. Though a deeply symbolic meeting, Ta'isi seems to have been taking poetic license about this meeting in a report to Sāmoa about his European travels. Richardson did pass through Paris but only for about six hours (from 4:00 p.m. to 10:00 p.m.) of sightseeing between transport connections, and he did not mention going to Versailles or seeing Ta'isi there. Report by O. F. Nelson, no. 19, December 7, 1928, ANZ, IT1 41, EX 1/23/8, part 20, R17961305; G. S. Richardson diary, June 13, 1928, Acheson Papers, box 9, item 5.2.1.1a.

83. G. S. Richardson to C. Berendsen, July 3, 1928, ANZ, AAEG W3240 950, box 28, part 7, R17708950. The press also reported on this detail: see "Samoan Troubles," *Daily News,* June 20, 1928.

84. G. S. Richardson diary, June 14, 1928, Acheson Papers, box 9, item 5.2.1.1a.

Chapter 9: "If There Is Any Justice at All"

1. Harold Grimshaw, the International Labour Organization (ILO) representative, was probably a person who met with Ta'isi privately. O. F. Nelson to J. Roberts, June 23, 1928, OFN 30.

2. O. F. Nelson to M. Pōmare, June 19, 1928, OFN 58; Patricia O'Brien, "Showdown in Geneva: Sāmoa, New Zealand and the League of Nations in 1928," forthcoming.

3. O. F. Nelson to Q. Roberts, June 15, 1928, OFN 56

4. O. F. Nelson to M. Pōmare, May 24, 1928, OFN 58.

5. League of Nations 41st Session of the Council, 3 September 1926, ANZ IT1 267 EX 25/13 R17961847.

6. See discussion about petitioners in chapter 7 of this volume.

7. G. S. Richardson to F. Bell, July 11, 1928, Bell Papers ATL MS 5210–068; G. S. Richardson to J. G. Coates, July 28, 1928, in ANZ, AAEG W3240 950, box 28, part 7, R17708950.

8. G. S. Richardson to C. Berendsen, July 3, 1928, ANZ, AAEG W3240 950, box 28, part 7, R17708950 [88/97]. *Journal de Genève* published four articles on Sāmoa around the time of the PMC hearings 1928 that furthered Ta'isi's position, www.letempsarchives.ch (accessed October 31, 2014).

9. Richardson's military reputation cited in *Proceedings of Fourteenth Meeting of the Permanent Mandates Commission June 1928,* 97, ANZ, IT 1, box 267, R1796184.

10. G. S. Richardson to C. Berendsen, July 3, 1928, ANZ, AAEG W3240 950, box 28, part 7, R17708950.

11. Pedersen, *Guardians,* chap. 6; Susan Pedersen, "Samoa on the World Stage: Petitions and Peoples before the Mandates Commission of the League of Nations," *Journal of Imperial and Commonwealth History* 40, no. 2 (2012): 231–261.

12. Richardson diary, June 14, 1928, Acheson Papers, box 9, item 5.2.1.1a. See by Gerald Chaudron, *New Zealand in the League of Nations:* chap. 12; "The League of Nations and Imperial Dissent: New Zealand and the British Labour Governments 1924–1931," *Journal of Imperial and Commonwealth History* 39, no. 1 (2011): 47–71 and "Obsession: New Zealand, Money and the League of Nations 1920–1935," *Journal of Imperial and Commonwealth History* 41, no. 1 (2013): 143–169.

13. H. Gilchrist, notes of meeting with Mr. Knowles of the New Zealand High Commission, London, March 16, 1928, LONA, R2322, series 709, dossiers 801 to 4,000, 6A/2872/709.

14. Richardson diary, June 14, 1928, Acheson Papers, box 9, item 5.2.1.1a.

15. Richardson diary, June 20, 1928, Acheson Papers, box 9, item 5.2.1.1a.

16. G. S. Richardson to F. Bell, July 11, 1928, Bell Papers ATL MS 5210–068.

17. Richardson's comments on petitions, June 15, 1928, LONA, box R2322, 1928–1932, series 709, dossiers 801 to 4,000, 6A/875/709.

18. *Transcript of the Thirteenth Meeting of the Permanent Mandates Commission,* June 20, 1928, 97, ANZ, IT1 series 1, box 267, R17961849.

19. G. S. Richardson to C. Berendsen, July 3, 1928, ANZ, AAEG W3240 950, box 28, part 7, R17708950.

20. Ibid.

21. Ibid.

22. Richardson diary, June 22, 1928, Acheson Papers, box 9, item 5.2.1.1a.

23. G. S. Richardson to J. G. Coates, July 28, 1928, ANZ, AAEG W3240 950, box 28, part 7, R17708950.

24. G. S. Richardson to C. Berendsen, July 3, 1928, ANZ, AAEG W3240 950, box 28, part 7, R17708950. Richardson diary, June 23, 1928, Acheson Papers, box 9, item 5.2.1.1a.

25. Richardson diary, June 23, 1928, Acheson Papers, box 9, item 5.2.1.1a.

26. Richardson diary, July 2, 1928, Acheson Papers, box 9, item 5.2.1.1a.

27. G. S. Richardson to J. G. Coates, July 28, 1928, in ANZ, AAEG W3240 950, box 28, part 7, R17708950.

28. J. Roberts to O. F. Nelson (at Regina Hotel, Munich) telegram, July 9, 1928, OFN 30.

29. J. Roberts to O. F. Nelson (at Hotel Baur au Lac, Zurich), July 9, 1928, OFN 30. Roberts told Ta'isi the court consisted of Lord Chancellor, Lord Hailsham, Lord Dunedin, Lord Sumner, Lord Darling, and Lord Atkin.

30. Memorandum for Secretary of Department of External Affairs, November 12, 1928, in ANZ, IT1 441, EX79/2/1, part 1, R17962644.

31. J. Parr to J. G. Coates, August 15, 1928, ANZ, IT1 441, EX79/2/1, part 1, R17962644.

32. Privy Council proceedings transcript, ANZ, IT1 441, EX79/2/1, part 1, R17962644.

33. J. Roberts to O. F. Nelson, July 9, 1928, OFN 30; J. Roberts to O. F. Nelson, July 20, 1928, OFN 30, enclosing note by Lionel Heald of July 20, 1928, explaining the Privy Council decision with the wording "the only legal remedy now remaining is that suggested both in Mr Cripp's opinion and by the Lord Chancellor . . . i.e. an action against the Administrator in the local Courts, probably commencing in Samoa and appealing thence to New Zealand, for a declaration that the order was invalid."

34. G. S. Richardson to F. Bell, July 11, 1928, Bell Papers ATL MS 5210–068.

35. J. Parr to J. G. Coates, August 10, 1928, ANZ, IT1 267, EX 25/14, R17961849.

36. J. Parr to Prime Minister's Department, cablegram, June 25, 1928, ANZ, G48 35 s/3 (1) R19162267.

37. J. Roberts to O. F. Nelson, June 29, 1928, OFN 30.

38. J. Roberts to V. Catastini, July 20, 1928, OFN 30.

39. "After the Bawl Is Over," *Samoa Times,* July 27, 1928, 4.

40. V. Catastini to J. Roberts, July 24, 1928, OFN 30.

41. There was one female commissioner from Norway, Valentine Dannevig, who served from 1928 to 1939.

42. "Affairs in Samoa," *New Zealand Herald,* August 4, 1928.

43. V. Catastini to J, Roberts, July 24, 1928, OFN 30.

44. Signed memorandum of agreement by Olaf Fredrick Nelson and Elizabeth Descours for a furnished flat at 20 Chalfont Court, Upper Baker Street, Marylebone, July 30, 1928, to September 24, 1928, OFN 30. The rent was "eight guineas per week" or "sixty-seven pounds four shillings for the whole period."

45. Account from Jacques and Co. to O.F. Nelson, July 25, 1928, OFN 30. Inflation calculator websites vary on the conversion rate of 1928 value to the contemporary value. The site http://safalra.com/other/historical-uk-inflation-price-conversion (accessed January 7, 2016) calculated the rounded figure of £719 in 1928 to be worth £40,264 in 2015. The site http://www.moneysorter.co.uk/calculator_inflation.html (accessed January 7, 2016) calculates £719 in 1928 to be worth £31,580 today. The site http://apps.nationalarchives.gov.uk/currency/default0.asp#mid (accessed January 7, 2016) calculates a value of £21,544.56 for £718 17s. 5d. for 1925. This site only allows a year selection

every five years. This site estimates the 1930 value of £718 17s. 5d. to be £24,024.66.

46. O. F. Nelson to J. Roberts, July 28, 1928, OFN 30.

47. Cripps' advice is outlined in the account from Jacques and Co. to O. F. Nelson, July 25, 1928, OFN 30.

48. O. F. Nelson to J. Roberts, July 28, 1928, OFN 30.

49. Richardson diary, July 26, 1928, Acheson Papers, box 9, item 5.2.1.1a.

50. G. S. Richardson to V. Catastini, July 27, 1928, LONA, box R2323, 1928–1932, Series 709, 6A/5037/709.

51. See the letters from N. E. Neter and Co. London to O. F. Nelson regarding copra prices from 1928–1932, OFN 34.

52. Messrs Otto Gierth and Co. Hamburg to R. T. Turnbull & Co. Ltd London (Ta'isi's London agents), September 22, 1928, OFN 60.

53. Receipts for tailoring and personal expenses from the 1928 European trip are in OFN 30, OFN 60, OFN 82, and OFN 91.

54. Secretary of House and Social Committee to O. F. Nelson, August 28, 1928, OFN 56.

55. "Nelson Blamed," *Auckland Star,* August 18, 1928; "Samoan Trouble, Dominion Exonerated: Mandate Commission, Mr Nelson Condemned," *Evening Post,* August 18, 1928.

56. O. F. Nelson to the Secretary General of the League of Nations, no date. Though this letter is undated, correspondence about it puts its date as October 2, 1928. Ta'isi also sent a copy to the New Zealand High Commission, who received it October 3 and then sent it on to Wellington, October 4, 1928, ANZ, IT1 441, EX79/2/1, part 1, R17962644.

57. The file OFN 30 contains a handwritten note on letterhead from Bryn-derwen, Llanrwst in North Wales expressing regret that Ta'isi had a "mishap" on the way back for staying with them and that they hoped he was now recovered. This is currently the location of a guesthouse and could be where Ta'isi and his party stayed en route.

58. "Eight Injured in Car Smash," *News* (Adelaide), September 4, 1928; "Mr Nelson Injured," *New Zealand Herald,* September 5, 1928; Report by Ta'isi, September 10, 1928, ANZ, IT1 41, EX 1/23/8, part 20, R17961305.

59. Several letters between O. F. Nelson and lawyer John Roberts in OFN 30 trace the aftermath of the car accident.

60. Ta'isi stayed in Monte Carlo October 13, 1928, at the Grand Hotel, receipts in OFN 60.

61. "Mr O. F. Nelson Arrival at Sydney," *Sydney Morning Herald,* November 23, 1928.

62. O.F. Nelson to R. T. Turnbull, December 12, 1928, OFN 60.

63. "Samoan Affairs: New Administrator," March 27, 1928 (clipping of newspaper article with no publication details recorded), ANZ, AAEG W3240 950, box 29, part 6, R17708952.

64. J. G. Coates to S. Allen, March 26, 1928, ANZ, AAEG W3240 950, box 29, part 6, R17708952.

65. S. Allen to J. G. Coates, June 28, 1928, ANZ, AAEG W3240 950, box 28, part 7, R17708950. For the official account of the "battle of Malautu," see S. Allen to J. G. Coates, May 29, 1928, ANZ, AAEG W3240 950, box 28, part 7, R17708950.

66. S. Allen to J. G. Coates, June 28, 1928, ANZ, AAEG W3240 950, box 28, R17708950.

67. "Mau Policy in Samoa: Passive Resistance," *Samoa Times,* August 17, 1928, 6. The tax collected 1926–1927 was £17,849 but only £2,460 was collected 1927–1928, the paper reported.

68. S. Allen to J. G. Coates, October 18, 1928, ANZ, AAEG W3240 950, box 33, R17708964.

69. Ibid.

70. Ibid.

71. Ibid. Allen mentions Williams, Westbrook, Meredith, Moors, Kruse, Baxter, and Slipper (and it seems he also wrote Gurr, though he was in exile at this time) as these European correspondents.

72. "The Cry of the Mau," *Samoa Times,* August 17, 1928, 5. For more on Thomas Henley, see O'Brien, "Bridging the Pacific."

73. S. Allen to Minister for External Affairs, October 30, 1928, ANZ, AAEG W3240 950, box 33, R17708964.

74. J. Parr telegram, November 1, 1928 copied to S. Allen and sent by J. G. Coates, November 8, 1928, ANZ, AAEG W3240 950, box 33, R17708964.

75. J. G. Coates to S. Allen, November 8, 1928, ANZ, AAEG W3240 950, box 33, R17708964.

76. S. Allen to External Affairs, November 14, 1928, ANZ, G48 35 s/3 (1), R19162267.

77. J. G. Coates to S. Allen, November 8, 1928, ANZ, AAEG W3240 950, box 33, R17708964; J. G. Coates to S. Allen, November 18, 1928, ANZ, G48 35 s/3 (1), R19162267.

78. S. Allen to J. G. Coates: this letter is dated November 12, 1928, though it was written over several days. The election was on November 14, and Allen refers to the results. The incident with Tupua Tamasese occurred on November 13, ANZ, AAEG W3240 950, box 33, R17708964;

79. S. Allen to External, November 17, 1928, ANZ, AAEG W3240 950, box 33, R17708964.

80. S. J. Smith to Minister for External Affairs, November 19, 1928, ANZ, AAEG W3240 950, box 33, R17708964.

81. J. G. Coates to S. Allen, November 19, 1928, ANZ, AAEG W3240 950, box 33, R17708964; S. Allen to J. G. Coates November 19, 1928, ANZ, AAEG W3240 950, box 33, R17708964.

82. S. Allen to External, November 27, 1928, ANZ, AAEG W3240 950, box 33, R17708964.

83. For events surrounding Tupua Tamasese's arrest, see Field, *Mau.*

84. S. Allen to Prime Minister's Department, December 5, 1928, ANZ, AAEG W3240 950, box 33, R17708964.

85. J. G. Coates to S. Allen, December 14, 1928, ANZ, AAEG W3240 950, box 33, R17708964.

86. S. Allen to J. Ward, December 11, 1928, ANZ, AAEG W3240 950, box 33, R17708964.

87. "Shipping," *New Zealand Herald,* December 27, 1928, 7.

88. "Samoan Affairs. Return of Mr Nelson," *New Zealand Herald,* December 18, 1928, 12; "Mr O. F. Nelson," *Evening Post,* December 17, 1928, 13.

89. "In Melting Pot," *Auckland Star,* December 17, 1928, 10.

90. "Mr Nelson's Silence," *Evening Post,* December 21, 1928, 8.

91. "Tamasese in Mt Eden," *Auckland Star,* December 27, 1928, 2.

92. O. F. Nelson to Minister for Justice and Prisons, December 28, 1928; Minister of Justice and Prisons to O. F. Nelson, December 28, 1928; O. F. Nelson to Minister for Justice and Prisons, December 29, 1928; Minister of Justice to O. F. Nelson, December 31, 1928: all in OFN 70.

Chapter 10: Slander, Abuse, and Calumny

1. Ian Fairbairn, "Samoan migration to New Zealand," *Journal of the Polynesian Society* u70, no. 1 (1961): 18–30. Fairbairn cites the 1921 New Zealand census, which estimated 164 Sāmoans lived in the country.

2. O. F. Nelson to A. Hall Skelton, April 7, 1930, OFN 64.

3. Ibid.

4. O. F. Nelson, *Samoa at Geneva: Misleading the League of Nations* (Auckland: National Printing Company, 1928); "New Zealand Notes," *Samoa Guardian,* February 14, 1929. For example, Ta'isi sent twenty-five copies to the US State Department, O. F. Nelson to Secretary of the State Department, Washington, DC, January 14, 1929, OFN 64.

5. S. Allen to External, telegram, January 9, 1929, ANZ, IT 441, EX79/2/1, part 1, R17962644.

6. "The Samoan Unrest, 'Mr Nelson's Silence,'" *Evening Post,* January 18, 1929, 6.

7. "Report on the Finances and Staff of the Samoan Administration," *Samoan Public Service and Finance Report* (hereafter *VPB* report), 50, ANZ, AAEG W3240 905, box 55, R17709025.

8. Ibid., 2.

9. Ibid., 31.

10. Ibid., 2. The report stated that the causes were derived from "the absence of any definite system of recruitment," the Sāmoan service had "for a long

period been cut off from contact with the New Zealand" service, and the men at the head of departments had "inadequate departmental training and experience." "The enervating effect of the Tropics also cannot be ignored. Too many officers have served in Samoa for too lengthy a period."

11. Ibid., 8, 14, 34.

12. Ibid., 10, 23.

13. Reference to "half-caste individuals" was made throughout the *VPB* report. General reference to their "inefficiencies" was made (ibid., 36).

14. Statement of Prime Minister Ward, February 11, 1929, ANZ, AAEG W3240 905, box 55, R17709025.

15. See "Samoan Finances: New Zealand's Burden," *Evening Post,* February 20, 1929; "Mandated Territory of Western Samoa (Extracts from Report on Finances and Staff) 1929," *AtoJsOnline,* Te Puna Mātauranga o Aotearoa—National Library of New Zealand, http://atojs.natlib.govt.nz/cgi-bin/atojs?a=d&d=AJHR1929-I.2.1.2.6&e=———-10—1———0—(accessed December 12, 2014).

16. "Drastic Action Necessary," *Auckland Star,* February 20, 1929.

17. "A Fresh Start," *Auckland Star,* January 26, 1929, 13.

18. "Mr Nelson's View," *Auckland Star,* January 26, 1929, 13.

19. "Reliability of General Richardson," *NZ Samoan Guardian,* June 27, 1929, 1.

20. "By the Way," *Samoa Guardian,* March 14, 1929 (annotated translation of the *Samoan Supplement,* Auckland Public Library), folio 903.

21. Q. Roberts to O. F. Nelson, February 27, 1929, OFN 56.

22. Q. Roberts to O. F. Nelson, April 24, 1929, OFN 56.

23. C. Berendsen to S. Allen, February 13, 1929, ANZ, AAEG W3240 905, box 55, R17709025.

24. "Samoan Policy," *Auckland Star,* February 1, 1929; the *Samoa Guardian* held out high hopes that Ward would cut through the impasse. The annotated transcription of the *Samoa Guardian* in the Auckland Public Library described these hopes as "overstated": "The Samoa Guardian," February 14, 1929, folio 882.

25. See O'Brien, "From Sudan to Samoa."

26. C. Fergusson to J. Ward, March 17, 1929, ANZ, G48 40 s/17 (1) R19162282.

27. Ibid.

28. A. Hall Skelton to G. Ward, March 9, 1929, ANZ, IT1 39, EX 1/23/8, part 13, R17961298.

29. S. Allen to the Minister for External Affairs, September 14, 1929, ANZ, AAEG W3240 905, box 55, R17709025.

30. "The Verschaffelt-Park-Berendsen Report," in *Supplement to the "NZ Samoa Guardian," NZ Samoa Guardian,* October 31, 1929.

31. Text of Ala Tamasese's address given in the Auckland Town Hall is filed

at ANZ, IT1 39, EX 1/23/8, part 13, R17961298. See Ta'isi's account of her "eloquent" speech, Report no. 25, March 20, 1929, ANZ, IT1 41, EX 1/23/8, part 20, R17961305.

32. "Tamasese's Arrest: Wife's Graphic Story," *Auckland Star,* January 21, 1929; "Tamasese's Wife Visits to Husband," *Auckland Star,* January 26, 1929.

33. O. F. Nelson to A. Hall Skelton, January 14, 1929, OFN 64; O. F. Nelson to A. Hall Skelton, January 16, 1929, OFN 64.

34. The full judgment is filed at ANZ, IT1 512, EX88/12, part 1, R17963052.

35. "Tamasese's Sentence," *New Zealand Herald,* February 22, 1929.

36. "Deadlock: Stale Mate in Samoa," *NZ Samoa Guardian,* September 4, 1929.

37. "Notes on Western Samoa for the use of the representative of New Zealand at the League of Nations and the Permanent Mandates Commission," 1929, 8–9, ANZ, G48 40 s/17 (1), R19162282. For discussion of the 1929 PMC meetings, see Pederson, *Guardians,* chap. 6.

38. S. Allen to External, May 18, 1929, ANZ, IT1 512, EX 88/12, part 1, R17963052.

39. C. Berendsen to J. Ward, May 22, 1929, ANZ, IT1 512, EX88/12, part 1, R17963052.

40. C. Berendsen to Secretary of Samoa Administration, May 16, 1929, ANZ, IT1 512, EX88/12, part 1, R17963052.

41. Ta'isi mentions Sir Maui's poor health and his having to cancel an appearance at a Town Hall meeting in March 1929 in, Report no. 25, 20 March 20, 1929, ANZ IT1 41 EX 1/23/8 part 20 R17961305.

42. "Impression of Tamasese," by Sir Maui Pomare, *NZ Samoa Guardian,* May 30, 1929, 5.

43. Reverend John Greenwood was a regular correspondent to the prime minister about the Sāmoan cause (see file series ANZ, IT1 36, EX1/23/8) and also a dedicated supporter or Ta'isi and other Sāmoans in Auckland. He appeared or was mentioned regularly in the *NZ Samoa Guardian.*

44. "Tamasese's Release," *Dominion,* June 5, 1929, ANZ, IT1 512, EX 88/12, part 1, R17963052.

45. *NZ Samoa Guardian,* May 1, 1930, 3.

46. *NZ Samoa Guardian,* August 1 and 8, 1929, covered Tupua Tamasese Lealofi's return to Sāmoa; A. Hall Skelton to J. Ward, July 10, 1929, ANZ, IT1 512, EX 88/12, part 1, R17963052; C. Berendsen to Assistant Crown Solicitor, May 22, 1929, and Notice of Petition to File, May 20, 1929, ANZ, IT1 512, EX 88/12, part 1, R17963052.

47. C. Berendsen to Secretary of the Samoan Administration, August 3, 1929, ANZ, IT1 512, EX 88/12, part 1, R17963052.

48. The Mau divided New Zealand and Australian Methodist Church clergy. In New Zealand Goldie, supported conciliation, while others, like Australian Reverend F. G. Lewis, appointed secretary of native affairs by Richardson, did not.

See chapter 8 of this volume. The cartoon with Reverend Goldie appeared in the *NZ Samoa Guardian,* July 11, 1929, 4.

49. "Samoan Affairs," June 19, 1929, *New Zealand Herald,* 10.

50. H. P. Richmond to C. Berendsen, October 11, 1929, ANZ, IT1 43, EX1/23/10, R17961311. This file is entitled "Agitation Slander Trial" and demonstrates the complicity of the government with the conservative press.

51. "Sir F. D. Bell's Modesty," *NZ Samoa Guardian,* October 17, 1929, 3; "The Silence of Sir Francis Dillon Bell," *NZ Samoa Guardian,* October 31, 1929.

52. O. F. Nelson to Citizens' Committee, Report 24, February 22, 1929, ANZ, IT 1 41, EX1/23/8, part 20, R17961305.

53. O. F. Nelson, Report 25, March 20, 1929, ANZ, IT1 41, EX 1/23/8, part 20, R17961305.

54. For the libel case preparation, he also asked Harry Holland for copies of the JSPIC report. O. F. Nelson to H. E. Holland, August 2, 1929, Pacific Manuscripts Bureau (hereafter PMB), 712. This report remained suppressed.

55. H. E. Holland to O. F. Nelson, August 28, 1929, PMB 712; H. E. Holland to J. Ward, August 15, 1929, ANZ, AAEG W3240 950, box 55, R17709025. Holland was handed the report on August 13 and returned it with a thank-you note to the prime minister August 15, 1929.

56. O. F. Nelson to W. Rappard, August 29, 1929, OFN 56.

57. Parr's notes were the fourteen-page "Notes on Western Samoa for the use of the representative of New Zealand at the League of Nations and the Permanent Mandates Commission." These briefing notes discuss events up mid-June 1929 and do not discuss any precise dates. ANZ, G48 40 s/17 (1), R19162282.

58. An abbreviated version (pages 1–3 and 8) of these briefing notes for Parr is at ANZ, AAEG W3240 950, box 65, part 9, R17709062, next to Parr's report from PMC meetings in November 1929. Page 8 of these notes contains the questions about use of force and bloodshed.

59. J. Parr to Prime Minister, cablegram, November 18, 1929, ANZ, AAEG W3240 950, box 65, part 9, R17709062.

60. See O'Brien, "From Sudan to Sāmoa"; chapter 9, this volume.

61. V. Catastini to O. F. Nelson, November 18, 1929, OFN 26.

62. Faumuina and Tuimalealiifano were photographed with Ta'isi in Auckland. The *NZ Samoa Guardian* ran the image on their front page, September 5, 1929.

63. O. F. Nelson to A. G. Smyth, November 18, 1929, OFN 61.

64. O. F. Nelson to A. Hall Skelton, December 27, 1929, OFN 64.

Chapter 11: Sāmoa's Gethsemane

1. As Sāmoa was on the eastern side of the dateline, events of December 28 occurred on December 29 New Zealand time. The most comprehensive accounts of the Black Saturday Massacre are by Michael Field. See Field, *Mau;* Michael

Field, *Black Saturday: New Zealand's Tragic Blunders in Samoa* (Auckland: Reed Publishing, 2006).

2. Luxford's inquiry was into the deaths of "William Abraham, High Chief Tamasese, Tapu, Faumuina of Safotu, Ainoa, Vele, Migao, Tuia and Leaota." Also see note 15 of this chapter. "Coroner's Findings in the Inquest Respecting the Fatalities in Western Samoa" (hereafter Coroner's Findings), *AtoJsOnline,* Te Puna Maasranga o Aotearoa—National Library of New Zealand, http://atojs.natlib.govt.nz/cgi-bin/atojs?a=d&d=AJHR1930-I.2.1.2.5&e=———-10—1———0— (accessed October 2, 2013), 1.

3. "Riot in Samoa," *New Zealand Herald,* December 30, 1930, 8; other papers' reports also followed the government's line as this was the sole communication from Apia. See "Mau Parade," *Auckland Star,* December 30, 1929, 7. See the Women's Mau petition to Prime Minister July 1930, ANZ, IT1 41, EX 1/23/8, part 19, R17961304. This petition outlines the Mau's sequence of events for December 28, 1929. The petition contends that the New Zealand police did not know until their firing had stopped that Constable Abrahams had been killed (15).

4. O. F. Nelson to A. Hall Skelton, December 30, 1929, OFN 64.

5. Ibid.

6. For a list of dates and occasions when members of the Mau as a body have marched into Apia, see ANZ, IT1 39, EX1/23/8, part 15, R17961300.

7. "Coroner's Findings," 15.

8. O. F. Nelson to A. Hall Skelton, December 30, 1929, OFN 64.

9. "The Clash in Samoa," *Evening Post,* December 30, 1929, 8.

10. O. F. Nelson to A. Hall Skelton, December 30, 1929, OFN 64.

11. See also O'Brien, "Ta'isi O. F. Nelson and Sir Māui Pōmare," 42; "What Is a Rebel," *NZ Samoa Guardian,* May 16, 1930; "Samoan and Maori: Te Whiti's fight in Taranaki," *NZ Samoa Guardian,* September 4, 1930; "Impression of Tamasese," by Sir Maui Pomare, *NZ Samoa Guardian,* May 30, 1929, 5.

12. M. Pōmare to O. F. Nelson, January 8, 1930, OFN 58. "Galumalemana" was the Sāmoan title bestowed by Ta'isi on Sir Māui as a term of endearment, which he used in their correspondence. See also O'Brien, "Ta'isi O. F. Nelson and Sir Māui Pōmare," 46.

13. O. F. Nelson to Lady Pōmare, January 15, 1930, and Lady Pōmare to O. F. Nelson, n.d., OFN 58.

14. "Martyred Mau Leader," *NZ Samoa Guardian,* January 9, 1930.

15. Mau figures put the dead at twelve, which accounts for nine who died of wounds inflicted from the December 28 massacre and others who died in the ensuing crackdown. See "More Poison Gas," *NZ Samoa Guardian,* March 27, 1930. The government monitored the condition of Molia, for example, whose health was very tenuous at the time the findings of the coronial inquest was due on January 24. Ta'isi used the phrase "has filled us all with horror" to describe the Sāmoan "atrocities"; see O. F. Nelson to M. B. Soljak, January 13, 1930, OFN 64.

16. C. Fergusson to F. Bell, December 13, 1927, BP 5210–067.

17. C. Fergusson to G. Forbes, January 30, 1930, ANZ, IT1 39, EX1/23/8, part 15, R17961300.

18. C. Fergusson, "Report for Quarter ending December, 31, 1929," January 28, 1930, NA, DO 35/331/8.

19. G. S. Richardson to J. Ward, January 12, 1930, ANZ, IT1 39, EX1/23/8, part 15, R17961300.

20. "Coroner's Findings," 16.

21. J. H. Luxford, *With the Machine Gunners in France and Palestine* (Auckland: Whitcombe and Tombs, 1923).

22. O. F. Nelson to A. Hall Skelton, January 6, 1930, OFN 64.

23. *The Samoa Seditious Organisations Regulations 1930 Order-in-Council,* January 11, 1930, ANZ, IT1 39, EX 1/23/8 15, R17961300.

24. A. Hall Skelton to O. F. Nelson, telegram, n.d., OFN 64. Faumuina of Safotu, Savai'i was killed as a result of firing on December 28, 1929.

25. "Witnesses Missing," *Evening Post,* February 5, 1930, 12.

26. "Samoan Libel Case," *New Zealand Herald,* March 15, 1930, 15.

27. "Samoan Atrocities," *NZ Samoa Guardian,* January 16, 1930, 1.

28. External Affairs to S. Allen, January 31, 1930, ANZ, IT1 39, EX1/23/8, part 15, R17961300.

29. "Black and Tan Terrorism," *NZ Samoa Guardian,* February 13, 1930, 1.

30. "Samoa's Gethsemane," *NZ Samoa Guardian,* February 29, 1930, 2.

31. "The Samoan Women: A Taste of British Justice," *NZ Samoa Guardian,* May 15, 1930; "War on Women and Children," *NZ Samoa Guardian,* May 22, 1930.

32. J. Carruthers to T. Slipper, April 9, 1929, Carruthers Papers, volume 17.

33. *Braisby v. Slipper,* compiled by Neroni Slade, *The Western Samoa Law Reports: Cases Determined by the High Court and the Supreme Court of New Zealand* (Apia: n.p., n.d.), 5.

34. *Braisby v. Slipper, the Western Samoa Law Reports,* 1–6.

35. "Mau Solicitor Gaoled," *NZ Samoa Guardian,* March 6, 1930, 4.

36. O. F. Nelson to P. Fitzherbert, November 27, 1930, OFN 5.

37. T. Slipper to Faumuina, May 18, 1931, OFN 63.

38. "O. F. Nelson Report No. 25," March 20, 1929, ANZ, IT1 41, I/23/8 20, R17961305.

39. O. F. Nelson to J. Carruthers, April 24, 1929, Carruthers Papers, volume 17.

40. J. G. Findlay to J. Ward, February 4, 1929, J. G. Findlay to J. Ward, February 5, 1929, ANZ, AAEG W3240 950, box 33, part 8, R17708964.

41. S. Allen to Minister for External Affairs, memorandum, October 13, 1930, ANZ, IT1 41, EX 1/23/8 19, R17961304.

42. "Personal History of O. F. Nelson written by A. L. Braisby at the Request of Sir James Parr," ANZ, IT1 44, EX1/23/20, R17961384. Braisby also claimed Priscilla was the "intimate friend" of US consul to Saigon Quincy Roberts, Ta'isi's friend and correspondent.

43. *Police v. Rosabel Nelson* and *Police v. Priscilla Muench, the Western Samoa Law Reports,* 11.

44. "Women's Processions," *Auckland Star,* May 14, 1930.

45. P. Fitzherbert to O. F. Nelson, May 27, 1930, OFN 5.

46. P. Fitzherbert to O. F. Nelson, May 15, 1930, OFN 5.

47. O. F. Nelson to P. Fitzherbert, May 29, 1930, OFN 5.

48. These letters are filed in ANZ, IT1 41, EX1/23/8, part 19, R17961304. The reports taken from Rosabel's chicken coop are most likely those filed in ANZ, IT1 41, EX1/23/8, part 20, R17961305.

49. P. Fitzherbert to O. F. Nelson, May 27, 1930, OFN 5; O. F. Nelson to P. Fitzherbert, June 11, 1930, OFN 5.

50. For further information about Malienafau (Olive's) academic achievements, see https://cdn.auckland.ac.nz/assets/fmhs/soph/pacifichealth/docs/talaga 01092009.pdf (accessed June 19, 2014). In 1931 she won the Butterworth Prize for the student with highest mark in jurisprudence; see also https://www .lawsociety.org.nz/news-and-communications/people-in-the-law/women-legal -pioneers (accessed September 29, 2015).

51. See correspondence relating to the girls' schooling in OFN 4, 46, and 47.

52. O. F. Nelson to H. W. Moors, March 12, 1931, OFN 19.

53. *Mandated Territory of Western Samoa Tenth Report of the Government of New Zealand on the Administration for the Year Ended the 31st March 1930* (Wellington: Government Printer, 1930) http://atojs.natlib.govt.nz. Accessed April 25, 2013, 5; Faamu Faumuina, Paisami Tuimalealiifano, and Ala Tamasese to the Administrator of Western Samoa, September 10, 1930, ANZ, IT1 41, EX1/23/8, part 19, R17961304.

54. See O'Brien, *Pacific Muse;* Patricia O'Brien, "Gender," in *Pacific Histories: Peoples, Oceans, Lands,* ed. David Armitage and Alison Bashford, 282–304 (Basingstoke: Palgrave Macmillan, 2014).

55. *Mandated Territory of Western Samoa Tenth Report,* 5.

56. Women's Mau to S. Allen, September 10, 1930, ANZ, IT A5, box 1, 25/1/1, R15386147.

57. S. Allen to Minister for External Affairs, September 12, 1930, ANZ, IT A5, box 1, 25/1/1, R15386147.

58. O. F. Nelson, Petition to the Parliament of New Zealand, August 25, 1930, ANZ, IT1 41 EX 1/23/8 19, R17961304. See also the dedicated file on this petition, ANZ, IT1 61, EX1/47, R17961455.

59. S. Allen to Minister, February 2, 1931, ANZ, IT1 41, EX 1/23/8 20, R17961305.

60. O. F. Nelson to Thomas Slipper, August 25, 1930, OFN 63.

61. After his brother was killed, Mea'ole assumed the Tupua title and a prominent role in the Mau, though Faumuina and Tuimaleiliifano were now the movement's official leaders. After 1936 Tupua Tamasese Mea'ole assumed the role of Mau president.

62. S. Allen to Minister, May 19, 1930, ANZ, IT 1 446, EX79/109, R17962696.

63. O. F. Nelson to Rosabel Nelson, May 27, 1930, PMB 712.

64. O. F. Nelson to Thomas Slipper, August 25, 1930, OFN 63. Includes extract from the letter Ta'isi wrote to Rosabel.

65. H. W. Moors to O. F. Nelson, May 2, 1931, OFN 19.

66. O. F. Nelson to P. Fitzherbert, June 11, 1930, OFN 5.

67. P. Fitzherbert to O. F. Nelson, May 15, 1930, OFN 5.

68. S. Allen to Minister, June 10, 1930, ANZ, IT 1 446 EX79/109, R17962696.

69. P. Fitzherbert to O. F. Nelson, May 27, 1930, OFN 5.

70. S. Allen to External, telegram, June 12, 1930, ANZ, IT 1 446, EX79/109, R17962696. S. Allen to External, July 17, 1930, ANZ, IT1 41, EX 1/23/8 19, R17961304.

71. "Coming By-Election," *Evening Post,* March 22, 1930, 10.

72. "Parnell Seat," *Auckland Star,* March 22, 1930, 12.

73. "Labour Candidate," *New Zealand Herald,* April 17, 1930, 12.

74. "Parnell By-Election," *New Zealand Herald,* April 17, 1930, 12.

75. O. F. Nelson to A. Hall Skelton, April 7, 1930, OFN 64.

76. "O. F. Nelson Sued," *Auckland Star,* May 1, 1930, 8; "In Defence," *Auckland Star,* May 2, 1930.

77. "In Defence," *Auckland Star,* May 2, 1930, 9.

78. "Damage Denied," *Auckland Star,* May 6, 1930, 10.

79. "O. F. Nelson Sued," *Auckland Star,* May 1, 1930, 8.

80. "Tenant to Pay," *Auckland Star,* June 26, 1930, 8.

81. M. Pōmare to O. F. Nelson, May 23, 1930, OFN 58. Many thanks to Malcolm McKinnon for the insights into the political ramifications Sir Māui referred to (e-mail to the author, September 19, 2012).

82. H. Holland, July 1, 1930, *NZPD,* volume 224, 90.

83. English translation of the Samoan language supplement, *NZ Samoa Guardian,* July 3, 1930, 5, ANZ, IT 1 284, EX 37/12; Cowan and Pomare, *Legends of the Maori,* 276.

84. English translations of *NZ Samoa Guardian,* September 4, 1930, and *NZ Samoa Guardian,* August 28, 1930, 5, ANZ, IT1 284, EX 37/12, R17961901.

85. S. Allen to Minister for External Affairs, memorandum, October 13, 1930, and Acting Prime Minister to Prime Minister Forbes in London, October 28, 1930, ANZ, IT1 41, EX 1/23/8 19, R17961304.

86. S. Allen to Minister for External Affairs, memorandum, October 13, 1930, ANZ, IT1 41, EX 1/23/8 19, R17961304.

87. O. F. Nelson to F. Wilson, August 6, 1930, ANZ, IT1 41, EX 1/23/8 19, R17961304.

88. S. Allen to Minister for External Affairs, October 18, 1930, ANZ, IT1 41, EX 1/23/8 19, R17961304.

89. I. Field to O. F. Nelson, July 3, 1930, OFN 5.

Chapter 12: Breaking Mr. Nelson in the Great Depression

1. O. F. Nelson to G. Forbes, May 13, 1931, ANZ, IT1 41, EX1/23/8, part 20, R17961305. Ta'isi also gave a similar explanation to J. Carruthers in O. F. Nelson to J. Carruthers, May 3, 1931, Carruthers Papers, volume 18.

2. This is according to the Judgment of Court of Appeal in *O.F. Nelson and Co. Ltd v. Police*, December 16, 1931, 337. In other files, twenty-seven transactions were recorded worth £238. See documents in ANZ, IT1 43, EX1/23/18, part 1, R17961381.

3. In his covering letter to the minister for external affairs, enclosing a cache of letters sent by Ta'isi "by the last Tofua," Administrator Allen described Ale Malu as "a taxi owner in Apia, married to a half-caste, of no standing but a very strong Mau adherent." He described the widowed Ala Tamasese as "widow of late Tamasese. A smug little Tokelau islander, well in the hands of the half-caste women." Other recipients—Faumuina, Mata'utia Karauna, Moananu, Poulava, Tunufai, Mele, Une, Tamasese, and Atoa—were also described with varying degrees of derogatory remarks. Allen to Minister, August 2, 1930, ANZ, IT1 41, EX1/23/8, part 19 R17961304.

4. O. F. Nelson to R. Nelson, May 27, 1930, PMB 712.

5. Ta'isi to A. Malu, July 11, 1930, ANZ, IT1 41, EX1/23/8, part 19, R17961304.

6. Ta'isi to A. Tamasese, July 9, 1930, ANZ, IT1 41, EX1/23/8, part 19, R17961304.

7. R. Nelson to O. F. Nelson, May 27, 1930, PMB 712.

8. O. F. Nelson to R. Nelson, May 27, 1930, PMB 712.

9. Ibid.

10. When Lucy was in London with Ta'isi in 1928, she racked up considerable bills for shoes and clothes, which her indulgent father settled. These receipts are in OFN 44.

11. "Adored" has been the word repeatedly used by all of Ta'isi's grandchildren to describe how their mothers felt about this father.

12. O. F. Nelson to R. Nelson, May 27, 1930, PMB 712.

13. O. F. Nelson to C. A. B. Joske, July 10, 1930, OFN 18.

14. O. F. Nelson to H. W. Moors, September 10, 1930, OFN 19.

15. O. F. Nelson to L. D. Stewart, July 14, 1931, OFN 62.

16. R. Bartlett to G. Forbes, August 8, 1931, ANZ, IT1 41, EX1/23/8 20, R17961305.

17. S. Allen to Minister for External Affairs, August 26, 1930, ANZ, IT1 41, EX1/23/8, part 19, R17961304.

18. The appeal signed by seventy-nine prominent New Zealanders was published in the *NZ Samoa Guardian* on October 9, 1930.

19. "Samoa Again," *Evening Post,* October 8, 1930, 10.

20. O. F. Nelson, *What Samoans Want,* October 23, 1930, ANZ, IT1 41, EX1/23/8, part 19, R17961304.

21. "Self Rule for Samoa: Unanimous Recommendations by US Congress Commission," November 6, 1930, ANZ, IT1 41, EX1/23/8, part 19, R17961304. This assessment was first published in the *NZ Samoa Guardian* and then reprinted as a pamphlet.

22. See ibid.

23. These photographs both appeared in *NZ Samoa Guardian,* September 25, 1930. See also "East and West in Samoa: Where America Differs from New Zealand," *NZ Samoa Guardian,* July 9, 1931, 6.

24. "America Frees Samoans," *NZ Samoa Guardian,* March 5, 1931, 5.

25. O. F. Nelson to D. B. Crane, March 12, 1931, OFN 71; D. B. Crane to O. F. Nelson, March 16, 1931, OFN 71; D. B. Crane to O. F. Nelson, April 14, 1931, OFN 71.

26. "American Samoa," *Evening Post,* October 16, 1930, 15; "Eastern Samoa," *Auckland Star,* October 20, 1930, 8; "American Samoa," *New Zealand Herald,* November 24, 1930, 3; "American Samoa," *Evening Post,* December 4, 1930, 8.

27. O. F. Nelson to E. A. Ransom, November 5, 1930, 12, ANZ, IT1 41, EX1/23/8, part 19, R17961304.

28. Ibid., 2.

29. O. F. Nelson to E. A. Ransom, December 2, 1930, OFN 40.

30. He expressed these views in letters with C. A. B. Joske, a leading trader in Suva (see OFN 18).

31. G. Westbrook to O. F. Nelson, December 29, 1930, Westbrook Papers, ATL MS 0061–13.

32. Allen probably heard this report from A. M. McCarthy. Westbrook told Ta'isi that "Mr McCarthy sometime acting as chief judge during the judge's absence or awaiting a new appointment to that position, Crown Solicitor, Crown Prosecutor, Official member of the Legislative Council and now Acting Chief of Police in the absence of Inspector Braisby now away on furlough"; George Westbrook to O. F. Nelson, December 29, 1930, Westbrook Papers, ATL MS 0061–13.

33. S. Allen to External Affairs, December 29, 1929, ANZ, IT1 41, EX1/23/8, part 19 R17961304.

34. G. Westbrook to O. F. Nelson, December 29, 1930, Westbrook Papers, ATL MS 0061–13.

35. O. F. Nelson to D. B. Crane, February 16, 1931, OFN 71.

36. "Mau Agitation: Prosecution at Apia," *Auckland Star,* January 23, 1931, 9. These documents may be those in restricted file ANZ, IT1, A3 box 6, R15386131. There is an ironically titled "the Empire exercise book" with names and notes and a receipt book with "lafoga o le Mau" [due to the Mau] printed on the dockets along with names, dates and amounts paid. The receipts are all dated 1929.

37. See the transcript of evidence at ANZ, IT1 43, EX1/23/18, part 1, R17961381.

38. O. F. Nelson to D. B. Crane, May 4, 1931, OFN 71.

39. O. F. Nelson to D. B. Crane, February 16, 1931, OFN 71.

40. S. S. Allen to External, January 29, 1931, ANZ, IT1 43, EX1/23/18, part 1, R17961381.

41. S. Allen to Minister for External Affairs, January 31, 1931, ANZ, IT1 43, EX1/23/18, part 1, R17961381.

42. G. Forbes (as Minister for External Affairs) to S. Allen, January 30, 1931, ANZ, IT1 4,3 EX1/23/1,8 part 1, R17961381.

43. See V. H. S. Meredith to Secretary of Department of External Affairs, March 30, 1931, regarding Ta'isi giving evidence in ANZ, IT1 43, EX1/23/18, part 1, R17961381. Telegram from External to Admor, Apia, March 20, 1931 ANZ, IT-A5 AO 25/12, R15386141.

44. Judgment by Luxford CJ in *Police v. O. F. Nelson and Co. Ltd,* April 21, 1931, *Western Samoa Law Reports,* 20–22. The minister wanted to think about the implications of canceling the license before taking action. External to Allen, April 22, 1931, ANZ, IT1 43, EX1/23/18, part 1, R17961381.

45. H. W. Moors to O. F. Nelson, May 2, 1931, OFN 19.

46. O. F. Nelson to G. Forbes, May 13, 1931, ANZ, IT1 41, EX1/23/8, part 20, R17961305.

47. Tuimalealiifano, Tupua Tamasese, Alipia, Pulepule to H. E. Hart, May 1, 1931, filed at ANZ, IT1 41, EX1/23/8, part 20, R17961305.

48. O. F. Nelson to G. Forbes, May 13, 1931, ANZ, IT1 41, EX1/23/8, part 20, R17961305.

49. O. F. Nelson to D. B. Crane, May 4, 1931, OFN 71.

50. H. H. Daniel to C. Berendsen, August 4, 1931, ANZ, IT1 41, EX1/23/8, part 20, R17961305.

51. J. A. B. Crawford, "Hart, Herbert Ernest," in *Dictionary of New Zealand Biography. Te Ara—the Encyclopedia of New Zealand,* http://www.TeAra.govt.nz/en/biographies/3h9/hart-herbert-ernest (accessed February 9, 2015).

52. O. F. Nelson to D. B. Crane, May 4, 1931, OFN 71.

53. O. F. Nelson to G. Forbes, May 13, 1931, ANZ, IT1 41, EX1/23/8, part 20, R17961305. There is no documentation of the meeting Ta'isi had with Hart in Auckland 1931.

54. O. F. Nelson to L. D. Stewart, July 14, 1931, OFN 62.

55. O. F. Nelson to D. Stewart (Suva), August 4, 1932, OFN 64.

56. O. F. Nelson to L. D Stewart, July 14, 1931, OFN 62.

57. A. G. Smyth to O. F. Nelson, May 28, 1931, OFN 61.

58. Ibid.

59. H. Buckleton to O. F. Nelson, September 7, 1931, OFN 23.

60. Memo for Crown Solicitor, October 8, 1931 in ANZ, IT1 43, EX1/23/18, part 1, R17961381.

61. O. F. Nelson to Messrs. Island Tifaga Ltd., December 16, 1929, OFN 24; C. S. James of Metro-Goldwyn-Mayer Wellington to C. C. Dean, Tifaga Playhouse, October 7, 1932, OFN 24, notifying him that MGM will supply Apia with only silent films.

62. O. F. Nelson to R. Kruse, April 23, 1932, OFN 79.

63. When she died Nimo Moors owed more than £700 that was to be repaid from her estate; see C. V. Allom to O. F. Nelson, December 2, 1931, OFN 7. Regarding the Wetzells, see H. W. Moors to O. F. Nelson, February 10, 1933, OFN 7; H. W. Moors to O. F. Nelson, June 27, 1932, OFN 7.

64. Ledgers of creditors for December 31, 1932, January 28, 1933, and February 25, 1933, are filed at OFN 23.

65. H. W. Moors to O. F. Nelson, June 30, 1932, OFN 7.

66. "A Letter from Ta'isi," October 2, 1931, ANZ, IT1 41, EX1/23/8, part 20, R17961305.

67. Letter from six chiefs to H. E. Hart, August 31, 1932, ANZ, IT1 EX1/23/8, part 21, R17961306.

68. O. F. Nelson to Vito Catastini, May 26, 1931, OFN 26.

69. "A Letter from Ta'isi," October 2, 1931, ANZ IT1 41 EX1/23/8 part 20 R17961305.

70. O. F. Nelson to E. J. Grey, October 29, 1931, OFN 13, in which Ta'isi mentions copies of the petition were sent to President Hoover, members of US Congress, and British MPs, and that the petition was "well ventilated" at the twentieth session of the Mandates Commission. Ta'isi was also in contact with former German governor Erich Schultz regarding this petition. O. F. Nelson to E. Schultz-Ewerth, April 9, 1932, OFN 64.

71. Quoted in Judgment by Luxford CJ in *Police v. O. F. Nelson and Co. Ltd,* April 21, 1931, *Western Samoa Law Reports,* 20.

72. A copy of the decision is filed at ANZ, IT1 43, EX1/23/18, part 1, R17961381.

73. "A Letter from Ta'isi," December 22, 1931, ANZ, IT1 41, EX1/23/8, part 20, R17961305. A copy of the majority judgment is filed at ANZ, IT1 43, EX1/23/18, part 1, R17961381.

74. "A Letter from Ta'isi," April 21, 1932, ANZ, IT1 41, EX1/23/8, part 20, R17961305.

75. Hart began this conversation about the return of Ta'isi and Gurr when he commenced his tenure as administrator. H. E. Hart, telegram, June 11, 1931, ANZ, IT 1 41, EX1/23/8, part 20, R17961305.

76. F. D. Baxter to G. Forbes, March 14, 1932, ANZ, IT 1 41, EX1/23/8, part 20, R17961305.

77. G. Forbes to F. D. Baxter, April 14, 1932, ANZ, IT 1 41, EX1/23/8, part 21, R17961306.

78. G. Forbes to H. E. Hart, April 14, 1932, ANZ, IT 1 41, EX1/23/8, part 21, R17961306.

79. "Translation of a letter read by Ala Tamasese at a big meeting of the Mau . . . 15 April 1932," ANZ, IT 1 41, EX1/23/8, part 21, R17961306.

80. H. E. Hart to G. Forbes, May 3, 1932, ANZ, IT 1 41, EX1/23/8, part 21, R17961306.

81. G. Forbes to H. E. Hart, June 28, 1932, ANZ, IT 1 41, EX1/23/8, part 21, R17961306.

82. Faumuina Fiame, Tuimalealiifano, Alipia, Tagaloa, K. Matautia, J. Tamasese to H. E. Hart, August 31, 1932, ANZ, IT 1 41, EX1/23/8, part 21, R17961306.

83. O. F. Nelson to Principal of Sacred Heart College Ponsonby, June 2, 1932, OFN 64.

84. O. F. Nelson to R. Kruse, November 19, 1931, OFN 79.

85. O. F. Nelson to Principal of Sacred Heart Ponsonby, February 8, 1933, OFN 64; O. F. Nelson to Principal of Sacred Heart Ponsonby, October 11, 1932, OFN 64; O. F. Nelson to Principal of Sacred Heart Ponsonby, May 23, 1932, OFN 64.

86. Manager O. F. Nelson and Co. to Principal of Sacred Heart Ponsonby, June 10, 1932, OFN 64.

87. O. F. Nelson to R. Kruse, October 29, 1931, OFN 79; O. F. Nelson to R. Kruse, telegram, February 1, 1933, OFN 79: "Inform Mrs Nelson that if she is not able to control Miss Joyce Nelson she should send [her] back to me immediately."

88. F. E. Syddall to O. F. Nelson June 30, 1930; O. F. Nelson to F. E Syddall, July 15, 1930, and August 6, 1930, OFN 64.

89. R. Kruse to O. F. Nelson, March 5, 1932, OFN 79; O. F. Nelson to Brother Benignus, September 12, 1931, OFN 31.

90. Telegram to O. F. Nelson, March 12, 1932, OFN 35.

91. O. F. Nelson to F. Meredith Nelson, February 23, 1932, OFN 35; O. F. Nelson to F. C. F. Meredith, February 10, 1932, OFN 35.

92. O. F. Nelson to Dr. G. Allen, January 5, 1933, OFN 84.

93. O. F. Nelson to L. (Viopapa) Nelson, December 14, 1932, OFN 35.

94. O. F. Nelson to Dr. G. Allen, January 5, 1933, OFN 84.

95. I. (Noue) Nelson to O. F. Nelson, January 24, 1933, OFN 35.

96. O. F. Nelson to C. Ross, January 12, 1933, OFN 56; O. F. Nelson to C. Ross, January 20, 1933, OFN 56; O. F. Nelson telegram to C. Ross, January 25, 1933, OFN 56; C. Ross to O. F. Nelson, January 27, 1933, OFN 56; O. F. Nelson to C. Ross, February 2, 1933, OFN 56.

97. Piliopo Maiai, interview with the author, July 16, 2014.

98. O. F. Nelson to C. Crowther, May 3, 1932; C. Crowther to O. F. Nelson, May 4, 1932, OFN 46; T. Henley to J. Carruthers, February 25, 1929, Carruthers Papers, volume 17.

99. O'Brien, "Bridging the Pacific."

100. Ta'isi to G. Forbes, November, 1932, republished in *NZ Samoa Guardian,* December 22, 1932, 3.

101. "Return of Samoan Deportees, Mr Nelson meets Mr Forbes," *NZ Samoa Guardian,* December 22, 1932, 2–3.

102. Partial transcript of November 23, 1932, meeting with Prime Minister Forbes and O. F. Nelson in "proceedings against Mr Nelson" in ANZ, IT1 44, EX1/23/20, part 2, R17961384.

103. O. F. Nelson to D. B. Crane, March 14, 1933, OFN 71.

104. Telegram to O. F. Nelson, February 23, 1933, OFN 7.

Chapter 13: Return to Sāmoa, Trial, and Exile

1. O. F. Nelson to Apia Head Office, May 3, 1933, OFN 10.

2. New Zealand commentary on an article, "German View of Situation in Samoa," published in *Deutsche Kalonial Zeitung,* says, "It is quite true that the Mau, comprising over 90 per cent of the Samoans, did not attend any of the functions prepared by the Administration in honour of the vice-regal visit. Nelson was in Auckland . . . and advised the Mau not to make hostile demonstrations" (ANZ, IT1 45, EX 1/23/20, R17961320). Conservative newspaper accounts described the reception as "inspiring." See "Welcome at Apia," *New Zealand Herald,* April 21, 1933, 10; "A Loyal Welcome," *Evening Post,* April 21, 1933, 8.

3. "Relations with Samoa," *New Zealand Herald,* April 28, 1933, 11.

4. "Going home," *NZ Samoa Guardian,* May 11, 1933, 1. This photograph was accompanied by an inflammatory article by Percy Andrews, "Here and There: Exiles Return Home," that compared the lot of Sāmoans with Māori and Hawaiians.

5. O. F. Nelson to General Manager Head Office, April 10, 1933, OFN 40.

6. O. F. Nelson to unknown, March 17, 1933, OFN 10.

7. O. F. Nelson to General Manager Apia, April 10, 1933, OFN 40.

8. Klinkmueller and Kronfeld Lawyers to C. V. Allom, February 21, 1933, OFN 24.

9. O. F. Nelson to General Manager Head Office, April 10, 1933, OFN 40.

10. " 'Stormy Meeting," *New Zealand Herald,* March 31, 1933, 10; "Chairman Deposed," *Auckland Star,* March, 1933, 3.

11. "Gen. Richardson Ousted," *NZ Samoa Guardian,* April 13, 1933, 1.

12. P. Andrews to O. F. Nelson, in extracted letter, n.d., filed in ANZ, IT1 45, EX 1/23/20, R17961320. See also "Divorce Suit," *Auckland Star,* August 16, 1933, 5.

13. "Tofa Ta'isi: Farewell Function at Auckland," *NZ Samoa Guardian,* May 11, 1933, 3.

14. The government claimed "1,528" women participated. Other numbers concur with the *NZ Samoa Guardian* view that thousands of Sāmoans turned out to see Ta'isi. See page 2 of secret report of Ta'isi movements from May 1933 in ANZ, IT1 44, EX 1/23/20, R17961383.

15. "An Exile's Homecoming," *NZ Samoa Guardian,* June 8, 1933, 3; "Feasting at Vaimoso: Great Receptions to Taisi," *NZ Samoa Guardian,* October 20, 1933, 3.

16. G. Forbes to H. E. Hart, October 9, 1933, 2, ANZ, IT 1 44, EX 1/23/20, R17961383.

17. This secret dossier is filed at ANZ, IT 1 44, EX 1/23/20, R17961383.

18. Prime Minister Forbes wondered whether this seeming bestowal of a title on Ta'isi could be another cause for proceeding against him, this time under the *Samoa Native Titles Protection Order* 1928; Dossier ANZ, IT 1 44, EX 1/23/20, R17961383, 13. See also G. Forbes to H. E. Hart, October 9, 1933, ANZ, IT 1 44, EX 1/23/20, R17961383.

19. A *ta'alolo* is an elaborate, formal presentation of gifts in support of an occasion and/or presentation of a VIP. The *ta'alolo* is composed of singers, dancers, and bearers of gifts. Those leading the *ta'alolo* are normally a *taupou* and/or *manaia,* who are both dressed in full traditional regalia. With thanks to Mea'ole Keil (e-mail to author, February 16, 2015).

20. *NZ Samoa Guardian*, October 20, 1993.

21. See correspondence around November 1933 about using evidence from spies in court in ANZ, IT 1 44, EX 1/23/20, part 1, R17961383. Also the restricted file ANZ, IT-A6, box 1, R15386148, contains information about intelligence collected by supposed spies.

22. "Is a Judas There?," translation of *Samoan Supplement to NZ Samoa Guardian,* January 12, 1934, 5, in ANZ, IT 1 284, EX 37/12, part 2, R17961902.

23. Arthur Braisby testimony on January 9 and February 12, 1934, in *Braisby v. Nelson* court transcript, ANZ, IT1 44, EX1/23/20, R17961383.

24. G. Forbes to H. E. Hart, October 9, 1933, ANZ, IT 1 44, EX 1/23/20, R17961383.

25. "Samoa's Lost Friend," *NZ Samoa Guardian,* October 20, 1933, 1.

26. "Leader's Tributes," *Auckland Star,* October 9, 1933, 9; "Labour Leader's Death," *New Zealand Herald,* October 9, 1933, 11; Hoare, "Harry Holland's Samoan Complex," 152.

27. Exhibit 73, "Record of Names of Samoans," December 1933, IT1 45, EX1/23/20, part 1, R1791320 46/102; IT 1 44, EX 1/23/20, part 1, R17961383.

28. Hart to External, telegram, November 1, 1933, ANZ, IT 1 44, EX 1/23/20, R17961383.

29. Solicitor general's legal opinion, November 7, 1933, five pages, IT 1 44, EX 1/23/20, R17961383. The identity of the "spies" are revealed in this file. Skepticism about administration intelligence is the basis for not naming names here.

30. O. F. Nelson to P. Andrews, November 11, 1933, 97/102 IT 1 45 EX 1/23/20 R17961320.

31. H. Labouchère, "Where Is the Flag of England?," referred to in O. F. Nelson to P. Andrews, November 15, 1933, ANZ, IT1 44, EX 1/23/20, part 1, R17961383.

32. O. F. Nelson to C. V. Allom, November 6, 1933, ANZ, IT 1 45, EX 1/23/20, R17961320.

33. O. F. Nelson to Friends of Samoa, November 15, 1933, ANZ, IT 45, EX 1/23/20, R17961320.

34. O. F. Nelson to P. Andrews, November 15, 1933, ANZ, IT 45, EX 1/23/20, R17961320.

35. "O le Fea'u" (Business) extract of document seized at Tuaefu dated October 13, 1933, filed at ANZ, IT1 44, EX1/23/20, R17961383.

36. Account of police raid from the Translation of *Samoan Supplement of the NZ Samoa Guardian,* December 15, 1933, in ANZ, IT1 284, EX37/12, R17961902.

37. Loloma Johnston (daughter of Atoa) and Siuga Paula Masoe (daughter of Masoe Tulele), who were both raised at Tuaefu, recounted stories of the alarm at Tuaefu when Ta'isi was arrested and the fear a Black Saturday–style massacre would be repeated. Translation of *Samoan Supplement of the NZ Samoa Guardian,* December 15, 1933, in ANZ, IT1 284, EX37/12, R17961902.

38. Translation of *Samoan Supplement of the NZ Samoa Guardian,* December 15, 1933 in ANZ, IT1 284, EX37/12, R17961902.

39. "Search warrant for house and grounds of Olaf Fredrick Nelson," November 15, 1933, ANZ, AAAR W3558 24460, box 1453, Exhibit 4, R23545287. The list of legal authorities were *The Maintenance of Authority in Native Affairs (No.2) Ordinance 1928,* the *Samoa Seditious Organisations Regulations 1930, The Samoa Administrator's Additional Powers Ordinance 1930,* and Section 102 of the Samoa Act 1921.

40. These exhibits seized at Tuaefu are filed at ANZ, IT1 45, EX 1/23/20, R17961320.

41. "Tuaefu Looted a Second Time," translation of *Samoan Supplement of the NZ Samoa Guardian,* December 15, 1933, in ANZ, IT1 284, EX37/12, R17961902.

42. Administrator Hart to External, November 16, 1933, ANZ, IT1 44, EX 1/23/20, part 1, R17961383.

43. Report for Secretary of Native Affairs on meeting with Faumuina, November 20, 1933, ANZ, IT-A6, box 1, R15386148.

44. Report on conversation with Faumuina, November 22, 1933, ANZ, IT-A6, box 1, R15386148.

45. Translation of *Samoan Supplement of the NZ Samoa Guardian,* December 15, 1933 in ANZ, IT1 284, EX37/12, R17961902.

46. "Arrest of Taisi," *NZ Samoa Guardian,* December 15, 1933, 5.

47. Justice Luxford judgment in *Police v. Autagavaia* and seven others, November 22, 1933, ANZ, IT1 44, EX 1/23/20, part 1, R1796383.

48. Administrator Hart to External, December 3, 1933, ANZ, IT1 44, part 1, R17961383.

49. "Trial of Second Malaga," *NZ Samoa Guardian,* January 12, 1934, 2. Apia to External, telegram, December 8, 1933, ANZ, IT1 44, part 1, R17961383. Tagaloa and Tauiliili were sentenced to six months. Fiu and Tilialo were discharged. Tuala Tulo and Maulalosa were given three weeks in jail or a fine; they opted for prison.

50. C. Berendsen to G. Forbes, December 4, 1933, ANZ, IT 44, EX 1/23/20, part 1, R17961383.

51. Details of the trial authored by Arthur Braisby for High Commissioner James Parr in 1934 are contained in a document dealing with "the period in Western Samoa from 1926 to 1934," hereafter referred to as "Braisby Trial Account" in ANZ, IT1 44, EX 1/23/20, part 2 R17961384; Ta'isi's perspective on the trial is contained in the *NZ Samoa Guardian.* See "Trial of Taisi Starts," *NZ Samoa Guardian,* January 12, 1934, 2.

52. "Latest News from Samoa," *NZ Samoa Guardian,* January 12, 1934, 3.

53. "Braisby Trial Account," ANZ, IT1 44, EX 1/23/20, part 2, R17961384.

54. Ibid.; See Field, *Mau* for another account of the trial.

55. C. Berendsen to S. Allen, January 23, 1934, ANZ, IT1 44, EX1/23/20, part 1, R17961383.

56. J. H. Luxford to H. E. Hart, March 10, 1934, ANZ, IT1 44, part 2, R17961384.

57. Ibid.

58. *Braisby v. Nelson* transcript, December 28, 1933, ANZ, IT1 44, EX 1/23/20, part 1, R17961383. The transcript of *Braisby v. Nelson* filed in ANZ (R17961383) is incomplete. The *NZ Samoa Guardian* also published court proceedings that are likewise incomplete.

59. Sir James Carroll was the member for Eastern Māori 1887–1893, the member for Waiapu 1893–1908 (a Pākeha seat), the member for Gisborne 1908–1919 (a Pākeha seat); Te Rangi Hiroa was the member for Northern Māori 1909–1914; Sir Māui Pōmare was the member for Western Māori 1911–1930.

60. *Braisby v. Nelson* transcript, December 29, 1933, ANZ, IT1 44, EX 1/23/20, part 1, R17961383.

61. Translation of *Samoan Supplement of NZ Samoa Guardian,* February 9, 1934, ANZ, IT1 284, EX 37/12, part 2, R17961902.

62. *Braisby v. Nelson* transcript, January 2, 1934, ANZ, IT1 44, EX 1/23/20, part 1, R17961383. 234/433.

63. Ibid., January 4, 1934.

64. Ibid., January 5, 1934.

65. "The Mau Case," *Samoa Herald,* January 12, 1934.

66. See the exchanges for February 14, for example, *Braisby v. Nelson* transcript, February 14, 1934, ANZ, IT1 44, EX 1/23/20, part 1, R17961383.

67. Ibid., February 19–23, 1934.

68. Ibid., February 21, 1934.

69. Ibid., February 23–26, 1934.

70. "Trial of O. F. Nelson," *Press,* March 1, 1934, 9.

71. A. McCarthy quoted in "The Mau Case," *Samoa Herald,* March 9, 1934, 9.

72. Ta'isi O. F. Nelson quoted in ibid.

73. "Samoa Trial Over," *Evening Post,* March 5, 1934, 9.

74. Justice Luxford, *Interim Judgment in Braisby v. Nelson,* March 3, 1934, *Western Samoa Law Reports,* 83–94.

75. "Samoa Trial Over," *Evening Post,* March 5, 1934, 9.

Chapter 14: Sāmoa Evermore

1. Taufau Nelson Meyer, "A Daughter's Grief (After Seeing My Father in Vaimea Jail March 3rd 1934." Copy of poem given to author by Meyer family.

2. "Summary of Nelson and Mau Events 3rd to 8th March 1934 Inclusive," ANZ, AAEG W3240 950, box 55, part 10, R17709024.

3. Justice Luxford, Final Judgment in *Braisby v. Nelson, Western Samoan Law Reports,* 102.

4. "The Mau Case: Final Judgment: An Historic Document: Some Scathing Remarks," *Samoa Herald,* March 16, 1934, 5.

5. Justice Luxford, Final Judgment in *Braisby v. Nelson, Western Samoa Law Reports,* 95–108.

6. "Summary of Nelson and Mau Events 3rd to 8th March 1934 Inclusive," ANZ, AAEG W3240 950, box 55, part 10, R17709024.

7. Ibid.

8. At this time Malietoa wrote to George Richardson asking him to return and govern Sāmoa. Malietoa to G. S. Richardson, January 13, 1934, Acheson Papers, box 9, item 5.2.1.1a.

9. This account comes from "Extract from Private Letter Dated Apia 16 March 1934," filed at ANZ, AAEG W3240 950, box 55, part 10, R17709024.

10. There is a large amount of correspondence relating to Hart's acceptance of the mat without granting the request of the *ifoga.* Hart was asked to return the mat, with Faumuina threatening to take legal action over its return. See documents filed at ANZ, IT-A6, box 1, part 1, R15386148, Restricted, and IT1 42, EX 1/23/8, part 22, R17961307.

11. "Summary of Nelson and Mau Events 3rd to 8th March 1934 Inclusive," ANZ, AAEG W3240 950, box 55, part 10, R17709024.

12. "Lauaki: A Samoan Statesman," *NZ Samoa Guardian,* March 9, 1934, 3.

13. *Samoa Publications Order* published in full in *NZ Samoa Guardian,* January 12, 1934, 1.

14. O. F. Nelson to Head Office Apia, memorandum, March 18, 1934, ANZ, AAEG W3240 950, box 55, part 10, R17709024.

15. C. V. Allom to H. W. Moors, March 9, 1934, OFN 10; C. V. Allom to J. Helg, March 9, 1934, OFN 10; C. V. Allom to A. Betham, March 9, 1934, OFN 10; J. Helg to C. V. Allom, March 10, 1934, OFN 10.

16. O. F. Nelson to Head Office Apia, memorandum, March 18, 1934, ANZ, AAEG W3240 950, box 55, part 10, R17709024.

17. Ibid.

18. P. B. Cooke to C. V. Allom, March 26, 1934, OFN 10.

19. O. F. Nelson to Atoa, August 6, 1934, ANZ, IT1 44, EX1/23/20, R17961384; O. F. Nelson to Atoa, July 26, 1934, ANZ, AAEG W3240 950, box 55, part 10, R17709024.

20. O. F. Nelson to Head Office Apia, memorandum, March 18, 1934, ANZ, AAEG W3240 950, box 55, part 10, R17709024; Prime Minister Forbes to Minister for Justice, March 9, 1934, ANZ, IT1 44, EX 1/23/20, part 1, R17961383.

21. "Report of Constable S. W. Burney No. 2446," March 24, 1934, ANZ, IT1 44, EX 1/23/20, part 1, R17961383.

22. "People and Their Doings," *Christchurch Star,* March 19, 1934; "O. F. Nelson Objects," *Evening Post,* March 19, 1934, 8.

23. He was staying at the New City Hotel with his two daughters.

24. O. F. Nelson telegrams to Head Office April 5, 1934, and April 11, 1934, OFN 10. "A Letter from Ta'isi," July 17, 1934, ANZ, AAEG W3240 950, box 55, part 10, R17709024.

25. The transcripts from these *fonos* are filed at ANZ, IT1 44, part 2, R17961384.

26. External to Admor, telegram, June, 29, 1934, ANZ, IT1 44, part 2, R17961384.

27. Judgment of Justice Blair in *Olaf Fredrick Nelson v. Arthur Braisby,* ANZ, IT1 44, part 2, R17961384, 20. Judgments of Justice Myer, Justice Herdman, and Justice Reid filed at ANZ, IT1 44, part 2, R17961384.

28. O. F. Nelson to Atoa, August 6, 1934, in ANZ, IT1 44, EX1/23/20, part 2, R17961384.

29. Interview with G. W. Forbes and O. F. Nelson, transcript, July 31, 1934, ANZ, AAEG W3240 950, box 55, part 10, R17709024.

30. Ibid.

31. These documents were sent to Wellington under cover of a letter by H. E. Hart to Minister for External Affairs, August 18, 1934, ANZ, IT144, EX 1/23/20, part 2, R17961384.

32. A. L. Braisby to G. S. Richardson, December 26, 1934, Acheson Papers, box 9, item 5.2.1.1a.

33. Taufau was not able to complete high school. Sina Schmalkuchen, interview with author, April 9, 2015.

34. H. E. Hart to External, telegram, October 29, 1934, ANZ, IT1 44, EX 1/23/20, part 2, R17961384.

35. O. F. Nelson to F. Langstone, September 16, 1937, ANZ, IT1 EX79/2/1, R17962644.

36. Fialaui'afualeafi Tamasese, interviews with author, November 10, 2012, and September 14, 2014; Piliopo Ma'ai, interview with author, July 16, 2014; Tui Atua Tupua Tamasese Ta'isi Efi, interview with author, June 6, 2012.

37. Fialaui'afualeafi Tamasese was born October 7, 1935.

38. This correspondence is in OFN 13.

39. Evatt, *British Dominions as Mandatories,* 17.

40. Mackrell, Maton, Godlee, and Quincey, Solicitors to New Zealand Crown Solicitor, March 28, 1935, ANZ, IT1 44, EX1/23/20, part 2, R 17961384.

41. O. F. Nelson to Atoa, July 26, 1934, ANZ, AAEG W3240 950, box 55, part 10, R17709024.

42. *Fourteenth Report of the Government of New Zealand on the Administration of the Mandated Territory of Western Samoa for the Year Ended 31st March 1934,* 3.

43. O. F. Nelson to G. Forbes, September 27, 1935, ANZ, IT1 42, EX 1/23/8, part 22, R17961307.

44. Police report by Sub Inspector Fell, October 9, 1935, ANZ, IT1 42, EX 1/23/8, part 22, R17961307.

45. O. F. Nelson to M. Savage, March 21, 1936, ANZ, IT1 441, EX79/2/1, part 1, R17962644.

46. "Return to Samoa," *Auckland Star,* April 4, 1936, 7; "Exile to End," *New Zealand Herald,* April 4, 1936, 14. Other papers covered this story at this time.

47. M. Savage to Governor-General, June 19, 1936; warrants signed by Governor-General Galway, June 20, 1936; Michael Savage to O. F. Nelson, June 29, 1936; all in ANZ, IT1 44, EX 1/23/20, part 2, R17961384.

48. Proclamation revoking *Samoa Seditious Organizations Regulations* 1930, June 24, 1936; proclamation revoking the declaration of numerous areas as "disturbed," June 24, 1936, ANZ, AAEG W3240 950, box 55, R17709024. A. C. Turnbull had been acting in this position since July 1935 when Hart's term ended.

49. "Natives Rejoice," *Evening Post,* June 26, 1936, 9.

50. O. F. Nelson to M. Savage, June 12, 1936, ANZ, IT1 44, EX 1/23/20, part 2, R17961384; see the report on Langstone and O'Brien's visit, filed at ANZ, IT1 4, boxes 7–14, R15930755.

51. O. F. Nelson to Faumuina, June 10, 1936, ANZ, IT1 44, EX 1/23/20, part 2, R17961384.

52. O. F. Nelson to M. Savage, June 12, 1936, ANZ, IT1 44, EX 1/23/20, part 2, R17961384.

53. "Second in Auckland," *Auckland Star,* June 26, 1936, 3.

54. "Back to Samoa," *Evening Post,* July 15, 1936, 13; "Returning to Samoa," *Auckland Star,* July 16, 1936, 11.

55. O. F. Nelson to M. Savage, September 30, 1936, ANZ, IT4, box 12, R15930755. There were about five hundred Chinese workers in Sāmoa at this time. See the report on Langstone and O'Brien's visit, filed at ANZ, IT1 4, boxes 7–14, R15930755, 24.

56. O. F. Nelson to M. Savage, October 14, 1936, ANZ IT4, box 12, R15930755.

57. O. F. Nelson-Taisi to Editor of the Western Samoa Mail, September 14, 1937, ANZ, IT1 EX79/2/1 R17962644.

58. A. Gozar to M. Savage, May 12, 1936, November 10, 1936, December 4, 1936, December 15, 1936, December 23, 1936, in ANZ, IT1 441, EX79/2/1, R17962644.

59. See numerous police reports in ANZ, IT1 42, EX 1/23/8, part 23, R17961308, and ANZ, IT1 42, EX 1/23/8, part 24, R17961309.

60. Priscilla Braisby incident report, July 22, 1937, ANZ, IT1 42, EX 1/23/8, part 23, R17961308.

61. "Mau Again," *Auckland Star,* January 21, 1938, 8.

62. A. C. Turnbull to Minister for External Affairs, July 28, 1937, ANZ, IT1 42, EX 1/23/8, part 23, R17961308.

63. "O. F. Nelson versus A. M. Gurau," *Western Samoan Mail,* March 26, 1938; O. F. Nelson to F. Langstone, March 7, 1938, ANZ, IT 441, EX79/2/1, part 1, R17962644.

64. Tui Atua Tupua Tamasese Ta'isi Efi, interview with author, June 6, 2012; Fialaui'afualeafi Tamasese, interviews with author, November 10, 2012, and September 14, 2014.

65. "Samoan Funeral," *Auckland Star,* March 19, 1937, 10. Viopapa's grave (the headstone was arranged by her sisters) does not acknowledge her married name. Her name reads "Lucy Viopapa Nelson." She died February 3, 1937.

66. "Samoan Affairs," *Evening Post,* January 24, 1938, 10.

67. "Mau Again," *Auckland Star,* January 21, 1938, 8.

68. A. L. Braisby, "Police Department Report on Mau Activity," January 10, 1938, ANZ, IT1 42, EX 1/23/8, part 24, R17961309.

69. Ibid., January 13, 1938.

70. Ibid.

71. "Mau Again," *Auckland Star,* January 21, 1938, 8.

72. "Satisfied Samoan Delegation," *Auckland Star,* February 2, 1938, 14; "Mau Again," *Auckland Star,* January 21, 1938, 8.

73. "Samoan Affairs," *Evening Post,* January 24, 1938, 10.

74. "Satisfied Samoan Delegation," *Auckland Star,* February 2, 1938, 14.

75. C. McKay, Secretary of Native Affairs, April 26, 1938 in "Mau Newspapers," in Fredrick Grattan Papers, ATL MS 4879–095.

76. A. C. Turnbull to C. A. Berendsen, November 10, 1938, ANZ, AAEG W3240 950, box 55, part 10, R17709024.

77. F. Langstone to O. F. Nelson, December 1, 1938, ANZ, IT1 441, EX 79/2/1, part 1, R17962644.

78. Ibid.

79. See the series of letters regarding these problems circa late 1938 and May 1939, ANZ, IT1 441, EX 79/2/1, part 1, R17962644.

80. Fialaui'afualeafi Tamasese, interview with author, November 10, 2012; Tui Atua Tupua Tamasese Ta'isi Efi, interview with author, June 28, 2013.

81. Sina Schmalkuchen, interview with author, April 9, 2015.

82. Ibid. Taufau was back in Wellington from Samoa in April 1943.

83. O. F. Nelson to T. (Calmar) Meyers, February 2, 1944, Meyer family papers.

84. Ibid., June 6, 1943.

85. Ibid.

86. With thanks to Siuga Paula Masoe for the detail about Ta'isi's use of the telescope to keep watch over Apia Harbor from Tuaefu.

87. O. F. Nelson to T. Meyers, September 29, 1943, Meyer family papers.

88. Malienafau had a history of rheumatic fever that compromised her health. Sina Schmalkuchen interview with author, April 9, 2015.

89. O. F. Nelson to T. Meyers, February 2, 1944, Meyer family papers.

90. Ibid.

91. R. Nelson to T. Meyer, n.d., Meyer family papers.

92. S. Annandale to T. Meyer, April 16, 1944, Meyer family papers.

Epilogue

1. Ta'isi, "What Samoans Want," October 23, 1930, ANZ, IT1 41, EX1/23/8 19, R17961304, 4.

2. O. (Malienafau) Betham to P. Fraser, February 14, 1945, ANZ, IT1 441, EX 79/2/1, R17962645.

3. P. Fraser to O. Betham, April 26, 1945, ANZ, IT1 441, EX 79/2/1, R17962645. There are numerous documents relating to the estate in this file.

4. Sina Schmalkuchen, interview with author, June 25, 2013.

5. E. Annandale to Secretary of Administration of Western Samoa, February 6, 1945, ANZ, IT 1 441, EX 79/2/1, R17962645.

6. "One Hundred Years of Service to Samoa," 8.

7. Fialaui'afualeafi Tamasese managed O. F. Nelson and Co. in its last years. Fialaui'afualeafi Tamasese, conversation with author, August 13, 2015.

8. "Portrait of the Patriot: Olaf Fredrick Nelson," *Samoana,* January 1, 1962.

9. F. M. Keesing, *Modern Samoa: Its Government and Changing Life* (London: George Allen and Unwin, 1934), 124–125.

10. F. M. Keesing to O. F. Nelson, November 6, 1930; M. Keesing to O. F. Nelson, January 8, 1931, OFN 27.

11. "Death of Mr O. F. Nelson: Mau Leader Who Fought NZ Officialdom for 15 Years," *Pacific Islands Monthly,* March 1944, 10, 30.

12. See historiographical notes in this volume's prologue.

13. With thanks to Piliopo Ma'ai and Joan Tamasese for these memories shared in conversation with author on August 4, 2015.

14. Davidson, in *Samoa mo Samoa,* leaves the reader with the distinct impression Ta'isi was a narcissistic man. Although Ta'isi objected to being referred to as "Fredrick the Great," as Davidson recounted, this sobriquet has been repeated out of context, particularly by Hugh Laracy in his *Te Ara (Dictionary of New Zealand Biography)* entry on Ta'isi.

15. "Full Text: Helen Clark's Apology to Samoa," *New Zealand Herald,* June 4, 2002, http://www.nzherald.co.nz/nz/news/article.cfm?c_id=1&objectid=2044857 (accessed May 12, 2012).

16. Leone Forsgren, conversation with author, July 20, 2015.

Bibliography

Oral Histories

As the heirs to Ta'isi's story, the Ta'isi *aiga*'s cooperation with this project has been critical. Many members of the Ta'isi family have shared oral histories with me. These oral histories took the form of formal interviews, as cited in the notes, as well as ongoing conversations since 2012. Countless meetings have taken place in Apia, Safune, Wellington, Auckland, Dunedin, and Canberra, where we have talked about the past. As well as face-to-face meetings, there have been countless phone calls, e-mails, and text messages, where conversations about the past have continued. Lectures I have given or documents I have found or been given by the family have often prompted memories and comments and produced rich historical detail. Distributed photographs have also stimulated memories and questions and fueled the conversations that underpin this book. I owe a great debt to all the Ta'isi grandchildren, each of whom helped me better understand this history. In terms of oral histories, I have relied in particular on testimony from Tui Atua Tupua Tamasese Ta'isi Efi, Fialaui'afualeafi Tamasese, Irene Piliopo Maiai, Tugaga Misa Telefoni Retzlaff, Papali'i Viopapa Atherton Annandale, Sina Schmaulken, and Lelani Keil. Cousins Siuga Paula Masoe and Loloma Johnston have also shared oral histories with me since 2012 and 2013, respectively. Siuga then shared written reminiscences of Tuaefu with me in May 2015.

Unpublished Ta'isi Family Papers

Irene Piliopo Maiai Letters
Meyer Family Letters

OFN Papers

The Ta'isi O. F. Nelson papers comprise 101 files numbered sequentially held at Tuaefu, Apia. They were all used extensively in this book. They mainly cover the period 1928–1933 and contain a wide array of correspondence, business-related documents, and other highly valuable material used extensively to piece together Ta'isi's life. These documents were consulted in their original form by the author from 2012 with the kind permission of His Highness Tui Atua Tupua Tamasese Ta'isi Efi. (Since 2015, the Pacific Manuscripts Bureau has commenced the process of digitizing these documents.)

Pacific Manuscripts Bureau (PMB) 712—Letters between O. F. Nelson and Rosabel Nelson and H. E. Holland.

Newspapers

Newspapers were consulted in two ways. First through focused searches using the invaluable research tool of Papers Past that has digitized New Zealand historical newspapers, and during the writing of this book, some Sāmoan historical newspapers also. The second method was "slow reading." The *Samoa Times* (or from 1931 the *Samoa Herald*) was read at the Nelson Public Library, Apia. The *Samoa Guardian* was read at the National Library of Australia and as an annotated translation from Sāmoan to English at the Auckland Public Library. Holdings of the *NZ Samoa Guardian* were consulted at the National Library of New Zealand, the Auckland Public Library, the Library of Congress, and the National Library of Australia (no holding is complete). Archives New Zealand files IT1 284, EX 37/12, part 1, R17961901 and IT1 284, EX 37/12, part 2, R17961902 provide translations of the Sāmoan language supplement for the *NZ Samoa Guardian for 1929 to 1934.*

Auckland Star
Brisbane Courier
Christchurch Star
Evening Post
Journal de Genève
News (Adelaide)
New Zealand Gazette
New Zealand Herald
Northern Advocate
NZ Samoa Guardian
Pacific Islands Monthly
Samoa Guardian
Samoana
Samoanische Zeitung
Samoa Times
Samoa Weekly Herald
Scotsman
Sydney Morning Herald
Western Samoan Mail

Archives

Archives New Zealand

Documents in Archives New Zealand have been used extensively. The author urges future researchers to use the unique "R number" to locate files on the Archives New Zealand "Archway advanced search" page.

Department of Justice

The AAAR W3558/1452 series contains ninety-four records relating to *Braisby v. Nelson* and the appeal. Most of these files are exhibits of evidence (eighty-nine exhibits), the contents of which are replicated in other files though not completely. Most of these files were consulted.

Customs

C1/84 29/53/2 R17944609. Smuggling of Spirits and Opium into Samoa.

Island Territories Department

IT1 EX 5/12, R17962091. Opium Traffic in Samoa 1922–1938.

IT1 EX 1/8, Part 1, R17961230. Legislative Council of Western Samoa 1919–1928.

IT1 5, EX 1/8/1, Part 2, R17961209. Legislative Council Minutes 1927–1929.

IT1 36, EX 1/23/8, Part 1, R17961334. Mau Agitation 1926.

IT1 36, EX 1/23/8, Part 2, R17961335. Mau Agitation 1926.

IT1 37, EX 1/23/8, Part 3, R17961288. Mau Agitation 1927.

IT1 37, EX 1/23/8, Part 4, R17961289. Mau Agitation March to May 1927.

IT1 37, EX 1/23/8, Part 5, R17961290. Mau Agitation June 1927.

IT1 37, EX 1/23/8, Part 6, R17961291. Mau Agitation July 1927.

IT1 38, EX 1/23/8, Part 7, R 17961292. Mau Agitation August 1927.

IT1 38, EX 1/23/8, Part 8, R17961293. Mau Agitation September to December 1927.

IT1 38, EX 1/23/8, Part 9, R17961294. Mau Agitation January 1928.

IT1 38, EX 1/23/8, Part 10, R17961295. Mau Agitation February 1928.

IT1 39, EX 1/23/8, Part 11, R17961296. Mau Agitation March 1928.

IT1 39, EX 1/23/8, Part 12, R17961297. Mau Agitation April to June 1928.

IT1 39, EX 1/23/8, Part 13, R17961298. Mau Agitation July 1928 to March 1929.

IT1 39, EX 1/23/8, Part 14, R17961299. Mau Agitation April to December 1929.

IT1 39, EX 1/23/8, Part 15, R17961300. Mau Agitation January 1930.

IT1 40, EX 1/23/8, Part 16, R17961301. Mau Agitation February 1930.

IT1 40, EX 1/23/8, Part 17, R17961302. Mau Agitation March 1930.

IT1 40, EX 1/23/8, Part 18, R17961303. Mau Agitation April to June 1930.

IT1 41, EX 1/23/8, Part 19, R17961304. Mau Agitation July to December 1930.

IT1 41, EX 1/23/8, Part 20, R17961305. Mau Agitation January 1931 to June 1932.
IT1 41, EX 1/23/8, Part 21, R17961306. Mau Agitation July to December 1932.
IT1 42, EX 1/23/8, Part 22, R17961307. Mau Agitation January 1933 to December 1935.
IT1 42, EX 1/23/8, Part 23, R17961308. Mau Agitation 1935–1938.
IT1 42, EX 1/23/8, Part 24, R17961309. Mau Agitation 1938–1939.
IT1 43, EX 1/23/10, Part 1, R17961311. Agitation Slander Trial 1929.
IT1 43, EX1/23/11, Part 1, R17961312. Mau Agitation-Riot 28 December 1929.
IT1 43, EX1/23/11, Part 2, R17961313. Mau Agitation-Riot 28 December 1929.
IT1 43, EX 1/23/18, Part 1, R17961381. Prosecution of O. F. Nelson & Co. Ltd.
IT1 44, EX 1/23/20, Part 1, R17961383. Braisby v. O. F. Nelson Trial.
IT1 44, EX 1/23/20, Part 2, R17961384. Braisby v. O. F. Nelson Trial.
IT1 45, EX 1/23/20, Part 1, R17961320. Police v. O. F. Nelson.
IT1 47, EX 1/33, Part 1, R17961392. Monthly dispatch from administration.
IT1 47, EX 1/33/1, Part 1, R17961393. Private correspondence between Sir G. S. Richardson and Sir Francis Bell, Minister for External Affairs.
IT1 60, EX 1/42, Part 1, R17961375. Private notes by General Richardson.
IT1 61, EX1/47, R17961455. Petition of O. F. Nelson to House of Representatives 1930–1931.
IT1 106, EX 2/9, Part 1, R17961623. Reports on Samoan affairs for governor general.
IT1 107, EX2/9, Part 2, R17961624. Reports on Samoan affairs for governor general.
IT1 251, EX25/1/8, 17961877. Mandates—Late German possessions in Pacific—South of the Equator (other than Samoa and Noura [*sic*]).
IT1 251, EX25/1/9, Part 1, R17961878. Mandates—Late German possessions in Pacific—North of the Equator.
IT1 255, EX25/1/23, R17962028. Permanent Mandates Commission—Discussion on Samoan Annual Reports.
IT1 266, EX25/9, R17961988. Mandate Report 1929.
IT1 267, EX 25/13, Part 1, R17961847. Questionnaire by Permanent Mandates Commission for Annual Reports—Hearing of Petitioners 1922–1926.
IT1 267, EX 25/14, R17961849. Action by Permanent Mandates Commission 1928 regarding Samoan situation.
IT1 267, EX25/15, R17961850. League of Nations—Permanent Mandates Commission—Forced Labour.
IT1 284, EX 37/12, Part 1, R17961901. NZ Samoa Guardian.
IT1 284, EX 37/12, Part 2, R17961902. NZ Samoa Guardian.
IT1 372, EX67/12/2, Part 1, R17962336. Constitution of Samoa 1919.
IT1 372, EX67/12/2, Part 2, R17962337. Constitution of Samoa.
IT1 372, EX67/12/3, Part 3, R17962351. Constitution of Samoa.
IT1 441, EX 79/2/1, Part 1, R17962644. O. F. Nelson, Death in Samoa.

IT1 441, EX 79/2/1, Part 1A, R17962645. O. F. Nelson—general correspondence.
IT1 443, EX 79/32, Part 1, R17962657. H. J. Moors—Apia.
IT1 443, EX 79/32, Part 2, R17962658. H. J. Moors—Apia.
IT1 445, EX 79/78, Part 2, R17962677. General Richardson 1923–1924.
IT1 446, EX 79/109, R17962696. P. B. Fitzherbert 1930–1937.
IT1 512, EX 88/12, Part 1, R17963052. Arrest of Tamasese and imprisonment in NZ 1928–1929.
IT4 boxes 7–14 R15930755. Visit of delegates from Fono of Faipules to New Zealand.

Island Territories Department, Restricted Access

IT-A3, Box 6, R15386131. Mau notes.
IT-A5, Box 1, AO25/2, R15386146. Samoa Royal Commission 1927–1928.
IT-A5, Box 1, AO25/3, R15386145. Political agitation-Deportations and Enquiries—O. F. Nelson, A. G. Smyth, E. W. Gurr, G. E. L. Westbrook, S. H. Meredith, S. V. Mackenzie.
IT-A5, Box 1, 25/1/1, R15386147. Women's Mau petition 1930.
IT-A5, AO 25/12, R15386141. Police v. O. F. Nelson and Company Ltd.
IT-A6, Box 1, R15386148. Political (Mau) Intelligence.

Ministry of Foreign Affairs

AAEG 950/2/E 311/9/9, Part 1, R17708883. Petition Evidence taken by the Royal Commission Concerning the Administration of Western Samoa 1927.
AAEG W3240 950, Box 28, Part 5, R17708949. Samoan Unrest 1928.
AAEG W3240 950, Box 29, Part 6, R17708952. Samoan Unrest 1928.
AAEG W3240 950, Box 28, Part 7, R17708950. Samoan Unrest 1928.
AAEG W3240 950, Box 33, Part 8, R17708964. Samoan Unrest 1928–1929.
AAEG W3240 950, Box 65, Part 9, R17709062. Samoan Unrest 1929–1933.
AAEG W3240 950, Box 55, Part 10, R17709024. Samoan Unrest 1933–1938.
AAEG W3240 950, Box 22, R17708933. Western Samoa-Social Affairs-Slavery 1922–1927.
AAEG W3240 950, Box 55, Part 1, R17709025. Report on the Administration of Western Samoa (VPB Report).

Ministry

Allen1 1 M1/1 R22319694. Ministerial Files—Brigadier General GS Richardson.

New Zealand Defence Force, Personnel Archives

AABK 18805/W5520, R22278688. Arthur Leslie Braisby WWI.

Office of the Governor-General

G48 6 R19162155. Tour of Cook Islands and Samoa by His Excellency Sir Charles Fergusson.

G48 35 S/3(1), R19162267. Samoa—General file (Visit by ex-German officials—Agitation created by Mr. Nelson).

G48 38 S/17, R19162280. Samoa—Agitation in up to end of 1928—Newspaper cuttings, etc.

G48 40 S/17(1), R19162282. Samoa-Agitation from 1929—Includes petition to HM the King.

League of Nations Archive (Geneva)

Col 100, 6A/15281/224–6A/4398/709.

R2321, 6A/708, 1928–1932, Series 701 to 709, dossiers 800.

R2322, 6A/2872/709, Series 709, dossiers 801 to 4,000.

R2322, 6A/875/709, 1928–1932.

R2323, 6A/5037/709, 1928–1932.

National Archives of Sweden

O. F. Nelson to Consul General Count Mörner, 10 June, 1908, Swedish Consulate archives from Sydney, series F1:25, The National Archives of Sweden, Arninge.

National Archives, United Kingdom

Despatches from New Zealand Governor General to Dominions Office

DO 35/4 1926

DO 35/24 1927

DO 35/48 1928

DO 35/69 1929

Samoa Lands and Titles Records

Alesoni to Mr. Harrison, February 2, 1921; Lands and Titles Court case, Savai'i File No. B/S 317/19 (High Court of Western Samoa at Vaisala, Savai'i).

Unpublished Manuscripts

Acheson, Frank O. V., Papers incorporating the papers of Sir George Spafford Richardson. MSS & Archives 96/1, Special Collections, University of Auckland Libraries and Learning Services.

Bell, Francis Dillon, Papers, Alexander Turnbull Library, Wellington.

Carruthers, Sir Joseph Hector, Papers, Mitchell Library, State Library of New South Wales.

Grattan, Fredrick, Papers, Alexander Turnbull Library, Wellington.

G. S. Richardson to M. E. J. Cocks, ML document 763, Mitchell Library, State Library of New South Wales.

Tate, Robert Ward, Papers, Alexander Turnbull Library, Wellington.
Westbrook, George, Papers, Alexander Turnbull Library, Wellington.

Government Records

"Confiscated Native Lands and Other Grievances." AJHR. 1928. Session 1, G-7. http://atojs.natlib.govt.nz. Accessed September 15, 2014.
"Coroner's Findings in the Inquest Respecting the Fatalities in Western Samoa." AJHR. 1930. Session 1, A-4B. http://atojs.natlib.govt.nz. Accessed October 2, 2013.
"European War: Occupation of German Samoa by an Expedition Force from New Zealand." AJHR. 1915. Session 1, H-19C. http://atojs.natlib.govt.nz. Accessed March 12, 2014.
"Mandated Territory of Western Samoa (Extracts From Report on Finances and Staff)." AJHR. 1929. Session 1, A-4B. http://atojs.natlib.govt.nz. Accessed December 12, 2014.
"Mandated Territory of Western Samoa (Report of Visit by Hon. W. Nosworthy)." AJHR. 1927. Session 1, A-4B. http://atojs.natlib.govt.nz. Accessed September 27, 2012.
New Zealand Legislative Council and House of Representatives Parliamentary Debates, 1927–1933.
Report of the Parliamentary Select Committee on Aboriginal Tribes (British Settlements). London: William Ball, 1837. https://books.google.com.au. Accessed February 2, 2014.
"Report of Royal Commission Concerning the Administration of Western Samoa." AJHR. 1928. Session 1, A-4B. http://atojs.natlib.govt.nz. Accessed May 13, 2012.
Reports of the Government of New Zealand on the Mandated Territory of Western Samoa to the League of Nations, for the Years 1921 to 1936. http://atojs.natlib.govt.nz. Accessed April 24–27, 2013.
"Samoan Epidemic Commission." AJHR. 1919. Session 1, H-31C. http://atojs.natlib.govt.nz. Accessed January 10, 2014.
"Visit of Parliamentary Party to Pacific Islands. February-March, 1920." AJHR. 1920. Session 1, A-05. http://atojs.natlib.govt.nz. Accessed March 19, 2014.

Legislation and Judicial Decisions

Commonwealth of Australia. *Naturalization Act*, 1903.
NSW Government. *Aborigines Protection Act*, 1909.
Samoa Act 1921.
Samoa Amendment Act 1927.
Samoa Constitution Order 1920.
Slade, Neroni (compiled). *The Western Samoa Law Reports: Cases Determined by the High Court and the Supreme Court of New Zealand*. Apia: n.p., n.d.

Unpublished Speeches

Tui Atua Tupua Tamasese Ta'isi Efi. Address to the Methodist Consultative Council of the Pacific, April 12, 2015, Fogaa, Faleula, Sāmoa.

Tui Atua Tupua Tamasese Ta'isi Efi. Speech given on Pōmare Memorial Day, June 29, 2013, Waitara Mārae, Taranaki, New Zealand.

Published Primary Sources

Adams, Romanzo. *Interracial Marriage in Hawaii: A Study of Mutually Conditioned Processes of Acculturation and Amalgamation.* New York: Macmillan, 1937.

Andrews, Percy, ed. *Samoa in the Shadows: A Pictorial Record of Recent Events in Western Samoa under a Mandate from the League of Nations to the Dominion of New Zealand.* Auckland: NZ Samoa Guardian, 1931.

Brown, John Macmillan. *Maori and Polynesian: Their Origin, History and Culture.* London: Hutchinson, 1907.

Brown, H. Runham. *Western Samoa: Imprisonment, Deportation and Shooting.* Enfield: War Resisters' International, 1930.

Chappell, A. B. *A Stir in Samoa: An Independent Review.* Auckland: Wilson Horton, 1928.

Churchill, L. *Samoa 'Uma: Where Life Is Different.* New York: Forest Stream Publishing, 1902.

Churchward, William B. *My Consulate in Samoa.* London: Richard Bentley and Son, 1887.

Cowan, James, with Maui Pomare. *Legends of the Maori.* Wellington: H. H. Tombs, 1930.

Cyclopedia of Samoa, Tonga, Tahiti and the Cook Islands, 1907. Reprint. Papakura: R. McMillan, 1983.

Dana, Julian. *Gods Who Die: The Story of Samoa's Greatest Adventurer.* New York: Macmillan, 1935.

De Decker, Paul, ed. George Pritchard (author), *The Aggressions of the French at Tahiti and Other Islands of the Pacific.* Auckland: Auckland University Press, 1983.

Dening Greg, ed. *The Marquesan Journal of Edward Robarts, 1797–1824.* Canberra: Australian National University Press, 1974.

Eustis, Nelson. *Aggie Grey of Samoa.* Adelaide: Hobby Investments, 1979.

Evatt, H. V. *The British Dominions and Mandatories.* Melbourne: University of Melbourne Press, 1935.

Holland, H. E. *Indentured Labour: Is It Slavery?* Greymouth: Grey River Coy, 1919.

———. *Samoa: A Story That Teems with Tragedy.* Wellington: Maoriland Worker Printing and Publishing, 1918.

Keable, Robert. *Tahiti Isle of Dreams.* London: Hutchinson, 1925.

Keesing, F. M. *Modern Samoa: Its Government and Changing Life*. London: George Allen and Unwin, 1934.
Knoll, Arthur J., and Hermann J. Hiery, eds. *The German Colonial Experience: Select Documents on German rule in Africa, China, and the Pacific, 1884–1914*. Lanham, MD: Universities of America, 2010.
Luxford, J. H. *With the Machine Gunners in France and Palestine*. Auckland: Whitcombe and Tombs, 1923.
Moors, H. J. *Some Recollections of Early Samoa*. Apia: Western Samoa Historical and Cultural Trust, 1987.
———. *With Stevenson in Samoa*. London: Collins Clear Type Press, 1910.
Nelson, O. F. *The Truth about Samoa: A Review of Events Leading Up to the Present Crisis*. Auckland: n. p., 1928.
———. *Samoa at Geneva: Misleading the League of Nations*. Auckland: National Printing Company, 1928.
Nelson, O. F., and J. C. Andersen. "Legends of Samoa." *Journal of the Polynesian Society* 34, no. 134 (1925): 124–145.
O'Brien, Frederick. *Mystic Isles of the South Seas*. London: Hodder and Stoughton, 1921.
———. *White Shadows in the South Seas*. New York: Century, 1919.
Owen, C. W. *The Samoan Massacre*. Hobart: Newman's Printery, 1930.
Rowe, Newton A. *Samoa under the Sailing Gods*. London: Unwin Brothers, 1930.
Stair, J. *Old Samoa: Flotsam and Jetsam from the Pacific Ocean*. London: Religious Tract Society, 1897.
Stevenson, Robert Louis. *Treasure Island*. London: Cassell and Co., 1883.
———. *The Strange Case of Dr Jekyll and Mr Hyde*. London: Longmans, Green, 1886.
———. *Kidnapped*. London: Cassell and Co., 1886.
———. *A Footnote to History: Eight Years of Trouble in Samoa*. London: Cassell and Co., 1892.
Turner, George. *Samoa: A Hundred Years Ago and Long Before*. London: Macmillan, 1884.
Watson, Robert. *History of Samoa*. Wellington: Whitcombe and Tombs, 1919.

Secondary Works—Books, Book Chapters, and Articles

Banivanua Mar, Tracey. *Violence and Colonial Dialogue: The Australia-Pacific Labor Trade*. Honolulu: University of Hawai'i Press, 2007.
———. *Decolonisation and the Pacific: Indigenous Globalisation and the Ends of Empire*. Cambridge: Cambridge University Press, 2016.
Bayliss-Smith, Tim, and Judith A. Bennett, eds. *An Otago Storeman in Solomon Islands: The Diary of William Crossan, Copra Trader, 1885–86*. Canberra: ANU E Press, 2012.

Belich, James. *I Shall Not Die: Titokowaru's War, New Zealand, 1868–9*. Wellington: Bridget Williams Books, 1989.

———. *Paradise Reforged: A History of the New Zealanders*. Honolulu: Hawai'i University Press, 2001.

———. *Replenishing the Earth: The Settler Revolution and the Rise of the Anglo-World, 1783–1939*. Oxford: Oxford University Press, 2009.

Binney, Judith. *Encircled Lands: Te Urewera, 1820–1921*. Wellington: Bridget Williams Books, 2009.

Bonnemains, Jacqueline, Elliot Forsyth, and Bernard Smith, eds. *Baudin in Australian Waters: The Artwork of the French Voyage of Discovery to the Southern Lands, 1800–1804*. Melbourne: Oxford University Press, 1988.

Boyd, Mary. "Coping with Samoan Resistance after the 1918 Influenza Epidemic: Colonel Tate's Problems and Perplexities." *Journal of Pacific History* 15, no. 3 (1980): 155–174.

———. "Military Administration of Western Samoa 1914–1919." *New Zealand Journal of History* 2, no. 2 (1968): 148–164.

———. "Racial Attitudes of New Zealand Officials in Western Samoa." *New Zealand Journal of History* 21, no. 1 (1987): 139–155.

———. "The Record in Western Samoa to 1945." In *New Zealand's Record in the Pacific Islands in the Twentieth Century*, edited by Angus Ross, 115–188. London: Longman Paul, 1969.

Brunt, Anthony. *To Walk under Palm Trees: The Germans in Samoa, Snapshots from Albums*. http://germansinsamoa.net/ebook/, 2016.

Buchanan, Rachel. *The Parihaka Album: Lest We Forget*. Wellington: Huia Publishers, 2009.

Burton, Antoinette, and Tony Ballantyne, eds. *Moving Subjects: Gender, Mobility and Intimacy in an Age of Global Empire*. Urbana-Champaign: University of Illinois Press, 2009.

Campbell, I. C. "New Zealand and the *Mau* in Samoa: Re-Assessing the Causes of a Colonial Protest Movement." *New Zealand Journal of History* 33, no. 1 (1999): 92–110.

Carey, Jane, and Jane Lydon eds. *Indigenous Networks: Mobility, Connections and Exchange*: London: Routledge, 2014.

Chappell, David. "The Forgotten Mau: Anti-Navy Protest in American Samoa 1920–1935." *Pacific Historical Review* 69, no. 2 (2000): 217–260.

Chaudron, Gerald. "The League of Nations and Imperial Dissent: New Zealand and the British Labour Governments, 1924–1931." *Journal of Imperial and Commonwealth History* 39, no. 1 (2011): 47–71.

———. *New Zealand in the League of Nations: The Beginnings of an Independent Foreign Policy, 1919–1939*. Jefferson, NC: McFarland, 2012.

———."Obsession: New Zealand, Money and the League of Nations 1920–1935." *Journal of Imperial and Commonwealth History* 41, no. 1 (2013): 143–169.

Cleary, Tania. *Poignant Regalia: Nineteenth Century Aboriginal Breastplates and Images*. Glebe, Australia: Historic Houses Trust, 1993.

Cody, J. F. *Man of Two Worlds: Sir Maui Pomare*. Wellington: Reed, 1953.

Conrad, Sebastian. *German Colonialism: A Short History*. Cambridge: Cambridge University Press, 2012.

Davidson, J. W. *Samoa mo Samoa: The Emergence of the Independent State of Western Samoa*. Oxford: University of Oxford Press, 1967.

Druett, Joan. *Petticoat Whalers: Whaling Wives at Sea 1820–1920*. Auckland: Collins, 1991.

Fairbairn, Ian. “Samoan Migration to New Zealand.” *Journal of the Polynesian Society* 70, no. 1 (1961): 18–30.

Field, Michael J. *Black Saturday: New Zealand's Tragic Blunders in Samoa*. Auckland: Reed Publishing, 2006.

———. *Mau: Samoa's Struggle for Freedom*. Auckland: Polynesian Press, 1991.

Foley, Dennis. “Indigenous Standpoint Theory: An Acceptable Academic Research Process for Indigenous Academics.” *International Journal of Humanities* 3, no. 8 (2005–2006): 25–36.

Gilson, Richard. *Samoa 1830 to 1900: The Politics of a Multicultural Community*. Melbourne: Oxford University Press, 1970.

Gunson, Niel. *Messengers of Grace: Evangelical Missionaries in the South Seas, 1797–1860*. Melbourne: Oxford University Press, 1978.

Hanlon, David. *Making Micronesia: A Political Biography of Tosiwo Nakayama*. Honolulu: University of Hawai‘i Press, 2014.

Harland-Jacobs, Jessica. *Builders of Empire: Freemasonry and the British Imperialism, 1717–1927*. Chapel Hill: University of North Carolina Press, 2007.

Haskins, Victoria. *One Bright Spot*. London: Palgrave Macmillan, 2005.

Hau'ofa, Epeli. “Our Sea of Islands.” *The Contemporary Pacific* 6, no. 1 (1994): 147–161.

Hempenstall, Peter. *Pacific Islanders under German Rule: A Study in the Meaning of Colonial Resistance*. Canberra: Australian National University Press, 1978.

Hempenstall, Peter, and Paula T. Mochida. *The Lost Man: Wilhelm Solf in German History*. Wiesbaden: Harrassowitz, 2005.

Hempenstall, Peter, and Noel Rutherford. *Protest and Dissent in the Colonial Pacific*. Suva: Institute of Pacific Studies, 1984.

Hiery, Hermann. *The Neglected War: The German South Pacific and the Influence of World War 1*. Honolulu: University of Hawai‘i Press, 1995.

Hiery, Hermann, and John Mackenzie, eds. *European Impact and Pacific Influence: British and German Colonial Policy in the Pacific Islands and the Indigenous Response*. London: Tauris Academic Studies, 1997.

Hoare, Nicholas. “Harry Holland's ‘Samoan Complex.’ ” *Journal of Pacific History* 49, no. 2 (2014): 151–169.

Huggins, Jackie. *Sister Girl: The Writings of Aboriginal Activist and Historian Jackie Huggins*. Saint Lucia: University of Queensland Press, 1998.

Hunt, Susan, and Paul Carter, eds. *Terre Napoleon: Australia through French Eyes, 1800–1804*. Sydney: Historic Houses Trust, 1999.

Jones, Ryan. "Environment." In *Pacific Histories: Ocean, Land, People,* edited by David Armitage and Alison Bashford, 121–142. Basingstoke: Macmillan, 2014.

Kame'eleihiwa, Lilikalā. *Native Lands and Foreign Desires*. Honolulu: Bishop Museum Press, 1992.

Kennedy, Paul. *The Samoan Tangle: A Study in Anglo-American Relations 1878–1900*. Saint Lucia: University of Queensland Press, 2011.

King, Michael. *Te Puea, a Biography.* Auckland: Hodder and Stoughton, 1977.

Lal, Brij V., Doug Munro, and Edward D. Beechert, eds. *Plantation Workers: Resistance and Accommodation*. Honolulu: University of Hawai'i Press, 1993.

Lergessner, James G. *Chief Bungaree: King of the Broken Bay Tribe*. Woorim, Australia: James G. Lergessner, 2008.

Linnekin, Jocelyn. "Ignoble Savages and Other European Visions." *Journal of Pacific History* 26, no. 1 (1991): 3–26.

Luker, Vicki. "Half Castes in Australia, New Zealand and Western Samoa between the Wars: Different Problem, Different Places?" In *Foreign Bodies: Oceania and the Science of Race 1750–1940,* edited by Bronwen Douglas and Chris Ballard, 307–335. Canberra: ANU ePress, 2008.

Mallon, Sean, Kolokesa Māhina-Tuai, and Damon Salesa, eds. *Tangata O Le Moana: New Zealand and the People of the Pacific*. Wellington: Te Papa Press, 2012.

Martin, Karen, and Booran Mirraboopa. "Ways of Knowing, Being and Doing: A Theoretical Framework and Methods For Indigenous and Indigenist Re-Search." *Journal of Australian Studies* 27, no. 76 (2009): 203–214.

Masterman, Sylvia. *The Origins of International Rivalry in Samoa 1845–1884*. London: George Allen and Unwin, 1934.

Maynard, John. "Circles in the Sand: An Indigenous Framework of Historical Practice." *Australian Journal of Indigenous Education* 36 (2007): 117–120.

———. *Fight for Liberty and Freedom: The Origins of Australian Aboriginal Activism*. Canberra: AIATSIS, 2007.

McNeill, John. "Of Rats and Men: A Synoptic Environmental History of the Island Pacific." *Journal of World History* 5, no. 2 (1994): 299–349.

Meleisea, Malama. "Introduction." *A Footnote to History: Eight Years of Trouble in Samoa,* by Robert Louis Stevenson, vii–xvi. Honolulu: University of Hawai'i Press, 1996.

———. *The Making of Modern Samoa: Traditional Authority and Colonial Administration in the History of Western Samoa*. Suva: Institute of Pacific Studies, 1987.

Meleisea, Malama, and Penelope Schoeffel Meleisea, eds. *Lagaga: A Short History of Western Samoa*. Suva: University of South Pacific, 1987.

Mohanty, Chandra Talpade. "Under Western Eyes: Feminist Scholarship and Colonial Discourses." *Feminist Review* 30 (1988): 61–88.

Moses, John, and Paul Kennedy, eds. *Germany in the Pacific and the Far East 1870–1914*. Saint Lucia: University of Queensland Press, 1977.

Nakata, Martin. *Disciplining the Savages: Savaging the Disciplines*. Canberra: Aboriginal Studies Press, 2007.

O'Brien, Patricia. "Showdown in Geneva: Sāmoa, New Zealand and the League of Nations in 1928." Forthcoming.

———. "Bridging the Pacific: Ta'isi O. F. Nelson, Australia and the Sāmoan Mau." *History Australia*, 14:1, 2017.

———. "From Sudan to Samoa: Imperial Legacies, Cultures and New Zealand's Rule over the Mandated Territory of Western Samoa." In *New Zealand's Empire*, edited by Katie Pickles and Catharine Coleborne, 127–142. Manchester: Manchester University Press, 2016.

———. "Gender." In *Pacific Histories: Peoples, Oceans, Lands*, edited by David Armitage and Alison Bashford, 282–304. Basingstoke: Palgrave Macmillan, 2014.

———. "Ta'isi O. F. Nelson and Sir Maui Pomare: Samoans and Māori Reunited." *Journal of Pacific History* 49, no. 1 (2014): 1–24.

———. *The Pacific Muse: Exotic Femininity and the Colonial Pacific*. Seattle: University of Washington Press, 2006.

———. "Think of Me as a Woman: Queen Pomare of Tahiti and Anglo-French Imperial Contest in the 1840s Pacific." *Gender and History* 18, no. 1 (2006): 108–129.

Okihiro, Gary. *Cane Fires: The Anti-Japanese Movement in Hawaii, 1865–1945*. Philadelphia: Temple University Press, 1991.

Osorio, Jonathon Kay Kamakawiwo'ole. *Dismembering Lāhui: A History of the Hawaiian Nation to 1887*. Honolulu: University of Hawai'i Press, 2002.

Paisley, Fiona. *The Lone Protester: A. M. Fernando in Australia and Europe*. Canberra: Aboriginal Studies Press, 2012.

———. *Loving Protection: Australian Feminism and Aboriginal Women's Rights*. Melbourne: Melbourne University Press, 2000.

Pedersen, Susan. *The Guardians: The League of Nations and the Crisis of Empire*. Oxford: Oxford University Press, 2015.

———. "Samoa on the World Stage: Petitions and Peoples before the Mandates Commission of the League of Nations." *Journal of Imperial and Commonwealth History* 40, no. 2 (2012): 231–261.

Pickles, Katie, and Catharine Coleborne, eds. *New Zealand's Empire*. Manchester: Manchester University Press, 2016.

Plomley, N. J. B. *The Baudin Expedition and the Tasmanian Aborigines*. Hobart: Blubber Head Press, 1983.

Ralston, Caroline. *Grasshuts and Warehouses: Pacific Beach Communities of the Nineteenth Century.* Honolulu: University of Hawai'i Press, 1978.

Riseborough, Hazel. *Days of Darkness: Taranaki, 1878–1884.* Wellington: Allen and Unwin, 1989.

———. "A New Kind of Resistance: Parihaka and the Struggle for Peace." In *Contested Ground: Te Whenua i Tohea: The Taranaki Wars, 1860–1881,* edited by Kelvin Day, 230–253. Wellington: Huia, 2010.

Rose, Deborah Bird. *Hidden Histories: Black Stories from Victoria River Downs, Humbert River and Wave Hill Stations.* Canberra: Aboriginal Studies Press, 1991.

Ross, Angus, ed. *New Zealand's Record in the Pacific Islands in the Twentieth Century.* London: Longman Paul, 1969.

Russell, Lynette. *Roving Mariners: Australian Aboriginal Whalers and Sealers in the Southern Oceans.* Albany: State University of New York Press, 2012.

Ryan, Lyndall. *Tasmanian Aborigines: A History since 1803.* Crows Nest, New South Wales: Allen and Unwin, 2012.

Salesa, Damon. "Misimoa: An American on the Beach." *Common-Place* 5, no. 2 (2005). http://www.common-place-archives.org/vol-05/no-02/salesa/index.shtml. Accessed June 6, 2013.

———. "A Pacific destiny: New Zealand's Overseas Empire 1840–1945." In *Tangata O Le Moana: New Zealand and the People of the Pacific,* edited by Sean Mallon, Kolokesa Māhina-Tuai, and Damon Salesa, 97–122. Wellington: Te Papa Press, 2012.

———. *Racial Crossings: Race, Intermarriage, and the Victorian British Empire.* Oxford: Oxford University Press, 2011.

Scarr, Deryck. *The History of the Pacific Islands: Kingdoms of the Reefs.* Melbourne: Macmillan, 1990.

Scott, Dick. *Ask That Mountain: The Story of Parihaka.* Rev. ed. Rosedale: Raupo, 2008.

Smith, Linda Tuhiwai. *Decolonizing Methodologies: Research and Indigenous Peoples.* 2nd ed. Dunedin: University of Otago Press, 2012.

Somerville, Alice Te Punga. *Once Were Pacific: Māori Connections to Oceania.* Minneapolis: University of Minnesota Press, 2012.

Spate, O. H. K. *The Pacific since Magellan.* Vol. 3 of *Paradise Found and Lost.* Canberra: Australian National University Press, 1988.

Spivak, Gayatri C. "Can the Subaltern Speak?" In *Colonial Discourse and Post-Colonial Theory: A Reader,* edited by P. Williams and L. Chrisman, 66–112. Hemel Hempstead: Harvester Wheatsheaf, 1993.

Starbuck, Nicole. *Baudin, Napoleon and the Exploration of Australia.* London: Pickering and Chatto, 2013.

Steel, Frances. *Oceania under Steam: Sea Transport and the Cultures of Colonialism, 1870–1914.* Manchester: Manchester University Press, 2011.

Stoler, Ann Laura. "Tense and Tender Ties: The Politics of Comparison in North American History and (Post) Colonial Studies." *Journal of American History* 88, no. 3 (2001): 829–865.

Suaalii-Sauni, Tamasa'ilau, I'uogafa Tuagalu, Tofilau Nina Kirifi-Alai, and Naomi Fuamatu, eds. *Su'esu'e Manogi—in Search of Fragrance: Tui Atua Tupua Tamasese Ta'isi and the Samoan Indigenous Reference.* Apia: Centre for Samoan Studies, National University of Samoa, 2008.

Teaiwa, Katerina. "Multisided Methodologies: Homework in Australia, Fiji and Kiribati" In *Anthropologists in the Field: Cases in Participant Observation*, edited by Lynne Hume. New York: Columbia University Press, 2004.

Trask, Haunani-Kay. *From a Native Daughter: Colonialism and Sovereignty in Hawai'i.* Honolulu: University of Hawai'i Press, 2012.

Tui Atua Tupua Tamasese Ta'isi Efi. "Clutter in Indigenous Knowledge, Research and History: A Samoan Perspective." *Social Policy Journal of New Zealand* 25 (2005): 61–69.

———. *Englishing My Samoan: Selected Speeches and Letters.* Suva: University of the South Pacific, 1995.

———. "The Riddle in Samoan History: The Relevance of Language, Names, Honorifics, Genealogy, Ritual and Chant to Historical Analysis." *Journal of Pacific History* 29, no. 1 (1994): 66–79.

Wanhalla, Angela. *Matters of the Heart: A History of Interracial Marriage in New Zealand.* Auckland: Auckland University Press, 2013.

Wareham, Evelyn. *Race and Realpolitik: The Politics of Colonisation in German Samoa.* Frankfurt: Peter Lang, 2002.

Weindling, Paul. "German Eugenics and the Wider World: Beyond the Racial State." In *The Oxford Handbook of the History of Eugenics*, edited by Alison Bashford and Philippa Levine, 315–331. Oxford: Oxford University Press, 2010.

Wevers, Lydia. *Reading on the Farm: Victorian Fiction and the Colonial World.* Wellington: Victoria University Press, 2010.

Dissertations

Eteuati, Kilifoti Sisilia. "Evaevaga a Samoa: Assertion of Samoan Autonomy 1920–1936." PhD diss., Australian National University, 1982.

Hoare, Nicholas. "New Zealand's Critics of Empire: Domestic Opposition to New Zealand's Pacific Empire, 1883–1948." MA thesis, Victoria University of Wellington, 2014.

Wendt, Albert. "'Guardians and Wards': A Study of the Origins, Causes, and the First Two Years of the Mau in Western Samoa." MA thesis, Victoria University of Wellington, 1965.

Web Sources

Buchanan, Rachel. "Te Rā o Māui Pōmare 2013: A Slow Reading." *rachelbuchanan100*. http://rachelbuchanan100.com/2015/05/25/te-ra-o-maui-pomare-2013-a-slow-reading. Accessed May 29, 2015.

Butterworth, Graham. "Pomare, Maui Wiremu Piti Naera." *Dictionary of New Zealand Biography. Te Ara—the Encyclopaedia of New Zealand*. http://www.TeAra.govt.nz/en/biographies/3p30/pomare-maui-wiremu-piti-naera. Accessed December 8, 2012.

Clark, Helen. "Full Text: Helen Clark's Apology to Samoa." *New Zealand Herald*. June 4, 2002. http://www.nzherald.co.nz/nz/news/article.cfm?c_id=1&objectid=2044857. Accessed May 12, 2012.

Crawford, J. A. B. "Hart, Herbert Ernest." *Dictionary of New Zealand Biography. Te Ara—The Encyclopaedia of New Zealand*. http://www.TeAra.govt.nz/en/biographies/3h9/hart-herbert-ernest. Accessed February 9, 2015.

Francis, Hywel. "Cook, Arthur James (1883–1931)." *Oxford Dictionary of National Biography*. Oxford: Oxford University Press, 2004. http://www.oxforddnb.com.virtual.anu.edu.au/view/article/32539. Accessed December 4, 2015.

"Ie Toga Från Samoa." *Kalmar Läns Museum*. June 2007. http://www.kalmarlansmuseum.se/samlingar/vara-samlingar/manadens-foremal/ie-toga-fran-samoa/. Accessed October 26, 2015.

Kirk-Kuwaye, Christine, and Lori Pierce. "Race and Ethnicity." *Local Sightings/Citing: Teaching and Learning through Local History & Culture*. 1999. http://localcite.manoa.hawaii.edu/themerace.html. Accessed February 6, 2014.

Laracy, Hugh. "Nelson, Olaf Frederick." *Dictionary of New Zealand Biography. Te Ara—The Encyclopaedia of New Zealand*. http://www.TeAra.govt.nz/en/biographies/4n5/nelson-olaf-frederick. Accessed April 8, 2014.

McGibbon, Ian. "Richardson, George Spafford." *Dictionary of New Zealand Biography. Te Ara—The Encyclopaedia of New Zealand*. http://www.TeAra.govt.nz/en/biographies/3r16/richardson-george-spafford. Accessed April 7, 2014.

New Zealand Law Society. https://www.lawsociety.org.nz/news-and-communications/people-in-the-law/women-legal-pioneers. Accessed August 29, 2016.

Wheeler-Bennett, John. "Fergusson, Sir Charles, of Kilkerran, Seventh Baronet (1865–1951)." Revised by Roger T. Stearn. *Oxford Dictionary of National Biography*. Oxford: Oxford University Press, 2004. http://dx.doi.org/10.1093/ref:odnb/33111. Accessed October 3, 2013.

Williams, Nuhisifa. "Talanoa." *Talaga* 2 (September 2009): 2. https://www.fmhs.auckland.ac.nz/assets/fmhs/soph/pacifichealth/docs/talaga01092009.pdf. Accessed June 19, 2014.

Selected Works from Ta'isi O. F. Nelson's Tuaefu Library

Beaslai, Piaras. *Michael Collins and the Making of the New Ireland.* London: Harrap, 1926.
Best, Elsdon. *The Maori—Memoirs of the Polynesian Society.* Wellington: Board of Ethnological Research, 1924.
Betchel, John H. *Things Worth Knowing.* Philadelphia: Penn Publishing, 1904.
Buchan, John. *Nelson's History of the War.* London: Thomas Nelson, 1915–1919.
Buick, Thomas. *The Treaty of Waitangi or How New Zealand Became a British Colony.* Wellington: Mackay, 1914.
Carnegie, Dale. *How to Win Friends and Influence People.* Sydney: Angus and Robertson, 1937.
———. *Public Speaking and Influencing Men in Business.* New York: Association Press, 1926.
Cavendish. *The Laws and Principles of Whist Stated and Explained and Its Practice Illustrated on an Original System by Means of Hands Played Completely Through.* London: Thos. De la Rue, 1905.
Cullen, J. H. *Young Ireland in Exile.* Dublin: Talbot Press, 1928.
Fletcher, Charles Brunsdon. *The New Pacific: British and German Aims.* London: Macmillan, 1917.
Gibbon, Edward. *The History of the Decline and Fall of the Roman Empire.* Edited by William Smith. New York: Bigelow, Brown, n.d.
Gill, William Wyatt. *Myths and Songs from the South Pacific.* London: H. S. King, 1876.
Grimshaw, Beatrice. *In the Strange South Seas.* London: Hutchinson, 1908.
Ireland, A. *Geography and History of Oceania: Comprising a Detailed Account of the Australian Colonies.* Hobart: W. Fletcher, 1861.
Leary, Leonard. *New Zealanders in Samoa.* London: Heinemann, 1918.
Lord, John. *Beacon Lights of History: The World Heroes and Masterminds.* New York: Fords, Howard and Hulbert, 1912.
Malinowski, Bronislaw. *Argonauts of the Pacific: An Account of Native Enterprise and Adventure in the Archipelagoes of Melanesian New Guinea.* London: G. Routledge and Sons, 1922.
Martin, John. *The Natives of the Tongan Islands in the South Pacific Ocean.* London: John Murray, 1818.
Melville, Herman, *Omoo: A Narrative of Adventures in the South Seas.* London: John Murray, 1847.
O'Brien, Frederick. *Mystic Isles of the South Seas.* London: Hodder and Stoughton, 1921.
Ogan, Ernest, ed. *The Wonderland of Knowledge: An Up-to-Date Illustrated Encyclopaedia.* London: Odhams, 1934.

Roosevelt, Theodore. *African Game Trails: An Account of African Wonderings of an American Hunter Naturalist.* New York: C. Scribner's Sons, 1920.

———. *Outdoor Pastimes of an American Hunter.* New York: C. Scribner's Sons, 1905.

———. *Theodore Roosevelt: An Autobiography.* New York: C. Scribner's Sons, 1920.

———. *Through the Brazilian Wilderness.* New York: C. Scribner's Sons, 1920.

Wawn, William T. *The South Sea Islanders and the Queensland Labour Trade.* London: Swan Sonnenschein, 1893.

Wells, H. G. *An Englishman Looks at the World: Being a Series of Unrestrained Remarks upon Contemporary Matters.* London: Cassell, 1925.

———. *The Outline of History.* London: Cassell, 1925.

Wilson, Marguerite. *Dancing: A Complete Instructor and Guide to All the New and Standard Dances.* Philadelphia: Penn Publishing, 1905 and 1924.

Index

Page numbers in **bold** indicate illustrations.

About the Author

Patricia O'Brien is an Australian Research Council Future Fellow in the School of History at The Australian National University. In 2012 she was the J. D. Stout Fellow in New Zealand Studies at Victoria University Wellington, and in 2011 she was the Jay I. Kislak Fellow in American Studies at the John W. Kluge Center at the Library of Congress, Washington, DC. From 2001 to 2013 she was a visiting associate professor in the Center for Australian, New Zealand and Pacific Studies and the Department of History in the Edmund A. Walsh School of Foreign Service at Georgetown University, Washington, DC. She is the author of *The Pacific Muse: Exotic Femininity and the Colonial Pacific* (Seattle, 2006), as well as numerous chapters and articles on colonialism, gender, and the cultural history of empire.